Praise for Feng Shui For Dummies

"David Kennedy is a master at translating the complex principles of Feng Shui into language we can all understand and really apply to our home and business environments."

— Dawn Dutcher Schwartzman,
Interior Services Incorporated

"David Kennedy's clear and concise understanding and explanation of this ancient Chinese art I suspect will be called the 'Bible of Feng Shui.' Finally one source that answers *all* the questions! *Brilliant!*"

— Martha Rohl, Feng Shui Consultant

"A true trailblazer in Feng Shui. David Kennedy has certainly come up with a gem with *Feng Shui For Dummies.* I highly recommend this read for all levels."

— James Moser, CEO, Feng Shui Warehouse

"David has a unique way of organizing the incredible amounts of Feng Shui information into clear, concise, easy-to-understand principles. Using these principles correctly, you will be able to make positive life changes, to improve your wealth, health, happiness, and more!"

— Ileen Nelson, Director of the Feng Shui Studies Department
– The Metropolitan Institute of Interior Design

"If you've ever wanted to know anything about Feng Shui, this is the book to read. It's extremely educational and practical. David Kennedy provides simple solutions that you can put into effect immediately. Read this book . . . the quality of your life is guaranteed to radically improve."

— Deborah Rachel Kagan, President, Sacred Interiors

" . . . David Kennedy is a modern Feng Shui master who skillfully blends Eastern wisdom with Western reality. Read this book cover to cover, apply the knowledge, and your life will change forever."

— Susan Levitt, author of *Taoist Feng Shui*

"David easily brings Feng Shui alive with straightforward clarity and details that are vital to real-life situations. This book is definitely essential reading for students at all levels."

— Diane L. Knepper, *The Feng Shui Connection*

Feng Shui
FOR
DUMMIES®

by David Daniel Kennedy

Foreword by Grandmaster Lin Yun

Hungry Minds™

Best-Selling Books • Digital Downloads • e-Books • Answer Networks • e-Newsletters • Branded Web Sites • e-Learning

New York, NY ◆ Cleveland, OH ◆ Indianapolis, IN

Feng Shui For Dummies®

Published by
Hungry Minds, Inc.
909 Third Avenue
New York, NY 10022
www.hungryminds.com
www.dummies.com

Library of Congress Control Number: 00-109409

ISBN: 0-7645-5295-3

Printed in the United States of America

10

1B/QR/QZ/QR/IN

Distributed in the United States by Hungry Minds, Inc.

Distributed by CDG Books Canada Inc. for Canada; by Transworld Publishers Limited in the United Kingdom; by IDG Norge Books for Norway; by IDG Sweden Books for Sweden; by IDG Books Australia Publishing Corporation Pty. Ltd. for Australia and New Zealand; by TransQuest Publishers Pte Ltd. for Singapore, Malaysia, Thailand, Indonesia, and Hong Kong; by Gotop Information Inc. for Taiwan; by ICG Muse, Inc. for Japan; by Intersoft for South Africa; by Eyrolles for France; by International Thomson Publishing for Germany, Austria and Switzerland; by Distribuidora Cuspide for Argentina; by LR International for Brazil; by Galileo Libros for Chile; by Ediciones ZETA S.C.R. Ltda. for Peru; by WS Computer Publishing Corporation, Inc., for the Philippines; by Contemporanea de Ediciones for Venezuela; by Express Computer Distributors for the Caribbean and West Indies; by Micronesia Media Distributor, Inc. for Micronesia; by Chips Computadoras S.A. de C.V. for Mexico; by Editorial Norma de Panama S.A. for Panama; by American Bookshops for Finland.

For general information on Hungry Minds' products and services please contact our Customer Care Department within the U.S. at 800-762-2974, outside the U.S. at 317-572-3993 or fax 317-572-4002.

For sales inquiries and reseller information, including discounts, premium and bulk quantity sales, and foreign-language translations, please contact our Customer Care Department at 800-434-3422, fax 317-572-4002, or write to Hungry Minds, Inc., Attn: Customer Care Department, 10475 Crosspoint Boulevard, Indianapolis, IN 46256.

For information on licensing foreign or domestic rights, please contact our Sub-Rights Customer Care Department at 212-884-5000.

For information on using Hungry Minds' products and services in the classroom or for ordering examination copies, please contact our Educational Sales Department at 800-434-2086 or fax 317-572-4005.

Please contact our Public Relations Department at 212-884-5163 for press review copies or 212-884-5000 for author interviews and other publicity information or fax 212-884-5400.

For authorization to photocopy items for corporate, personal, or educational use, please contact Copyright Clearance Center, 222 Rosewood Drive, Danvers, MA 01923, or fax 978-750-4470.

Hungry Minds™ is a trademark of Hungry Minds, Inc.

About the Author

David Daniel Kennedy is a direct disciple of Grandmaster Lin Yun, and the founder of the International Institute for Grandmaster Lin Yun Studies. Mr. Kennedy is a Feng Shui teacher, speaker, and professional consultant, whose client list ranges from individuals to Fortune 500 companies. An expert at making Eastern concepts easily accessible, David has spent the last fifteen years showing people how to make simple life changes that dramatically improve their wealth, relationships, and happiness. His unique and entertaining approach not only has led him to hundreds of speaking engagements and creative workshops across the United States and abroad but also has established him as one of the best-known consultants and writers on the subject. David is the personal teacher and mentor of numerous successful Feng Shui consultants, as well as the author of the best-selling book, *Feng Shui Tips for a Better Life*. David is a columnist for *Feng Shui Journal* and a frequent contributor to *Natural Health* magazine.

About the Author's Mentor

His Holiness Grandmaster Lin Yun is highly regarded as the leading authority on Feng Shui. His Feng Shui theories, also known as the Black Sect Tantric Buddhist Feng Shui School, are the most widely practiced Feng Shui school in the United States. For the past forty years, Grandmaster Lin Yun has lectured extensively on the subject of Feng Shui at many distinguished universities, businesses, and professional organizations throughout the world. Due to his introduction, transmission, and continuous promotion, Feng Shui has drawn tremendous interest; its popularity continues to grow worldwide. Numerous Feng Shui authors, teachers, and consultants are his disciples and/or students. Grandmaster Lin Yun's pioneering contribution to spreading the knowledge of Feng Shui has earned him the reputation as the father of Feng Shui in the West. In 1997, he received an honorary Ph.D. in Human Psychology from Northern California Graduate University. In 1998, he was enthroned as His Holiness of Black Sect Tantric Buddhism in its current and fourth stage of development.

Author's Acknowledgments

The author gratefully acknowledges these individuals for their assistance and guidance:

His Holiness Grandmaster Professor Lin Yun, my Feng Shui and spiritual teacher, for writing the foreword to this book, bringing Feng Shui to the West, and tirelessly helping countless people worldwide have better, happier lives through Feng Shui; Crystal Chu, CEO of the Yun Lin Temple, for her abundant support; Sarah Rossbach, whose books introduced Feng Shui to an English-speaking audience; Frances Li, the staff, and volunteers at the Yun Lin Temple and the Lin Yun Monastery; Teacher Ho Lynn Tu; colleagues Seann Xenja, who did a great job as technical editor, Lillian Garnier, James Moser, and my Feng Shui students and clients. Special thanks to Shelagh Keleyhers, Marge and Angelo DeVivo, Connie Jo DeLashmutt Phelps, Tom and Debra Margrave, Krissa Lee-Regier, Dell Hipp, BJ and Michael Adams, Lin and Michael Vernon, Diane Knepper, Dawn and Michael Swartzman, and DKLA.

My agent, Carol Susan Roth, for bringing this book to Hungry Minds and sticking with the project through thick and thin; editorial guru Doug Childers; and promotional wizard David Bucksner. Thanks also to Stephan Bodian, Shelley Sparks, and Judith Pynn.

The talented, wonderfully organized, and fearsomely competent staff at Hungry Minds: Acquisitions Editors Tami Booth for committing to this project, Stacy Collins, and lifeline Karen Young; Project Editor Alissa Cayton and Copy Editor Mary Fales for their dedicated work and great contributions; and the legions of unseen but important production staff.

Professional artist Chi Chung, for drawing the illustrations for this book, working in record time, enduring countless revisions, and coming through with the best illustrations imaginable.

Teachers Lama Ole Nydahl and Haidakhan Baba.

My beautiful partner, Jaqui.

Publisher's Acknowledgments

We're proud of this book; please register your comments through our Online Registration Form located at www.dummies.com.

Some of the people who helped bring this book to market include the following:

Acquisitions, Editorial, and Media Development

Project Editor: Alissa D. Cayton

Acquisitions Editor: Stacy Collins

Associate Acquisitions Editor: Karen Young

Copy Editor: Mary Fales

Technical Editor: Seann Xenja

Editorial Manager: Jennifer Ehrlich

Editorial Assistants: Carol Strickland, Jennifer Young

Cover Photo: The Image Bank © Mahaux Photography

Production

Project Coordinator: Emily Wichlinski

Layout and Graphics: Amy Adrian, Beth Brooks, Sean Decker, Julie Trippetti, Jeremey Unger

Proofreaders: Corey Bowen, Jennifer Mahern, Susan Moritz

Indexer: Liz Cunningham

Special Help
Andrea Boucher, Amanda M. Foxworth, Maureen Kelly, Elizabeth Kuball

General and Administrative

Hungry Minds, Inc.: John Kilcullen, CEO; Bill Barry, President and COO; John Ball, Executive VP, Operations & Administration; John Harris, CFO

Hungry Minds Consumer Reference Group

    Business: Kathleen A. Welton, Vice President and Publisher; Kevin Thornton, Acquisitions Manager

    Cooking/Gardening: Jennifer Feldman, Associate Vice President and Publisher

    Education/Reference: Diane Graves Steele, Vice President and Publisher

    Lifestyles/Pets: Kathleen Nebenhaus, Vice President and Publisher; Tracy Boggier, Managing Editor

    Travel: Michael Spring, Vice President and Publisher; Suzanne Jannetta, Editorial Director; Brice Gosnell, Publishing Director

Hungry Minds Consumer Editorial Services: Kathleen Nebenhaus, Vice President and Publisher; Kristin A. Cocks, Editorial Director; Cindy Kitchel, Editorial Director

Hungry Minds Consumer Production: Debbie Stailey, Production Director

◆

The publisher would like to give special thanks to Patrick J. McGovern, without whom this book would not have been possible.

◆

Contents at a Glance

Cartoons at a Glance

By Rich Tennant

Fax: 978-546-7747
E-mail: richtennant@the5thwave.com
World Wide Web: www.the5thwave.com

Table of Contents

· ·

Foreword

. . . .

From the time I was about fifteen or sixteen years old, I began studying with Black Sect Tantric Buddhist masters Hui Chieh-fu and Chang Kuei-ying. In addition to spiritual studies, meditation, calligraphy, poetry and painting, secret cures and holistic healing, and divination, I was most captivated by the study of Feng Shui. In later years, I spread the teaching of Feng Shui to Taiwan, Hong Kong, Europe, and the United States. In the last thirty years, I have combined the knowledge of modern architecture, psychology, medicine, spirituality, folkloric cultures of China and Taiwan, and the knowledge of traditional and modern Feng Shui schools to establish a new school in the study of Feng Shui, which is the Black Sect Tantric Buddhist Feng Shui Perspective (referred to as Grandmaster Lin Yun's Feng Shui school in this book). From 1973 to the present, I have been lecturing, teaching, and providing spiritual guidance in Europe, the United States, Australia, and Africa.

Many books are now available on the study of Feng Shui, and each one has its own specialty. Now that I have read David Daniel Kennedy's second book, *Feng Shui For Dummies*, I feel that this guide is like an instamatic camera, readily usable and easily understood by anyone and everyone without the need for a teacher.

After reading this book, the reader can completely understand the true meaning, explanation, and applications of Feng Shui through the Ba-Gua, Five Elements, and the power of the Three Secrets Reinforcement. This book also places special emphasis on the visible elements of Feng Shui, namely the chi (or energy) of the land, the shape of the land, the shape of the house, the floor plan, the interior factors, and the exterior factors. In addition, the reader can understand how to adjust the Five Elements and how to use Exterior and Interior House Blessings, the Method of Minor Additions, and the Constantly Turning Dharma Wheel to make modifications and improvements to his or her living and working environments.

The publication of *Feng Shui For Dummies* is much anticipated. The author, Mr. Kennedy, has a smooth penmanship and clear and precise ideas. His writing style and concepts are concise and refreshing, and easy for the reader to understand and accept. This book contains theories of Black Sect Tantric Buddhism Feng Shui Perspective as well as meditation methods to improve one's spiritual powers, practical applications, and both mundane and transcendental solutions. Through this book, the author has made great contributions to society. These contributions can help many people who feel at loss, and they can strengthen the stability of society, increase the well-being of the nation, and create happiness in mankind. Therefore, the publication of Mr. Kennedy's new book is indeed a great and joyous event for the Black Sect Tantric Buddhist School.

H. H. Grandmaster Lin Yun
Translated by Mary R. Hsu

Introduction

• •

*T*ake a look around you. What do you see? Whether or not you're aware of it, your environment profoundly impacts your health, wealth, family life, relationships, and, yes, even your destiny.

Feng Shui (pronounced fung shway) is the ancient Chinese art of improving every aspect of your life by enhancing your environment according to the principles of harmony and energy flow. Within the last ten years, Feng Shui has gained widespread popularity in the West, and today, more and more people from all walks of life are practicing Feng Shui and experiencing the positive benefits of auspicious placement. Many successful individuals now create harmony and happiness in their relationships, increase their prosperity, and dissolve chronic patterns of failure, difficulty, and stress by rearranging their living and working environments according to ancient Feng Shui principles.

By implementing the practical and effective Feng Shui methods in this book, you see your surroundings in a new light and notice how your home environment influences your job, your relationships, your personal health, and every aspect of your daily experience. You make new and amazing connections between obstacles in your physical space and recurring difficulties in your financial, professional, emotional, or creative life. Following Feng Shui principles, you can design living and working environments that can help you achieve the success and happiness you deserve. In short, you experience how a harmonious environment allows more energy to flow through your whole being. And most importantly, you can understand why Feng Shui has been practiced for thousands of years: It works!

Feng Shui is neither superstitious magic, nor a passing fad. The Chinese have known for millennia that our physical surroundings affect every aspect of our inner and outer lives. They've long recognized the distinct relationship between success in life and good Feng Shui. For example, the location of your bed affects your marriage, and the position of your desk affects your attention and work performance — which perhaps means the difference between a job promotion or demotion. Employed effectively by emperors and sages of the East for thousands of years, the timeless Feng Shui principles presented in this book are as effective today as ever. And now Grasshopper, you can find out how to make them work for you!

About This Book

Yes, many valuable Feng Shui books crowd the bookstore shelves these days. But finding the right one for you can be a real challenge. Some of the books are more suitable for advanced practitioners and scholars, while others contain valuable, but highly complex details of historical, cultural, and theoretical significance. Trying to determine which ones actually work for you can sidetrack you from the pressing goal at hand — changing your home and office for the better.

Enter *Feng Shui For Dummies,* your do-it-yourself guide to no-kidding, cut-to-the-chase-and-hit-the-ground-running Feng Shui. I wrote this book with you, the on-the-go reader in mind. This book is focused on helping you apply Feng Shui principles and techniques to the nitty-gritty reality of your daily life. It guides you through the fascinating, mysterious art of Feng Shui and gives you the practical knowledge you need to improve your environment and life — starting today. It allows you to take charge and literally turn things around by designing your environment to suit your purposes and needs. I've stuffed, shoe-horned, and packed this book with the most effective methods, tips, and techniques available, ones that address the issues and concerns you encounter in your daily life. I explain each method clearly, and tell how and why it works. So roll up your sleeves, continue to read, and prepare for action!

This book is your step-by-step guide to effective Feng Shui. The easy, practical steps are:

- ✔ Feeling and assessing the energy of your own home or office — it's easier than you might think!

- ✔ Recognizing specifically how your environment is impacting your life right now — and is it ever. Your mouth may drop open in amazement as you recognize unmistakable correlations between environmental features described in this book and specific conditions in your daily life.

- ✔ Properly executing the specific solutions necessary to change your environment, so that you can feel the before-and-after differences (in short order!).

For each environmental matter I address, I describe the ideal state and function of that feature. (When I use the word environment in this book, I mean your personal environment, not the rainforest or the ozone layer.) I then give the ways your situation can vary from these ideal principles and explain the potential negative consequences. But I won't leave you high and dry; I provide you with one or more practical solutions for each problematic condition. And I tell you which parts of your life are directly benefited by performing the recommended solutions.

How to Use This Book

This book isn't meant to be read from cover to cover, although you can read it this way if you want. For first-time Feng Shui-ers, the first chapter in this book answers the big question, "What is Feng Shui?" This overview gives you the understanding you need to implement the practical suggestions found throughout the book. If you're already familiar with the basic concepts of Feng Shui, you can use the Table of Contents or the Index at the back of the book to direct you to the chapter that provides the information you need. Also, be sure to follow the references and links I provide within the book; these resources lead you to related material located in other chapters.

Chi Chung's helpful illustrations sprinkled throughout the text clarify key points and demonstrate exactly how to perform specific cures. If an illustration differs from your particular situation, simply adapt the suggested remedy to fit your particular circumstance. On the other hand, in many cases, specific details can mean the difference between an effective solution and one that produces less than adequate results. For instance, if I recommend using a bamboo flute, don't use a chopstick and expect that you'll get the same result! If I emphasize particular details as important, stick with them to the best of your ability. I also use real life stories from my client files to illustrate the effectiveness of the methods you'll be learning.

Conventions Used In This Book

The following conventions are used throughout the text to make things consistent and easy to understand:

- ✔ All Web addresses appear in `mono font`.
- ✔ New terms appear in *italic* and are closely followed by an easy-to-understand definition.
- ✔ **Bold** is used to highlight the action parts of numbered steps.

The Feng Shui method in this book — called Grandmaster Lin Yun's Feng Shui school — is unique in several respects. First, it combines both ancient Eastern and modern Western thought. Second, it is highly practical and emphasizes remedies that demand very little of your time, money, and effort. For more on this type of Feng Shui, and how it differs from traditional Feng Shui (also very effective and valid) see Chapter 1.

Foolish Assumptions

In this book, I make several assumptions about you, the reader.

- ✔ You're interested in finding out how your surroundings affect you and how you can affect them, and improve your life by doing so.

- ✔ You want to make your home and/or work environments more beautiful and harmonious, improve your luck, nurture your relationships, and increase your prosperity.

- ✔ You don't want to be overwhelmed by overly mysterious or complex theories and methods that require years of study to understand.

- ✔ You have an open mind and are eager to learn new and interesting ways to improve your life.

- ✔ You're ready to act, move, and make things happen.

Feng Shui is action-oriented. And you'll find that you get more out of it than you put into it. When you prime a pump, it takes some initial effort before the water starts to flow. In the same way, once you prime your Feng Shui pump by arranging your environment according to Feng Shui principles, the energy of harmony, creativity, and abundance starts to flow into every area of your life!

How This Book Is Organized

Like all *For Dummies* books, *Feng Shui For Dummies* is organized to make tons of useful information easily accessible. This book includes five main parts. Here's how I divvied it all up:

Part I: Getting Started: Feng Shui Basics

Part I explains the basic Feng Shui principles you need in order to apply the practical methods found throughout this book. I explain what Feng Shui is — and what it definitely is not. I also explain how the main schools of Feng Shui differ from each other and where Grandmaster Lin Yun's Feng Shui school fits into the general scheme of Feng Shui. Also, I define core concepts of Feng Shui: *chi,* the energy of Feng Shui; *cures,* Feng Shui solutions; and *intent,* the force which dramatically strengthens the impact and effectiveness of your cures. I also show you how to map the energy of your personal space using the Feng Shui Octagon.

This section provides easy ways to sense energy in a space to determine if the energy is positive or negative. Interestingly, the Chinese were talking about energy and space 3000 years B.C. — Before California — although they didn't say "Dude!" I also introduce two key Feng Shui concepts: *symbolism* and *patterns.* These are two important ways your subconscious mind interprets your space and influences your moods and your actions. I also show you which areas of your house affect the well-being of your children, your career, your finances, your personal health, and so on.

Part II: Outdoor Feng Shui: Energizing Your Home's Exterior

Part II deals with the great outdoors — the outside of your house, that is. Just as you live in your house, your house lives in the land or property it sits on. From your neighborhood to your street, right up to your front door, I show you how to use the energies of nature to assist your personal progress. In addition, this section gives you tips on the best siting for your house, how to counteract nearby negative features, and how to use the beneficial effects of vegetation and flowing water.

In this part, I deal with the vital matter of shapes. The shape of your lot and your house powerfully influence your life path in that residence. I also show you how to make the most of your approach, or the path by which energy (and money) either flows in to nourish your dwelling, or is obstructed or blocked. You'll find that it's important to design this area with care and attention, to leverage a fortunate future.

Part III: Indoor Feng Shui: Boosting the Energy of Your Home and Office

Part III takes you indoors to consider your home's interior assets. I show you how to read your home's floor plan to see how the layout is either benefiting or harming your life. I walk you through each individual room and give you practical tips for improving its energy. In addition, I explain the importance of key individual features including doors, stairs, windows, beams, and more. I also explain how to improve your home's energy with lighting, color, removing clutter, and everyday maintenance.

The last chapter in this section includes suggestions on how to create the unfair advantage that everyone deserves at work. Whether you work out of your home or in a cubical on your office building's twenty-third floor, I show you how to apply easy Feng Shui cures to make the most of your work environment.

Part IV: Special Feng Shui: Performing Ceremonies and Personal Cures

In Part IV, I present powerful ceremonies that help clear unwelcome energies from your home and that increase your good fortune. (No, this is not a recipe for getting rid of your significant other!) Part IV also deals with a unique and effective branch of Feng Shui, performing special cures directly on yourself, rather than your home or workplace, to enhance your personal energy.

Part V: The Part Of Tens

The *Feng Shui For Dummies* Part of Tens section provides a wealth of powerful, practical, and quickly applicable Feng Shui information in the areas of health, wealth, and personal relationships. I've also included helpful hints on selling, finding, and buying a house, tips for successful apartment and condo living, and key principles for getting the most out of your Feng Shui cures. Closing out Part V is a special treat, 10 calligraphy blessings by Grandmaster Lin Yun.

Icons Used In This Book

In the margins of this book, you find several helpful icons that can make your journey easier:

Tip: Text marked with this bull's-eye icon gives helpful Feng Shui pointers and information.

Remember: This icon sits next to key details you need to keep in mind in order to have success with your Feng Shui adjustments.

Heads Up: This icon tells you when to sit up and take notice. Something in your environment may be harming you, and changing it will save you a heap o' trouble down the road.

Advanced Cure: If you want to tackle more involved Feng Shui tips, follow the special cures given next to this icon. These remedies are some of the most potent solutions out there!

Real Life Example: This icon indicates a real life Feng Shui story illustrating some aspect or result of using Feng Shui. You can discover a lot from the experiences of others and apply their knowledge to your own life. The details are true, although the names have been changed to protect the fortunate.

Part I

Getting Started: Feng Shui Basics

The 5th Wave · By Rich Tennant

©RICHTENNANT

Meditations, Inc.
BOOKS · SEMINARS · TAPES

"Sales on the Web site are down. I figure the server's chi is blocked, so we're fudgin' around the Feng Shui in the computer room, and if that doesn't work, Ronnie's got a cure that should do it."

In this part . . .

Feng Shui is the interaction between you and your environment. Feng Shui in action is jumping out of your current mold and applying tips, tricks, and techniques to reform your living environment, to forge a new relationship with your space, and to become happier in the process. Sound intriguing?

First you need some of the basics (just a few), and then you can move on to the really heavy Feng Shui firepower. Part I gives you the lowdown on Feng Shui and the key principles that make it work. You're then fortified to move on and discover how to map the energy of your home (it's a lot easier than it sounds). You can also grab an armful of effective Feng Shui tools — I call 'em cures — you can apply anywhere you want. Last but not least, I let you in on Feng Shui's biggest secret of all: How to use intention to make your Feng Shui solutions really zing.

Chapter 1

Discovering the Benefits of Feng Shui

In This Chapter

▶ Orienting yourself to Feng Shui

▶ Getting grounded in basic Feng Shui principles

▶ Grasping the Feng Shui principles in this book

▶ Preparing to find solutions to your life problems

▶ Choosing the life areas you want to begin with

*E*veryone appreciates the benefits of beautiful, comfortable living environments; America's billion-dollar interior decorating industry attests to this fact. But Feng Shui says that your surroundings affect not just your level of material comfort but also your physical and mental health, your relationships, and your worldly success.

Feng Shui (pronounced fung shway) examines how the energy flow in your living environment is affected by the placement of things and objects within it, and how these objects interact with and influence your personal energy flow. Your personal energy flow affects how you think and act, which in turn affects how well you perform and succeed in your personal and professional life. *Remember:* Feng Shui affects you every moment of the day — whether you're aware of it or not.

The purpose of this book is to help you perform effective Feng Shui corrections. In this chapter, you get a firm grounding in the essential concepts. I present a brief overview of traditional Feng Shui methods and then show you how Feng Shui can bring order, clarity, and newfound power to your daily life. Keep in mind that beginning students of Feng Shui need to have an open mind and should use the methods that are most comfortable for their particular circumstances.

Demystifying Feng Shui

If you've already read through several Feng Shui books, you may be somewhat confused by the seemingly contradictory advice you've encountered. Before I discuss the essence of Feng Shui, I help clear up some common Feng Shui misconceptions and apprehensions. Feng Shui isn't any of the following:

- A get-rich-quick method of Oriental interior design that guarantees impossible results for mystically rearranging your furniture
- A superstitious or magical belief system or a New Age fad that disconnects you from reality or from your daily life
- A simple home and garden makeover
- A quick fix to be tackled in one afternoon
- A luxury only the rich and famous can afford

Now on to the million-dollar question: What is Feng Shui?

- On the surface, Feng Shui is the simple interaction of humans and their environments. Taken a step further, Feng Shui allows you to influence these interacting energies to achieve specific life improvements. This influence is achieved by positioning or designing your surroundings in harmony with principles of natural energy flow. As a result, you (and your life) can achieve harmony with your surroundings. Feng Shui is practical and grounding, and it helps you right where you live and work.
- Feng Shui is often referred to as the art of placement. How you place your furniture, possessions, and yourself within your surroundings largely determines your life experience at every level. Feng Shui offers a unique way of looking at yourself and your environment, and it provides a way of bringing balance, comfort, and harmony into your environment in a manner that is difficult to achieve by any other means.
- Feng Shui is the study of the relationships between the environment and human life. Discovered by the Chinese, Feng Shui has been practiced for centuries to design environments that enhance conditions for success in life.

Interesting bits of historical Feng Shui confirmation are starting to emerge. For example, recent scientific research indicates that 28,000 years ago, Neanderthal cavemen (located in present-day Croatia) chose which caves to live in based on three criteria: The caves held the high ground in the area, the surrounding area was easily seen from the entrance of the cave, and the water source was easily accessible. These findings show that even our ancestors were naturally aware of the effects of placement in their environment. Interestingly enough, all three of these criteria are in harmony with the basic principles of Feng Shui, which has evolved and become more sophisticated along with humankind. Thus, Feng Shui is as relevant and beneficial to humankind today as it was 28,000 years ago. (And the books are a lot better, too!)

The environment rules! Feng Shui factors have determined the path of human culture

Many respectable, successful, and highly intelligent Western individuals are recognizing and applying in their own lives the basic premise behind Feng Shui — that your immediate environment affects you on a daily basis and influences your long-term destiny. One individual who's deeply aware of these ideas has written a great book on the subject. Jared Diamond, biologist and author, won the Pulizter Prize for nonfiction for his book *Guns, Germs and Steel.* Written after years of research, his book explains why some societies and peoples developed farming, then writing, then steel, and finally higher technologies, while other societies remained in hunter-gatherer mode.

Previous theories that attempted to explain this difference of cultures included racial factors, intelligence differences among peoples, an evolutionary head start or lack of the same, and other theories. After examining all these factors, Mr. Diamond realized that none of them explained the puzzling differences of human evolutionary, cultural, and technological progression. Though his book doesn't discuss Feng Shui directly, he finally comes to this conclusion: Throughout human history, the dominant factor that has determined the evolutionary destiny and rate of progress among human societies has been the environment in which they live. Feng Shui strikes again!

Feng Who? The Meaning of the Term Feng Shui

Feng Shui is a term composed of two Chinese words: *feng* (wind) and *shui* (water). Wind and water are the two natural elements that flow, move, and circulate everywhere on Earth. They are also the most basic elements required for human survival. Wind — or air — is the breath of life; without it, we die in moments. And water is the liquid of life; without it, we die in days. The combined qualities of wind and water determine the climate, which historically has determined our food supply and in turn affects our lifestyle, health, energy, and mood. These two fundamental and flowing elements have always profoundly yet subtly influenced human individuals and societies.

The essence of these life-giving elements is *chi,* or life force. Wind and water are direct carriers of chi, as their flowing quality reflects their essential nature. All living organisms are largely composed of these two elements. Thus, Feng Shui is the art of designing environments in harmony with the flow of chi through one's living space, and this flow supports and enhances one's personal chi or life force. (Read more about the energy called chi in Chapter 2.)

Ancient Chinese Secrets: The Big Picture View of Feng Shui

Feng Shui is rooted in a holistic worldview. It sees all things and creatures as part of a natural order, a vast environment that is alive and in flux, ever moving and changing. Each thing in this natural order is equally alive and has an energetic value or component. So everything — plants, animals, people, and things — exists in a vast landscape that swirls with vital energy. The same energy that flows through the world flows through you as well. In fact, according to this view, your *essence* — the part of you that makes you alive, unique, and vital — is this energy. And your body is the vehicle or environment in which this essence flows.

Feng Shui divides the vast environment or landscape that is the universe into more manageable units — like human beings and their homes, property, offices, living rooms, and bedrooms. You can't control the Feng Shui of the world at large. But Feng Shui enables you to design your personal environment according to the same universal principles of energy flow by which planets spin in their orbits and galaxies wheel through space. I delve deeper into this energy, the basis for Feng Shui, in Chapter 2.

Historical origins of Feng Shui

Feng Shui has been practiced in one form or another for several thousands of years. Its origins reach back to China's ancient shamanic practices and nature-based religions. The earliest Feng Shui comprised a mixture of divination, ritual, magic, and ancestor worship. It was practiced as a means of integrating one's earthly life, embedded in nature, with the world of chi or spirit. In these ancient times, gravesites were carefully selected according to energetic (or Feng Shui) principles with the thought that happy ancestors were likely to create favorable fortunes for their descendents. Eventually these principles were brought into common use and applied for the benefit of the living to improve the quality of their daily lives.

Feng Shui energy principles were also used to predict the weather; to determine the best times to plant crops; and to fix dates, times, locations, and positions for building sites. These principles were also used to decide when to wage war, and where battles ought to be fought. (Even today, military strategies and campaigns are designed according to the principles of positioning and placement of troops in relation to the others of the battlefield environment. This strategy also uses Feng Shui.)

Systems similar to Feng Shui have evolved in other cultures throughout the world. In India, practices used to create harmony with the environment are called *Vastu Shastra* and *Sthapatya Veda* (both methods of aligning one's living place with the natural forces of the universe). The Japanese use a related method. And Celtic and medieval European cultures used magical and divinational methods such as *geomancy* (literally "earth magic") to influence their relationship with their environment, align themselves with the power of the land, and improve their earthly lives.

Unearthing Basic Feng Shui Principles

Let me present a few basic Feng Shui concepts that can help you start thinking in Feng Shui terms. These basic Feng Shui principles can help you better understand your environment and its effects on you. (Don't worry, I keep it short and sweet.) If you're already aware of the basics of Feng Shui, you can skim the rest of this chapter and move on to Chapter 3, if you want.

The ancient Chinese determined that the universe was composed of two complementary qualities: *yin* and *yang*. They further assigned three categories into which these two essences flowed; the three categories are Heaven, Earth, and Human. Then the ancient philosophers made an intensive study over generations to learn how these interconnected categories could be manipulated or influenced in order to improve one's personal life, fortune, and destiny. Feng Shui was developed out of this prolonged and profound consideration. Read on to further examine these primary elements.

Yin and yang: The complementary opposites

Everything in the universe is composed of two opposite yet complementary principles or qualities: yin and yang. Yin symbolizes the passive side of nature, while yang represents the active side. But yin and yang don't exist independently; they simply describe the two primary qualities in which all existing things partake. Although nothing is 100 percent yin or 100 percent yang, all things contain relative amounts of both yin and yang energy. This concept is an important key to Feng Shui. Figure 1-1 shows the symbolism of yin and yang interacting. The white fish symbolizes yang, and the black fish shows yin. Note how each quality carries the color of its opposite within itself, showing that within all things is the seed for potential change.

Figure 1-1:
The interaction and harmony between yin and yang.

Things with characteristics such as passivity, receptiveness, silence, darkness, and inwardness are said to represent yin. In contrast, things with active, hard, projecting, loud, and bright characteristics represent yang. Neither one is better than the other, and both are absolutely necessary for life and the universe to exist. As philosophical concepts, yin and yang poetically describe the dualistic world. Nothing is completely good or pure, just as no one is totally evil or without redeeming qualities. (Darth Vadar has the cutest little dimple!) Everything that exists is a mixture in some measure of yin and yang.

In Feng Shui terms, a too-yang environment is disturbing and leads to the loss of peace and harmony. For example, a bedroom facing a noisy street can rob you of the quality rest you need. But a too-yin area — say an office looking out onto a dark narrow alley — can cause you to become overly subdued and lethargic, and can limit your energy and efficiency. An overly yin entrance to a residence — one that is hidden and dark — may not attract enough money or energy.

Yin and yang can also describe activities, events, and even emotions. For instance, a funeral is usually yin in nature: quiet, sober, and subdued. On the other hand, the famed Mardi Gras festival held in New Orleans is the epitome of yang energy: active, colorful, noisy, and exuberant. If you are overly yang, your emotional state is angry or explosive. But if you are overly yin, you can become withdrawn or depressed. To help you counteract or enhance certain qualities and tendencies, you can design your living environment according to Feng Shui. At their essence, all the Feng Shui cures you discover are ways of balancing the yin and yang in you and in your environment.

The Three Realms of Influence: Heaven, Earth, and Human

Another important Chinese model for looking at life is called the Three Realms of Influence. This concept relates to Feng Shui, because Feng Shui is a way of improving the destiny a person starts with. Three realms of the universe influence you — Heaven, Earth, and Human. These areas are both literal (they actually exist) and figurative (they symbolically influence people's lives). To get the most out of your life circumstances, you need positive conditions in each of these realms. On the other hand, a way of improving your circumstances is to pay close attention to these three areas and begin to move into alignment with the best they can offer.

Through the centuries, these three realms have become associated with three types of luck, one for each realm. According to Chinese belief, aligning your life — your activities and thoughts — with the natural order of all three realms brings you good luck and success. Feng Shui is a fundamental method that follows this principle. The following sections can help you better understand each of the Three Realms of Influence.

The Heaven Realm

Heavenly energy literally influences you daily through the climate, atmosphere, and air quality, and it influences you metaphorically through the place and time of your birth. Miracles and other unexpected interventions from above are also considered to be the workings of heaven. You've probably heard someone exclaim, "The heavens opened!" when describing an inspiration or a narrow escape from danger.

Positive timing — a bit easier to control than heavenly help — also comes under the category of the Heaven Realm. To achieve the greatest chances for prosperity and good fortune, any plan should be started at the proper time (meaning the time with the most favorable chance for success). To have Heaven luck is to have proper or auspicious timing for your endeavors.

The Earth Realm

The Earth Realm provides humans with all the materials needed to sustain life — food, shelter, clothing, and so on. According to Feng Shui beliefs, the way humans position and orient themselves relative to their surroundings enormously impacts their welfare and destiny. Applying Feng Shui to your environment maximizes the positive influences and minimizes the negative influences of the environment on your life. Early Chinese thinkers described the good fortune that was achieved by powerful and positive positioning as Earth luck. (Of course, humans impact the earth as well. And the best practice of Feng Shui helps humans live in harmony with the environment.)

The Human Realm

The third realm that affects your life is the Human Realm. In addition to timing (Heaven luck) and positive positioning (Earth luck), you need the right people around you to create success in your projects. The actions you and your associates undertake — and the harmony between all parties — is the factor that completes the picture. To be blessed with Human luck, you need the right people around you supporting you in your efforts.

Analyzing Western life in light of the Three Realms of Influence shows that most people rely first on themselves and their associates or family (Human luck), then on providence (Heaven luck), and very little or none at all on environmental circumstances (Earth luck) — that's Feng Shui to you and me — mainly because they don't know it exists. In reality, all three realms are equally important for success. By waking up to the power and influence of Feng Shui, you have a chance to increase your luck and grow into your fullest potential.

Five top factors affecting your fortune

Another way to look at life's equation for success is to consider an historical concept from Chinese culture called the Five Factors That Contribute To Life Fortune. This information has been distilled over several centuries of empirical observations by Chinese sages with a burning question on their minds: What are the key factors for human success? The Five Factors concept is the *CliffsNotes* version of their answer.

I explain these factors, in order of importance, in the following list:

- **Fate (or destiny).** The time in history, the country you're born into, your family type, and the socioeconomic status of your family are all elements that combine to set you on a particular life route from the start. Fate or destiny comprises about 70 percent of one's life destiny. Three types of fate generally affect humans: good, fair, or poor. Traditionally, you are stuck with the one you're handed at birth. The best you can do is try to improve your basic situation by using the four other factors listed in this list. (Read on for a way out of this dilemma!)

- **Luck.** According to the Five Factors concept, luck is neither chance nor random coincidence striking like a bolt out of the blue. Luck is a discernible, if mysterious, pattern of influences on your life path. Some people seem to have a luckier path through life than others do. If destiny is the time, place, direction, and speed with which you hit the road at birth, your luck is the pattern of events that impact you as you head down your path.

- **Feng Shui.** The third key factor affecting the quality of your life is your placement (positioning) on the earth. How you situate yourself in life impacts you so strongly that the ancient seers rated it as number three on Life's Hit Parade! Here's the payoff: If your fate and luck are poor, you can improve things by properly applying Feng Shui in your life and environment. In fact, practicing good Feng Shui makes it substantially easier than other known methods (besides winning the lottery) to overcome even poor fate and bad luck.

- **Charitable actions.** The positive actions you undertake — especially to serve others — are the fourth important factor that influences the quality of your life. Performing good deeds, without hoping for reward or recognition, makes your actions even more beneficial to you and others.

- **Self-improvement.** More than a Dale Carnegie course (which can also help), self-improvement refers to improving one's character and moral fiber. To improve yourself in this way invites good people, events, and well-being into your life.

How the East came West

During the latter half of the twentieth century, the Oriental mindset infiltrated the West through several different vehicles. In the 1950s and early 1960s, the Beat Generation discovered Zen Buddhism, and in the 1970s, Oriental martial arts (including karate and kung fu) started to gain popularity. In the 1970s and 1980s, acupuncture, acupressure, yoga, and tai chi also became very popular, and their use and influence still grows by leaps and bounds. Then in the 1990s, Feng Shui burst onto the scene, and its popularity has grown continuously. More than a passing fad, the main reason for this surge in Feng Shui awareness is that people in the West started to experience amazing and exciting results from their applications of Feng Shui. Many Westerners have experienced the positive life benefits that come from arranging their homes and offices according to the timeless principles of Feng Shui. And all of the Oriental systems I mention (martial arts, acupuncture, tai chi, and so on) are based on the same fundamental insights into the energy (chi) that flows everywhere in the environment, including throughout your body and the universe itself.

As you can see from the previous list, when determining causes of success in life, the influence of Feng Shui ranks as the third most important factor of all! If the ancient Chinese were correct (and why shouldn't one take seriously the longest continuously existing civilization on the planet), your environmental surroundings affect your success more than the good deeds you do or even the attempts you make to improve yourself. Can the environment you're in continuously have massive and pervasive impacts on your thoughts, feelings, actions, and life results? My answer is an emphatic yes!

Of the Five Factors, the first one on the list you can do something about is your Feng Shui. Think about this for a second: You can't choose which family you're born into, and you can't change your luck pattern on a whim, right? Of course not. But you can move your furniture around or start changing the colors in your house — both are Feng Shui methods you can implement today — and see the positive results tomorrow, or not long after. The truth is that all Five Factors affect you all the time. The point to grasp is that Feng Shui (the interaction between you and your environment) plays in life's big leagues. It affects you powerfully, and doing something about it is one of the most powerful and direct methods of life improvement the human species has discovered.

Understanding the Schools of Feng Shui

Though many schools of Feng Shui exist, all of them maintain the same basic purpose — gaining life improvement through improving the energy of the environment. Most traditional schools of Feng Shui use a combination of two basic methods: the Landform Method and the Compass Method.

A lesser-known school of Feng Shui is called BTB or Black Sect Feng Shui, the type of Feng Shui used in this book. In this book, BTB is referred to as Grandmaster Lin Yun's Feng Shui school. This style of Feng Shui was further developed and brought to the West by Grandmaster Lin Yun, my teacher, of Berkeley, California.

Landform and Compass Method Feng Shui

Landform Feng Shui reads the lay of the land and notes the contour, climate, shape, and other factors to determine the best locations for living and working. For example, in China, living with a mountain at your back and with your house facing south was recognized over the centuries as a safer living position. Why? The mountain helped the residents on at least three levels: The mountain gave protection from warring bands of infidels swooping down upon them; and it provided a strong psychological feeling of support and stability — this continuous influence helped the family's fortune grow over time; finally, the mountain was a protective barrier against the storms and cold that could sweep down from the north in winter. (This barrier helped preserve the croplands and the personal health of the occupants.) The Landform Method was easier to apply in the countryside, but today, many of its observations are still highly useful for city living.

Compass Method Feng Shui studies the direction (east, west, north, and south) your front door faces and compares this direction with your personal life directions, which are calculated from the time and date of your birth. Both simple and complex formulas exist to determine your personal directions. Other areas of the house that are aligned to positive directions include the bed, the stove, the desk, and the back door. The Compass Method says that directions and timing are the two of the most critical factors that affect your Feng Shui.

Grandmaster Lin Yun's Feng Shui school

One of the chief characteristics of Grandmaster Lin Yun's Feng Shui school is its eclectic nature. With roots in the teachings of India, China, and Tibet, it pulls from multiple sources, weaving together a combination of traditional

Feng Shui, Grandmaster Lin Yun's energy theories, and Chinese folklore. This school also benefits from the addition of Western concepts and explanations from various fields including physiology, psychology, ecology, sociology, and many others. Its working philosophy is that the best result comes from a marriage of Eastern and Western viewpoints and knowledge.

Grandmaster Lin Yun's Feng Shui school is

- An easy-to-grasp form of Feng Shui
- Highly practical and effective
- Focused on creating beneficial results quickly with the least expenditure of time and money

In this book, I focus intently on solutions that produce noticeable effects but are relatively easy to perform. Feng Shui is one of the most effective methods available to change your circumstances and achieve more of want you really want out of life. You can pick it up, put it into practice immediately, get new results, and create a brand new flow of life and energy.

Two key differences exist between traditional Feng Shui and Grandmaster Lin Yun's Feng Shui school. First, traditional Feng Shui employs a physical compass to diagnose the key directions of the home and relate them to the residents through astrological calculations. Grandmaster Lin Yun's school, while acknowledging the validity of the traditional Compass Method, uses a different approach. It does not use a physical compass but instead uses a mental compass called the Ba-Gua or Feng Shui Octagon to read the energies of the house and the lot (see Chapter 3 for more details on how to apply the Feng Shui Octagon to your environment). Grandmaster Lin Yun's Feng Shui school also emphasizes the *Theory of Relative Positioning*, which states that the areas of the environment that are physically closest to you most affect your energy (see Chapter 2).

Second, Grandmaster Lin Yun's school differs from traditional Feng Shui schools because it metaphorically uses *intention* (a way to dramatically enhance the effects of the Feng Shui cures you apply) as a sixth sense on top of the traditional five: sight, hearing, touch, smell, and taste. In Chapter 6, I detail how to use intention and visualization to make your cures more effective.

With this information, you hold the power to change your circumstances. No life scenario is hopeless or unworkable; you can always do something to improve your situation — if you choose. If you read other Feng Shui books, keep in mind that other schools of Feng Shui may use different principles and methods. This difference is okay — all methods of Feng Shui hold value and effectiveness.

Using Feng Shui to Your Advantage

The following list describes ten important ways that Feng Shui is influencing you right now. Using this book, you can discover how all these factors — and more — can be used to your advantage:

- ✔ **Your front door.** This area receives most of the subtle energy in your home, influences your opportunities and the amount of income you command.

- ✔ **The people who previously lived in your house.** They probably left behind some invisible vibes when they moved. The subtle traces of their feelings and experiences can hinder you for the first several years you live in the house.

- ✔ **The placement of your stove.** This location can influence your cash flow and physical health. A chronically dirty stove can significantly affect your financial status.

- ✔ **Clutter in your home or office.** Junk blocks vital energy, leading to dozens of frustrations and subtle obstacles.

- ✔ **The locations of bathrooms.** This situation can result in leaking money from your life or can raise significant health issues.

- ✔ **Your bed position.** This condition influences your love life to an amazing (and unseen) degree.

- ✔ **The air quality and lighting levels.** In your home and office, these circumstances directly affect your thinking patterns and endorphin levels, which in turn influence your performance, attitude, and results.

- ✔ **The colors you see.** The colors around you powerfully influence your moods, energy level, and effectiveness.

- ✔ **Your desk position.** This situation can make or break your career. The desk is the number one Feng Shui factor for success on the job.

- ✔ **Seeing your front door from the street.** You may have to struggle hard for the opportunities you receive if your front door is hidden from plain view. (Feng Shui to the rescue!)

A Midwestern dentist located in a small town was frustrated because of his difficulties in hiring additional staff to expand his practice. After performing Feng Shui in his office, he was pleasantly surprised to find that quality hygienists came from out of the woodwork to apply for positions. Ultimately, changing the Feng Shui of your environment creates new options and choices. Feng Shui can create a whole realm of possibilities that you never considered or didn't believe possible. Yet, real as life, here's an example of Feng Shui's power to influence and change your life experience.

Fortunately, by applying the easy and sensible Feng Shui principles provided in this book, you can reverse negative patterns and strengthen positive ones to maximize your chances of success. The bottom line is that Feng Shui can help you improve your environment easily, directly, and powerfully. And if applied correctly, your life can become easier and happier in essential areas — relationships, career, wealth, family connections, and so on. You may be amazed at how many life obstacles can be cleared with simple energy shifts you can perform in your home or office.

Using Feng Shui to Find Life Solutions

When you have a problem in life, you can seek solutions through multiple avenues. For example, if you have a problem with your car, you can buy a new car, repair it yourself, have someone else repair it, hope the problem goes away, or decide to live with the issue. Each of these options holds advantages and disadvantages. Which option you choose depends on your level of cash on hand, your expertise with cars, and your current life status. In almost any situation, you can choose from a range of solutions. You almost never have only one road to follow.

For life problems in general, your solutions can include:

✔ Working harder and/or smarter; acquiring new information

✔ Calling in an expert

✔ Calling on a higher power and praying

✔ Trying to learn from the situation, becoming a better person, and building character

✔ Improving the environment to create change (performing Feng Shui adjustments)

You may be surprised to find out that the best choice on the list is often the last one: Adjust the Feng Shui of your home or office to change your situation and resolve your problem.

The Feng Shui process

The school of Feng Shui presented in this book involves identifying energetic problems (or opportunities for improvement) in your environment and coming up with a solution that is viable for your needs, including your taste, budget, aesthetic values, and temperament. To really work, your solutions should be both practical and effective.

You can approach Feng Shui in your life in two basic ways: Consider them carefully. Though both of them are effective, the general approach (detailed in the following section) can sometimes lead to frustration and confusion. I personally recommend the second, or the specific method, because of its clarity, power, and straightforward progress toward tangible results. However, as usual in Feng Shui, the best method is the one that personally feels right for you — and creates the results you need.

The general approach: Improving the environment at random

The first Feng Shui strategy is to look at your house in Feng Shui terms — without necessarily taking your current life needs into account. Then apply solutions to improve the overall energy of the environment with the general intention of making things better for you and your home. This method is more of a general approach, because you're not analyzing your life to determine the direction you want to take. It produces results; however, because you don't set specific intentions, the results may not be as powerful as desired. Using this method can make it more difficult to see how well your cures are working or what additional improvements you need to make.

The specific approach: Setting your goals and achieving them

If powerful results are highly attractive to you, I recommend the specific approach, which requires you to perform two basic steps:

1. **Examine your life.** Pinpoint the parts of your life (relationship, work, money, and so on) that aren't working and are screaming for improvement. Decide specifically how you want these areas to improve.

2. **Adjust your environment.** Use the information crammed chock-a-block into this book to determine how you can adjust your environment to achieve changes directly in the life areas you want to improve. Pick the cures that work for you and your lifestyle and implement them.

Overall, this approach is effective as well as specific and is focused on getting you the results you want. You know your goals and targets, and you can hone in and hit them. Rather than making just general improvements to the environment and hoping they can help, you know the specific practical purpose of each cure — vastly extending the power of your efforts. The specific approach puts you firmly in the driver's seat. You can select which areas of your life to improve and which areas are fine for right now. Because you set goals and implement changes to create them, you also can easily track your results to see how well your Feng Shui is working. Finally, you can adjust your cures, over time, to fine-tune the energies for even more results.

Intention: The real power behind Feng Shui

Feng Shui can be divided into two parts — the visible and the invisible — both of which are important for success in life and in Feng Shui. Visible factors include the walls, doors, streets, and other tangible elements that are analyzed and altered with Feng Shui. The invisible factors include *chi* (life force energy), *predecessor influences* (the energies of the people who previously lived in your house), ghosts and spirits, the energies within the land that impact you, and other factors.

The most important invisible factor is *intention*, or the simultaneous strong desire and visualization of what you want a cure to produce. Everything you do in life involves an intention and an action. The action is the physical side of the process. In Feng Shui, this means some tangible activity like moving the bed to a better location, changing a wall color, or decorating with healthy potted plants. Intention is the invisible or spiritual side of Feng Shui. Intention is the reason why you move the bed — what life change you hope to accomplish when you make this change. Intention includes two parts: what you want and how clearly you want it. If you move the bed to improve your marriage, and you visualize the improvement while changing the bed position, your cure will be much more effective. (See Chapter 6 for powerful methods of empowering your intention.)

The range of available cures

You can perform a wide range of possible cures to transform a Feng Shui malady. For any situation, the appropriate cure can range anywhere from simple, quick, and easy (rearranging your existing furniture) to complex, difficult, and expensive (buying a new house!). In this book, I keep things as easy and inexpensive as possible.

Feng Shui isn't necessarily cheap or inexpensive, but you can find creative ways to implement low cost Feng Shui cures in many situations. Most importantly, I recommend choosing a practical and effective solution for your personal situation.

Choosing the Life Areas to Improve

Okay! Now you're ready to begin. You can start by deciding what you want to change or improve in your life. You don't necessarily need to change or correct every possible Feng Shui issue in your home or office. The list can extend to hundreds of cures. No house or building is perfect, and they can't be made perfect in terms of Feng Shui. What you want to do is focus on how your dwelling (or office) is currently benefiting or stopping your progress.

In this book, you can find dozens of practical ways to create the new results you want. Most significantly, focus on what you can do now. By taking action, sooner or later you will create new results. Begin by filling out Table 1-1 to find out what areas of your life you want to improve first by practicing Feng Shui. This Self-Assessment Exercise gives you a clear look at the status of several areas of your life and helps you decide which ones you want to improve. For each area of your life listed in the first column, write one or two words describing the general situation for the area. Use the final column to prioritize the urgency of improvement by assigning 1 (high priority), 2 (medium priority), or 3 (low priority) to each area. Photocopy the worksheet before using it so you can use it again later.

Table 1-1	Self-Assessment Exercise	
Life Area	*Description*	*Priority (1, 2, 3)*
Wealth		
Marriage		
Health		
Career		
Fame/Reputation		
Family		
Children		
Helpful People		
Knowledge		

When you've completed the Self-Assessment Exercise, select (from the areas you've rated as high priorities) the ones you want to focus on immediately. Keep these Life Areas firmly in mind, and as you read this book, notice the cures you can perform to improve these areas. This awareness keeps you focused on finding practical techniques you can implement immediately.

Getting Started: The Steps to Success

Be sure to get a scale or close drawing of your house and lot to use with this book. (Hey, if you're going to practice Feng Shui, do it right.) Find the architectural drawings you stashed in the garage, or make a drawing of your house including the internal walls and the doors. This tool is your guide when using Feng Shui to actually make something happen (instead of just thinking about making a change).

In the following list, I present nine steps you can use to perform highly powerful Feng Shui, using a life example (improving the marriage) in each step:

1. **Choose which life areas you want to work on first.** (See Table 1-1.) For example: You want more harmony and closeness with your partner.

2. **Make a commitment to seeing new results (changes!) in your life in the chosen areas.** Realize that you need to make changes in your home, office, or property to get the new results you desire, and commit yourself to finding and correcting the imbalances. (Or, following the example, add energy to Marriage Areas if no problems are obvious.) At this point, you may recruit your spouse to help with the Feng Shui endeavor or proceed to make the changes yourself.

3. **Scan your environment as you read this book to see where you need to implement Feng Shui adjustments.** To improve your marriage, note the placement of your bed and the amount of clutter in your bedroom.

4. **Select the best cure options for each environmental problem you notice.** For example, you may choose to cure the situation by moving your bed to the best possible position in the room and clearing items out from under the bed.

5. **Implement the chosen cures.** Move the bed and clear the clutter.

6. **Perform the Three Secrets Reinforcement on your cures.** I explain this important mental step that empowers the cures you perform in Chapter 6.

7. **Pay attention to changes that occur in your life after you implement your cures.** Keep on the lookout for the new effects you desire. Hopefully, you and your spouse will experience greater harmony and increased communication after you put your cures in place.

8. **Based on the feedback you're getting from your life, perform additional cures for the same area of your life if necessary.** If things have improved somewhat, but you want further benefits, jump back into the book and apply some more marriage cures.

9. **Start the whole process again focusing on another area of your life.** Now that you have a success under your belt, you can target another area of your life — like career or income — that you want to improve.

How and when results come isn't something you can directly control. However, keep in mind that even if you see quick or immediate benefits from your cures, they continue to work indefinitely and provide you with ongoing energy and results for years to come — unless of course you move, in which case you can begin anew.

Getting Additional Help

Occasionally, a situation is so laden with Feng Shui problems that you can't decide where to begin. Or you may perform some good cures and gain incremental improvement but feel that you still have a long way to go. If you need help to tackle your issues fully, you can take a Feng Shui course, or you can call in a professional Feng Shui consultant for assistance (see the Feng Shui Resource page at the end of this book). Meanwhile, make any improvements that you can right now and better your odds of creating positive effects — inevitably, things will begin to shift.

Chapter 2

Key Feng Shui Principles

Feng Shui is about becoming aware of your environment and applying energetic principles to your surroundings. Whether you know it or not, you're affected by the Feng Shui of your environment at all times. The energies of your residence and workplace have been constantly contributing to your successes and/or failures in life, so practicing Feng Shui isn't really taking on something new. Feng Shui is conscious participation in a natural process that has been going on as long as human beings have been alive; Feng Shui is you intentionally interacting with your environment. The information in this book gives you Feng Shui eyes. You can start to see practical changes that you can make in your living and working environments to improve your life situation, and you can make these changes according to principles and techniques discovered in ancient China and refined over centuries.

An underlying premise of Feng Shui is that energy flows freely in a harmonious environment but is obstructed in a disharmonious environment. Whether this premise seems mystical or academic to you, this Feng Shui concept is a reality that continuously affects your life in direct and tangible ways. So prepare to find out some unusual ways of thinking about life, energy, and feeling, and get ready to perceive living environments in a way that gives you a whole new level of understanding and control over your life.

In this chapter, I introduce the essential principles of Feng Shui that explain how and why *cures* (alterations to your environment that result in desired life changes) work. You can certainly get results without mastering all these principles, but this crash course in Feng Shui concepts can help you make sense of everything that follows. Start reading, and you can soon find yourself growing and changing with your environment. Feng Shui can be fun! So strap yourself in for an adventure in the realms of space (your space, that is), energy, and improved living circumstances.

Chi: The Energy of Feng Shui

Chi (pronounced chee) is the fundamental principle without which Feng Shui (or you and me for that matter) cannot exist. Chi, a Chinese word that has no direct translation in English, holds several meanings at once: cosmic energy, life force, breath, and vapor. (In this book, when I say energy, I'm referring to chi.) Chi is the invisible energy that animates all living things. Chi flows continuously: through pathways (or *meridians*) in your body (the practices of acupuncture and Oriental medicine are based on these flows); through your home, through the Earth, the heavens, the atmosphere, and the cosmos. (See Figure 2-1 for a stylized view of human energy circulation.) Chi is the flow of life itself, and if the chi stopped flowing through you for even one second, you would cease to live. Based on Chinese folklore, energy channels that run inside the earth are called dragon veins. These veins are similar to the body's energy meridians. The chi that flows through these channels is metaphorically called the breath (or energy) of the dragon.

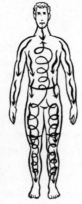

Figure 2-1:
Energy
flowing
within the
body.

The flow of chi in your environment affects every area of your life, influencing your health, your outlook, your decision making, and even your sex life. The flow of chi in turn is influenced by the interior and exterior elements of the physical environment. Colors, shapes, orientation, lighting, objects and their positions and arrangements, the use of space, and the degree of cleanliness or clutter all impact and collectively determine your home's energy flow. And this flow (or lack of flow) affects you continually, conditions your experience in your home and workplace, and significantly influences your future for good or for ill.

Millions of people worldwide and thousands of people with whom I've worked over the years are applying the principles and practices taught in this book in their daily lives and are experiencing positive results. So whether you prefer the philosophical approach to understanding chi ("This whole chi metaphor really gives me a useful new way to look at and reorganize my life.") or you take the tangible route ("Whoa, I'm really feelin' somethin' here!"), you can receive profound and practical benefits by arranging your living and working environments according to Feng Shui principles.

A new, yet old, way of seeing the world

At this point, you may be wondering, "How real is this mysterious, all-important force called chi?" Many Westerners don't understand chi because modern science doesn't acknowledge that it exists. The rationalist worldview denies the reality of whatever can't be weighed on a scale or measured by an instrument. By this rational logic, a life force that animates all living things doesn't exist, because no meter exists to measure it. By further extension, happiness, sadness, joy, love, and pain aren't real for the same reason. Yet the most sophisticated instrument in the universe already exists that possesses functions for registering the flow of chi. This instrument is the human being, and the functions are feeling and intuitive sensing.

An interesting fact about chi is that it works for you whether or not you believe it's real (kind of like gravity and oxygen). For example, how exactly are you able to move your arm? Modern science says that the food you digest releases energy (calories of heat) that powers your cells

and enables your nerves to fire and your muscles to contract. Voila! You can grab your morning cup of coffee. But how exactly does this process occur? And why, when the body dies, can't you simply shove a hamburger into it — or zap it with electricity — and make it rise and walk again? These mysteries are what drive both science and religion.

Chinese theory explains the phenomena of movement from a different perspective. Your life force — your personal chi — originally came from your parents. (Before your parents, it came from the universe, but that's a much longer story.) Chinese theory says that the chi activates your brain to perceive and think and then flows through the body, allowing the body to move and function. "Gimme a cup of coffee!" Mr. Brain says. And the chi stimulates the muscles of your arm to grasp, lift, carry the cup to your lips, and swallow the sips. But even when you're buzzing on coffee, you're still running on chi, like everything else in the universe.

(continued)

(continued)

Or look at it this way: Modern electricity is essentially electrons flowing through wires. Electricity leaves the power plant at very high voltages. When the electricity reaches your house, the energy has stepped down enough to power your home's wiring without blowing it out. This basic energy is then adapted to run a wide variety of appliances (furnace, air conditioner, refrigerator, computer, stereo, TV, and so on) that perform a diverse range of functions. By now you're used to it, dependant on it, and probably even take its numerous benefits for granted — until the power goes out or the monthly bill arrives — and yet you don't really understand what energy is or how it works. In fact, no one really does! The most interesting thing about electricity is that you know how to harness it, but you ultimately don't know what it is. (So you call it electricity.) The same can be said for chi: You ultimately don't know what chi is, but the energy runs your body, courses through your emotions, and dances mysteriously in your thoughts, inspirations, and dreams.

And remember, even the greatest masters of the East haven't completely conquered the subtlest mysteries of the life force. Nor have the greatest Western scientists. They simply find workable theories that allow them to effectively manipulate forces they ultimately do not understand or need to understand. (Scientists are still searching diligently for approximately 65 to 90 percent of the mass of the universe, which they have termed *dark energy*. So if you find it, please let them know where it is.) Even as we speak, Einstein's theories are being overturned by new ones, which will also be overturned in time. So take heart: Using the Feng Shui principles and methods in this book, you can employ the mechanics of chi just as you employ aerodynamics every time you get on a plane, even if you lack a Ph.D. in aviation theory. Oh, I almost forgot . . . did you know that according to the principles of aerodynamics, bumblebees shouldn't be able to fly? (Luckily, bees are unable to read the dense aerodynamics manuals.)

So think of chi as a useful metaphor, like $E=MC^2$. And for the purposes of this book, visualize it as a river of energy that runs through your home and your body. Where the river flows smoothly and powerfully, you're able to navigate the path of your life with confidence and power, and you tend to be fortunate, happy, and successful. But where the river is blocked, cramped, or stagnant, you tend to get bogged down and overwhelmed by obstacles, problems, and frustrations.

Start by examining the ways that your body absorbs chi on a daily basis. Chi comes to you from multiple environmental sources that include:

- The food you eat
- The air you breathe
- The water you drink
- The land and its vegetation
- The sun and other celestial bodies
- Your living environment
- Your working environment

These multiple sources in the environment supply your body with chi (energy) to sustain itself. Your body then transforms the energy and directs it into multiple activities: digestion, breathing, moving of muscles, thinking, working, sensing, worrying, complaining, lounging around the house, watching TV, and a myriad of other important (and not-so-important) human activities. But all these activities are powered by the same basic energy that flows through your system, your environment, and the universe itself.

The Types of Chi

According to Feng Shui theory, several varieties of chi exist, all of which affect you on one level or another. The following sections cover some of the more-important varieties.

The chi of the heavens

Heavenly chi includes the chi of the air, the weather, the sky, the stars, and other heavenly bodies. The amount and quality of chi in the air helps determine the quality, freshness, and vitality of the oxygen you breathe. Chi of the sky and atmosphere includes climatic influences that affect humans and other life forms. Cosmic chi is the energy of outer space and its celestial bodies: the sun, the moon, and the stars. Without solar chi (the chi of the sun), no life can exist on earth.

The chi of the earth

The chi of the earth is the realm of Feng Shui. While civilization is not advanced enough to change things in space (it can send out satellites, but it can't rearrange the planets), civilization can certainly alter the chi of the Earth, for both good and ill. The energy of the Earth is divided into many different categories; Feng Shui masters have delineated hundreds of specific distinctions about the types of chi of different pieces of land. The most important distinction in Feng Shui is whether the energy (chi) of a parcel of land is healthy and supportive of the humans who live in the area. At the extreme ends of the spectrum, the chi of the earth can be two forms:

✔ **Lively, vibrant, and nourishing:** This type of chi is abundant in locations like Hawaii, in old-growth redwood forests, or by healthy, moving streams. Such an environment generates lots of negative ions (which are actually positive for your health), contains high levels of oxygen, and helps create a positive mental attitude.

✔ **Arid, barren, and hostile:** The chi in these conditions is unsupportive
of human life and can actually drain life from the people who stay in the
area for long periods of time. These locations may feature negative magnetic fields, unbearable temperatures (hot or cold), and a lack of life
forms. Examples include the Arctic and Antarctica, the Gobi Desert,
Death Valley, and the Dead Sea (the names of these last two are certainly
no coincidence!).

The chi of your house and living environments

The chi of homes can vary widely, depending on the energies of the residents
and the general and specific details of the structure and the lot. The interaction between the chi of a living environment and the chi of the humans within
this space is Feng Shui; the house itself and the people living in it synergistically
create the house chi, which in turn continuously affects and conditions the
residents' energy, actions, and to some degree, their destinies. Amazingly, the
way your home is situated can mean the difference between experiencing long-
term happiness and good fortune versus enduring missed opportunities and a
more-difficult life path. Deciding between these two options and taking concrete actions to bring about the one you desire is the purpose of Feng Shui.

Table 2-1 gives you an overview of some of the types of energy that can be
found in various residences. Note that the chi type refers to the overall feeling that continuously permeates the environment. All homes, over time, have
variations in their energy patterns. However, the chi types listed in the table
are a quick-and-dirty way of discussing the general energy characteristics of a
home as it relates to humans. For example, if a home has gambling chi, this
influence can be felt by the residents even when they're not currently sitting
at the poker table. And if someone has died recently in the home, the general
energetic feeling may be death chi for some time — regardless of whether the
residents are conscious of the feeling.

You don't have to worry about correctly analyzing your home's specific chi
type. This job is better left to a professional Feng Shui consultant. You can
simply determine what areas of your life you want to change and apply effective cures to meet your goals. Through this process, rest assured that the chi
type of your home can inevitably change and improve.

Table 2-1	Types of House Chi
Chi of House	*Life Effects on Occupants*
Studious chi	Atmosphere of learning and cultivation
Noble chi	Honor, principles, and worthiness are tangible
Angry chi	Feeling of tension, arguments, and bitterness
Fighting chi	Clashes, violence, and a feeling of fear in the air
Wealthy chi	Feeling of prosperity and abundance
Gambling chi	Fortunes can rise or fall rapidly
Lucky chi	Good fortune and happiness prevail
Unlucky chi	Something bad may happen in this area
Death/dying chi	Change this chi!

The chi of humans

The chi states of people are measured against an ideal chi state and have many variations. The human chi states are classified according to their demeanor or dominant behavior patterns. For example, someone who's prickly, pushy, and displays sharp edges around others has porcupine chi; a person who is physically present, but mentally absent, has daydreamer's chi. (The lights are on and the dog is barking, but no one's home.) See Table 2-2 for a glimpse at some of the other types of chi that can characterize your fellow humans.

Table 2-2	Types of Human Chi
Human Chi Type	*Personal Characteristics*
Ideal chi	Energy is uplifted, smooth, balanced
Choked	Unable to speak the truth
Talkative	Unfortunately, speaks the truth too much!
Self-Defeating	Deluded, prevents their own success
Distracted	Moves in too many directions at once
Introverted	Overly focused within themselves, easily becomes suspicious

The Flows of Chi

One of the most important things to remember about chi is that it flows like wind and water. Think of the flow of chi in your body and in your home as a river of energy. The main source of this energy river is your mouth; for your home, the front door. To manipulate the flow of chi in your environment is to practice Feng Shui. Ideally, your flows of chi should meet the characteristics described in the following sections.

Ideal chi state for the physical body

For the human body, the ideal state of chi is strong, smooth, and positive energy that is uplifted and evenly distributed through the body — it flows from the ground (feet) up to the head. You receive chi from many sources, but the main source is through your mouth; food, air, light, and chi all enter the body through the mouth to provide nourishment, sustenance, and energy. (The fact that your mouth plays a key role in your ideal chi state reveals why breathing exercises and changing what you eat for the better are so important.) The best chi condition occurs when chi flows strongly through the whole body without any blocks, distortions, or flow problems.

Ideal chi state for the house

To explain house chi, I use the metaphor of an energy bank account. Ideally, the chi in a house circulates smoothly and freely through every part of the house, filling it with positive energy. This energy — which comes mainly through the front door — is the energetic income of the house. The front door is the main energy source because this point is where the people enter. (See Chapter 9.) When your house chi is ideal and flowing (see Figure 2-2), it conducts sufficient energy to provide you with beneficial life circumstances. Your energy bank account is in the black. You prosper and flourish. Life is good. But if the house contains obstructions (for example, if the front door is blocked), the flow of chi is disrupted, and areas of the house can become energetically depleted, which in turn affects the people who live in the house. Generally, a house that has depleted or distorted energy patterns (low energy account balance) results in disharmony and various life problems.

Figure 2-2:
Energy
circulating
in house
and land.

To sum up, the beneficial characteristics of ideal chi flow are as follows:

- Powerful
- Positive
- Uplifting
- Flowing
- Smooth

Negative characteristics of chi flow include:

- Rushing energy (comes too fast, is unbalancing, and can lead to injuries)
- Stagnant chi (prevents your goals from happening)
- Blocked chi (can stop you in life)
- Leaking chi (leads to loss of energy)
- Piercing chi (can threaten your health and welfare)

Any of the previous negative energy patterns can create harmful influences on your body, mind, and life circumstances. However, Feng Shui cures — which I detail throughout the book — exist to remedy negative energy conditions. Properly applied, the cures transform negative energy states into positive ones, resulting in new and beneficial influences that help create the life conditions you desire: peace, harmony, and prosperity.

Cultivating Chi

You know that everything affects your energy, so what can you do about it? According to ancient Chinese philosophy, one of the most important things in life is cultivating one's chi. You can call your chi cultivation personal Feng Shui. You cultivate chi in the same way you cultivate anything else — with time, patience, attention, and careful steps. For example, to cultivate a vegetable garden you do the following things: Pay close attention to how the garden is doing; feed, water, and care for it; protect it from pests and intruders; continuously create the conditions where the things you want (kinds of plants, wildlife, and so on) can flourish; and you may also want to increase your knowledge of gardening techniques and principles. (Oh, and by the way, you may want to plant a few vegetable seeds.) Read on to find out how to apply the cultivation principle to your own personal chi.

Chi cultivation: Benefits and rewards

Chi is life, so cultivating your chi enhances and improves your life in all areas and expands your sphere of influence in life, at home, in relationships, and at work. The many and desirable results of chi cultivation include:

- ✔ Improved physical health
- ✔ Enhanced mental health
- ✔ Increased intellectual ability and wisdom
- ✔ Increased spiritual and psychic power
- ✔ Better luck
- ✔ Improved family and personal relationships
- ✔ Character benefits, such as becoming more calm, tolerant, patient, honest, and so on

Eight factors affecting your personal chi

In addition to the sources of chi and its movements (or flow) inside your body, you can also pay attention to the forces that condition your personal chi. To *condition* means to affect or influence the quality of something. Consciously conditioning your chi is what the Chinese call chi cultivation. And chi cultivation is necessary because everything influences your chi. If you don't take charge of your chi, other factors take control whether you like it or not.

You can cultivate your personal chi by manipulating the eight main factors that affect your personal chi. These factors include:

- **Your inner self:** You exert the biggest impact on (and bear the greatest responsibility for) your own energy. Your thoughts, moods, and choices continuously affect and modify your chi, for good or ill. So observe and discipline your inner self. Change your thinking habits for the better. Self adjustment in this way cultivates your chi, and it really works.

- **The people around you:** The people you spend time with affect you profoundly. Every teacher of human growth throughout history has said that one of the most important factors determining the quality and course of your life is the people you surround yourself with. So spending more time in good company and less time in bad company is chi cultivation.

- **Your environment:** Your environment conditions your energy continuously and relentlessly. Because you can't stop these influences, deciding to change them sticks you in the driver's seat of life and allows you to assert more control over your own destiny. This control is where Feng Shui enters the picture. Conscious and mindful modification of your environment is definitely cultivation of your chi.

- **Events:** Things that happen in life affect your energy. A car accident, falling in love, a job loss, a promotion, a divorce . . . all these things directly, profoundly, and noticeably affect your chi. You can't stop things from happening, but you can somewhat influence and determine your response to what happens. This influence is also chi cultivation and naturally leads to the following factor, conduct.

- **Conduct:** Your actions throughout life continuously affect your chi. Your conduct leaves lasting impressions in your own mind and emotions as well as in the minds and emotions of others. These impressions become perpetual conditioning factors on your personal flow of chi.

- **Spiritual demeanor:** Your religious or spiritual perspectives significantly influence your energy (not to mention your character). So consciously developing this area of your life and living in harmony with spiritual principles and values is chi cultivation.

- **Political climate:** Do political events affect your personal energy? Cuban Missile Crisis. Cold War. Watergate. Monica Lewinsky. Political events clearly affect your energy to one degree or another. You can also say that who you vote into office helps to determine the nation's Feng Shui. (So vote energetically!) Actively participating in the larger life around you to promote positive change is chi cultivation.

- **Others:** This sector includes all the many unknown factors that constantly impact you . By continuing to grow in life and wisdom, you can discover more of these factors.

The previous factors influence everyone to one degree or another. However, your personal Feng Shui is one of the easiest of the eight areas to change. So forget about trying to change other people for a while and focus on improving yourself and your personal environment. Cultivate your own chi. Take responsibility for your personal Feng Shui. Then watch the positive changes stream into your life.

The Language of Feng Shui

If chi is the power of Feng Shui, symbols and patterns are the language of Feng Shui. These aspects can reveal how your environment affects you, and, believe me, these effects are big. Like a fish in water that is unknowingly affected by the water, your environment conditions your daily experience without your awareness in a holistic and encompassing manner. Symbols and patterns are the ways your psyche subconsciously interprets and relates to your environment.

- ✔ **Symbolism:** Something that represents or stands in for another thing. Symbolic images reveal correspondences between patterns in your environment and patterns in your life.

- ✔ **Patterns:** The structural relationships between the events in your life and the realities of your home and workplace. These patterns — when you're aware of them — show you exactly how your environment is influencing your experience. Patterns can also point the way to making changes quickly and powerfully.

Read on for a closer look at symbols and patterns.

Symbols: The environment is talkin' (to you!)

Symbols affect you on three different levels — universal, cultural and personal — all of which involve your living space. The Feng Shui of your home (and office) addresses all three of these levels of symbolic effect.

- ✔ **Universal symbols:** Representations that hold true for everyone. For example, your stove symbolizes nourishment and health. Regardless of individual cultural conditioning, the stove or cooking fire represents the same thing to all human beings, so the stove is a universal symbol. In the same way, the bathroom symbolizes cleansing and elimination, the bed symbolizes relationship and marriage, and so on.

✔ **Cultural symbols:** Connections between objects and meanings that are valid only in a particular culture. The Liberty Bell is a uniquely American cultural symbol. Any American who sees this bell with its characteristic crack in the side thinks — let freedom ring. A member of another culture may not make the same association.

✔ **Personal symbolism:** A connection between objects, events, and meanings that is valid only for you or your family. For instance, a picture of your relatives on the wall or the image on your family coat-of-arms has unique symbolic value for you, but means little to a stranger visiting your home.

Whether you realize it or not, symbolic connections permeate and exert a profound influence in your life. They condition your thoughts, moods, actions, and energy, all of which greatly determine how others see and treat you. Personal or cultural symbols can be used in Feng Shui, but in this book, I present mostly universal symbology that applies to everyone. (However, I do use various Chinese cultural symbols that have long-standing meaning in Feng Shui practice and can work effectively for anyone.)

Symbols you live by

The primary level of symbolism in Feng Shui is the relationship between you and your living environment. This connection is universal symbolism; everyone has a fundamental relationship to his or her living space. Thus the Feng Shui saying, "Your house is you." Of course, this saying isn't literally true but is a *metaphor* — a symbolic way of communicating the importance and impact your dwelling has on you and your family. Symbolically speaking, your house (its structure, shape, condition, and so on) represents and reflects you, your body, and your mind and spirit on various levels. But don't think of this metaphor as only a concept. The state of your house strongly influences the state of your psyche and your life.

To continue, the main door of your residence represents your self, your security and safety, and your voice. Doors inside the home represent the voices of the adults, while the windows represent the voices of the children. The doorknob symbolizes your grip on life, and the list of correlations goes on and on. (Symbolic correlations of this type are given throughout this book to keep you conscious and aware of how the changes you're making in your environment directly and indirectly affect your life situation.)

You can also apply the symbolic principle by keeping in mind two metaphors: "Your environment is your mirror" and "your house symbolizes your body." Saying that your environment is your mirror means that everything in your surroundings reflects back to you something about who you are. With this newfound awareness, you start to see what kind of conditioning you're experiencing day in and day out. Not that you're necessarily on the lookout for new things; rather, you have a different mindset, awareness, and attitude. For instance, you may shockingly realize that the permanent piles of clutter in your bedroom likely pertain to the relationship frustrations you've been experiencing. (In Feng Shui, the bedroom correlates directly to relationship.)

The other powerful metaphor — your house symbolizes your body — relates to an entire branch of Feng Shui concerned with the relationship between your house and the different parts of your physical body. For example, the main beam of the house represents the spine, the walls represent your skin, the plumbing relates to your body's elimination system, and so on. In Chapter 14, I provide cures you can perform to improve things in these areas.

Seeing and changing your patterns

As you apply the techniques in this book, look for *patterns* (or correspondences between your living environment and the ongoing events in your life). When you can spot these patterns, you enter into a conscious, effective relationship with your environment; this relationship is the purpose of Feng Shui. Seeing these patterns lets you connect what's happening in your life (your obstructed career and dire financial situation) with the conditions in your home (a cluttered front entrance and badly arranged Wealth Area). Noticing patterns reveals the causal relationships between your surroundings and your life. And this awareness allows you to take concrete actions and create positive changes in any part of life you desire.

Steve and Josie, my clients in California, were having a hard time financially and in their careers. They did make money, but it always seemed to leak away. (It came in like molasses and went out like water.) When I looked at their house, the pattern became clear. In Feng Shui, water symbolizes money. Leaks in your house or other plumbing problems can negatively affect your finances. Well, the Burkes had a roof leak in the Wealth Area of their home. Bingo! Direct correlation. They also had a broken hot tub in the Wealth Area, another obvious connection between their personal experience (life effects) and their living environment (contributing cause). They immediately remedied these conditions and then proceeded to recieve more income in the next few months than they had made in the previous year. This effect is Feng Shui in action. (You were expecting something more mystical?)

Scores of these correlations exist in your life as well. You may not notice them now, but the further you read, the more glaringly obvious they can become. And you're able to do something about it. (Even if this book just gets you to keep your house clean and in good repair, you'll get far more than your money's worth!) So as you read on, look more deeply at both your life and your home. Start thinking in terms of pattern, correlations, and connections, and you can go a long way in Feng Shui.

Positioning: Your Place in the Scheme of Things

A Feng Shui principle is that the importance of a position is determined by the amount of time you spend in the positioned area. *Positioning* is how you relate personally to any environment you find yourself in. On average, humans spend one-third of their time working (at the desk), one-third sleeping (in bed), and one-third taking care of everything else. You may not have thought of this concept before, but the positions of your bed and desk determine your orientation during two-thirds of your life. Needless to say, these positions strongly impact your health, happiness, success, and financial fortune.

Two theories of positioning — Relative Positioning and Commanding Position — can help you understand how to apply the concept. (In Chapters 11 and 16, you can find cures to help you gain strong personal positioning.)

The Theory of Relative Positioning

As I explain in Chapter 1, traditional Feng Shui relies on the physical compass to determine directions, starting with the all-important front door. I call using the physical compass *absolute* (or global) positioning because it uses the magnetic field of the earth to orient the house correctly by using the absolute directions on the face of the compass (east, west, north, and south). Grandmaster Lin Yun's Feng Shui school (the type of Feng Shui in this book) uses another method called the Theory of Relative Positioning to orient and analyze your environment. This method is easier for most people to pick up quickly and perform effectively.

Two principles guide the Theory of Relative Positioning.

✔ **Local interrelations are more important than global positioning.** The first principle of the Theory of Relative Positioning says that the interaction between the parts of your environment (their orientation relative to each other) is more important than their orientation to absolute direction (east, west, north, or south). In practical usage, this school emphasizes the interrelationships between your house and your neighbors, your driveway and the street, your house and the lot, and numerous other parts of your environment over the importance of compass directions. (*Note:* Grandmaster Lin Yun's school does consider the compass method to be a highly valid and effective Feng Shui system, but prefers to use his own unique method to analyze and diagnose the environment.) This method has the added benefit of getting you to examine more closely and understand more deeply the symbolic connections that exist between the various parts of the environment in which you live and how interrelated they truly are. This system also allows you to see the symbolic connections of all the areas in your personal life and to understand more clearly the ways in which they impact you.

✔ **What's closer to you is more important than what's farther away.** The second principle of the Theory of Relative Positioning is that the closer an area of the environment is to the human beings that are in it (that's you!), the more the area affects them and their life experience. Keep in mind that the closer an area of your environment, the more it affects you.

Taking the Commanding Position

The Commanding Position principle is used in several different contexts. The main idea of the Commanding Position is that you sit, stand, or otherwise situate yourself in the best and most powerful position available in any situation. The Commanding Position provides fundamental assistance to these areas of your life:

✔ General success (bed position)

✔ Career and projects (the desk position)

✔ Health and money (stove position)

✔ Social life (living room couch)

The Commanding Position helps keep you safe, strong, and in charge. Many modern Westerners have forgotten the need for protection or for taking extra precautions in life. The truth is that, on a basic level, you're still the same being who fought to survive in the jungle, forest, and savanna; the evolutionary advantage still goes to the person in the more protected and empowered position. I show you how to put the Commanding Position principle into action with your bed in Chapter 11, your stove in Chapter 12, and your desk in Chapter 16.

One way to apply the Commanding Position to your home is with the classic armchair position, using the following guidelines.

Say a hill or mountain sits behind your house. This setup provides a solid backing in life. Say a hill, slightly lower than the one in back, sits to the left of the house; and a still lower, yet substantial hill sits to the right of the house. In front of the house is an open place with a pleasant view, including a view of water in the middle distance (see Figure 2-3). This position protects the house on three sides, keeping out intruders and protecting the residents. The house's inspiring front view bodes well for good fortune. This classic example is a powerful Commanding Position in Feng Shui.

The Commanding Position is also used in the interior of the house in several key areas, although the applications are slightly different. In order of importance, these areas are the bed, the stove, the desk, the dining table, and the couch. The following guidelines are the interior Commanding Position principles in a nutshell:

- ✔ Have a solid backing for your position.
- ✔ See the entrance from wherever you are situated (command the room visually).
- ✔ See the widest possible part of the room.
- ✔ Don't situate yourself in the direct onward path of the door into the space.

Figure 2-3:
Classic
positive
Feng Shui
house
positioning.

The Three Life Pillars

I have created the term *Three Life Pillars* to embrace a very important and fundamental Feng Shui concept, which comprises the three most vital parts of any residence — the front door, the master bed, and the stove. By focusing on the Three Life Pillars of your home, you can ensure that the basic energy of your home and life stays strong and solid. If you have Feng Shui issues in just one of these three areas, multiple life problems can result, and if you have issues in more than one of the Life Pillars — watch out!

Recognizing the importance of the entry

The front door — the *Mouth of Chi* — is the first and greatest of the Life Pillars. The front door is the chief entry point for your home's energy; it affects money, relationships, health, people, and so on. The condition of the front door tells a good deal about your life and sets the tone for the Feng Shui of the entire house. If the conditions of your front door prevent sufficient energy from entering the house, all areas of your life can suffer. In Chapter 9, I cover the front door and entryway in great detail.

Improving the place of rest and rejuvenation

The second Life Pillar is the master bed, which relates directly to rest, relationships, and health. The bed also relates to your financial success because your sleeping position and the quality of your rest impact your ability to acquire money. You can find out more information about the bed and bedroom in Chapter 11.

Activating your home's energy generator

In Grandmaster Lin Yun's Feng Shui school, the Third Life Pillar and chief energy generator of the home is the stove, which generates health and prosperity. In the kitchen, the position of the stove and the cook are vitally important to your health and finances. I cover the stove, the kitchen, and the position of the cook in Chapter 12.

The Psychology of Feng Shui

Attitude determines the potential for success in any endeavor, including performing Feng Shui in your home. How you approach your Feng Shui practice helps determine how much it contributes to your increased life energy and success. Use the following attitudes and modes of thinking to attain success and fulfillment through your Feng Shui efforts.

Improvement is possible in any situation (especially yours)

Like gravity, Feng Shui works equally for all things. Whether you're rich or poor, happy or sad, atheist or Christian, the same energy is available and the same principles apply. No situation is hopeless, and something can be done to remedy any environment and life circumstance. At worst, you may need to move. Moving is a Feng Shui remedy, as long as you move to the right place — the right change of environment can change your life. No matter who you are, whether you're Donald Trump or Donald Duck, you can benefit from arranging your living and working environments according to Feng Shui principles. The results may be subtle; they may be dramatic. But you can see positive results.

Maximizing your current situation

The idea of maximizing your current situation follows on the heels of improving any situation. A special magic derives from pulling out all the stops and using everything available. When you know that you've done all (not almost all) that you can, a burden lifts, your psyche shifts, and the situation changes. Something new and unexpected comes into the picture. And you — sitting in the catbird seat (Feng Shui equals being in the best position!) — are able to grab the opportunity by the collar and slide graciously into a realm of greater harmony, prosperity, and happiness.

You've heard the saying, "Pray as if everything depends on God and work as if everything depends on you." This truly great advice equals a Feng Shui belief: "Take action as if the Feng Shui of your house determines your life course. Apply every reasonable option and then stretch it a bit further. Then prepare for great results."

Action without knowledge is no recipe for success. Feng Shui is not merely furniture juggling or random interior decorating. Feng Shui combines aesthetics with time-tested energetic principles. So take the ropes. Apply the principles in this book with wisdom. Choose the appropriate cure(s) after observing your environment and considering your needs. And above all, listen to your intuition.

You are the center of the equation

Whether you believe in science or in a higher power, life is still a mystery. No one controls all events in his or her life. However, you have free will, so you can take positive actions to influence the areas you want to affect. In Feng Shui, you are the central factor in your environment. And your actions can make the differences that lead to substantial and beneficial life changes.

Choosing to change your life for the better

After you realize that you can act to improve your situation, the next step is to decide to begin. The decision to act is made by anyone who ever accomplishes anything worthwhile in life. Now it's your turn. Look closely at your present situation; you're reading a book that gives you easy, practical methods for creating changes that can lead to a better life. All you need to do is put these methods to use.

Being open to change and receiving the new

When you put Feng Shui into action, prepare for changes! Some life shifts may be dramatic and sudden; others may be subtle and gradual. The key is to be open to new things and ideas, to be willing to act, and to be receptive to change. The mind is like a parachute: It works best when open. The people who get the best results from Feng Shui proceed with an open mind, a positive outlook, and a clear intention (qualities that are also Feng Shui principles).

Pointers for Feng Shui Success

If you do nothing else, at least apply the following Feng Shui principles as a minimum. Herewith, please find and follow the six points of Feng Shui 101:

- ✔ **Enliven the door and entrance.** The door is the key point of the entire house. Appoint it well — there's a lot of leverage at this spot. See more in Chapter 9.

- ✔ **Energy must flow.** If your situation is blocked or stagnant, you may find it hard to get and keep moving. Keep your pathways (hallways, driveways, and so on) open and clear for free-flowing energy.

- ✔ **Improve your bed position and quality.** The bed is the most important place in the house after the door and affects all parts of life, including the key areas of health and marriage. You can improve your life by improving the Feng Shui of the bed. (See Chapter 11 for details.)

- ✔ **Protect your back.** Take the Commanding Position for strength and safety. See Chapters 10, 11, and 16 for more information on this concept.

- ✔ **Cleanliness is next to godliness.** Need I say more? Okay, just a little more: A clean house provides you with fresh, clean energy, just the kind you truly need to stay happy, healthy, and vigorous.

- ✔ **Improve balance and harmony at every opportunity.** Whenever and wherever you detect a lack of balance in your space, make an effort to correct it with Feng Shui cures, and you may be surprised by the benefits.

Chapter 3

Reading the Vibes and Using the Feng Shui Octagon

*T*his chapter introduces you to sensing the energy in your space and using energetic maps to make sense of what's going on in your environment — the two steps of performing Feng Shui. The first step involves using your body and feelings; the second step involves mapping your space with a special tool that I call the Feng Shui *Octagon*. After grasping the basic methods of analyzing the energy characteristics of your space, go to Chapter 4 for the Mr. Fix-It toolbox of cures to make the appropriate life and energy changes.

Pay attention to your senses by using your *intuition* — everybody has it — and receive a new level of awareness and insight into what's energetically happening in your environment. The sensory methods described in this chapter may seem a bit foreign at first (or they may feel like old hat), but as you give them a whirl, you'll see that they really work. The value of this approach is that it provides you with general, overall input about the energy of your space.

The Octagon, on the other hand, gives you a visual tool that you can apply to any space you encounter. It helps you divide your home or office into nine areas, referred to in this book as Life Areas. In this chapter, I show you how to overlay the Octagon on your home floor plan. (Refer to chapter 16 for information on using the Octagon in your office.) By applying the Octagon to your home, you acquire a strong tool for pinpointing where to take action to create your desired life changes.

Both of these methods (feeling the energy and using the Octagon) are important and valuable; by using them together, you can develop an awareness of what's happening in your space and gain insights about where to apply your Feng Shui adjustments for maximum benefits. This chapter gives you tips for becoming more consciously aware of the information that your body already picks up all the time and then gives you tips for using the information to understand which changes are the best for your home.

Sensing the Energy: Good Vibes and Bad

Being able to sense energy, feel it in your body, and act on these feelings is an essential part of Feng Shui. Feng Shui is the relationship between the energy in your space and the energy in your body. If you're already proficient at feeling energy, you have a head start on the information in this chapter. Everyone can feel these energies after he or she figures out how to simply pay attention. When you can feel what's going on in your personal space and correlate what you're feeling with what's happening in your life, a picture begins to develop of what changes your space needs. (See Chapter 2 for more on the correlations and patterns between your life and your house.)

Sensing energy is something that all humans do unconsciously and continuously 24 hours a day, 7 days a week. When you walk into an environment that gives you the creeps or makes you feel peaceful, reflective, or sad, you are definitely sensing the energy of the space.

The first ways to read energy are intuitively and physiologically. Everything you encounter registers in your body as feeling. When you become sensitive to your feelings, you find that they're giving you correct readings of the energy in any space you enter. In other words, your body and feelings are incredibly accurate barometers for spatial energetic realities. And you don't have to be a special kind of person to read energy; this ability is common to all humans. All you do need is an open mind, patience, and the willingness to try and practice the methods in this book. The ability to read energy, like any other ability, improves and becomes natural with practice.

The information in the following sections gives you a wealth of insight into a place and its inhabitants. With practice, you can become more comfortable and skilled in applying the upcoming techniques. I recommend that you choose the methods that work best for you; then apply them to sharpen your energy-sensing abilities, which are natural and nothing to be scared of.

Observing the energy patterns of your environment

Many signs exist telling you whether a specific place is favorable or unfavorable to live in. Detecting the signs simply involves knowing what to look for, how to feel your environment, and what questions to ask. Imagine that you and your family are looking to buy a home, and a realtor is showing you around the neighborhood. The following factors and questions can help you evaluate the energies of any place. (But keep in mind that you don't need to know the answers to every question to make a valid evaluation of an environment.)

- **Weather:** Is the climate in the area nourishing, pleasant, moist, damp, arid, and so on? Is it severe or harsh in any way? How does the climate feel in each season?

- **Vegetation:** Is the plant life around the house lush and green or dry and desolate? Is the soil rich and fertile, sandy and sterile, rocky, or predominately clay?

- **Animals:** What kind of animals (pets or wild ones) inhabit the environment? Do you observe any animals as you approach? Crows, vultures, black cats, mangy dogs, and dead animals are obvious negative signs. Positive signs include deer, fox, eagle, magpie, or healthy, well-fed, friendly and happy animals.

- **People:** Take a look at the two-legged animals who surround the place. (And I don't mean ostriches and kangaroos.) Are the people in the area well-educated, balanced, well-groomed, employed? Do they seem bright, energetic, alert, and happy? Lethargic, standoffish, or unhappy?

- **Others' environments:** How do your neighbors' environments look? Are their gardens tended and their lawns raked and mowed? Are their cars dismantled and lying in pieces on their front lawns? Are there bullet-holes in the stop signs? Do you feel excited and uplifted when exploring the area? Or do you have a feeling of unease or even dread? Do you get a sudden urge to lock your car door while you're still moving?

- **Omens or spiritual occurrences:** What happens when you show up at a house? First impressions are important, so pay close attention. Noticeable or out-of-the-ordinary events are called *omens* in Feng Shui. For example, say the realtor tries to open the front door and the key breaks in the lock, preventing you from entering. Not the best of signs! Or suppose you enter the kitchen and the overhead light burns out. Or you find a dead rat under the kitchen sink. What, too mild, you say? Well then, suppose you glance out the window to see that a hearse with two coffins has broken down in front of the house. The driver changing the tire is wearing a black hooded shroud. His car stereo is blasting a current pop hit: *Soon You'll Be With Me*. And it isn't even Halloween. Now some people may make an offer on the spot. Personally, I recommend that you consider passing on this house!

Okay, so I exaggerated a bit. But you get the point. These events are called signs and omens for a reason. And observing and feeling the energy of the little things that happen can help you assess the qualities of a place.

✔ **Fortunate and lucky chi versus unfortunate chi:** Ask around about the lives of the neighbors of the house you're considering. If negative events (divorce, job loss, recent death, major illness, robbery, bankruptcy, major lawsuits, and so on) are highly prevalent on the same block as the house in question, you may want to keep looking.

Sensing energy with your breathing

Breath is intimately connected with chi, so a good way to sense an environment is to notice if your breathing changes when you enter a place. If abundant, positive chi is flowing freely in the space, your breathing expands and opens. If the chi of a space is stagnant, restricted, blocked, or noxious, your breathing feels more difficult or restricted when you enter. Just like changes in feeling, changes in breathing naturally occur whenever you change environments. You may not have paid attention to it before, but changes to your breathing are a simple and effective way of sensing the energy in a space. As with all the other methods, you should consciously feel and pay attention to what your body is telling you.

Using your body to feel energy

Reading energy is based on the following simple principle: Your body always tells you the truth. The only problem is that your body doesn't shout at you; it speaks quietly, so you have to quiet down and listen to your body to hear its invaluable messages. So the next time you enter a new environment, stop, pay attention, and feel what's going on inside yourself. Whatever input your body gives you, try to accept it without judging or second-guessing it. Just notice it and feel it.

In addition to paying attention to the rate, ease, and depth of your breathing (see the preceding section, "Sensing energy with your breathing"), be aware of other ways to sense your body's reactions to environmental energies. Again, the best time to use these techniques is immediately upon entering a location, as humans tend to adjust rapidly and seamlessly to their environments. After you've been in a place for an hour or more, you're less consciously sensitive to its effects than in the first minute or two after entering.

Because the easiest way to sense energy is through the body's kinesthetic or feeling mode, I offer techniques in this vein that allow you to feel energy immediately.

Keep in mind that you may have acclimated or adjusted to the energetic effects of the spaces in your home, so being in them now feels normal and regular. If this is the case, pay particular attention to your feelings just after you perform Feng Shui cures. Cures change the energy of the space, so the altered chi will have new impacts on you that you can notice if you pay attention. (Cures are Feng Shui techniques that improve the energy flow of a space, with improved impacts on your life.)

The following methods are ways to sense energy with your body:

- **Quiet yourself and feel your emotional impressions.** All emotions register in the body as physical sensations that are usually felt from the stomach up through the chest and throat. So open yourself and feel the effect of the space in your body. Notice any sensation in this key area and any emotion associated with it. Your body can give you extremely accurate emotional information about the energy of the space. If you are quiet and receptive — and trust the data you're receiving — you'll know what needs to be done to remedy any space using the various cures I describe in this book.

- **Check your body's stability in the location.** Do you feel a slight wobble as you stand? A lethargy or heaviness? Do you feel grounded and stable? Off-balance or spacey? Restless or calm? Closely observe whatever you feel. If you feel unstable, the energy is probably not balanced in the location. See if you can determine why. (Perhaps the structure itself is slightly tilted on its foundation, a fact that normally can't be discovered without an engineer. But your body's subtle lean can tell that something is off even if you don't know exactly what it is. And this situation unfortunately can keep unknowing residents off-kilter for years!) If you feel comfortable, rooted, calm, and balanced, the energy of the space is most likely harmonious and positive.

- **Observe your thoughts in the space.** Thoughts reflect the body's feelings and emotions, so changes in thinking can serve as a barometer of how the space is impacting your energy. Notice your thoughts or frame of mind before entering a space. Try to enter clear and calm. Do your thoughts change when you enter? Does your frame of mind shift either positively or negatively? Pay attention.

- **Pay attention to your body's reactions.** Entering an area with negative chi tends to register more in your stomach or head than in other body parts. So if you feel a sudden discomfort, an ache or dizziness in your head, or a tightening in your stomach after entering a space, it can be a sign of negative chi. Conversely, if you feel relaxed, open, happy, or clear-headed, it can be a sign of positive chi. Also notice if you feel suddenly hot or cold upon entering the space or if you get a strange taste in your mouth. These temperature and taste changes are not definitive signs of good and bad chi, rather they're like a cloudy day versus a sunny day — they give you valuable information about what's happening in a space. Interpreting this information is a matter of intuition and practice.

✔ **Observe your energy level.** Figuring out what your energy level is telling you is really quite simple. If a space has good energy, you feel energetically good, whether calm, happy, alert, or even excited. If an area has low energy, it can suck energy from its occupants. In such a space you are likely to feel low, tired, lethargic, lazy, or down.

Discovering the Magic of the Octagon

Using the Ba-Gua, or what I call the Feng Shui Octagon, is an instrumental element of Feng Shui analysis. The *Ba-Gua* (pronounced bah-gwah) enables you to discern how the areas of your space (house, yard, office, and rooms) are impacting the corresponding areas of your life. All spaces affect you; the important question is, which area affects what? The Feng Shui Octagon provides the first key to answering this question.

What is the Feng Shui Octagon?

The Feng Shui Octagon is an energetic map (or a tool used to diagnose energy qualities in your space) that applies the wisdom of the I-Ching (an ancient book of Chinese knowledge) to human spaces. Using the Octagon, you divide any definable space into nine sections or areas, each with its own corresponding set of influences and energies. A definable space must have specific boundaries and one discernible main entrance. I recommend that you commit the Octagon to memory so you can apply it mentally whenever you enter a room or house and, therefore, more easily discern its Feng Shui qualities.

The nine Life Areas of the Octagon

The Octagon divides the floor plan into nine areas (called *guas* in Chinese). Each of the areas — hereafter called areas of the Octagon or Life Areas — holds a different energy and corresponds to a specific area of your life. If your home is square, the sizes of these areas are equal. In odd shaped houses, the sizes of the areas vary. (But the actual size of each of the nine areas is less important than what is happening energetically in these areas.) The Octagon enables you to pinpoint the areas you need or wish to work on and then to proceed with knowledge and awareness.

For example, suppose you need more money. First use the Octagon, pinpoint the area of your house that affects wealth; then assess the energy conditions of this area, and make changes or adjustments (cures) to improve its energy. (This process is Feng Shui in action, and you'll use it throughout the book to make simple, easy, and effective changes.)

The nine Life Areas of the Octagon and their corresponding locations in the environment are as follows:

- **Helpful People:** Located in the right front area of the space
- **Career:** Located in the center front
- **Knowledge:** Located in the left front
- **Family:** Located in the center left
- **Wealth/Money:** Located in the back left
- **Fame/Reputation:** Located in the back center
- **Marriage/Partnership:** Located in the back right
- **Children:** Located in the center right
- **Health:** Located in the center of the Octagon

Look at Figure 3-1 to see the nine areas of the Octagon — eight sides plus the center. In the following sections, I go through each of the nine areas along with their life associations and other important correlations. You can apply the Octagon to both your home (including the lot) and your office. To this effect, I include correlations for the business world in case you want to place the Octagon on your floor plan (office, cubicle, and so on) at work or in your home office. (For actually placing the Octagon on your floor plan, see the "Placing the Octagon on Your Floor Plan" section later in this chapter.)

Locations of the Octagon Areas in Figure 3-1 are in relation to the front door and front of the house. So when I say "back left of the house," the position is figured from the front door.

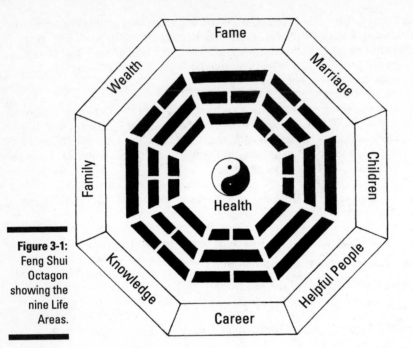

Figure 3-1:
Feng Shui Octagon showing the nine Life Areas.

You can also use the Octagon for physical healing and good health, so I also list the body parts that correspond to each area of the Octagon. For example, the Marriage Area is connected with the internal organs, so the proper cure placed in the Marriage Area can help energize an organ that is out of balance.

Time for a personal disclaimer. I am not a qualified health care practitioner! In fact, I'm not even a witch doctor. So do not use these Feng Shui cures as substitutes for professional medical care. If you have a medical problem, do consult a qualified health professional. Meanwhile, you can also use Feng Shui cures both proactively and in a supplementary fashion.

In Feng Shui, everything is energetic and interrelated with everything else. Color is another form of energy and has profound affects on your life. Feng Shui associates certain colors with each area of the Octagon. I include the associated colors for each Octagon area in the following section, and in Chapter 15 I give you specific tips on how to use color to create changes in your environment.

In Feng Shui, no one Octagon Area is more important than any other. The areas all interrelate and, when aligned to Feng Shui principles, contribute to a balanced, full, and prosperous life. Deciding which area to focus on at any given time is entirely up to you (and likely depends upon which corresponding area of your life you wish to remedy or enhance).

Also, the correlations given for each issue are by no means the only ones. For example, family issues are affected not only by the Family Area of the Octagon, but also by rooms in which the family spends time together (or should), such as the living and dining rooms. In other words, there is a natural energetic overlap.

Without further ado, the nine Life Areas of the Octagon:

The Helpful People Area of the Octagon

Location: Right front

Chinese name: Ch'ien (pronounced chyen)

Colors: Gray, white, and black

Body part association: Head

The Helpful People Area relates to any travel you do. If you travel a lot or plan to travel more and you wish to be safe on your trips, I suggest enhancing this Life Area with Feng Shui cures as detailed throughout this book. Helpful People is also associated with benefactors or people who help you in life. (Actually, because anyone and everyone can be a helpful person, adjusting the Helpful People Area can benefit all of your life relationships.)

Enhancing this area can also improve your networking, your business associations (colleagues, employees, clients, customers, suppliers, and so on), other worldly contacts, or even a circle of friends. This area is also associated with the fortunes of male members of the family, such as a husband, son, or brother.

The Career Area of the Octagon

Location: Front center

Chinese name: Kan (pronounced kahn)

Colors: Black and midnight blue

Body part association: Ears and kidneys

The Career Area of the Octagon concerns your work, career success, and how you make a living. This Life Area is a great one to cure if you want to find a better job, get a promotion, make better relationships with your co-workers, or receive increased recognition at work. This area of the house can impact your career more than your business office does. Because the Career Area is in the front of the house, this area is also connected to your relationship with the world outside of your home. (And what is a career, if not a relationship to the outer world?)

The Knowledge Area of the Octagon

Location: Front left

Chinese name: Gen (pronounced guhn)

Colors: Blue, green, and black

Body part association: Hand

The Knowledge Area affects the mental/inner/spiritual/personal areas of your life. If you desire to become smarter, wiser, or quicker-witted — look here! Because this Life Area is associated with knowledge, information, and insight, it is also associated with your spiritual/religious life, personal growth, and self-development, so adjusting the Knowledge Area can be very helpful in these areas.

In a business context, the Knowledge Area is concerned with business data, competitive intelligence, good decision making, and computer networks. (See also the Children Area for computers.) If you deal with the Internet and its deluge of data, curing the Knowledge Area can help you keep up with the continuous change and flow of information.

The Family Area of the Octagon

Location: Center left

Chinese name: Jen (pronounced jen)

Colors: Green and blue

Body part association: Foot

The Family Area concerns your nuclear family as well as all your relatives. Family is the Feng Shui arena to work on to resolve interpersonal family conflicts or to promote family harmony.

In business, the Family Area affects both employees and management. To a smaller extent, its influence extends to customers, vendors, and others who regularly interact with the business (the extended family of the business).

The Wealth Area of the Octagon

Location: Back upper-left

Chinese name: Sun (pronounced shuhn)

Colors: Purple, green, red, and blue

Body part association: Hips

The Wealth Area correlates directly to the prosperity and abundance in your life; this area concerns your cash flow and your financial status. For financial improvement, focus your attention here. (Because most people approach Feng Shui for this issue, I call the Wealth Area the Feng Shui end zone.) Keep in mind that in addition to the Wealth Area, your front entrance and your kitchen stove also strongly affect your money chi (see Chapters 9 and 12). And of course, in a business site, the Wealth Area is of primary concern.

The Fame Area of the Octagon

Location: Back center

Chinese name: Li (pronounced lee)

Color: Red

Body part association: Eyes

Yes, this Life Area affects fame, acclaim, and public attention. I'm talking about the Hollywood type of fame, complete with paparazzi, talk show appearances, and magazine articles, though harmonizing this Feng Shui space can't guarantee the above-mentioned results. This area also has a more practical, even mundane side. Fame in this area also means your personal reputation — how your peers, your neighbors, and your community see you. Not everyone can be famous, after all. (You didn't really want to deal with the paparazzi, did you?)

Everyone, including you, has a reputation of some kind. Having a good reputation brings many benefits in life; a poor reputation is an obvious stumbling block. The Fame Area also influences how you envision your life, so this area is good to enhance if you're setting goals or planning your future.

In the business world, this area relates to marketing, public relations, market position, and word of mouth about your company. To improve your business or corporate reputation, be sure to pay some Feng Shui attention to this area.

The Marriage or Partnership Area of the Octagon

Location: Back upper-right

Chinese name: Kun (pronounced kuhn)

Colors: Pink, red, and white

Body part association: Internal organs

The Marriage Area is specifically related to the status of your marriage or significant relationship. This area affects the quality of your existing relationship and also affects your ability or chances to find a new partner, if you so desire. According to Feng Shui energetics, this area is associated with the nurturing energy of the Earth and is also connected to the females in the household — the wife and mother, daughters, sisters, and so on.

In business, this area is called the Partnership Area, and it affects your primary business partnerships, whether internal business partnerships (such as two partners who own a business together) or the key external partnerships with which the business engages.

The Children Area of the Octagon

Location: Center right

Chinese name: Dui (pronounced dway)

Color: White

Body part association: Mouth

The Children Area is connected to the health, well-being, and progress of your children. If you're having trouble conceiving a child, apply Feng Shui cures to this area. The Children Area also impacts your creativity, whether artistic or otherwise, and the clarity and quality of your communication.

In a business, the Children Area connects to employees as well as to work creativity and communication.

The Health Area of the Octagon

Location: Center

Chinese name: Tai Chi (pronounced ty chee)

Colors: Yellow and earth tones

Body part association: Any body part not associated with the other eight areas

The Health Area of the Octagon is primarily concerned with physical health. Enhance this area with Feng Shui cures if you want to boost your physical vitality and stamina. Because this area's position is in the center, the Health Area also relates to the self (that's you!) and affects all areas of your life at once. The Health Area is the hub of the wheel where all the spokes (or areas) connect; the energies of the other eight areas all pass through and connect to the center.

In a business, the Health Area relates both to the physical health of the people in the area and to the financial health of the business itself.

Placing the Octagon on Your Floor Plan

The Feng Shui Octagon is always set up in relation to the main front door of the house, never to a side or back or garage door. Each house has only one front door, which in Feng Shui terms is called the *Mouth of Chi*. The Mouth of Chi is where the main flow of energy enters the house. (For more on the Mouth of Chi, see Chapter 9.) For individual rooms, the trigram is oriented according to the main (most used) door to the room.

Determining the line of the front door

To determine the line of the front door, draw a line on your floor plan running from left to right, directly through the plane of the front door. This line of the front door is important for two reasons: First, the line helps you to orient and place the Octagon. Second, it tells you which parts of the structure are energetically in front of the front door.

Positioning the Octagon

If your home has a complicated shape, you may want to first practice the following exercise on a simple square house drawing, and then apply it to your house plan. See also the following section, "Missing areas and projections," to understand how irregularities in your floor plan affect the Octagon and, therefore, affect you.

1. **Determine the front wall of the house.** The front wall contains your front door.

2. **Draw the line of the front door.** See preceding section for more information.

3. **Determine if your door is in the right, middle, or left of the front wall of the house (Helpful People, Career, or Knowledge position).** A door on the right-hand side of the front wall of the house is in the Helpful People Area of the Octagon. A door in the front middle area is in the Career Area. And a door on the left-hand side is in the Knowledge Area. In this Feng Shui system, these Octagon Areas are the only three which can contain the front door (meaning that the front door, for example, can never be in the Wealth Area or Children Area). See Figure 3-2.

4. **Draw the front three Areas of the Octagon across the front line of the house.** The Helpful People Area is always in the front right. The Career Area is always in the front center. And the Knowledge Area is always at the front left.

5. **Draw the rest of the Octagon on the floor plan accordingly.** See Figure 3-3.

The Feng Shui Octagon is applicable to any space that you can define (or determine the perimeter of) and that has a clear front (or main) entrance. The Octagon can be placed on multiple spaces of your environment (including each room of the house), giving you an increasingly detailed understanding of your Feng Shui causes and effects. An Octagon reading is typically centered on the house itself, but you can also place the Octagon on other chief spaces in your life, such as an office, a workout area, or a garden. (The method of applying multiple Octagons for the same home is unique to Grandmaster Lin Yun's Feng Shui school.)

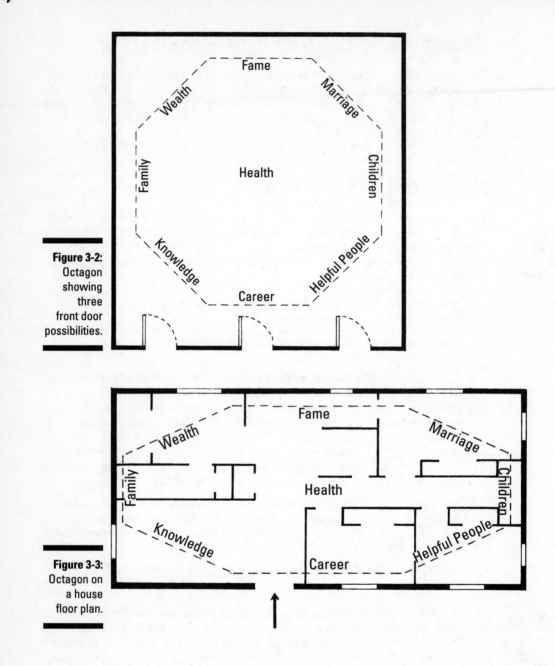

Figure 3-2:
Octagon
showing
three
front door
possibilities.

Figure 3-3:
Octagon on
a house
floor plan.

Two additional ways you can use the Octagon to analyze the environment and change its influences include:

✔ **Placing the Octagon on your lot.** You can place the Feng Shui Octagon on your property plan to determine which areas of the lot to adjust to improve the corresponding areas of your life (see Figure 3-4). I give cures for your lot in Chapter 7.

✔ **Placing the Octagon on the individual rooms of your house.** The most important room is the master bedroom. Feng Shui lore says that the Octagon of your bedroom impacts your life even more than the Octagon of your house and property. In Figure 3-5, I show how the Octagon can be used for any and all rooms of the house.

A powerful Feng Shui technique is to use the Octagon to perform cures for the same issue in every room of the house at once. For example, if you want to increase your wealth, you can perform cures in the Wealth Area of each room of your house. This method has the potential to improve your home and your life dramatically.

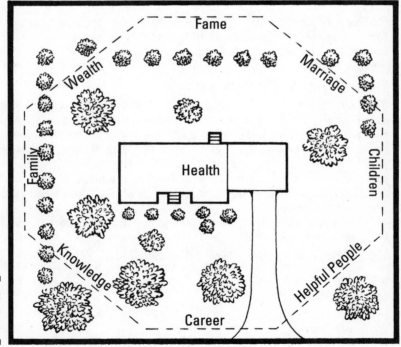

Figure 3-4: Octagon on lot plan.

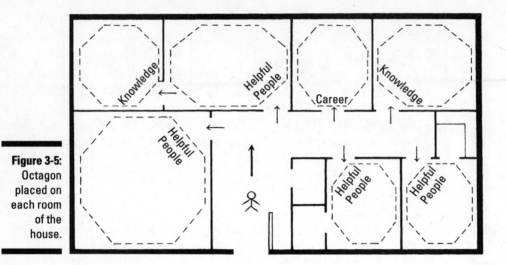

Figure 3-5:
Octagon
placed on
each room
of the
house.

Troubleshooting the Octagon

For many homes, placing the Octagon on the floor plan is easy and straight-forward. However, questions arise in several common situations. I cover a few of these situations in the following sections.

Missing areas and projections

The ideal house shape is a regular one — square or rectangle. A regular shape supports a natural, positive balance. Yet an irregular house shape isn't necessarily negative, but can bode either good or ill for the home's occu-pants depending upon the shape and on the Feng Shui cures you use or fail to use. *Missing areas* of your floor plan are negative features that block chi flow in the corresponding life area. *Projections,* on the other hand, represent extra areas where energy circulates, providing additional chi, thereby improving one's fortune in that life area. You can have both at once in the same floor plan. To illustrate, if you have a missing area in the Children Area of the Octagon and a projection in the Fame Area, you are likely to have a good rep-utation, but may have problems with your children (or with conceiving chil-dren). These principles hold true for the shape of your lot as well. For instruction on determining if your home or lot shape has either missing areas or projections, see Chapter 8.

Difficult floor plans

If your floor plan is too complex, correctly placing the Octagon can be diffi-cult. Or your floor plan may be unusually odd-shaped, also making correct Octagon placement difficult. A potential solution for such cases is simply to use the Octagon on each room in the house. Or you may want to seek a pro-fessional Feng Shui consultant for assistance.

Entrances with turns

The situation can be a little tricky if you enter the house in one direction, yet turn to continue into the body of the house in another direction. In such cases, I recommend that you orient the Octagon according the direction of greatest traffic flow coming into the house (see Figure 3-6).

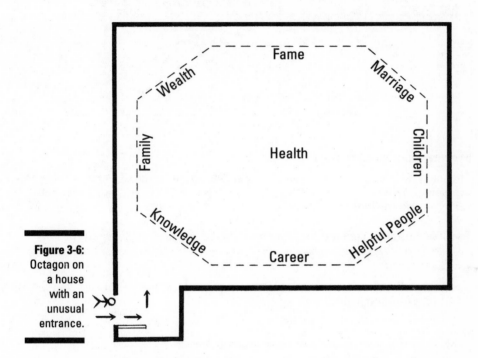

Figure 3-6: Octagon on a house with an unusual entrance.

Angled entrances

A front door at a 45 degree angle presents two possible ways to place the Octagon on the floor plan. Which is correct? The solution comes in two steps: First, determine which of the two sides of the house experiences greater traffic flow (either by foot or vehicle). Then, place the Octagon at a 90-degree angle to this direction. See Figure 3-7 for two examples. (In Chapter 14, I talk more about Feng Shui challenges caused by angled doors.)

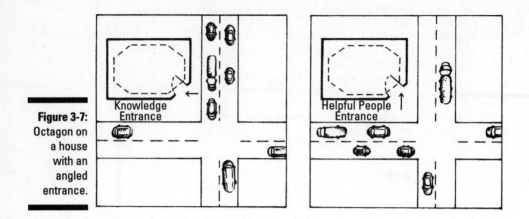

Figure 3-7:
Octagon on
a house
with an
angled
entrance.

Placing the Octagon upstairs and down

The main floor of the house is the most important in terms of Octagon assessment. If you wish to place the Octagon on an upper floor or basement, keep in mind these tips:

- ✔ The entrance (main door/Mouth of Chi) of any floor other than the ground level floor (meaning a floor accessed by stairs) is its landing (see Figure 3-8).

- ✔ Internal stairways constitute missing areas of the Feng Shui Octagon of both floors that the stairway connects.

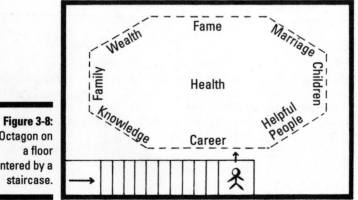

Figure 3-8:
Octagon on
a floor
entered by a
staircase.

Changing Your Life with the Octagon

Now that you're able to place your Octagon correctly, the next step is putting it into use. A good way to use the Octagon is to select the areas that correspond to the most important life changes you want to make. If you want to increase family harmony, the Family Area is a good place to begin. Go to this area of your home. Quiet down and take a look. Feel the energy using the methods from the beginning of this chapter. Things may jump out at you and clamor for changes and cures.

Another good way to use the Octagon is to look for correlations between each Octagon Area of the house and the corresponding life patterns you're experiencing (see Chapter 2.) For example, if the Wealth Area of your house is cluttered and messy and your finances are in complete disarray, the correlation is easy to make. Cleaning up the area (and keeping it clean) can bring about some noticeable effect in your financial circumstance (check Chapter 15 for more). Not to mention that the room looks much nicer. Feng Shui is nothing if not practical.

Chapter 4

Exploring Your Feng Shui Cure Toolbox

*I*n Chapters 1 through 3, I cover how Feng Shui works with an energy called *chi* that continuously flows throughout your home and affects your daily life, for good or ill. Changing the way this energy circulates in your home and life is where the rubber meets the road in Feng Shui.

To get a different result in life you need to change something. Cures are Feng Shui adjustments that positively shift the energy of your house, lot, or office. When you change the energy of your environment with a cure, you can experience new, positive influences from your environment. Cures put the power of Feng Shui directly into your hands. By applying them, you can change your life in any area you wish.

The enormous array of solutions in Feng Shui can seem a little bewildering at first, so in this book, I focus on the ones I've found to be the simplest, easiest, and most effective. This chapter presents the stuff that really works — reliable methods that you can apply without arduous training or having to learn Chinese. Time to put Feng Shui into action!

So What Is a Feng Shui Cure?

At the simplest level, cures are ways of changing your life by altering your space. You can also say that cures are solutions to Feng Shui problems. Performing cures changes the flow of energy in your space, shifting the chi in your environment — and in you — to a more beneficial and prosperous energy state.

Motivations for performing Feng Shui cures

You can use cures to fix an environmental problem, improve a weak life area, or further improve a life area that's already in good shape. If you're looking for motivation or inspiration, check out the three main reasons for performing cures.

- ✔ **To remedy an energetically weak or problematic area of your surroundings.** Say you assess your bedroom using Feng Shui principles and discover that your bed sits in a position bad for your health. And you connect this situation to health problems you've been having. If you were an ostrich, you'd simply stick your head in the sand and hope the problem goes away. (Unfortunately, Ostrich Feng Shui works only while your head remains nestled comfortably in the sand.) But being a person and not an ostrich, you want your environment to support your health, so you decide to perform a cure.

- ✔ **To improve an area of life that is challenging or troubling you, or remedy a life problem.** In keeping with the bedroom, say that you've been arguing a lot with your spouse or significant other lately, and you therefore decide you want to perform a cure to improve your relationship. (Performing such cures is also a good idea even if you haven't been experiencing marital tension. I'm a firm believer in proactive cures.) The next step would be to consult the areas of your house, lot, bedroom, and so on that affect your relationship, and perform specific cures in these areas. You can cure an existing Feng Shui defect (perhaps an exit door in the Marriage Area is allowing chi to leak away from the relationship). Or, if you can't detect any relevant Feng Shui problems, you can perform a cure that energetically enhances or activates an area relating to marriage. For example, place fresh flowers or something with the color pink in the Marriage Area of the bedroom or other parts of the house. (See Chapter 3 for more information on the Life Areas of the Octagon.)

✔ **To further empower or strengthen an area of your life that is already strong.** Say your career is going gangbusters. Your latest movie hits number one at the box office. Your CD tops the charts. Your MTV video has made you a Gen-X icon. And your new fashion line is all the rage in Paris. What, you want a Pulitzer Prize, too? Well, go for it! To assist your career, you can perform cures in the Career Areas of your house, lot, bedroom, and other applicable areas. (On a practical level, if you're going for a Pulitzer, I suggest that you write a novel or something, in addition to the cures, just to increase your odds.)

Five types of Feng Shui cures

To remedy or enhance any life situation, you can always choose from a range of options. Fixing a car problem may entail buying a new car, overhauling the engine, rotating the tires, or simply replacing the windshield wipers — the remedy depends on the nature of the problem (and your financial situation). If you get a new car, what kind do you want? And if you fix up the old one, how much fix is it worth? Do you want it in perfect running condition, or reliable for another year or two, or just functional enough to drive until it falls apart on its own?

Feng Shui cures work in much the same way; the cure you choose depends on the nature of the problem, your particular goals, and your financial circumstances. Each level of cures has advantages and disadvantages and requires varying expenditures of time, energy, and, yes, sometimes, cash. As with many decisions, budget is often the bottom line. ("Say, these solid gold, diamond encrusted bathroom fixtures would make marvelous Feng Shui accouterments. But you know, I think I'll go with the brass.")

The following list gives you five levels of solutions you can use to bring your home into tip-top Feng Shui shape. To save you time and money and keep things practical, I focus on the final three bullets in the list below, and refrain from suggesting the more expensive options in the first two bullets.

✔ **Move to a different house or build a new one.** This cure is the most radical you can perform and is also quite expensive, so if you choose this option, make sure that you do it right. (Meaning make sure your new home has better Feng Shui than your old one.) In my work with clients, I suggest this cure only as a final alternative when their current home can't be sufficiently cured (say you have an up-close, picture-window view of Chernobyl and, yes, it glows in the dark).

✔ **Perform major remodeling or landscaping to fix the problem.** This cure is an excellent option for effectiveness, provided that you perform it according to valid Feng Shui principles. This solution, like moving to a different house, has obvious drawbacks: expense, time investment, and inconvenience. However, it also has obvious advantages. And as with the costly option of buying a house, if you go this route, make sure that you do it right! Nothing's is worse than financing a ten-, twenty- or even forty-thousand dollar non-cure.

✔ **Devise an energetic placement or adjustment that changes the chi flow.** Now I'm talkin' really cost effective ways of solving Feng Shui problems without making structural changes in your house. Most cures in this book fit into this category. I focus on practical methods you can use now to create noticeable, desired effects, so you can perform cures with minimal expense. (But you'll have to do without the solid gold bathroom fixtures.)

✔ **Conduct a blessing ceremony to change, clear, or shift the energy.** In contrast to the method given just before, Feng Shui ceremonies work on the energy of your house or lot at once, giving them great power. Ceremonies work on a purely energetic level affecting the invisible elements of the site. These invisible elements include spiritual and emotional energies as well as energetic residue left by previous occupants or spillover from surrounding occupants. Blessing ceremonies help remove negative energies, calm chaotic chi, and instill prosperity and well-being. Blessing ceremonies are one of the most effective and least expensive Feng Shui methods. Though they typically involve no physical changes on the site, they can profoundly and positively impact your physical and mental health, well-being, and safety. Solutions of this type are found in Chapter 17.

✔ **Adjust your personal chi directly.** This method involves special personal energy adjustment practices you can use to change your life experience directly, without necessarily altering your house or environment. Personal chi cures work on your personal inner environment, and work very much like blessing ceremonies do for your house and lot. These potent cures are also highly effective and inexpensive. I include a wealth of these solutions in Chapter 18.

Using the Two Phases of Your Cures

In this section, I discuss the two phases of Feng Shui cures. One of the most important things to understand about cures is that they work in two realms at the same time: the *visible* (or material) realm, and the *invisible* (or intangible) realm. Each cure has two parts that correspond to these two realms. By paying equal attention to both parts of the cure, you can get maximum benefits and results from your cures.

Phase I: Performing the action of the cure

The first phase of the cure relates to the visible, material realm. This phase involves making physical changes in your environment; for example, painting a room a new color, rearranging your furniture, or cleaning out a closet. The visible part of the cure accounts for perhaps 10 to 30 percent of a cure's power. Phase I definitely creates an effect, but for maximum results, you need another powerful ingredient — intention. So read on!

Phase II: Activating the intention of the cure

The invisible, intangible part of the cure deals with your thoughts, emotions, and feelings as you perform the cure. The secret of effective Feng Shui is your intention — the most important factor in effectiveness of the Feng Shui cures you perform! The intention of the cure generates 70 to 80 percent of its effectiveness. So take a closer look at this thing called intention.

On one level, intention is your awareness of your personal reasons for performing the cure and your desire to accomplish it. What do you want the cure to create, and how clearly do you want it to happen? These questions are a matter of intention. But intention is more than mere desire. On a second level, intention encompasses a combination of sincerity, will, visualization, and faith. These factors work synergistically to activate or reinforce the physical portion of the cure, taking its power to new heights.

The combination of these two components — action and intention — can create cures with more than 100 percent effectiveness. What does over 100 percent mean? Over 100 percent means that a cure can not only fix a particular life problem, but can also make things better than they were before the problem started.

Find out more about activating your intentions for your cures with the special method called the Three Secrets Reinforcement in Chapter 6.

Cures are not mere mechanical adjustments that you make in an environment. Feng Shui changes involve your heart and mind as well as your house and lot. If you feel that you don't fully understand just yet, that's ok! As you perform your cures and practice the Three Secrets Reinforcement (see Chapter 6), you can start to understand how this process creates new energy states and new life paths.

Opening the Feng Shui Toolbox: Creating Your Cures

I now put five key methods at your disposal that you can use to create cures. The method you implement depends on such things as your particular needs and wishes, your budget, and your sense of aesthetics. The following sections outline these methods.

Creating positive placement

Creating positive placement means putting things in their right places or most favorable locations. Good or bad placement affects you in important ways. The arrangement of your things determines how the chi (or energy) circulates through your environment. And this chi flow directly affects your body and mind. Your bed location, for example, impacts many life areas, including your marriage, your level of pep and vitality, and how much income you enjoy.

In the same way, the placement of your office desk is important because it dictates where and how you sit and appear, as well as how you interact with the people and energy entering your office. Important placement areas include your bed, desk, stove, and others. You can find more information on placement factors in Chapters 11 through 13 and 16.

Adding what's needed, minor and otherwise

The next category of cures involves adding objects to your environment. These cures range from planting a new tree or constructing a flowerbed to adding furniture or a mobile or installing a mirror. Think of the cures in this category as the acupuncture needles of Feng Shui. The proper addition at the right point in your space can create dramatic changes in the energy and in your life. See the section "Making Minor Additions to Bring About Major Changes" in this chapter for detailed explanations of many different additional cure tools that you can apply for fun and profit.

Clearing the path for energy to flow

Another important strategy involves removing whatever isn't needed, whatever's in the way, and anything that simply needs to go. Almost everyone is to some degree a packrat. You belong to a culture of compulsive collectors, and lightening the load can free up your energy and your life considerably.

The problem with clutter is that it blocks the energy circulation in your home and in you, especially if the offending items sit in hallways or other common areas and also if the clutter is hidden in a closet or garage. Superfluous junk burdens your psyche, holds you back, and trips you up. Shoes sitting behind the front door need to be moved. Useless objects cluttering the closets and garage are better thrown out or donated to a charitable organization. (Need more motivation to donate? Here's one: Someone else may use your stuff, you'll feel freer, and donating is tax deductible!) Great de-cluttering tips are found in Chapter 15.

Adjusting cures: Repairing, cleaning, and changing

This category involves altering and adjusting existing items in your house to improve their energy value. Examples of this type of cure include repairing broken things, replacing burnt-out light bulbs, and, of course, the all-important cleaning. What's important about these changes? Simply this: Whatever's out of order in your environment provides a subtle or profound influence for you to be out of order. Broken or unmaintained features of your home provide a continuous subconscious influence of malfunction and decay. So be sure to dig into Chapter 15, where you can find many solutions.

Changing the spirit of the place: Using ceremony to create a new feeling

Ceremony was the first human science and is still an essential part of human experience. A woman putting on her make-up and a dash of perfume before a date; a man putting on his power suit for an important meeting; a pitcher tugging his baseball cap with every new batter; even fans and players singing the national anthem before each game. What are these habits if not ceremonies, particular actions performed to trigger specific effects? But awareness of ceremony has been pushed out of modern awareness due to society's current fixation on technology and science. Feng Shui definitely hasn't forgotten, and still makes good use of the power and influence of ceremonies.

Ceremonies unite the material world in which we live with the unseen realms of energy to which we are also connected. Feng Shui ceremonies are energy procedures that change the spirit and feeling of your home's chi. They purify unseen (but felt!) negativity, remove bad luck, provide protection, create new beginnings, and add cheerful energy to your environment. You can find ceremony procedures in Chapter 17.

Making Minor Additions to Bring About Major Changes

In the preceding section, I give five major types of Feng Shui cures. In the category of adding things to the environment ("Adding what's needed"), one of the easiest approaches is the Method of Minor Additions. The Method of Minor Additions operates on the principle of *xie di* (shyeh dee), which means "a little bit." The principle is akin to using four ounces of positive energy to deflect a thousand pounds of negative force. For example, say you're walking across the street and look up to see a speeding car coming right at you. Do you a) go into your immovable martial arts stance, lean forward with your hands outstretched, and prepare to stop the car in its tracks? Or do you b) step lightly out of the way. If you chose the second example, by golly, I think you're starting to get it. Not to mention you're still in one piece!

Minor Additions cures involve adding one of several kinds of "natural chi" (such as light, sound, and water) to adjust the energy of a location. These cures allow you to create tangible, desired changes without the need for remodeling, buying a new home, or turning your current home around on its foundation to face a different direction. Minor Additions cures are simple, practical, and above all, effective. They work immediately, and you can feel their energetic effects on the environment and on you. (See the Feng Shui Resources page at the end of this book for cure sources.)

Minor Addition cures use the energies of

- Light
- Sound
- Living energy (or spirit)
- Water
- Color
- Movement
- Weight
- Bamboo
- Power
- Fragrance
- Touch

Light cures

Light cures come in three main types: lights, faceted crystal spheres, and mirrors. These cures add beneficial energy qualities to spaces in need, including additional light, brilliance, expansion, and cheer. Lighting levels and lighting quality naturally affect humans in many ways making light cures a powerful tool in your Feng Shui toolbox.

Lights

Lights, such as overhead lights, lamps, incandescent lights, or other kinds, can add brightness and cheer to an area. With light, the general rule is the brighter, the better. Lights used in Feng Shui cures don't have to be on at all times, but they should remain in good working condition. If the bulb in your Feng Shui cure burns out, the cure is nullified.

Faceted crystal spheres

Faceted crystal spheres (made by adding 30 percent lead oxide to pure glass) have many useful Feng Shui applications. Faceted crystal spheres come in a range of sizes. For the cures in this book, I recommend 50-millimeter diameter or larger crystal spheres (2 inches or larger) — 40-millimeter spheres (1.5 inches) if you're in a pinch. (See the Feng Shui Resources page at the end of this book to find crystal sphere sources.) When sunlight hits these crystal spheres, prismatic rainbows scatter beautifully throughout the house. (See Figure 4-1.) Crystal spheres shift the energy of a space in several important ways including:

- Adding light, expansion, and new energy.
- Redirecting energies towards a more beneficial direction.
- Harmonizing confusing or chaotic flows of energy.
- Protecting you from poison arrows of energy by refracting and diffusing energy flows (see more on poison arrows in Chapter 7).
- Empowering and aiding in visualizations.
- Attracting and drawing energy to a location.
- Looking so darned beautiful! (Beauty is an important Feng Shui element.)

Quartz crystals (geodes from the ground) can also be employed for Feng Shui cures, but because their methods of use are more complex (and faceted crystals are highly effective), I don't cover quartz crystals in this book. Also, leaded *crystal spheres* (leaded glass) are important because the lead is what creates the prismatic effect. (Regular glass spheres don't provide the same level of curing power.)

Mirrors

Mirrors are a key Feng Shui tool as useful as a Swiss Army Knife. Mirrors are best used in one of four shapes: square, rectangular, octagonal, and circular. (See Figure 4-1.) Any of these four shapes are effective. Square and rectangular mirrors symbolize balance, while circular mirrors represent wholeness, oneness, and unity. Octagonal mirrors denote power and have the positive symbology of representing the Feng Shui Octagon. However, mirrors used for regular viewing (not just for décor) and mirrors hung on doors are best rectangular or square. Generally, large mirrors create stronger cures than smaller mirrors.

Depending on the need, mirrors can be used to

- ✔ Add light and brightness.
- ✔ Attract new energy to a space.
- ✔ Repel negative or harmful chi.
- ✔ Redirect an energy flow.
- ✔ Expand an area, energetically creating more space.
- ✔ Magnify or strengthen one's image.
- ✔ Empower an Octagon Area for a particular life need.
- ✔ Restore a missing area of a room or house. (The space can have a missing area if it is not a complete square or rectangle; see Chapter 8.)

Check your mirrors before purchasing. Avoid buying mirrors with visible ripples or flaws in the glass (or frame). To check a mirror for visible distortions, stand to one side and look into the mirror and then pick out a specific reflected object. Holding your eye steady on the object, sway your body back and forth evenly from left to right. If the object seems to move in a wave-like manner or appears deformed in any way, the mirror is distorted. Such a mirror is better replaced or not bought in the first place. Mirrors symbolize your self-image and clarity of mind, so distorted mirrors can have subtle and unpleasant effects on your psyche.

Avoid using mirrors that are smoked or darkened, odd-shaped, or have etchings or any other embellishments on them. Mirror tiles are also best avoided. The ideal mirror is a plain, flawless surface. A small bevel around the edges is fine. You can frame your mirrors or use no frame at all. Feng Shui recommends replacing antique mirrors that are scratched, pitted, or marred. If you're attached to the beauty of an antique mirror frame, whose glass is flawed or visibly aged, keep the frame and replace the mirror portion.

Figure 4-1:
Various
cure tools.

Sound cures

Sound cures are very effective for clearing old, negative energy and bringing new, positive energy into a space. You can choose from two types of sound cures: ones with a ringing quality or ones with any other kind of sound. Ringing cures are more powerful, but you can use almost any sound-emitting tool to create a cure. Tools for ringing cures include wind chimes, bells, and gongs. Modern day ringing devices include telephones, alarm clocks, and classroom bells, which never fail to grab your attention.

Sound cures create beneficial effects by

- Stimulating new energy
- Awakening, arousing, and alerting
- Calling forth a message
- Sending a reply
- Strengthening the energy of a location, person, or Octagon Area
- Providing protection (Burglar alarms are just glorified bells.)
- Creating harmony, peace, and balance

Special powers of the red ribbon

When hanging Feng Shui cures like faceted crystal spheres, wind chimes, or mobiles, use a red string, ribbon, or cord for best results. The color red is the most potent transformative color in Feng Shui. Red symbolizes fire and the energy that makes changes happen. (See Chapter 9 for information on red front doors.) The red string practice may also harken back to the shamanic roots of Feng Shui, as red string is used even today by native medicine men and women in their ritual healing work.

In addition to the color red, another key factor is to cut your hanging ribbon or string to a multiple of 9 inches long, such as 9 inches, 18 inches, 27 inches, and so on. Nine is the most powerful number in Feng Shui theory; it symbolizes completion and peak accomplishment. Therefore, using a red cord with a 9-inch multiple in length for your cures adds the two potent energetic elements of color and number to your cures.

Wind chimes

Wind chimes can be used for a multitude of curing purposes, both indoors and out. Chimes help attract new energy, stimulate opportunities, and blow out obstacles in your life. Be sure to hang your wind chimes with a red ribbon or cord for the greatest effect (see sidebar "Special powers of the red ribbon").

Wind chimes used as cures are best made of metal and chime clear tones. (Refer back to Figure 4-1.) Metal chimes truly ring, whereas those made of other materials do not ring and thus have less curing power. Brass is the favored metal for chimes.

However, sound quality — the clarity and tone of the ring — is the most important chime factor. So listen to your chimes before purchasing them to ensure a high-quality ring. Also, a chime sound should be pleasing to you to be highly effective in adjusting your energy. Don't hang a chime that you don't love simply because someone gives it to you. (One man's chime is another's aggravation.) If you detest the sound of a chime, its energy may be less helpful to you.

If the chimes inside your house don't ring, don't worry! Interior wind chimes are still very effective. If you wish, you can activate a wind chime by ringing it as you pass by, creating chi on demand.

Bells

A brass bell is a good cure for an area where a chime is inappropriate. (You don't need to hang chimes everywhere.) A brass bell sitting on a desk or counter can provide activation where needed. Gongs are excellent solutions for entrances to homes, properties, or buildings.

Living cures

Living cures utilize the vitality and energy of plants and vegetation to boost the chi of a space. They provide nourishing, healthy chi for your home or office. Living cures are also easy to perform, highly effective, and aesthetically pleasing.

Plants and flowers

Plants add color to your space and symbolize new life and growth. The best plants to use for cures are full, lush, and vibrant. Rounded leaves are generally better than long, pointed ones. Avoid dagger-like plants, such as cacti, which create symbolic spears in your environment. If you have plants that are sparse, weak, sickly or dying, heal them or replace them as soon as possible with fresh, healthy plants. Also, plants with flowers and/or fruits create more effective cures than those without.

When utilizing a plant for a Feng Shui cure, you can get best results if you go out and buy a new, fresh, vibrant plant specifically for the cure; buying a new plant proves more effective energy than using a plant you already own. However, if plants you already own are all you can afford, use them!

Get rid of the dead, dying, and dried

Dead wilting plants, flowers, and decorative sticks (except for bamboo flutes) create negative Feng Shui, as they are antilife signs. Even wreaths and dried flower arrangements, however beautifully designed, symbolize death to the subconscious mind and can create a subtle drag on your energy. This principle holds true even if you personally like them. Dried flowers are dead, regardless of how they look or how much you paid for them, and according to Feng Shui principles, they can negatively influence your environment and you. The recommended cure is to remove them. A stronger cure is to replace dead and dried flowers with living, colorful plants or flowers. Replacing death with life is a wonderfully symbolic act, and you can feel the positive, energizing effects of this cure immediately.

Creating good luck with plant symbology

An exciting aspect of using plants as cures is learning the specific symbolism of various plants. Certain plants are renowned for their positive effects when placed in the environment.

Bamboo is the king of plants. When grown or displayed on the premises, bamboo denotes safety, harmony, and a strong future. The Chinese say that when one lives with bamboo, one's life will improve in stages over time.

Because the green *jade plant* resembles the jade stone, this plant is considered one of good luck or good fortune and wealth.

The *money plant (Lunaria annua)* is a Feng Shui favorite, symbolizing wealth and abundance coming to its owners.

For more on specific plant symbology, see Table 7-2 in Chapter 7.

Freshly cut flowers make another great living energy cure, as they stimulate life, cheer, and positive chi. But be sure not to let them wilt and die on the premises.

Generally, an odd number of plants creates a stronger, more active energy than an even number. But an even numbers of plants is still very effective.

Artificial plants can be used as cures, but make sure they look real. The best silk plants are indistinguishable from the real ones, except to the touch. So if you choose artificial plants, use silk ones for Feng Shui cures. The best artificial plants always seem fresh and thereby symbolize continuing life. A nice touch is to put a convincing silk plant in a pot of real soil. *Remember:* If your plants — silk or otherwise — look fake, their cure value is lessened.

Fish

Aquariums, which combine water and living energy, are powerful Feng Shui cures. They wonderfully spruce up an area, bringing in new vitality and stimulating energy flow. They are also natural mood-enhancers. Aquariums are renowned for bringing luck and good fortune to a residence and generating a stream of wealth for the occupants, which is why so many restaurants — one of the most difficult of all businesses to succeed in — use them.

Aquariums also contain fish that continuously circulate, are apparently peaceful, and never get stuck. They stimulate a similar flow in your life, flexibility and ease in your endeavors, and fewer blocks and obstacles. Also, bright, lively, multicolored fish represent you getting along with many different types of people.

To maintain the positive chi of your aquarium, make sure that your fish remain healthy, that the water stays clean rather than murky, and that any fish that die are replaced as soon as possible with healthy new ones.

An even stronger aquarium cure given by Grandmaster Lin Yun, is to stock your tank with nine goldfish, eight of them red and one black. If any of these fish die, replace them at once. If the black fish dies, it means a misfortune headed your way has caught the fish instead of you.

Water cures

Water represents connection, sustenance, wealth, and the flow of life. Humans have always chosen to live near sources of water, but today, sealed in our homes and workplaces, most people are cut off from contact with naturally flowing water and because of this lose something psychologically and energetically profound.

The Feng Shui solution is to add water to your environment, either on the property or inside the home. Flowing water creates soothing sounds (the babbling brook), and the movement of water over stones and rocks (streams and waterfalls) instigates a healthy, refreshing release of negative ions, which provide a sense of well-being, and make breathing easier.

Fountains and waterfalls

Fountains and waterfalls create a new energy flow in any environment. Moving water is both surprising and pleasant to encounter indoors, and a well-placed fountain has a refreshing and beneficial impact in any home. However, avoid placing a fountain in the Fame Area of the Feng Shui Octagon (see Chapter 3). The Fame Area is the natural location of the fire element, and because water puts out fire, a fountain in this area can have a dampening effect on your reputation.

The best fountains are ones in which you can see the flow of water and in which the water pools visibly rather than disappearing immediately. A particularly potent fountain is one in which the water's flow performs work, such as turning a water wheel. Flowing water means flowing money, and this factor symbolizes that money not only comes to you but also that your funds are effective and create results. Another nice energetic touch is a fountain that incorporates a light in its design.

Ponds and pools

Still bodies of water represent stored wealth on the property as well as clarity and depth of knowledge. Ponds, lakes, and swimming pools generally enhance the chi of a property. However, the following key principles should be observed:

✔ The body of water shouldn't be too large compared to the house, or it can energetically overwhelm the house and weaken the occupants' chi.

✔ The shape and placement of the body of water are also important to note.

  • A sharp angle of a swimming pool pointed towards the house resembles a cutting edge and can stimulate accidents in the residence.

  • A crescent-shaped pond positioned with the tips of the crescent pointing away from the house symbolizes money leaving the site.

  • Kidney shapes are positive because they are rounded, and the kidney relates directly to the water element in the body. Kidney-shaped ponds are best situated so they appear to hug the house, meaning wealth gathers and remains in the house.

✔ The clearer your still water feature, the better for your finances and clarity of mind. Murky water on the property can result in funky financial deals and confusion.

Color cures

Color affects every area of life, and opportunities for using color to improve your home's energy are innumerable. Color can be used to adjust the energy of an entire room by painting the walls, added in various ways to an Octagon Area for energetic effects, or can be used in clothing to adjust your personal Feng Shui. Color is a powerful way to change a mood or activate the emotions and subconscious mind for success.

Keep in mind that the attributes listed in Table 4-1 are Feng Shui color representations. Many different color systems exist throughout the world (Western, Indian, and Native American, to name a few). Add this color information to your existing knowledge and make your own choices about which color schemes are right for you. For more on color, see Chapter 15; additional color information is also given in Chapter 5.

Table 4-1	Key Colors and Their Attributes
Color	*Symbolizes*
Green	New life, new beginnings, growth, energy, vitality, spring, hope
Purple	Wealth, royalty, the extreme value of red (The Chinese saying, "That's so red it's purple," means great energy and power.)
Red	Power, protection, energy, activity. The most active of all colors and is used many ways in Feng Shui.
Pink	Love, the heart, marriage, motherhood
White	Cleanliness, purity, righteousness, death (Chinese wear white mourning gowns when grieving departed loved ones.)
Gray	Neutrality, absence of color, hidden things, benefactors
Black	Power, authority, absorbing energy, respect (Too much black represents despair and gloom.)
Blue	Knowledge, the sky, royalty, life, hope
Yellow, earth tones	Health, the earth, ground, connection

Mobile cures

Mobiles are objects that swirl and move, stimulating and circulating energy while projecting a uniquely calming effect. Mobiles rely on air currents for their movements. You can use mobiles, windsocks, flags, banners, pinwheels, and whirligigs. Mobile cures create new flows of energy, harmonize and balance chaotic energy, stimulate action and new thinking, and clear stagnation.

Mobiles

Mobiles are an excellent addition to a space needing circulation, movement, or clearing. The mobile's gentle swaying rotation soothes and settles. Mobiles can also diffuse sharp energies, like those caused by the protruding corner of a desk, counter, bookshelf, or wall. Another effective use of a mobile is to fill an area that lacks definition, or create balance by bringing down or filling in a ceiling that is too high.

The significance of flagpoles and light poles

A commonly recommended cure in many Feng Shui situations is to place a flagpole or light pole in a key location. Besides adding color, motion, and light energy to the area, flagpoles and light-poles play another very important role. They act as earth needles, tapping into the chi of the earth and lifting it high above the surface. Raising the chi is an important function in Feng Shui. Energy with an upward motion promotes life and growth, while downward energy promotes decay and decline. Flagpoles and light poles thus have dual effects of uplifting and enlivening. Also, a hollow flagpole is more powerful than a solid one; a hollow pole acts as an attractor for earth energy, uplifting the chi of the earth, which blesses and uplifts the property.

Flags and banners

Flags add unique qualities of color and symbolism to your cures. A green flag (favored in Feng Shui) denotes health, vitality, life, and money. Other colors can be used according to your needs and the design of the space. (See the "Adding Life with A Splash of Color" section in Chapter 15.) Designs or emblems on your flag or banner are fine, as long as they appeal to you. Such emblems may include your family crest, a state or national flag, your alma mater or favorite football team, sunflowers, lady bugs, or any other image that pleases or energizes you. Use your gut feeling as a final arbiter in choosing your Feng Shui flags.

Windsocks

Windsocks are effective tools for both interior and exterior cure applications. Because they combine motion with color, windsocks help stimulate, activate, and enliven dead energy areas, such as alleys and dead-end roads. Road traffic moving too quickly past a house (excess chi) pulls away the house's chi. But placing a windsock (or three) in strategic locations, such as near the offending road can calm the negative effects of this excess chi and stabilize the area.

Pinwheels and whirligigs

Pinwheels are a quick, inexpensive way to enliven a garden path or draw chi along a driveway or walkway. Whirligigs are small yet effective energy generators that are also useful for calming or counteracting excess traffic chi.

Weight cures

These cure tools provide needed weight or solidity to a space by literally adding substantial mass or presence to a site, generating feelings of stability and calm. Heavy cures can also be used to emphasize or give form to a certain area or point. For example, a heavy rock or statue can be used to energetically complete a missing area of a house. (See Chapter 8 for details on missing areas.) A heavy cure can emphasize and strengthen a needy area of the property or fill in a missing area. The weighty cure can also be a heavy desk or other piece of furniture or even an outbuilding added to the property like a greenhouse, garage, or toolshed. (See Chapter 7 for the best locations for outbuildings.)

A more mystical form of a weight cure is called a *yu* (pronounced you). A yu is a small bowl with a shallow base, a wide body and a shallow mouth (Refer back to Figure 4-1.) If a yu is properly prepared, it can cure many problem areas. Steps for preparing a yu bowl can be found in Chapter 18.

Bamboo flute cures

Bamboo flutes are a very powerful cure tool with many positive aspects. Few cure items carry as much significance and effectiveness as the bamboo flute. (Refer back to Figure 4-1.) Flute cures are potent remedies for numerous life problems. My clients use them, and many of them report amazing life changes as a result. The best type of bamboo flute yields the following benefits:

- ✔ **Delivers peace and safety:** Bamboo is renowned in Chinese culture for bringing luck and strength if grown or displayed on the premises.

- ✔ **Provides support:** Everyone can use more support in life, and bamboo, one of the strongest and hardiest of plants, is a potent energetic symbol of support for your ongoing endeavors.

- ✔ **Fights off evil spirits:** Whether you call them spirits, ghosts, heebie jeebies or just plain old bad vibes, humans can sense negative energies. When hung as shown in Figure 4-2, the flute, which represents the symbolic angle of a sword, helps to scare away negative energies and promote calmness and peace of mind.

- ✔ **Drives away evil, negative, and scandalous persons:** The flute cure is a powerful way to banish or nullify the negative energy of those who harm, harass, or harangue you.

Angling your flute

An important aspect of a flute's power is the angle at which it is hung (the hanging angle associates with the angles of the Feng Shui Octagon). To understand this, visualize the Feng Shui Octagon, not placed on a floor plan as usual, but placed vertically on a wall. The actual angle at which you hang your flute depends upon the angle of the Octagon sector or Life Area you want to remedy or enhance. For example, if you want to accentuate wealth, you naturally hang a flute in the Wealth Area.

To make your flute cure stronger, also hang it at the Wealth Angle. This additional detail makes a real difference in the effect of the cure. The following table (Table 4-2) is an easy guide to the flute hanging directions for each of the Life Areas of the Octagon. See Figure 4-2 for specific details.

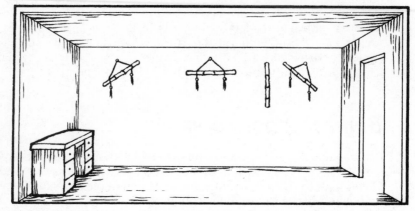

Figure 4-2:
Flute
positions.

Table 4-2	Beneficial Angles For Hanging Bamboo Flutes
Life Area to Emphasize	*Hanging Direction/Orientation*
Wealth or Helpful People	45-degree angle; left side lower, right side higher
Marriage or Knowledge	45-degree angle; right side lower, left side higher
Children or Family	Vertical; smaller sections of the flute downward
Fame or Career	Horizontal
Health	Use any of the four above angles

Important flute pointers

Here is a laundry list of things to consider when purchasing and hanging your flute.

✔ The flute recommended in Feng Shui is made from a special kind of bamboo in which each section grows longer than the previous one. This symbolizes life climbing upward step by step, meaning that things get better for you tomorrow than they are today, even better the day after, and so on.

✔ The sections of bamboo are segmented by the visible ridges in the bamboo stalk. (Refer back to Figure 4-1.) The ridges themselves are a key part of the flute's energy, symbolizing power and strength. For maximum effectiveness, use a bamboo flute that has its ridges still intact. If the ridges are sanded off (making the bamboo flute smooth and unsegmented), the flute makes a much weaker cure to implement. Hang your flutes with the shorter segments lower and the longer segments higher.

✔ Flutes work most effectively when hung by a red ribbon with two red tassels, one connected to each point where the ribbon attaches to the flute. (Refer back to Figure 4-1.) Leave the ribbon on the flute even if you hang it vertically. Also, the recommendation of having the length of your red ribbon measure in multiples of 9 inches (9, 18, 27, and so on) also holds. (See the sidebar "Special powers of the red ribbon" earlier in this chapter.)

✔ The only type of flute I recommend can be purchased by mail order by phoning 510-841-2347, and it already comes with a red ribbon attached. Ask for a flute — they only carry one kind.

✔ A flute used for a cure should be treated with respect and never be played with, handled roughly, or blown into. If this happens, the flute becomes simply an object of décor rather than an energetic cure.

Powered cures

Powered cures often utilize electrical objects such as appliances featuring generators or motors. The energy generated by these appliances can be used to activate particular areas of your space. Powered cures are used mainly to generate energy or create activity in a specific Life Area of the Feng Shui Octagon (see Chapter 3).

Firecrackers can also be used as a powered cure. Placed symbolically over the front door (on the inside of the house), firecrackers help to protect the home and its occupants. Depending on your intention when placing them, firecrackers can also activate new sources of revenue, enhance an occupation, and attract important business connections. (Find a source for symbolic firecrackers on the Feng Shui Resource page at the back of this book.)

Fragrance cures

Smell, one of the most powerful and evocative senses, directly stimulates the limbic system and often triggers the instant recall of rich and long-forgotten memories. Pleasant odors are frequently related to good feelings, higher states of well-being, and increased awareness. In the East, it is commonly believed that good spirits prefer environments that have pleasant, uplifting odors. Cures in this category include incense, essential oils, and flowers.

Incense

When using incense as an energy adjustment, I strongly recommend high-quality incense rather than inexpensive brands that commonly incorporate synthetic oils and perfumes. Synthetic incense is not only less effective but is also much less enjoyable and can even be irritating to the senses.

Essential oils

With essentials oils, quality is definitely the watchword for effectiveness. When essential oils are processed, heat and exposure to light rapidly degrade their subtle molecular structure and destroy their vital qualities. With oils, you definitely get what you pay for, and quality essential oils are worth the extra price. Two excellent brands of oils are Young Living and Tisserand (check the Internet for sources). Fragrant oils can improve your health and your mood as well as your environment. For more on the benefits and applications of fragrance, I recommend the excellent *Aromatherapy For Dummies* by Kathi Keville (published by IDG Books Worldwide, Inc.).

Touch cures

Touch cures engage your kinesthetic sense to awaken or adjust your energy. For instance, place a green vine around the hand rail of a stairway so each time you ascend or descend the stairs, your hand brushes the vine and tangibly connects to its symbolic life energy. Touch cures can give a boost to your recuperative powers and stimulate good health.

Chapter 5

Tapping the Power of the Five Elements

*I*n Chapter 1, I present two conceptual energy systems the Chinese use to explain the natural order of things. The first system is the principles of yin and yang — the concept that everything is divided into two big categories. The second system, the Three Realms of Heaven, Earth, and Human, refers to the cosmos, which is above, below, and within everyone. Chapter 3 presents the Feng Shui Octagon, a tool for mapping your home's energy by dividing it into nine important Life Areas.

Now I present another powerful method for understanding and shifting the energy of your environment — the Five Elements. According to Chinese energy theory, everything in the universe is made up of varying combinations of five *elements,* or forms of energy. The Five Elements are Wood, Fire, Earth, Metal, and Water. The Five Elements system offers a way of looking at the natural cycles of the world and coming into balance with them. Energetically speaking, you contain some of each of the Five Elements, and so does your environment.

The Five Elements have corresponding natural locations on the Octagon. If the Elements are situated in the proper positions in your home, the energy circulates and helps you achieve harmony and abundance. But each Element also has a location in the environment where it can conflict with another Element in the area. When Elements are situated in these negative locations, you may experience conflict, lowered income, and even psychological or health problems.

In this chapter, I explain the basic energies of each of the Elements, as well as their positive and negative placements. Then I give you several ways to create powerful cures using the energies of the Five Elements.

The Energies of the Five Elements

Each Element is a form of energy with unique characteristics, feelings, and various *correspondences* (meaningful and important connections) to the natural world. These correspondences include colors, seasons of the year, and geometric shapes. (See Table 5-1 for a quick summary.) The Five Elements are also connected to the psychological and interpersonal aspects of human life. In the following sections, I provide the correspondences of each of the Elements to help you understand how they function, and I explain their energetic qualities.

The energy of Wood: Growth

Wood chi is the energy of expansion and new growth. Represented by the color green, the Wood Element is related to the liver and the season of spring. Its corresponding geometric shape is a column or rectangle (positioned upright); skyscrapers are common examples of Wood-shaped buildings. On the Octagon, Wood is located in the Family Area. Wood is good to apply when you want to add the energy of growth, expansion, and vitality to your life. Associated with new beginnings, Wood cures are like adding a touch of spring, the season you feel young, energetic, and motivated.

The energy of Fire: Expansion

Fire chi is upward, burning, hot energy and is moving, bright, and fiery. Of the five energies, Fire represents maximum expansiveness and activity, the peak of energetic intensity. Fire is related to the summer season, the color red, and the heart. Its corresponding geometric shape is a triangle or pyramid. And Fire energy's natural position is in the Fame Area of the Octagon. Perform Fire cures when you want to create more expansion in your life and experience increased recognition.

The energy of Earth: Stability

Earth chi stabilizes, balances, and grounds you (pun intended). In times of intense life change, Earth helps you become centered and connected to bedrock (oops — pun again). Earth is related to the harvest season, the color yellow, and the stomach. Its corresponding geometric shapes are the square, the rectangle (positioned horizontally), and the cube (3-D). Earth's natural location is the center or Health Area of the Octagon. Perform Earth cures when you want to slow down in life, become more centered, and feel connected and stable.

The energy of Metal: Contraction

Metal chi is cold, contracting, dense energy associated with communication, creativity, detail, symbols, signals, and noise. Corresponding with the color white, metal is related to the lungs and the fall season. Its geometric shapes are the circle, sphere, and dome. Metal is located in the Children Area of the Octagon. Apply Metal cures when you want to improve communications, empower your children, or stimulate your projects.

The energy of Water: Stillness

Water chi is the energy of maximum concentration and stillness. Water is the energy of things moving downward and coming to rest. Also, Water is related to the season of winter, to the colors black and dark blue, and to the kidneys. The shapes of Water are elusive, imprecise, undulating forms that are flowing and difficult to describe. Water is naturally positioned in the Career Area of the Octagon. Perform Water cures when you want more peace and clarity of mind or want to increase the flow of people and cash into your life.

Placing the Five Elements in the Environment

If you know the positions of the Feng Shui Octagon (or if you don't know these positions, take a look at Chapter 3), finding the natural locations of the Five Elements is easy. The Five Elements are located on the Octagon as follows:

- **Fire:** The center back area of the environment (Fame Area)
- **Earth:** The center area (Health Area)
- **Metal:** The center right area (Children Area)
- **Water:** The center front area (Career Area)
- **Wood:** The center left area (Family Area)

The Cycles of the Five Elements

The Five Elements relate to and interact with each other according to two distinct cycles: the Creative (Generative) Cycle and the Destructive (Transformative) Cycle. You can use not only the Elements themselves but also the Creative and Destructive Cycles for Feng Shui cures.

In the Creative Cycle, the Elements create one another in a continual cyclical process. In the Destructive Cycle, the Elements cyclically consume each other in a similar process, but nothing is truly destroyed. Instead, the energy is simply transformed into another state. For example, when you apply heat to ice, the ice changes into water. The ice seems to be destroyed, but nothing is really lost. The material simply changes form. Apply more heat, and the water turns into steam — another change in form with no real destruction.

Both the Creative and the Destructive Cycles can be used beneficially for your Feng Shui cures. In the type of Feng Shui I present in this book, neither cycle is necessarily better than the other. Despite its name, the Destructive Cycle is not negative or harmful. Nothing actually gets destroyed but is merely transformed into another state of energy. Later in this chapter, however, I give you a couple cautionary tips on Five Element relationships you should be on the lookout for in your environment. The following two sections describe how the two Element Cycles work.

The Creative Cycle of the Five Elements

In the Creative Cycle, the Elements generate, create, or lead to one another in a continuous chain of creative energy (see Figure 5-1). The Creative Cycle superficially resembles the Destructive Cycle except for one difference — each Element changes from one form to another. The following ring-around-the-rosey example clearly illustrates the Creative Cycle.

- Wood, as it burns, is the fuel for Fire.
- Ashes, the result of Fire, return to and replenish the Earth.
- The Earth gives birth to Metal.
- Metal, heated sufficiently, becomes liquid like Water.
- Water nourishes Wood (the tree).

And the cycle continues forever . . . .

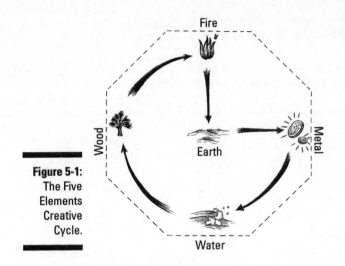

Figure 5-1:
The Five
Elements
Creative
Cycle.

The Destructive Cycle of the Five Elements

In the Destructive Cycle, the Elements symbolically destroy each other in a continuous pattern. (See Figure 5-2.)

✔ Wood is cut by the axe (Metal).

✔ Metal is burned by the blacksmith's Fire.

✔ Fire is extinguished by Water.

✔ Water is absorbed, subdued, and evaporated by the Earth.

✔ Earth is penetrated by growing trees (Wood).

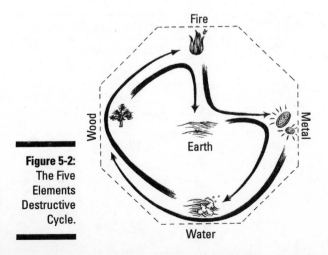

Figure 5-2:
The Five
Elements
Destructive
Cycle.

The following table gives you the corresponding physical representations, colors, and shapes for each of the Five Elements.

Table 5-1	The Five Elements' Corresponding Physical Representations, Colors, and Shapes		
Element	*Physical Representations of the Element*	*Color of Element*	*Shapes of the Element*
Fire	Candle, fireplace, light	Red	Triangle, pyramid
Earth	Pottery	Yellow, earth tones	Square, cube
Metal	Metal sculpture or metal table	White	Round, spherical, dome
Water	Fountain, stream, pond	Black	Undulating, wavy
Wood	Living tree, plant	Green, blue	Rectangular, columnar

Creator and Offspring Elements

In the following section, you can find out how to empower any Element simply by placing it in its natural location. Alternatively, you can create cures by using the Element that creates the Element you want to empower; I call this Element the Creator Element. A third cure option is to use the Element created by the Element you want to help; I call this Element the Offspring Element. Table 5-2 gives you the Creator and Offspring Elements for each of the Five Elements.

Table 5-2	Creator and Offspring Elements of the Five Elements	
Creator Element	*Element*	*Offspring Element*
Water	Wood	Fire
Wood	Fire	Earth
Fire	Earth	Metal
Earth	Metal	Water
Metal	Water	Wood

Using the Five Elements for Cures

The Five Elements theory explains how natural forces combine and interact to either help or hinder your life. When the Elements are in balance, your daily life reflects peace and harmony, but when your home has conflicts between Elements, you may experience disharmony and chaotic life patterns. In the following sections, I go over four different cure methods that you can apply to create powerful energetic shifts in your environment along with corresponding beneficial changes in your life.

This principle is the basic formula for balance: When the Elements are located in their natural positions and, more importantly, are not located in positions of conflict with other Elements, balance is enhanced.

When applying the Five Elements to create particular life results, you can use any of the following correspondences:

- ✔ The physical representation of the Element
- ✔ The corresponding color of the Element
- ✔ The corresponding shape of the Element

(See Table 5-1 for a reminder of the Five Elements' correspondences.)

Five Elements Cure Method 1: Placing Elements in their natural locations

With this cure method, you simply place a representation of a chosen Element in its natural location. If you need more Fire energy in your life or desire a boost in your reputation, add the Fire Element to the Fame Area of your house, bedroom, or yard.

For example, if you want to apply the Fire Element, you can add a candle to the natural location of Fire or the color red, or you can place a triangular or pyramid-shaped object in the area.

Five Element Cure Method II: Removing and counteracting offending Elements

When any of the conflicts listed in the following list are present in your environment, watch out! An Element positioned in the natural location of a conflicting Element can create particular life problems. You may want to remedy these Element relationships, especially if they correspond to an area of your life that you want to improve with Feng Shui.

- Wood located in Earth's natural location can harm your health.
- Fire located in Metal's natural location can harm your communication.
- Earth located in Water's natural location can harm your career.
- Metal located in Wood's natural location can harm your family life.
- Water located in Fire's natural location can harm your reputation.

For best results, remove an Element from a position where it conflicts with another Element (one symbolically consumes and destroys the other), particularly if you're experiencing challenges in the corresponding Life Area. For example: Water destroys Fire, so a fountain (Water) located in the fire location (Fame Area) of your house causes an Element conflict that can negatively affect your reputation. The cure? Simply remove the fountain. (Who says Feng Shui needs to be complicated?)

If a Destructive Element relationship can't be moved, you can still cure the problem in one of two ways:

- **Counteract the offending Element by adding a counter Element to the area in question to symbolically destroy the offending Element.** For example: If a fireplace (Fire) is located in the Metal position of your home (the Children Area) and your child is experiencing problems in school, cure the fireplace by adding Water — which destroys Fire — to the Children Area. Try adding a fountain to the Metal position to dampen the effect of the fireplace and relieve the negative effects on your child. Instead of adding actual water, you can also use the color of Water by placing something black in the area, or you can use an object with Water's wavy, undulating shape. Better yet, use a black object with Water's shape. (But please, don't use black water. There is such a thing as going overboard!)

- **Add more of the attacked Element to its natural location to increase its strength and help it overcome the offender.** Continuing with the example of a fireplace in Metal's natural location, use this method by adding more Metal to its natural location to boost Metal's power. Accordingly, you can add an object made of metal, the color white, or something round or spherical to the Metal location. (You can combine these effects by adding a spherical white metal object, if you can find one.)

Five Element Cure Method III: Utilizing the Creator and Offspring Elements for added power

Another way to perform Element cures is to add either the Creator or the Offspring Elements (or both) to an Element's natural position (see the earlier section "Creator and Offspring Elements" for more detail). For example, say you want to boost family expansion (with another kid!) and family unity. Wood is the Element you need to apply for these results. Water creates Wood, and Fire is the offspring of Wood. Therefore, to increase Wood, you can add either a fountain or the color red to Wood's natural position. Get it?

Five Element Cure Method IV: Using all the Elements together for power and creativity

To create balance, harmony, and power, you can add all Five Elements to an Element's position or to any room that needs its energy positively adjusted. This cure is good for a bedroom, the living room, or an office environment. With all Five Elements in place, you can create an atmosphere of wholeness, peace, and creativity. The Elements can be placed individually in the room or Octagon Area, or all the Elements can be contained in one item, such as a painting that presents each of the Five Element colors or an object that combines all the Elements in shape, color, and/or material.

When combining all the elements, no negative Destructive relationships ensue. When all the elements are together, they work in harmony, so the situation is energetically complete and whole. Just like this chapter!

Chapter 6

The Magic of Intention and Reinforcement

In This Chapter

▶ Defining intention

▶ Taking a look at the Three Secrets Reinforcement

▶ Performing the Reinforcement

▶ Answering some of your questions about Reinforcement

Nearly everything that humans do in life requires *intention* — a combination of will, motivation, and desire. According to Grandmaster Lin Yun's Feng Shui school, intention plays a key role; in fact, intention is the starting point for your Feng Shui efforts. First you decide what you want (you intend a result). Then you focus your intention as you create a change (a cure) in your environment designed to bring about the result. If your intention is clear, your desired outcome is much more likely to occur.

Intention magnifies the energy of the cures and increases their power and effectiveness in your life. Feng Shui cures work whether you perform them with focused intention or not, but if you want the maximum results, don't just go through the motions when you perform your cures. Give them your full intention.

Feng Shui has a special technique for empowering the intentions of your cures — thereby making them much more potent — called the *Three Secrets Reinforcement*. The Reinforcement is a short and easy-to-perform procedure (1 to 2 minutes in length) that you can apply with each Feng Shui cure that you perform. It utilizes aspects of your body, speech, and mind to energetically strengthen the cure.

This chapter presents the key elements of intention as well as the specific method (the Three Secrets Reinforcement) for strengthening your cures. So apply this Reinforcement when you perform your cures to greatly increase their effectiveness.

The Ingredients of Intention

Feng Shui works because its philosophy is based on the principles of energy flow to which all environments are subject. However, you can add rocket fuel to your Feng Shui by connecting a particular intention to each cure that you perform. By applying specific intentions to cures, you actually infuse them with added energy.

Applying intention to cures consists of three key elements:

1. Knowing exactly what you want

2. Visualizing and feeling the desired result before it happens

3. Expecting the result to happen

To the degree that any of these ingredients are missing, your cure can be less effective. But to the degree that these ingredients are present, your cures can be much more effective. In the next sections, I cover these three ingredients in detail, so you can feel absolutely clear about using this powerful aspect of Feng Shui practice.

For the best results, pay attention when you apply intention!

Know exactly what you want

Knowing what you want is the single most important factor in the realm of intention. If you're unclear about your goal, you can still get positive results from your cures, but they may be more general than particular. Clarity about your goals focuses your intention and empowers your cures to accomplish specific desired results. (But you can still perform beneficial cures with general intentions like improving your health, or increasing your wealth, or bringing harmony into the home, and so on. The point is to have a strong, clear, and focused intention.)

A very important factor of knowing what you want is the strength with which you want it; your intention is most effective when you desire with great intensity. Weak or wishy-washy intentions ("Gee, it'd be nice for that to happen, but it's really okay if it doesn't") do not greatly magnify your cures. Passion infuses your intentions with power and effectiveness. So the more passion you put into achieving your goal, the more energy your intention has, and the more effective your cure can be.

I recommend that you write down your intentions when you practice Feng Shui. Write down not only what you want, but why you want it and how intently you want it. This simple step makes your goal more real and the cure more meaningful. Writing also helps you generate the intention that you need to produce results. (See Chapter 1 for an exercise on writing down the areas of your life that you want to improve.)

See and feel the result before it happens

The human brain and imagination are the most powerful tools that the universe has yet developed. They allow us to vividly see desired future outcomes and then create them. Visualizing the intention is almost a prerequisite for manifesting an intention in any field of endeavor, such as art, science, business, and so on. Moreover, the clarity with which you visualize an intention makes your goal more likely to happen as you foresee it. So visualizing the desired results of a cure – while you perform it – makes it substantially more effective. When visualizing, endeavor to make your internal pictures so vivid that you actually feel, emotionally and physically, how wonderful and exciting your new life can be when the result is attained. (I give some visualization tips in the next section.)

Expect the result to happen

When you know what you want and can visualize it happening, the final step is to proceed in life with the confident assumption that your cures are effective as soon as you apply them — act as if! In other words, seal the deal with certainty. Align your actions, thoughts, attitudes, and words to the new life situation or result that you desire. Then watch your life change come into being before your eyes. Feng Shui cures, when performed in this manner, open up new energy pathways that allow your intentions to be realized in ways you never dreamed possible!

Expecting a result isn't wishing upon a star (or magical thinking) where you sit back and relax while expecting some higher power to magically work everything out. Nor is it stubbornly folding your arms or dragging your heels with an "Oh yeah, prove it to me!" attitude, doubting the result until your Feng Shui cures cough up and give you what you want. Neither passive wishful thinking nor aggressive skepticism is clear intention.

Simply perform the cures that you feel are right for you and your house with strong intention, and assume (see, hear, and feel inside) that they are effective. Remember, for best results, perform your cures without actively (or subconsciously) holding back. Act as if your cures are working and expect results. Not only do your cures work faster, but you're also happier while they do. Oh, yeah! Don't ya just love it?

A friend recently told me about the marvelous benefits she received after performing just two cures using a positive mindset. A year before our visit, she painted red the door of her own home and the door of the rental house she owned while visualizing more prosperity and expecting results. Because she applied intention, she just completed the purchase of yet another home (hello!) in addition to a share in another house. And her personal transformation was obvious; her energy was stronger and more vibrant, and she even looked younger than the last time I saw her. Did I mention she's happier? (And she didn't even have the opportunity to read *Feng Shui For Dummies*! I wonder what may happen if she performs 10 or even 20 cures!)

A final point about intention

After you choose your intended result and then act by performing the cures, you can't control the final outcome. You're simply setting in motion a powerful process that possesses its own energy and unfolds in its own way. But have faith that your intentions and actions, empowered by Feng Shui methods, can generate the desired results, even if you don't (and can't) know exactly how this process can occur. Final results may differ somewhat from your specific expectations, but they can fulfill them in some tangible (and agreeable) form.

Revealing the Secrets of the Three Secrets Reinforcement

One of the most powerful techniques taught by Grandmaster Lin Yun is the Three Secrets Reinforcement. The Three Secrets Reinforcement is the second, vitalizing half of each cure you perform and is the key enhancing technique for creating effective, successful cures.

Grandmaster Lin says simply, "If you do your cures without using the Three Secrets Reinforcement, your results are likely to be weak. If you do your cures with the Three Secrets Reinforcement, your results will be very strong." End of story. Without the Reinforcement, a cure is like a flashlight operating on a weak battery. The beam of light can only be so bright and shine so far, before it starts to fade. On the other hand, the Three Secrets Reinforcement is like a nuclear reactor empowering the cure — it makes the beam like a laser cutting through the energetic obstacles within you and in your personal environment. And it only takes two minutes! Do you have the time?

In Grandmaster Lin Yun's Feng Shui school, every cure involves two parts. First, each of your cures includes *visible* (tangible) elements — the changes you make in your physical environment. Second, they contain *invisible* (spiritual) elements — your energy, intentions, desires, and goals.

The physical portion of the cure is the physical change you perform in your environment: hanging a wind chime, moving the bed, and so on. However, the physical part of the cure gives only a fraction of the cure's effectiveness. The invisible part of the cure — strengthened by the Three Secrets Reinforcement — uses and focuses your intention to turbocharge the energy of the physical change. In fact, the invisible part of the cure contributes more to the cure's overall strength than the physical part does, so including the Reinforcement in each cure you perform pays off.

Both parts of the cure, however, are essential for full success, and combining them is the best method of all. You can call combining both parts the letter (outward actions) and the spirit (invisible energies) of Feng Shui. Both parts hold value in their own right, and together they form an unbeatable combination.

Feng Shui is about improving your life by altering your environment to create beneficial effects on your mind, body, and spirit and to achieve positive results in your daily life. Harnessing your energy and intention to empower your cures strengthens their effects on your life. Changing the outer environment is external Feng Shui; performing the Reinforcement is internal Feng Shui.

Ta da! The Three Secrets Reinforcement defined

The Three Secrets Reinforcement adds the power of body, mind, and speech actions to the physical Feng Shui adjustments of your environment. The three elements of the Reinforcement are called the Body Secret, the Speech Secret, and the Mind Secret. Each element engages a different part of your bodymind system and channels its unique power into the Reinforcement. In the following sections, I detail each of the secrets individually; then I show you how to combine them into one simple package with great relevance and potency.

The Body Secret: The physical you

The Body Secret uses a *mudra,* a spiritual hand gesture, position, or action that aligns the energy of your body to help create the desired energetic effect. Hand gestures have both a symbolic as well as an energetic value. To understand the power of hand gestures in daily life, consider how the infamous one-fingered salute can trigger anger and even violence in a total stranger; how both hands raised overhead can save your life in wartime; and even how clasping your hands in front of you can make you feel more relaxed, calm, and aware.

When applying the Body Secret in your Reinforcements, feel free to use a hand gesture from your personal spiritual tradition or any other gesture that feels comfortable and effective for you. (No hand gesture is superior to another.) I recommend any of the following mudras for your Reinforcements:

- ✔ **The Expelling or Ousting Mudra:** The most often recommended for the Three Secrets Reinforcement, this mudra is performed by pointing the first and pinky fingers straight up and then holding the middle and ring fingers against your palm with your thumb. Then repeatedly flick the middle and ring fingers out from the palm. Repeat the flicking motion nine times. (See Figure 6-1a.) This creates wonderful blessings by removing obstacles from your life. (Women use their right hand for this mudra; men, their left.)

- ✔ **The Heart-Calming Mudra:** This mudra invokes peace, calm, and contentment. Perform the Heart-Calming Mudra by placing your left hand on top of your right, with palms facing up and the tips of your thumbs touching. (See Figure 6-1b for details.)

- ✔ **The Blessing Mudra:** Bringing blessing, safety, and good luck, this mudra is physically the trickiest of the lot. To perform the Blessing Mudra, imitate the hand position in Figure 6-1c. Here are some pointers: Start with your palms up. Cross the little fingers. The thumbs hold down the tips of the crossed little fingers; the ring fingers stand straight up and side-by-side; and the index figures curl over and hold down the tips of the crossed middle fingers. (For another view of this mudra, see the photo of Grandmaster Lin Yun on the "About the Author" page.)

- ✔ **The Prayer Mudra (and other options):** Other sacred gestures that are effective in your Reinforcements include the Prayer Mudra (palms together) or any other meditative or spiritual hand position that has personal meaning or simply feels good to you. (See Figure 6-1d.) If you don't practice a religion, you can create your own hand gesture or position, or simply stand or sit with your eyes closed in a comfortable, balanced position until you feel a sense of clarity and calm. (Then leap upright and expertly practice kung fu. Only kidding!)

Don't worry about picking the right mudra. You can't do this process wrong or accidentally create bad results. (This is Feng Shui, not the Internet.) You simply need to choose a mudra you like for each Reinforcement that you perform. Any one you choose that feels right can work for any cure that you do.

To perform the Body Secret step of the Reinforcement, simply hold your hand gesture (if using the Expelling Mudra, flick nine times) as you do the next two Secrets.

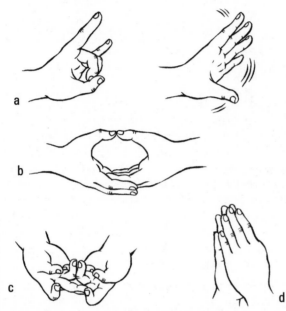

Figure 6-1:
Sacred
hand
gestures.

The Speech Secret: The power of the spoken word

The Speech Secret utilizes sacred words and sounds to enhance cures. All sounds and words have power, and sacred words have the most power of all. *Sacred words* are ancient containers of spiritual vibrations, meanings, and intentions made potent through ceremonial use over time. If you're wondering how spoken words can possibly affect your cures, think of how hearing a four-letter curse word can affect your mind and emotions and consider how other words can soothe, reassure, and calm turbulent emotions and distress. (And yes, the clear intention with which you speak such words does affect their potency.) True stories tell of several different horse trainers who are able to calm, tame, and train even wild horses simply by whispering certain words and sounds into their ears.

The sounds used in the Three Secrets Reinforcement are called *mantras* (sacred words of power). To perform the Speech Secret step of the Reinforcement, repeat aloud your mantra or prayer nine times.

Sacred speech is not the same as affirmations or repeating sentences stating your desire. Affirmations are good to use, but mantras used in the method described in the following section can be even more effective. Correctly used, a mantra (or prayer) uses sounds or words to take you beyond the conscious mind and connect you to your spirit, where the majority of your power resides.

I most often recommend that my clients use the following mantras with their cures:

- ✔ **The Six True Words:** The sacred speech that usually accompanies the Three Secrets Reinforcement is the Six True Words: *Om Ma Ni Pad Me Hum* (pronounced ohm-mah-nee-pahd-mee-hum). The Six True Words is also called the Mantra of Compassion. This mantra has the power to improve luck, uplift your mind, correct negative thoughts, enhance wealth and prosperity, and help you perform better in your daily life.

- ✔ **The Heart-Calming Mantra:** The beneficial effects of this mantra include creating peace and calm, invoking feelings of ease and contentment, and releasing fears and anxieties. The Heart-Calming Mantra has four lines to recite (reciting the four equals one time through the mantra):

Mantra	*Pronunciation*
Gate gate	**gah**-tay **gah**-tay
Para gate	**pair**-uh **gah**-tay
Para sum gate	**pair**-uh **sum gah**-tay
Bodhi swaha	**boh**-dee **swa**-ha

Note: Bold markings indicate stressed syllables.

Feel free to use mantras, prayers, or chants from other spiritual traditions for your Three Secrets Reinforcements. As always, repeat the one you select nine times when performing the Reinforcement.

The Mind Secret: See the result to receive it

The Mind Secret involves *visualization,* seeing the results of your cures before they happen. Thousands of books emphasize the power of visualization — an effective method for invoking beneficial changes in your life.

Visualization is standardly used by professionals of all types (including business people, top athletes, and even astronauts) to help them dissolve limitations, see results before they happen in order to make them happen, and excel in their chosen fields.

Whether you're consciously aware of it or not, you're continuously creating your future with mental visualization, so you may as well start using it to your advantage. (Because many of your mental pictures are formed outside of your awareness, figuring out how to consciously direct your mental imagery gives you greater control and is highly beneficial in terms of creating positive results and life changes.)

Visualization is the part of the Reinforcement in which you mentally see your desire — your motivation for performing the cure — coming true. In this step, you visualize in concrete and realistic detail the events, conditions, and scenes that you desire in your life. The more powerful and intense your mental pictures are, the better and more effective your cures can be. But for some of you who may have difficulty visualizing clear mental images, don't worry. All you need to do is to imagine and feel (or mentally hear) the desired results and the effect is the same. The present energetic imagining of the future desired result is what does the trick.

To illustrate, if you want greater wealth, visualize or imagine your future wealth and the things you can enjoy with wealth flowing into your life. The pictures, feelings, or imaginings should be moving, involving, and exciting. If you want a new relationship, visualize yourself together and happy with your new and right partner. Imagine what you want with such intensity, as if your desire is already happening in your life.

Keys to effective visualization

Two other important principles are taught in Grandmaster Lin Yun's Feng Shui school to increase the power of your visualizations.

> ✔ **A master key to effective visualization is detail.** See your desired goal occurring in as much detail as possible. Detailed visualization directs the subconscious mind, the chi, the universe, and your own belief system to create the life scenarios you desire. Involve other senses internally for even more oomph. For instance, if a new car is your goal, you can visualize the model, the color, the year, the sleek design, and the details of the instrument panel. You can feel the leather grain of the seat, hear the purr of the engine as you see yourself driving to your office, and smell the new car scent (one of the greatest smells in the world).

✔ **See in your mind's eye that your desired life situation occurs in three stages of development.** New things in life don't often drop out of the sky the moment you ask for them. Most things in life have a beginning, a middle, and an end. So I recommend that you see your desired results happen in the same manner. This three-stage visualization method imitates life's natural progression by setting up a path of energetic expectation in the subconscious mind that leads you into the new life situation you desire. For example, say that you want to buy a new car. The following steps demonstrate how you can put the three stages of development into effect to achieve your desire:

1. **See the initial circumstances that lead to what you want.** You're at the dealership checking out and test-driving the car you really want.

2. **Visualize the development phase of the process.** You acquire the down payment and sign the loan papers for the car. The whole process is smooth and enjoyable.

3. **See the wonderful completion of your goal.** The payoff, the dream, the victory. You're roaring down the freeway with YOBABY on your license plate. Life is sweet!

Performing cures with the Reinforcement

The moment you've been waiting for has arrived! You can now perform the entire cure by including the physical aspect and applying the Three Secrets Reinforcement.

First you can physically change your environment (hang a crystal, move the bed, or make whatever change). Now do the Three Secrets Reinforcement to empower the physical part of the cure in three easy steps:

1. **Perform the Body Secret.** Hold the mudra of your choice. (If you use the Expelling Mudra, perform the flicking motion nine times.)

2. **Perform the Speech Secret.** While holding the mudra, repeat the mantra of your choice nine times.

3. **Perform the Mind Secret.** Visualize your intended desire transpiring in as much detail as possible.

That's it! Congratulations, you've just completed a cure! Now go perform another cure, take other productive practical actions toward your goal, or simply relax. ***Remember:*** A watched pot never boils. Sitting around worrying about your cure after you've performed it is unnecessary. Go and enjoy your life already!

Hey! I don't see pictures in my head!

Rest assured, everyone is capable of performing visual imagery. What differs is that some people don't consciously see the pictures in their heads. If you can't visualize, don't sweat. If you can strongly feel the joy and satisfaction of achieving your intended result or even mentally hearing the sounds associated with your outcome, you can perform the Reinforcement effectively. In the third step of the Reinforcement (the Mind Secret), substitute feelings or sounds for the visualization. You may be pleased — and amazed — at the results!

Frequently Asked Questions about the Reinforcement

Here are some answers to basic questions on the Reinforcement process.

How long should my Reinforcements take?

You don't need to spend long periods of time performing your Reinforcement. Quality, not duration, is the general rule. One or two minutes is sufficient if you really feel the emotion. Internal intensity and realism are more important than the length of time you perform your Reinforcements.

Is how I'm thinking and feeling important during the Reinforcement?

You should be as focused and sincere as possible and should trust the process — everything will work out well. Perform each Reinforcement with sincerity, energy, intention, and positive emotion. The element of sincerity is particularly fundamental for a high level of effectiveness with your cures. Involve your heart in what you're doing, and you'll do fine. Also, your visualizations are ideally so exciting and powerful that your nervous system lights up like a Christmas tree. (If yours aren't this strong yet, don't worry, you'll get better at visualizing with time. Your level right now works fine!)

How do I know if I'm doing the Reinforcement right?

Don't get caught up in performance anxiety over the Reinforcement. Every person has his or her own natural way that works. Perform the Reinforcement as well as you can right now. Release all concern and feel confident that your Reinforcement is effective, and it will be effective. As with any skill, your ability naturally grows with practice.

The red envelope tradition

The red envelope tradition has long been practiced throughout Chinese history and stems from Chinese culture and folklore. The red envelopes symbolize good luck, power, and protection from evil. In Feng Shui, red envelopes that include a token amount of money — even a coin — are respectfully offered to energetically protect the giver of Feng Shui cures. By giving a red envelope, you protect the consultant or teacher from harm for sharing their sacred and traditionally exclusively oral knowledge. Giving red envelopes also increases the strength and effectiveness of the cures provided to you.

To perform this tradition, place money (a token amount or coin) inside a new red envelope and then present the envelope to the person who gives Feng Shui cure information. When professional Feng Shui practitioners perform consultations, their fees are presented inside of red envelopes to honor this practice. If you teach a Feng Shui cure to someone else, I recommend that, in exchange, you receive one or more red envelopes containing money from the person. This symbolic gift honors the importance of what you have shared and also helps to ensure continued good luck for you.

If you feel inclined to participate (completely optional) in the red envelope tradition in honor of what you learn from this book, you can send any sum of money of your choice in a new red envelope (again, a token amount or coin is fine) to your favorite charity.

How many times do I need to perform the Reinforcement?

You need to perform only one Reinforcement for each cure. (Several of my clients went around their house reinforcing each of their cures every day! Not necessary. And though they received fabulous results with their Feng Shui, so did many other of my clients who performed a single Reinforcement following all the steps in this chapter.) The Reinforcement you perform with the cure empowers the cure energetically and is sufficient to hold the energy of the cure indefinitely. If you want to apply the Reinforcement again for a cure (especially if an area of your life really needs a boost or you simply want the practice), feel free. An extra Reinforcement can't hurt, and it may help improve your situation. Some people enjoy reinforcing each of their cures monthly, weekly, or even daily. But again, while the Reinforcement is both fun and helpful, you don't need to repeat it to bring about your desired result.

Part II
Outdoor Feng Shui: Energizing Your Home's Exterior

The 5th Wave   By Rich Tennant

©RICHTENNANT

I was kind of hoping to harmonize the elements in the backyard with a pond or a tree – <u>not</u> an A-frame for pulling engine blocks!

In this part . . .

Now you can get down and dirty — outside. Your outside environment (including your neighborhood, house lot, and house exterior) affects your life in a major way. Part II shows you secret ways to whip your lot into energetic shape without lifting a single shovel. I show you how to conduct incredibly beneficial new flows of energy right into the front door of your house. Meanwhile, you can paint your front door and the neighbor's dog Chinese red. (And you think this exercise is going to be all work and no play.)

Chapter 7

Improving the Energy of Your Lot, Landscape, and House Exterior

. . . .

In This Chapter

▶ Examining the energy of your neighborhood

▶ Curing nearby negative energies

▶ Defusing the ill effects of poor house placement

▶ Using the postive energy of plants, color, and water to liven up your lot

▶ Effectively positioning outbuildings on your lot

. . . .

*W*hy focus on the outside of your house? Because with Feng Shui, you can read a good deal about the quality of the energy (or *chi*) that affects you from the conditions you see outside.

Things that you see as you come and go from one place to another affect you psychologically. Imagine this: On your way to work you experience the usual bump over the pothole in front of your driveway. You pass by the eyesore that is your neighbor's home with its peeling paint and untended yard. Then with a grumble, you pass the vacant lot at the end of the street that now serves as a local dumping ground for irresponsible citizens. Next you're delayed in a traffic jam and late for an important meeting at work. By the end of the day, you only want to relax at home, but first you must face the rush hour traffic snarl again, pass the same neighborhood eyesores, and hit the same irritating pothole to get into your driveway. A typical day, right? Experienced repeatedly over time, these conditions can provoke irritability and energetic discomfort.

The same experience — continuous environmental influences on your psyche and life — happens on a more subtle level with smaller obstacles that you encounter daily as you move in and out of your personal environment — your own home. What's the point? Every thing you see in your external environment, whether you notice it or not, affects you energetically. In this chapter, I discuss your outside environment, including the neighborhood and streets. So come along as I show you how to read the energies of your exterior surroundings and perform cures for the problem features found in the exterior of your house and property. Performing the cures in this chapter can increase the energy quotient of your property, and smooth your path to increased success and happiness.

Looking around the Neighborhood

Your neighborhood is the context or local container of your personal environment, the space in which your home is contained. Your neighborhood plays a large role in determining the overall feel, mood, and energy of your home, as well as the energy of you within your home.

Reading the chi of a neighborhood or place

Everyone (including you) can read energy. Sensing energy is a basic human ability; it doesn't require mountaintop mystical training. When you sense energy, you allow your feelings to come to the surface so you can recognize them and notice how they make you feel. Making the following observations can tell you plenty about the energy of a place and can let you know whether the energy is positive or negative.

- ✔ **Observe the local animals and wildlife.** Do you see healthy, bright animals and pets? For example, seeing a deer as you enter an area is a positive sign. A negative animal sign is a mangy, unleashed, roaming dog. (A black cat crossing the road smoking a cigarette and using a Ouija board is definitely a bad Feng Shui sign!)

- ✔ **Observe the plants and vegetation.** Are they lush, vibrant, and healthy? Or sickly, brown, and dried up? Healthy plants are a sign of living, flourishing energy — just the kind you want to surround yourself with. Dying plants symbolize a lack of abundant chi in the environment, which can make you wonder if enough energy is present to support your life and success.

- ✔ **Observe the people.** Seeing the inhabitants of a location can tell you a lot about the energy of an area. Are the people friendly, cheerful and happy, or suspicious, dour, and unhappy? Generally speaking, friendly people demonstrate a much higher quality of energy in the environment than do unhappy and angry people.

✔ **Observe the life patterns of the neighborhood.** Find out the general levels of harmony and happiness in your area. Notice how wealth is distributed and whether personal lawsuits are filed frequently. Also keep in mind the number of premature deaths, car accidents, divorces, and so on. These factors tell you a lot about the history of the neighborhood, as well as its current standing, and how living in the area influences you energetically. The lives of families in surrounding houses are powerful factors and indicators of the kind of energy circulating in the neighborhood. A sign of upheaval in a neighborhood is that many homes in the area have recently been sold. (Love Canal became a ghost town for a reason!) Check the institutions in the area; the presence of a graveyard, funeral home, or hospital can symbolize negative energy.

Noticing how street energy charges your home

Your residential street is one of the main exterior sources of energy for your property, house, and life. Streets are like arteries of a city that conduct the connecting energies of a society by funneling traffic and chi to the individual neighborhoods and homes. In American society, ninety percent of the population lives in metropolitan areas, and consequently, the homes receive a good deal of their chi from the street.

Of course, the most important street is the one leading directly to your house. The nature and power of the flow of energy (traffic) on your street is a prime indicator of whether your house is energetically well fed. Your street feeds the mouth of your driveway and front walk, your driveway and front walk feed your front door, and your front door feeds chi into the entry and hallways of the body of your house.

Enjoying the ideal street situation

From the Feng Shui point of view, the ideal residential street situation is one that has brisk, lively, creative energy. The general feeling should be cheerful and uplifting. The overall energetic quality of the street leading to your house should not be too active or too still, but just right. Too little energy coming to your house from the street can mean an energy deficit, which is detrimental to your finances and even your physical health. On the other hand, excessive street energy (rushing chi) tends to bring chaos and disruption into your life and results in negative consequences that can potentially rob your property of vital energy. Luckily, you can counteract any of these conditions with the Feng Shui cures in the following sections.

Curing street problems

If you live at a T-intersection, near a cul-de-sac, on a sloping or one-way street, or on a dead end road, you and your home may be suffering from the negative effects of these conditions. To transform the negative energy to positive energy, perform one of the cures in the following sections.

Escaping the dreaded T-intersection

If you live on a T-intersection, a street ends at your front yard, and the on-coming street traffic heads straight toward your house (see Figure 7-1a). The energy bombarding your home is dangerous due to its rushing or attacking qualities. (This onrushing energy can take the form of onrushing cars, which occasionally run into this type of house!) The energy here moves too fast and too forcefully for the well-being of the occupants.

The continuous effects of the street's chi crashing into the house can wreak havoc on the residents' lives. The results can range from subtle feelings of depression, paranoia, and being attacked to more serious psychological effects and even to accidents, sickness, or death in the household. Over time, life in a T-intersection house can progressively deteriorate. Also, the house can prove harder to upkeep and maintain.

You can cure the effects of rushing chi at a T-intersection by planting a tall hedge across the front line of the property to protect the house, or you can build a fence in the same location (see Figure 7-1a). Additional solutions include hanging a wind chime over the front door to disperse the onrushing chi, and placing a Ba-Gua mirror over the door for protection (see "The Power of the Ba-Gua Mirror" sidebar later in this chapter). The same problems and solutions apply to a home located at a Y-intersection.

One of my Feng Shui clients moved into a new house, which happened to face a T-intersection. The unfortunate effects of the location were compounded by the fact that the road leading towards the house came down a steep incline, making the oncoming rushing energy much more forceful.

The saving grace was a large tree that stood at the curb between the street and the front door. Usually, a tree directly in front of the door is a no-no, but in this case, the tree was an excellent energetic and literal buffering agent for the attacking chi of the street. I prescribed a supplemental cure; she hung a metal wind chime in the tree, directly between the center of the road and her front door. The ringing sound of the chime helped diffuse the oncoming chi and provided safety and protection. Located in the Career Area of her property (the front center section, as discussed later in this chapter), the chime also activated the career energy of the household. Shortly after implementing this cure, her financial picture improved. She felt stronger and healthier, her husband's business took an upward turn, and they bought the new car that they had wanted for some time.

Moving energy through a cul-de-sac

Cul-de-sac streets imply stagnation and a lack of energy rather than rushing or overwhelming chi. Because cul-de-sacs provide no outlet for traffic to flow through or past the house (as shown in Figure 7-1b), much less energy flows to houses built on a cul-de-sac than to ones built on a typical street. Therefore, cul-de-sacs and their houses face dead or stuck energy and risk becoming low on vital chi. Life effects that come from living on a cul-de-sac include lower physical vitality and difficulty receiving opportunities. Residents may find it difficult to move forward and make positive life changes.

Energetic cures for a cul-de-sac home counteract this stagnation by activating or awakening the chi. To wake up cul-de-sac chi flow, add motion, color, and activity to the home to stimulate incoming chi and invite opportunities and money towards you.

A moving water cure with a strong upward spray is a great antidote to stagnation and lethargy. Placing a fountain on your property is a good way to encourage flow, activity, and abundance in your life. Fountain cures stimulate income and connections with new and old friends, and they also protect the property. The best location for this fountain is near the mouth of the driveway (see Figure 7-1b). This position stimulates chi to enter the entire property. Alternate placements for the fountain are in the center of the yard near the front of the house or near the front door.

Two additional ways to compensate for a cul-de-sac is to use color and motion to stimulate energy at the property entrance. A flagpole bearing a colorful flag or a bright windsock near the mouth of the driveway is a good solution for this condition.

One of my Feng Shui clients, the CEO of a technology company, moved into a new dream home. The home was great in most aspects, except that it was located on a cul-de-sac. To keep his family and personal chi moving in this new location, the gentleman placed an energetic outdoor fountain near the front door of the house. I recommended that he orient the water flow towards the front door to invite cash flow into the house (instead of away from the door or away from the property to cause wealth to leave the family). Needless to say, he's still doing booming business.

Slowing the energy of sloping and one-way, streets

Living on a sloping or one-way street can create two energetic problems.
Generally, energy tends to moves faster on these streets, sometimes too fast
for ideal Feng Shui conditions. First, energy can pass through the street too
rapidly to enter and nourish the property and, therefore, deprive the residents of desperately needed chi. Second, the rapidly flowing chi can rob or
strip away vital energy from your yard and life. The effect of these factors is
that your career, opportunities, and your health can suffer.

Because the front of your lot (the part nearest the street) corresponds to the
Life Areas of Helpful People/Travel, Career, and Knowledge (see Chapter 3),
rushing street energy can create unfortunate results in these areas. The solution is to slow down the street energy at your property and absorb some of
its force for your own benefit. For an easy cure, you can plant bushes along
the front property line. (See Figure 7-1c.)

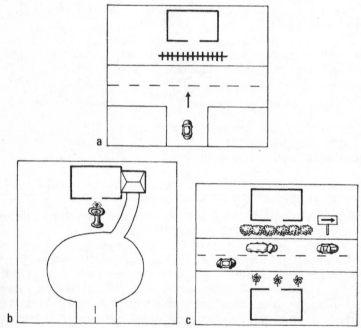

Figure 7-1:
T-intersection,
cul-de-sac,
and one-
way street
with cures.

Another cure that works wonders for slowing the chi of a sloping or one-way
street is a strong exterior fountain. You can place it in the Career Area of your
property or near the mouth of your driveway to both counteract and utilize
the rushing chi of the street. Yet another excellent solution involves using
moving cures, such as windsocks, pinwheels, or whirligigs. Apply these solutions along the front line of your property (at the street). The moving energy

of these cures beneficially uses up the rushing chi of the street by simultaneously absorbing it for the property's benefit, and preventing the street from pulling energy away from the lot. (See Figure 7-1c.)

An outerwear wholesale company found itself in a puzzling situation. The partners were confused, because they couldn't decide whether to move their business to another location and rent out their existing office and warehouse, to sell the business, or just retire and head to Fiji. They preferred to rent out the building, but they couldn't find any takers.

Upon inspecting the exterior of the property, their Feng Shui problem became obvious. The building was located on a busy highway just outside of town. The traffic on this highway consisted of huge fast moving trucks that zoomed by their office throughout the day. They couldn't decide (lack of clarity — a Knowledge Area problem) what business direction to move in (a Career Area issue) and were struggling to find potential renters and to keep a good staff (direct correlation to the Helpful People Area). The diagnosis was clear — the rushing chi of the trucks was pulling energy away from the front of their building, damaging their Helpful People, Career, and Knowledge Areas.

I recommended that they utilize colorful windsocks. They already had several tall light poles in front of the business, so they hung an odd number of large windsocks on the poles. (According to Feng Shui beliefs, odd numbers of cure items such as 1, 3, 5, 7 and so on can hold more curing power than even numbers 2, 4, 6, 8 and so on.) Not long after hanging the windsocks, the partners received a call from a company that had passed on renting their building months prior. They were interested in the property and wanted to move in immediately. So the path was clear, and the partners moved to a new location with relief. (Another windsock victory!)

Living on a dead-end street

A dead-end street receives even less inflow of energy than a cul-de-sac. Hence the name dead-end, meaning the street is dead energetically — and you're at the end. Now I ask you, is this image the symbology you want running your life?

The main problem with dead ends is that — by definition — no energy can flow through. Because no traffic can pass, the energy is lower and less active, creating stagnation and dullness. The lives of residents living in homes on dead-end streets are often lower in energy, wealth, and opportunities. Getting to work in the morning and succeeding in life can be more difficult.

Awakening and enlivening the energy of the lot is vital to transform the energy of a dead-end house. You can start by cutting back all overgrown bushes and vegetation. Make sure all outdoor lights are working. Keep your yard and street clean of debris and old belongings, including any junk cars, spare bulldozers, and dismantled 747s.

To attract and create a new flow of positive energy, do your best to enliven, energize, and awaken your property with sound, movement, color, and life.

- ✔ Use energy activators such as windmills and windsocks, which feature motion and color.

- ✔ Hang wind chimes to activate and awaken the area to create more energy and movement in your environment and life.

- ✔ Install bird feeders to attract the lively energy of fine-feathered musical friends. In Feng Shui, lovebirds and songbirds bring opportunities and messages that create new activity, movement, and harmony in your life.

Investigating and Curing Potential Nearby Negatives

Another way to determine the energy level of your environment is to pay attention to certain institutions that, if located near your house, can have negative effects on you and your family. Be aware of buildings or organizations in your neighborhood that can radiate negative energy. It can prove harder to maintain your health, career, marriage, and family if you live near a cemetery or any one of the areas mentioned in the following sections.

A negative element located across the street, next door, or directly behind your house is the most detrimental situation. One located on the same block can affect you with nearly as strong an impact. The next level out is a building that can is visible from the house or yard on a regular basis. When in doubt (doubt is always a feeling to listen to and address), perform a cure to feel safer and more protected.

All the institutions mentioned in this section are important and are rightfully placed in society. They aren't bad or evil; they simply aren't necessarily temples of cheer, elation, celebration, and affirmation of life. However, a prudent student of Feng Shui realizes that events and buildings near his or her home must inevitably influence their home, for better or worse. Feng Shui, of course, offers cures for alleviating these unfortunate effects. You can still live near one of these institutions and enjoy happiness, peace and prosperity. Read on.

Cemeteries and funeral homes

Cemeteries are places where dead people are buried. Lots of them. Feng Shui says that disembodied spirits can wander in graveyards and, sometimes, haunt nearby houses and their residents. If the spirits are unhappy, mischievous, or even malicious, they can cause no end of trouble for your home's occupants. Health problems as well as mental anguish can plague the residents of homes near cemeteries. Even if no ghosts or spirits are haunting the house, living close to a cemetery can cause depression.

The very yin (depressing and low) energy of a cemetery continuously impacts the subconscious mind and exerts a cumulative affect. Funeral homes and mortuaries give off similar vibrations, which continuously feature the energy of death, grieving, and sorrow.

Hospitals and convalescent centers

Hospitals, though important institutions, can negatively affect the health of the people living nearby due to the continuous stream of sickness, death, emergency, suffering, and grief that passes through and resides in the hospitals.

Police and fire stations

Police stations and fire stations can seem advantageous, and some people find living next to them exciting. Yet police and fire stations both house the energies of emergency, alarm, and fear. Police stations can especially radiate the negative vibes of criminals, crime, and suspiciousness. (Fire stations tend to emanate less toxic energies.) Although you may feel more secure — on the surface — living near these places, their energy never rests. As a result, you may find resting and relaxing difficult in your home, and you may always feel on edge waiting for the next emergency alarm to go off.

Schools and churches

A school can influence your home positively or negatively. The influence depends on the type of energy found at the particular school and whether you like the generally excited, happy — and admittedly hyper — energy of children.

A church carries negative energy similar to that of a funeral home only if it holds funerals on the church site. If a church doesn't hold funerals on its premises, living near one isn't a negative influence. And if the church features numerous weddings, it can positively influence your home.

If you live by a nearby negative, you may choose to perform a cure for the protection of your home and family, particularly if you've experienced a run of bad luck since moving into your house. Remember that whatever is happening to your lot and house (both known and unknown) has a simultaneous

The power of the Ba-Gua mirror

The Feng Shui Octagon is not only a tool for mapping the energy of your house and lot but also a powerful symbol of protection. The *Ba-Gua mirror* is usually octagon shaped, framed in wood, and measures about 4 to 6 inches across, with the Octagon trigrams marked around the outside in red and green, and with a round mirror in the center. (See "The poison arrow" sidebar later in this chapter for an illustration.) The Ba-Gua mirror is an easy and inexpensive protection method, typically hung above the front door of the house, on the exterior side. An even stronger variation of this mirror uses a convex mirror (which curves outward) instead of a flat one. Find sources in the Feng Shui Resources page at the back of this book.

and corresponding effect on you and your family. These results occur in the physical, mental, interpersonal, and financial realms. You can reap great benefits by observing these patterns and taking action to alter and improve your environment and your life.

A good all-around protection and blessing cure is to place a Ba-Gua mirror over the front door on the outside. (See "The power of the Ba-Gua mirror" sidebar previously in this chapter.) Or you can hang a set of five symbolic red firecrackers above the front door on the inside of the house. The firecrackers ward off negative people, energy, and events. (See the Feng Shui Resources page for firecracker sources.)

One of the most powerful Feng Shui cures that cleanses the energy and protects your house and family is called the *Rice Blessing* (also called the *Exterior Chi Adjustment*). This blessing is designed to remove negative chi, reverse bad luck, and generally create a new start in life. I detail this blessing ceremony in Chapter 17.

Eliminating House and Lot Problems

Besides nearby negatives, the following section details some other important house and lot conditions. Check these situations to see whether they apply to your life.

Too close for comfort

If your home is positioned too close to another building, especially a taller one, you can potentially experience feelings of oppression and victimization. I recommended curing the situation by hanging a Ba-Gua mirror on the wall of your house nearest the larger building, or even on the roof closest to the other structure (see Figure 7-2). The mirror should face the opposing build-ing. A particularly good Ba-Gua mirror for this situation is one featuring a concave (curving inward) mirror in the center. Hanging the mirror on your wall or roof can relieve any feelings of oppression and pressure, and provide newfound freedom and ease. For full effects with this cure, apply the Three Secrets Reinforcement, and visualize your desired results (see Chapter 6).

Figure 7-2:
Oppressed
house with
mirror cure
on roof.

Whole 'lotta shakin' goin' on

A major disturbing element close to the house structure itself, such as a main thoroughfare street or dingy alley, creates turbulence and chaotic energy. The continuous motion of cars and people passing by creates subtle (or pro-found) shakes, and rattles, and rolls, which translate into aggravation and unease. The rushing sounds and intense energy tend to upset the sleep, moods, and psychological balance of the residents. If the disturbing element is a train track, subway, or freeway overpass, the problem can be greatly intensified depending on the volume of traffic. Life results can range from lack of rest and health issues to clashing arguments, unnecessary accidents, and frequent absence from the home.

You can counteract this situation by creating a visual block, such as planting a tree (or trees) or tall shrubs that can hide the negative element and provide energetic protection for the home. If the problem is a nearby train or street, a good cure is to place sizeable pinwheels or windmills near the offending ele-ment (see Figure 7-3), which disperse the chaotic chi, and create a peaceful antidote to the noise and confusion. You can also cure this situation by plac-ing one or more flagpoles (the taller, the better) waving colorful flags near the disturbing element.

Problematic neighbors

If your neighbors are loud, antagonistic, dangerous, or otherwise bothersome, Feng Shui offers some simple solutions to help you protect yourself.

First, consider planting a row of hedges between your home and your neighbor's home. This cure buffers the problem neighbor's energy and even helps bring peace into the situation.

A second option is to hang a wind chime at the property line between your house and your neighbor's. The sound of the chime helps to disperse conflicting and aggressive feelings, replacing them with a melody of harmony and balance.

Figure 7-3:
Train near house with windmill cures.

If a situation is particularly intense and calls for strong help, mirrors can be effectively employed. A mirror on a fence or on the side of your house facing the neighbor can create an energetic boundary of protection and safety for you and your family. If even more oomph is needed, you can place a Ba-Gua mirror facing the neighbor's house.

The mirror can help protect you and your home from negativity that may come flying your way. As usual with Feng Shui, be sure to employ this solution in a spirit of compassion and desire for mutual harmony, never with the intention of malice, or returning negative energy to the other party. The mirror's purpose is to create safety and ease for your household, not to do something to or against your neighbor.

Sitting Pretty: Ideal and Not-So-Ideal House Positioning

The ideal house position is located in the center third from front to back of a regularly shaped, symmetrical lot; in the middle of the lot from left to right; even with the road or above the road; and with flat land or sloping-upward land behind the house. A house in this position is in a balanced and protected location and is set up for good fortune. (See Figure 7-4.)

Figure 7-4:
Ideal house position in center of lot, with protective hill behind.

The three thirds of the lot from front to back energetically represent the following:

- ✔ **The front third symbolizes planting or beginning.** This area is where opportunities and energy begin, germinate, and sprout.

- ✔ **The middle third represents growing.** This is where situations develop, progress, and begin to mature.

- ✔ **The rear third of the lot symbolizes harvest, cultivation, and completion.** Wealth is symbolically and energetically stored in this general area of the property.

Locating problems with your home's location

The following deviations from the ideal lot site can create obstacles and life problems.

- ✔ **If your house is in the front third of the lot, it sits too close to the street and can be vulnerable.** You can plant a large tree or place lights in the back and sides of the yard to balance the lot energy. See Figure 7-5.

- ✔ **If your house is located in the back third of the lot, it sits too far from the street and, therefore, lacks energy.** Also, the area behind the house is symbolically where the money of the family is stored. A house in this position does not have a large area between it and the rear property line; this small or nonexistent area for wealth can negatively influence the fortunes of the household. A tree or light placed in the front of the property is a balancing cure. The same cure can apply if the house is too close to either side of the lot. Simply place a light on the side opposite the house.

Positioning the house topographically

Another key factor is the contour of the land that the house sits on. The first general principle is that a house should not be placed too high or too low. If your house is positioned on a pinnacle of a hill, this location is called king of the mountain. Unfortunately at this position (the top), the only one way to go is down, and residents may find plenty of volunteers to push them off their perch.

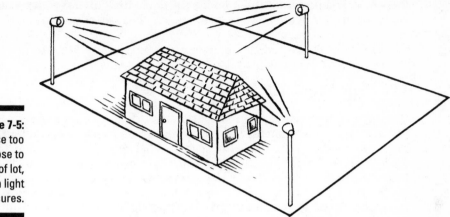

Figure 7-5:
House too
close to
front of lot,
with light
cures.

You can also experience negative energetic effects if you live in a very low area, such as the bottom of a valley or the base of a very high, steep hill. These effects can include depression, lack of energy, and failure to vigorously pursue your goals. Dismal spirits tend to gravitate to such places and can make prospering difficult.

The second general principle highlights the importance of the home's backing. The backing or shield behind the house represents support and protection for its occupants. The ideal backing includes a hill behind the house, which keeps invaders from approaching unawares. Land that slopes upward behind the house can also help hold wealth for the occupants. The space between the house and the hill is the wealth pocket, where money energy can pool and remain. Table 7-1 rates four common house positions.

Table 7-1	Influence of House Position on Occupants
House Position	**Life Influence**
On a flat piece of land	Neutral or good
On a gently rising slope	Good, offers protection
On a flat area with rising land or a hill behind	Excellent, increases protection and wealth
Land slopes away behind the house	Negative, decreases wealth and energy

The best cure for land that slopes away behind the house is a bright light mounted (the higher the better, and as high as the roof is best) on a tall pole or on a tree behind the house. The light should shine at the roof of the house. (See Figure 7-6a.) The energy of this cure keeps precious chi from rolling away from you downhill, and it uplifts the chi in back of the property and energetically fills in the missing land. The result is better wealth and health for your home's occupants.

Living high up or low down

Your positioning vis-a-vis the road is also important. The general Feng Shui rule states that your house is better positioned above the road rather than below the road. If you live in a house placed below the road, you may find your career and other life areas blocked by various obstacles. If you live below the road, rising each day to go to work may require extra effort. Also, you may subconsciously feel below the action — sensing that others are carrying on at a higher level than you — making life unnecessarily difficult.

The cure for the house-below-the-road syndrome is to place a bright light behind the house shining up towards the roof (see Figure 7-6b). You can also uplift the house by placing a flagpole, antenna, or weathervane on the roof to raise the height of the house above the road. Or you can install bright lights on top of the house that shine upward to uplift the energy of the house and improve your overall situation. This cure is more effective if you put an upward shining light on each corner of the roof. The lights don't need to be on at all times, but must be in good working condition to be effective.

In addition, you can also energize the driveway to symbolically reach the street easier. Line the sides of the drive with lights, colorful flags, or windsocks. The energy of light and motion make it easier for you to get up to the street, an important factor for career success.

Diffusing projecting roof ridges

A neighbor's roof ridge pointing toward the front of your house, and in particular toward your front door, can project piercing energy. This situation can bode ill for your future. (See Figure 7-7.)

One practical solution includes hanging a wind chime between your front door and the neighbor's roof ridge. Use a red ribbon or cord cut to a multiple of 9 inches in length to hang the chime. Make sure the chime is made of metal and has a pleasant, ringing sound. The power of sound disperses the invisible but harmful poison arrows of energy. (See "The poison arrow" sidebar later in this chapter.)

For particularly threatening circumstances, hang a Ba-Gua mirror with a convex (rather than flat) mirror in the center above your front door on the outside of your house. (See Figure 7-7.) The mirror protects you not only from the roof ridge but also from negative persons, events, and threats, and allows only positive and helpful energies to enter your home.

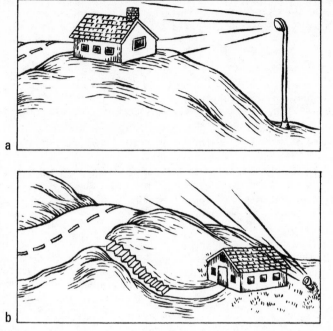

a

Figure 7-6:
Land sloping
away from
house with
cure; house
below road
with cure.

b

Figure 7-7:
Neighbor's
projecting
roof ridge
with Ba-Gua
mirror cure
over door.

The poison arrow

A *poison arrow,* also known as a secret arrow, piercing arrow, or heart piercing chi, should be remedied as soon as possible. This energetic arrow is generated by sharp points or edges directed at the house, front door, bed, people, and so on. The points can be generated by roof ridges, corners of houses, protruding wall corners inside the house, and other similar factors. Not surprisingly, the energy of the arrow is penetrating and, according to Feng Shui, can have very negative effects. The cure includes blocking the arrow-point. You can plant a tree in front of a neighbor's projecting corner. Or place a potted plant inside the house covering an interior offending arrow-point. Also, you can hang a decorative curtain in front of a protruding corner.

One key cure for a poison arrow is to use a Ba-Gua mirror (pictured here) for protection. Place a Ba-Gua mirror above your front door to deflect the poison arrow and any other forms of bad luck away from the area. Another cure is to hang a wind chime in line with an offending arrow to deflect and disperse its negative energy.

You can choose additional tools for counteracting secret arrows as well. Mount a weathervane in the path of the area with the vane pointed towards the poison arrow, one arrow virtually neutralizing the other. You can also employ a gazing ball (a mirrored sphere about 12 to 14 inches in diameter), which also reflects the negative force away. Search the Internet for gazing ball sources.

Enlivening Your Lot with Healthy Trees and Plants

Trees and vegetation are important because they provide green color, oxygen, and vitality to both outdoor and indoor environments. Green exerts a positive influence on the psyche, creating hope, growth, and new life. Adding healthy plants to your home and yard is one of the easiest ways to increase the living energy enjoyed daily. This cure can immediately affect your health, moods, and actions.

Avoid a barren yard, which symbolizes a lack of growth, attention, and stability. A client in California applied some Feng Shui cures on her own to her home and noticed significant life improvements. However, her husband had been locked into an unenjoyable night shift at his job for several years. When she came to me for advice, I pointed out that she had removed all the flowers in the Career Area of her front yard, leaving it barren, she quickly replenished the area with healthy flowering plants. Not long after this, her husband was offered a new work shift, which allowed them to spend more time together.

Trees in particular provide beauty and privacy. They can also serve as effective traffic screens and privacy shields. In addition, trees produce oxygen, which helps clean the air of pollution and toxins. However, be careful not to completely screen the front of the house from the street, which can block vital energy from coming to you and can cause stagnation and frustration.

Utilizing positive tree energies

Table 7-2 lists the energy effects of some specifically beneficial trees. Plant the following trees to enhance their special qualities in your life.

Table 7-2	Trees and Their Energy Effects
Tree Types	*Positive Effects*
Pine	Resilience, integrity, dignity, longevity
Willow (only good in front)	Gracefulness, scholarly atmosphere
Banana Palm	Scholarly ambitions
Persimmons	Joy, luck in business, good start for new endeavor
Apple	Safety
Orange	Good luck
Pomegranate	Fecundity, fertility
Pear	Sweetness
Olive	Peace
Peach-plum	Compassion

Helpful tree-selecting hints

When selecting trees, keep in mind the following helpful hints:

- Positive trees are ones with umbrella-shaped canopies. These trees provide a symbolic covering of protection and safety.

- Evergreen trees are better than deciduous trees, whose leaves fall in autumn and stay bare all winter. (Of course, deciduous trees are much better than no trees at all!)

- Upward reaching trees are better than downward reaching ones, such as weeping willows.

- Trees featuring flowers and fruits are more beneficial than ones that don't bear fruits or flowers.

Avoiding negative tree situations

Trees uplift the energy of the earth, bringing vitality and life to an area. Trees also provide symbolic and energetic protection against evil energy or bad influences (both physical and nonmaterial) in the neighborhood. Growing in the wrong place, however, trees can have unintended negative effects. For best results, follow the following tree rules:

- **Avoid planting a mulberry tree in the front yard.** The Chinese believe death can occur in your home. Also, because mulberry leaves are fed to hungry silk worms, your property and career can be chewed up!

- **Avoid planting a weeping willow tree in the back yard.** This tree symbolizes weeping, parting, slipping away, and energy flowing downward. As a result, occupants of the house may leave, lose money, or worse. (I leave it to your imagination.)

- **Avoid planting trees and bushes that contain thorns near a main entrance or on the pathway to your front door.** These trees/shrubs include rosebushes and cacti.

- **Avoid planting trees directly in front of the front door.** A tree in this location blocks the door, which can energetically harm every area of life.

- **Tend barren or stripped trees, either healing or removing them.** The subconscious influences of these decaying trees on your psyche can result in sickness or general failing health.

Curing dead or dying trees

A dead tree near the front of the house symbolizes death or decay for the household. Replace the dead tree with a new healthy tree. If the dead tree is impractical to uproot, wrap a green artificial vine around the tree trunk starting at the ground and circling upwards to at least as high as the tallest member of the household. A good additional step is to plant a healthy new tree or bush nearby.

If a tree is alive but dying, perform this cure to offset the negative energy:

1. Mix a bowl of rice with 99 drops of high-proof liquor and one packet (about ¼ teaspoon) of cinnabar powder. (Visit your local Chinese store for cinnabar.)

2. As you mix these ingredients together, repeat a prayer or mantra of your choice nine times.

3. Sprinkle this mixture on the ground around the entire tree.

4. Then sprinkle the mixture from the tree all the way up to your front door.

5. Perform the Three Secrets Reinforcement (detailed in Chapter 6) and visualize new health and life for all in your household.

Using Color to Empower Property Life Areas

An effective and enjoyable way to empower exterior areas of your property is by using color in the landscaping of your yard. As a first step, apply the Octagon to your property. (See Chapter 3 for Octagon information.) Then apply plants or shrubs featuring the appropriate colors for the Octagon Life Areas that you want to empower. Table 7-3 tells you which colors to use to empower each Life Area.

Table 7-3	Using Color to Empower in the Yard		
Area of Lot	*Octagon Life Area*	*Colors Options*	*Improves, Aids, Empowers*
Front center	Career	Black, dark blue	Connections, career
Front left	Knowledge	Black, blue, green	Thoughts, thinking, spiritual and personal growth
Center left	Family	Green, blue, blue-green	Immediate family relations, community

(continued)

Table 7-3 *(continued)*

Area of Lot	Octagon Life Area	Colors Options	Improves, Aids, Empowers
Back left	Wealth	Green, blue, purple, red	Money, prosperity, abundance
Back center	Fame	Red	Reputation, vision for the future
Back right	Marriage	Pink, red, white	Marriage, key partner in home or business
Right center	Children	White	Children, communication, creativity, creative projects
Right front	Helpful People	White, gray, black	Benefactors, travel helpers, networking
Center	Health	Yellow, orange, Earth tones	Physical, mental and emotional health, all parts of life

Engaging the Power of Water

In Feng Shui, water has two separate aspects: dynamic (or moving) and still. Each aspect holds a different energy, activity, and meaning.

Moving water brings flow

Flowing water represents flowing money, so water cures are excellent for improving your cash flow and financial circumstances. Moving water also represents social connections. Therefore, adding flowing water to your environment improves your level of personal friendships as well as your business contacts and networking connections. Streams, rivers, fountains, and waterfalls create dynamic water.

Choosing good areas for fountains

Fountains and waterfalls help humidify the air and create beneficial psychological effects by releasing negative ions that add soothing white noise to an area. They also make excellent additions to your landscape and can be beneficial in the following areas:

✔ **Near the entrance of the driveway:** A fountain here can stimulate more inflow of wealth and energy.

✔ **Near the front entrance of the house:** This position is one of the all-time best moving water cures, creating a host of life benefits.

You can also choose a spot based on the Octagon as applied to your property (laid out previously in Table 7-3).

✔ **The Career Area:** (Front center sector of the property) According to the Five Element Theory (see Chapter 5), the natural location for water is in the Career Area of the Octagon, so moving water is an especially potent cure.

✔ **The Knowledge Area:** (Front left sector) Helps create fresh, clear thoughts

✔ **The Family Area:** (Center left sector) Increases family harmony and flow

✔ **The Wealth Area:** (Back left sector) Attracts additional money

✔ **The Children Area:** (Center right sector) Stimulates increased creativity

✔ **The Helpful People Area:** (Front right sector) Invites more folks to your aid — you can't have too many beneficial friends and helpers!

One of my consultations involved the owners of an office furniture firm. They applied the power of flowing water to their business and received amazing results. Their cure was to place a large fountain outside the main door of the business. Shortly thereafter, the pace of the business quickened. New sales increased so rapidly, they soon had to hire new staff to handle the new incoming business.

Avoiding fountains in these areas

Two areas to avoid placing either moving or still water are

✔ **The Fame Area:** (Back center sector.) Water features in this area can cause damage to one's reputation and name.

✔ **The Marriage Area:** (Back right sector.) Fountains in this area can cause excess emotion in the primary partner relationship. If you have a water feature in this area, you can apply a cure by placing healthy potted plants near the water feature.

The soothing and clarifying effects of still water

Still water has dual connotations — one is increased wisdom and knowledge and the other is stored or contained wealth. Still water brings peace and serenity, and if clear, depth and clarity of mind. Still water features include ponds, lakes, and both natural and artificial pools (including swimming pools).

Still water features should be kept as clear and clean as possible. Stagnant, cloudy, or debris-filled water creates negative energy in any Octagon Area (and corresponding Life Area) of the property, which promotes confusion, unnecessary life entanglements, and shady dealings with money. If your property contains muddy water, get it cleaned up as soon as possible.

Still water features are beneficial in any area of the property, except for the Fame and Marriage Areas of the Octagon.

Positioning Outbuildings

The locations of outbuildings is another important part of your exterior Feng Shui. An outbuilding is a structure on the property such as a tool, garden, or storage shed, green house, guest house, a detached garage, or other building. Outbuildings represent added weight, significance, and value on the property.

Outbuildings reflect additional growth and expansion on the property and in their corresponding Life Areas. An outbuilding is a development of the property area. And as you may know, in real estate, buildings on a property are called improvements. (For detailed info on which parts of your property influence which areas of your life, see the Feng Shui Octagon section in Chapter 3. For a quick reference, see Table 7-3.)

A storage shed in the Wealth Area of your property symbolizes increased money in your future. Another positive outbuilding location is a detached garage in the Children Area as long as the garage is near the edge of the property, not right next to the house. This outbuilding can mean that another curtain-climber (a child) may join the household.

The following sections discuss outbuilding situations that can create negative results, and I provide helpful cures for each situation.

Who's that sneaking 'round my back door?

An outbuilding can be negative if located in the Marriage/Partnership Area of the yard. This building placement indicates that one spouse (or both) can start a separate relationship or even a separate household on the side. A cure for avoiding this unhappy event is to mount a spotlight on the outbuilding. Make sure it shines at the main house, ideally at the roof, to energetically connect the two buildings. The light doesn't need to shine at all times, but it should be in good working condition. Installing the light can transform the negative situation into a positive image of energetically connected yet independent structures, and the marriage can prosper and flourish.

My clients erected a children's playhouse on the Family Area of the property and then placed a tool shed on the Children's part of the lot. They soon found themselves in the somewhat unusual (and enjoyable) position of owning a second home 30 minutes from their main residence. This home is closer to the beach, and they enjoy meeting their relatives (the Family Area influence) and playing with their kids (the Children Area influence) at the new house. Of course, your mileage may vary.

Stuffed shed syndrome

Buildings on your lot that are run-down or in disrepair (or lovingly stuffed-to-the-gills with all-important junk) can quickly become a negative force on your lot. Simply keep your outbuildings shipshape, tidy, and shiny.

Honey, I can't see what's out there

When a building blocks your view of the street or a good portion of the view from a bedroom, living room, or kitchen window, moving it to a better spot on the property can free up your vision of the future. If moving the building is impractical, you can hang a wind chime between the building and the window to disperse the building's blocking influence.

Losing it: Fixing exterior drains

Drains on the property are an important aspect; improperly located, they can be, well, draining! Drains can pull down energy and water, both symbolizing money, and cause it to vanish to who knows where. Therefore, a visible drain can represent loss of wealth. Many lots don't have visible drain covers. If your lot contains a visible exterior drain, you can place a lively new plant on top of the drain.

If the drain is close to (or in a straight line with) the front door, the problem is even worse. An advanced solution for an auspiciously located exterior drain is to apply the special cinnabar and liquor cure given previously in the "Curing dead or dying trees" section of this chapter.

Chapter 8

Making the Most of Your Lot and House Shape

● ●

In This Chapter
▶ Dwelling in interesting shapes
▶ Balancing irregular house shapes
▶ Locating and curing missing areas and projections

● ●

*T*hroughout the ages, people have been fascinated with geometric shapes: their creation, their texture, and their meaning. Feng Shui also looks at these aspects of different shapes as well as the influence they exert upon us. In fact, shape is one of the most influential factors in Feng Shui. The shapes of our personal environments affect us energetically and psychologically, consciously and unconsciously. The shapes of particular living environments include the outlines of the house and lot (top down view), the elevation of the house (side views), and the contours of the land. These key aspects largely determine how the energies flow within our personal living environment.

The shapes of your house and lot are important. Whether positive or negative, these shapes strongly influence your immediate experience and your long-term destiny. You may have a perfectly shaped house and an irregularly shaped lot, or vice versa. This situation can enhance certain life areas and hinder others. The trick of Feng Shui is to discern which areas may be holding you back energetically so you can cure them.

This chapter examines the nature and effects of various shapes to see how they impact your career, relationships, prosperity, and other key areas of your life. You can find out how to distinguish positive and negative shapes and how to create effective cures for your particular situation. If you've read the previous chapters, you're now familiar with these tools. If you've been playing hooky, you can now take a quick make-up class while exploring the all-important matter of shapes. Then you can jump right in and change things for yourself.

Discovering What Shapes Mean to You

Two of the most important Feng Shui factors in your environment are the shapes and sizes of your lot and your house. These factors directly influence the boundaries of the space and determine key Feng Shui characteristics, including placement and orientation. (Room shapes and sizes also impact your chi and the energy flows in your house, though interior spaces tend to be more uniform and standardized.)

These overall shapes (lot and house) influence general life factors such as the ease or difficulty of life, the presence or lack of obstacles, good fortunes or bad, and health or the lack of same. The same general principles apply to the shapes of both houses and lots; the difference is the cures that are applied to correct the problems.

The shapes you inhabit mold your actions, feelings, and daily life path. Shapes determine energy flow and represent important symbology that act continuously on the subconscious mind.

According to the Theory of Relative Positioning (see Chapter 2), defects in the shape of your house affect you more than defects in the shape of your lot. This condition is due to the principle of proximity, meaning that the house is closer to you than is the perimeter of the lot, and therefore, the shape of your house affects you more profoundly and immediately (but both are important).

The same principle applies for apartment dwellers. According to the Theory of Relative Positioning, the shape of your apartment is more important than the shape of the lot your apartment building stands on or of the building itself. (However, these factors still influence the lives of the tenants in the building.) Plus, the shape of your apartment is something you can energetically alter with Feng Shui; you can't change the shape of your entire apartment building and its lot — unless, of course, you own them.

Enjoying Balance: The Positive Effects of Regular Shapes

In Feng Shui terms, regular shapes are the most favorable for houses and lots. Regular shapes include squares, rectangles, circles, and octagons. These shapes all promote even, balanced, and harmonious living. Because everything in your environment corresponds to your body and mind, the positive qualities of these four shapes have similar effects on you. Circular and octagonal houses and lots are rare (they're difficult to build and find), so square or rectangular lots and house shapes are the most common, favorable, and practical shapes.

Admittedly, many uneven or asymmetrical shapes can be interesting to look at, to visit, and to design. An asymmetrical shape is initially more arresting to the eye than a regular, balanced shape. But the problems with unbalanced shapes come not from looking at them but from living in them. Over time, the imbalance of the shape tends to produce an imbalance in the physical and mental well-being of the residents. (And I don't mean that if you live on a triangular lot you'll wind up looking like a pyramid!)

In terms of shape, the Feng Shui truth is that interesting isn't necessarily better and, in fact, is often worse. An ancient Chinese curse that says, "May you live in interesting times," can be paraphrased in Feng Shui as, "May you dwell in interesting shapes." Unfortunately, unbalanced and irregular shapes can generally result in unbalanced lives and problem circumstances.

Living foursquare: Squares and rectangles

A square represents a solid, even, and stable existence. A rectangle has the same basic energy, however if the rectangle is much longer in one direction, the main entry to the house or lot (for example the front door, driveway, or foot path) is best located on one of the short sides of the rectangle. If the entry sits on one of the long sides, the energy can quickly exit the property without nourishing it, leading to a loss of good fortune for residents. (The entry of the lot is the mouth of the driveway; the entry of the house is the main front door.)

Before you celebrate the wonderful fortune of having a square or rectangular house or lot, make sure your lot or house is a true square or rectangle — not an imposter! Follow this rule: A true square or rectangle has only four flat, even sides and four 90-degree corners with no indentations, protrusions, or slants. If your house or lot isn't a perfect square or rectangle (with houses, these shapes are rarer than you may think), the irregularities can either be helping or hindering you. Read on in this chapter to determine if your shape features *projections* (generally favorable), or *missing areas* (not so good). And of course, Feng Shui always provides a cure for enhancing the positive and countering the negative.

Round and round: Circles and octagons

Round shapes denote unity, wholeness, and balance. A circle has a pleasing symmetry that is good for life in general. Octagonal shapes are powerful, strong, and lucky, and they have a special association with the Feng Shui Octagon. Round and octagonal houses reflect the positive aspect of having a strong, whole shape, but often their interiors have many unusually shaped rooms. Round and octagonal shaped houses and lots are quite rare in real life, so if you happen to live in one, I suggest you contact a Feng Shui professional to assist you with your home cures.

Diagnosing Projections and Missing Areas

When you place the Feng Shui Octagon on any regular shape (see Chapter 3), all the Life Areas are somewhat evenly represented, indicating balance and harmony. However, if one or more sides of your house or lot shape is not completely even (say your shape is not exactly four flat sides with four 90-degree angles on the corners), you may have either a projection or a missing area in one or more corresponding Life Areas. (Of course, elements inside the house can also affect these areas; see the chapters of Part III.)

Are you projecting?

The short version of this principle is that projections expand the space in the house or lot and allow more chi to circulate, resulting in better fortune in the corresponding Life Area. For example, a projection in the Wealth Area of your house can positively influence your financial situation. But a missing area in your house or lot shape (as detailed in the following section) produces the opposite effect (missing wealth or financial trouble).

Oops! My areas are missing!

A missing area means proportionally less area for the all-important *chi* (life-force energy) to circulate or reside in any particular part of your house or lot shape. This situation implies probable negativity or lack of good fortune in the corresponding Life Area. Thus, a missing area in the Helpful People Area of your lot shape may explain why your network of supportive helpers and friends has shrunk since moving into your current residence. By the same token, a missing area in the Marriage Area can mean marital troubles or can make dating or finding the right partner difficult. (And entertaining a blind date in a missing area is the Feng Shui equivalent of flying a small plane into the Bermuda Triangle during a hurricane!)

In the following sections, take a look at these two contrary features and see what you can do to enhance the positive effects of projections and minimize or transform the negative effects of any missing areas you may have. (Before diving in, you may want to review the Feng Shui Octagon section in Chapter 3, because you'll be putting its theories into action right about . . . now.)

Locating Projections and Missing Areas

You may be able to figure out if the sides of your house and lot contain projections or missing areas simply by comparing your diagrams to the illustrations given in this chapter. However, if you prefer the step-by-step method, read on.

Keep in mind that many Feng Shui factors other than shape influence your life — otherwise, this book would be just one chapter long. Nevertheless, follow these easy steps to analyze your house and lot shapes to see how they may be helping or hurting you.

1. **Obtain or create scale drawings of your house and lot plan.** You can measure the house and lot yourself and draw it on graph paper, or use the architect's drawings, blueprints, or plot maps you've got stashed in a box in the garage or closet, or for you tidy types, in an actual filing drawer. If the measurements are given on the drawings it can speed up the process. (The quick-and-dirty version of the following process is to measure the distances by evenly walking them off. Estimate 3 feet for each step you take.)

2. **If any side of the house or lot is completely flat and even, with no variations at all, the side is fine.** Skip it.

3. **Apply either the 50% Rule or the 33% Rule to any side that is not completely flat.** How do you determine which rule to use? Follow these tips: If you have an apparent missing area in the center area of a wall — that is, if the side reminds you in any way of a U-shape — apply the 33% Rule to the side. Otherwise, you can safely apply the 50% Rule.

Using the 50% Rule

Measure the entire length of the side in question with a ruler. Say the length is 6 inches on paper with a 1:5 ratio, meaning 30 feet in real life. (Once again, your drawings must be to scale for this process to work correctly.) The following guidelines show you how to use the 50% Rule (the key concept to grasp is "less than half"). Check out Figure 8-1.

✔ If the part of the house or lot side that appears to be sticking out is less than half of the entire length of its side (3 inches or 15 feet in this example), call it a projection. (See Figure 8-1a.) Translation: Projections enhance the Octagon Life Area they're located in. Throw a party! Then continue reading.

✔ If the part of the side of the house or lot that appears to be indented is less than half of the entire length of its side (again, 3 inches or 15 feet in this example), call it a missing area. (See Figure 8-1b.) Not quite so good, but don't panic. The cures are given in the "Curing Missing Areas" section.

If the process I just described reads like Egyptian hieroglyphics to you, here's how to look at applying the 50% Rule another way:

- If the part of the side which appears to be indented or missing is more than half the length of the entire length of its side (again 3 inches or 15 feet) then you do not have a missing area, but a projection. The part of the wall that appears to be sticking out is your projection. (See Figure 8-1a.) Yippee!
- If the part of the house or lot side that appears to be indented or missing (not sticking out) is less than half of the entire length of its side (3 inches or 15 feet), then it truly is a missing area. (See Figure 8-1b.)

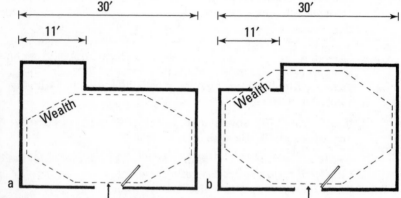

Figure 8-1: Projections and missing areas: Using the 50% Rule.

Fame area 38% Projection 62% indent Wealth area = Back Bedroom.

Using the 33% Rule

If the side of the house or lot in question appears U-shaped, or has two parts sticking out with an area that looks like it may be missing between them, apply the 33% Rule.

You need to measure the entire length of the side, or you can read the length from your accurate diagram. Using Figure 8-2, say you're working with the backside of the house or lot, which features the Wealth, Fame, and Marriage/Partnership Areas. Say the length of the side is 6 inches on paper (30 feet in actual distance). Your eagle eye spots an indented area in the center of the side (around the Fame Area), which looks like it may be missing. Now, determine which of the following measurements describes the indented area:

✔ **The area that appears indented is more than 33% of the total length of its side.** See Figure 8-2a. If your indented area meets this description, you don't have a missing area. What you have instead are two projections, one on each side, each reflecting a positive influence in its corresponding Life Area. If you wish, you can perform the Three Secrets Reinforcement for these projections to further enhance their positive influence. (See Chapter 6 for Reinforcement info.)

✔ **The area that appears indented is less than 33% of the total length of its side.** See Figure 8-2b. If your indented area fits this description, you officially have a missing area in the Life Area of the Feng Shui Octagon, and you may want to perform a cure for it. (Cures are described in the next section.)

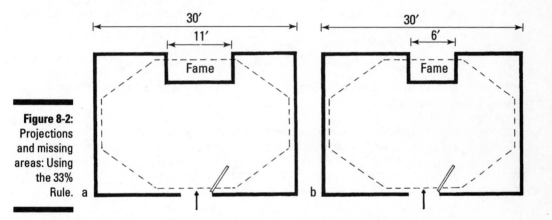

Figure 8-2:
Projections
and missing
areas: Using
the 33%
Rule.

Enhancing the Benefits of Projections

Because a projection helps its corresponding Life Area, you don't need to cure anything, right? That's correct! But wait — don't retire just yet. You can do at least one thing to enhance the benefits of a projection. Find out how in the following section.

Say you have a projection in the Family Area of the house. Say that things are pretty darn fine in your family right now. Why mess with a good thing, you ask? Well, let me ask you, is there such a thing as too much of a good thing? Can it hurt if things get just a little bit better? Enough said. Now for the technique: To increase the beneficial influence of the projection in the Family Area, you can perform the Three Secrets Reinforcement for this area. (Yep, performing this simple Reinforcement can significantly enhance the beneficial effects of your projection.)

The Three Secrets Reinforcement, typically performed right after you apply the physical portion of a Feng Shui cure, fully activates the power of the cure. In this case, the positive physical element (the projecting area of the shape) is already in place. You can magnify the positive effects of your projection using the Three Secrets Reinforcement. (See details on how to perform the Reinforcement in Chapter 6.)

Curing Missing Areas

If your house or lot includes a missing area, this area can create problems in the corresponding Life Area of your Feng Shui Octagon. For example, a missing area in the Children Area of your lot or house can contribute to one or more of the following effects depending on your particular life circumstances.

- Problems conceiving or bearing children
- Health difficulties with the children in your household
- Communication difficulties or a lacking feeling of creative energy or inspiration

Similar types of problems can ensue for any Life Area associated with a missing area. A missing area can hold you back from realizing your full potential in its corresponding Life Area. So the important question is, "What can I do right now to minimize or counterbalance any negative effects and to positively influence my situation in this particular Life Area?"

I recommend two cure options for missing areas in houses: interior (inside the house) cures and exterior (outside the house) cures. Generally, exterior cures are a bit stronger than interior cures. But use the ones that work the best for your overall situation. You rarely need to perform both an interior and an exterior cure for the same missing area (except when you really want or need to go for the strongest effect).

Exterior solutions for missing house areas

The exterior cure for a missing area symbolically completes the area that is missing. As shown in Figure 8-3, determine the spot where the corner would be if the house were complete. This point is the one you want to activate with your cure. The principle is that, by placing your cure here, you symbolically fill in the whole area (or you can actually fill in the hole in the area — take your pick). Thus, you restore energy to the structure and, more importantly, to the Life Area in need. Then you're off and running. You can activate the magic spot by performing one or more of the following cures.

✔ **Place a bright light on a tall pole at the indicated corner.** The light should point towards the house (generally at a 45-degree angle) and shine at the roof if possible. The taller the light, the better, although a light of any height is better than no light at all. The chi of the light fills the missing area, creating energy where a void once reigned.

The light doesn't need to shine all the time, especially if it can bother your neighbors. (Bothering neighbors is bad Feng Shui!) But the light does need to be in good working order for the cure to be effective.

✔ **Place a flagpole rather than a light at the indicated corner.** This cure serves to uplift the chi and complete the area. If you wish, you can choose a flag with the color scheme of the associated Octagon area for extra oomph! (See Chapter 3 for Octagon Area color details.) Otherwise, a green flag is generally effective, because green symbolizes life, healing, and energy.

✔ **Position a smooth heavy rock, boulder, or statue at the corner.** The heft and solidity bring energetic weight to the area to fill the gap. Size is important in this situation, and bigger is generally better. A five-pound rock or six-inch statue can't do much, although you don't need to reproduce Stonehenge or the Statue of Liberty in your back yard. See Figure 8-3.

✔ **Plant a healthy tree or other large plant (or bush) at the corner spot.** Or you can fill the area with flowers the colors of the missing Octagon Area. For example, planting white flowers in the Children Area can do the trick.

Figure 8-3:
Missing area of house with statue cure.

You can mix and match any of the previous solutions and apply more than one at the same time for an additional punch. If a large stone statue at the corner area combined with a patch of appropriately colored flowers suits your fancy, who am I to argue?

Interior solutions for missing house areas

You can choose from two main options for correcting a missing area inside the house. One option is to remodel the house and fill in the missing area. This cure can be the most effective cure. But unless you're a professional contractor with lots of free time or have piles of cash to spare, remodeling may not be the most practical option. Plus, remodeling tends to disrupt the household, can take two to three times longer than planned, and costs 20 to 30 percent more than you imagined.

The second choice — easier, faster, and cheaper — is to complete the missing area by performing an energetic cure, as given in the following list, rather than a structural modification. The energy solutions I give are quite effective, even though you haven't moved any of the walls in the house.

If you live in an apartment, you likely can't get permission to apply an exterior cure for a missing area inside your apartment. Besides, if the apartment is higher than the ground floor, the missing area is floating somewhere in space. So an interior cure is just the thing for you.

Fortunately, you can choose from several effective interior cures (see Figure 8-4) such as the following:

- ✔ **Line one wall (good) or both walls (better) with sizeable mirrors to energetically expand the area to make up for the defect.** (See Chapter 4 for important mirror tips.)

- ✔ **Hang a wind chime or large faceted crystal sphere (2 inches in diameter or larger) right at the interior corner in question.** As with many Feng Shui cures, use a red ribbon cut to a multiple of 9 inches for the greatest results.

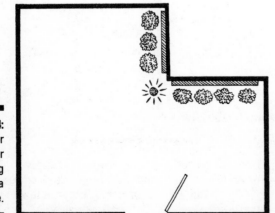

Figure 8-4:
Interior
cures for
missing
areas of a
home.

✔ **Position an odd number (a bit stronger than using an even number) of healthy new green plants along the two walls of the missing area.** The vital, living chi of the plants attract energy to the space and help compensate for the missing area.

Cures for missing lot areas

A missing area of the lot is a little trickier to cure because you can't get outside the lot to put something at the missing corner. (The exact corner spot is part of someone else's lot!) Fortunately, you can fix this problem in several ways:

✔ Place a bright spotlight on a tall pole at the corner of the missing area. The light ideally shines at the roof of the house. Another version of this cure is to place a flagpole with a colorful flag at the corner. Green is always a good choice, or you can use the color of the Life Area you're improving (see in Chapter 3). The taller the flagpole, the stronger the cure. The added light chi or the color and motion of the flag energetically compensates for the missing space of the lot.

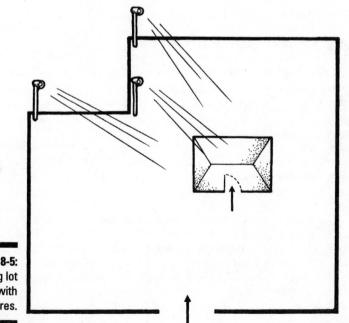

Figure 8-5:
Missing lot area with light cures.

✔ **Install three lights or flagpoles, one at each of the three corners.** This cure is a stronger version of the one in the previous example. (See Figure 8-5.) Shine the lights towards the house. This cure will help energetically compensate for the missing space of the lot.

✔ **Plant healthy green plants or a lively hedge along the perimeter of the missing area to put life chi in the area.** This cure uses the power of living energy to compensate for the missing area, and jazzes up the corresponding Life Area. For extra credit, plant flowers the color associated with this Octagon Area. *Remember:* Fruit-bearing plants generate even stronger Feng Shui cures! The living energy of the plants adds needed chi to the area by replacing what's missing and boosting your energy quotient in the Life Area.

Fixing Irregular House Shapes

The reality is that most people don't live in perfectly shaped houses. If your house fits one of the following descriptions, you can balance the shape with the proper cure.

L-shapes and boot shapes

An L-shaped house or lot is missing one-fourth of an area. An L-shaped house can negatively affect one Life Area greatly and negatively affect the three other Life Areas to a lesser degree. The suggested exterior cure for an L-shaped house is to place a tall spotlight or flagpole (for both: the taller, the better) where the corner would be if the house were a complete shape. The spotlight should shine towards the roof of the house. This cure serves to balance and complete the shape of the house and provides the area with additional energy. You can also place a water feature at the location where the corner would be if the house was complete.

If you live in an L-shaped apartment or, for some reason, can't apply an outside cure to your L-shaped house, interior cures can set you straight. Place mirrors at points along the walls of the missing area to energetically complete it. In addition, you can place a bright light or a faceted crystal sphere at the interior missing corner point to strengthen the area. (Refer back to Figure 8-4.)

The boot shape, similar to the L-shape, can also kick up trouble. A door, bed, or stove located at the ball or toe of the boot can cramp your style — and I mean hard, pardner! Results can prove harmful to your health, relationships, and finances. The cure for this situation is to move the door, bed, or stove away from the danger zone. (Moving the door means creating a new front door in a better position. I know, very difficult.) If implementing this option isn't possible, I recommend the mirror solution described in the following section on cleaver shapes. The mirror pulls the door, bed, or stove away from the ball of the foot to relieve the pressure (as shown in Figure 8-6a). A good exterior cure to balance the boot shape is to place a pool of water at the point where the corner would be complete (see Figure 8-6a).

Cleaver shapes

This house shape — a Chinese cleaver — can have unfortunate effects if the stove, the front door, or the bed is placed along the cutting edge. This placement can lead to fortunes being cut or lacerations of the body. Accidents involving visible blood are possible. To apply a cure for this situation, you can

- **Move the stove, bed, or front door away from the cutting edge.** For example, the bed can be moved to another wall of the bedroom that is not the cutting wall.

- **Place a mirror in line with the stove, door, or bed.** The mirror pulls the stove away from the cleaver's sharp edge. This solution can dramatically relieve any negative effects from the unfortunate placement. (See Figure 8-6b.)

One tricky cure for a cleaver-shaped house is to place the main entrance in the end of the cleaver's handle. (Obviously, easier if you're designing a house.) This way, you can control plenty of active energy and can use the cleaver shape to your advantage. (See Figure 8-6b.)

Dustpan and moneypurse lot shapes

Your cleaning habits aside, you may be living in a dustpan if your house or lot is shaped like Figure 8-7a. The dustpan shape can attract chaotic or negative energy. Likewise, the moneypurse shape, shown in Figure 8-7b, is not completely ideal, though it is far better for attracting money to the site. Of these two shapes, a moneypurse ranks more preferable than a dustpan. However, balance for both shapes is awkward, because each shape has two slanted sides.

One cure for a dustpan lot is to change the entrance to the other side so the shape resembles the money purse. This way, although the front of the lot is pinched, it widens at the back and symbolically holds wealth energy. If moving the entrance is not feasible, you can place spotlights or flagpoles featuring green flags (for either solution, taller is better) in the corners, as shown in Figures 8-7c and 8-7d.

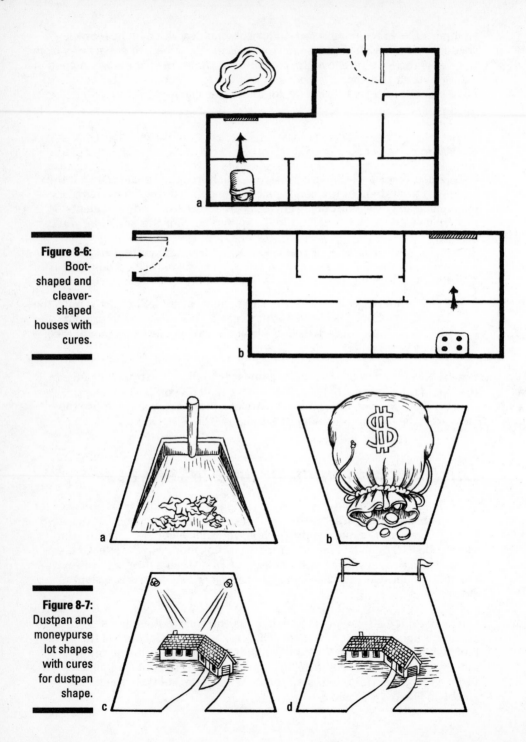

Figure 8-6: Boot-shaped and cleaver-shaped houses with cures.

Figure 8-7: Dustpan and moneypurse lot shapes with cures for dustpan shape.

To further empower the moneypurse shape, place lights in the front lot corners, shining toward the house.

Triangular shapes

Triangle shapes, though great for pyramids, are lousy for houses and lots. The sharp corners and angled sides promote conflicts and accidents in the household. The house orientation shown in Figure 8-8a is negative, because the path away from the front door leads to a vanishing point in the lot, foreboding a diminishing future. If your house and lot have this shape, you can choose from the following effective cures:

- ✔ **Place cures in each corner of the triangle.** Cure items include plants, bushes, or trees.
- ✔ **Place a bright shining light inward or a flag on a tall pole at the vanishing point.** (See Figure 8-8a.)
- ✔ **Place flagpoles in each of the three corners.** The most effective flagpoles are tall ones bearing green flags.

Reinforce these placements using the Three Secrets Reinforcement to receive the full effects from your solutions. (See Chapter 6.)

Angled lot side

If one side of your lot is angled, unbalanced living can result. You can cure this by planting healthy plants or bushes along the angled side, infusing this area with healthy, living chi. (See Figure 8-8b.)

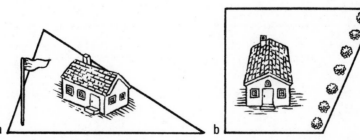

Figure 8-8: Negative lot shapes and cures.

a

b

Multicornered and oddly shaped lots

With rare exceptions, an odd number of corners (or any number greater than four) and slanted sides are negative conditions for a lot or house, because they can result in confusion and imbalance. These shapes are common in, but not limited to, cul-de-sacs. A recommended cure is to place spotlights or green flags on flagpoles at each corner of the lot or house exterior. This cure balances the energy of the lot, promoting harmony, cohesion, and forward progress for the residents.

Chapter 9

Open Sesame! Your Entryway and Entrance

. . . .

In This Chapter

▶ Discovering the importance of your entries

▶ Checking out the view from the road and from your front door

▶ Maximizing driveway chi

▶ Alluring energy to your front door — the Mouth of Chi

. . . .

The entry is the first energetic impression that your home makes on you and anyone who comes to see you. And the first impression is important. This chapter helps you create the best possible first impression and invite maximum energy and good feeling into your home. The payoff is desired improvements in important areas of your life.

Focusing on the Front Door and Foyer

Feng Shui considers the front door and entry to be the most important points in your home environment. The approach and entry determine the amount and quality of energy that flows into the home, and whether this energy nourishes or depletes the house, thereby helping or hindering the aspirations of the residents. A smooth, grand, open entry and approach supports free-flowing prosperity and vitality. Conversely, a convoluted or difficult approach can create corresponding unpleasant effects in various parts of your life.

The front door is the first and foremost of the three Life Pillars, a concept I introduce in Chapter 2. The Life Pillars provide fundamental energies to the home and its residents, so focusing your attention on the condition of your front door is important. Imagine going through life with your jaw wired shut — now you have an idea of the problems you can encounter if the main door is blocked.

The energy of the entry is mediated by the approach to the door, the entryway itself, the physical door and doorway, and the first room or thing you see upon stepping inside. The front door, the controlling point of the house's energy, is a crucial fulcrum point. Seemingly minor flaws at your front door can affect you negatively, while improvements made at the entry can significantly impact your life in positive ways. To paraphrase an old nursery rhyme, "When it's good, it's very good. But when it's bad, it's verrry bad."

Your entryway should be open, inviting, attractive, and look and feel positive. As you clear your entryway of blocks and activate its chi, you may notice more energy flowing into your life, obstacles melting, and opportunities knocking on your door (in more ways than one). An entryway that is gloomy, dark, overrun, or difficult to approach has subtle, and in some cases profound, negative effects on your life, including diminished opportunities, constriction of your cash flow, difficulties in making important contacts, and others.

If you think of the house as a body, then the front door would be considered the mouth, the point where energy enters to nourish the body. Of course, additional energy comes in through the other doors and the windows, and some natural energy enters through the walls, floors, and roof. But the major source of energy in the home is the *Mouth of Chi,* your front door. If a door is physically or energetically blocked, the house is metaphorically starved and suffocated, which creates problems in your life.

If the only place in your home you improve is the entry, you're still way ahead of the game. Something good, perhaps very good, may come of your improved door. Try it and see. No matter how fabulous the interior of your home is, if the approach, entry, and/or front door is problematic, you can see corresponding life effects. The fixes are quite easy compared to the inconveniences an improper entry can generate.

Viewing Your House from the Street

To practice this technique, visit a new neighborhood, stop at random in front of a house you've never seen, and look at it. But don't think; just feel. Notice your first gut impression. How do you feel within the first second or two? This simple exercise can give you an initial grasp of the energy of any residence and the kinds of influences it may be having on its occupants.

The impression a house makes from the street is a key indicator of its energy. For example, suppose you look at the front of a large, dark house and feel a sudden sense of gloom or foreboding. This gloom is probably the dominant effect you would feel from the house if you lived there, and the effect it may well be wreaking on its present occupants. The long-term energetic effects of living in this house may include lethargy or sluggishness, or feelings of oppression, depression, or sadness.

Try this technique on your own house. First, clear your mind of all preconceived notions. Let your thoughts stop for a moment and simply feel as you gaze at the front of your home. Notice how it makes you feel. If the answer is "like home," "proud," or some other familiar emotion, you're off track, still relating to the home you already know. Pretend you don't live in the house. See it with new eyes. Take a fresh look at the house, without conjuring up previous associations and memories. How does this place make you feel inside?

As you blank your mind and let your senses take over, you may notice sensory impressions. You may smell jasmine or grass or burning rubber, or you may hear the sounds of the wind in the trees and feel the pavement beneath your feet. But you get the most information visually. So notice your instant impression. Do you feel calm, excited, confused, numb, cheerful, scared, uneasy? As I explain in Chapter 2, the house is like a second body that you wear. Performing this exercise is like looking into the mirror to see what that second body looks like and how it feels.

This exercise gives you an indication of the kinds of impressions and effects that you receive each time you come home, effects that strongly influence your daily psychology. The most effective time to do this exercise is when arriving home after being away for several days.

As a professional Feng Shui consultant, I get many opportunities to see homes for the first time. And reading my feelings in this way, whether or not I have anything conscious to base them on, lets me know how the energy is functioning on the site. For example, I remember approaching one house with a client who was deciding whether or not to buy it. The instant I saw the house, without knowing exactly why, I had a bad feeling. Those feelings were verified when I saw a dead bird lying in the driveway. Upon entering, we were taken aback: The house was in total shambles and had an awful smell. This was our hint to head for the hills.

Looking Out from the Inside

Another important factor is the view you see as you exit your house from the front door. As you stand in the front doorway of your home and look out, what do you see? A vacant lot across the street? A factory? A condemned building? (The city dump? Relocate!) A beautiful home across the street? A door across the hallway of your apartment building? Are you lucky enough to see a pleasant green field stretching in front of you with a beautiful view of water in the distance? This last example is a Feng Shui concept of an ideal view.

Taking a look out from the inside helps, in part, to define your relationship with the outside world. You may not have stopped to consider it before, but your first view when you open your door is essentially how you see the world. Needless to say, this view does affect you. If your first daily glimpse of the world outside is of mangy buzzards congregating on the twisted limbs of a dead tree in your front yard, guess what? It's not good Feng Shui! Surprised? Knowing the importance of this first impression of the outside world may motivate you to create a vision of beauty, serenity, and charm. If a charming sight is what greets you each day when you leave your home, the world tends to look brighter; your attitude and actions tend to reflect this perception, which naturally boosts your energy and participation at work, resulting in positive, practical benefits.

Dealing with Driveway Issues

Your driveway is the main source of energy and societal chi — connections, money, and helpful people — for your property and home, and by extension, you. Your house is also fed energy by the front walkway. (If your house doesn't have a driveway, the main source of energy flowing into the property is the front walkway.) If you live in an apartment, the ease and accessibility of the path you take to the front door of your apartment is what counts. In the following sections, I give the ideal driveway conditions, then help you cure your drive if you have any of the problems detailed here. When energy flows freely onto your property and into your house, life feels much smoother, and more flowing.

Positive driveway conditions

The best kind of driveway is one that is flat or slopes gently upward, and is slightly winding, rather than arrow-straight or convoluted. (Though a short straight drive leading to the garage as found in many homes is fine.) The driveway should be smooth-surfaced rather than bumpy or difficult to navigate. The house and front door should be clearly visible from the front entrance to the property (the beginning of the driveway at the street). And the sights you see when driving up to the house should be uplifting or inspire positive feelings.

Problem driveway conditions and their solutions

Problematic driveways include steep drives, blind drives, shared drives, cracked or broken drives, and driveways that face a neighbor's drive that is wider or goes down. (Alas, not all construction contractors and architects are fully Feng Shui savvy — yet.) So consider a few common problematic driveway scenarios and their Feng Shui implications and cures.

Steep drive going up or going down

If your driveway goes down steeply, your house is probably below the road. In this situation, leaving the house — whether for occasional errands or for work each day — is difficult because you tend to strain to climb up and out of the property each day. The effect is subliminal yet real. This situation can generate career difficulties, not to mention the practical problems of leaving the driveway itself. A cure is to place your trusty energy generators along the drive to help move energy up to the street. Energy generators include lights, windsocks, and wind chimes (see Chapter 4). These cures also help protect the house from excess energy that can roll down the drive and impact the house. (See Figure 9-1.)

Being above the road is generally better than being below it. However, a house sitting high above the road typically has a steep drive leading up to it, which fosters two kinds of problems. First, energy has a hard time getting up the driveway to the house, making it hard for people and energetically hard for money to reach you. Second, whatever energy (money and people) does make it to the house has an easy time rolling back down the drive and being lost.

A good cure for a drive that descends sharply from the house down to the street is to place bright lights on each side of the drive where it meets the street. Another cure for a steep drive going up to a house is the same as the cure for a steep, descending one — activate the driveway with windsocks or other motion stimulators. (Generally, a house sitting above the road is in a good position. Problems arise when a house is very high above the street, with a steep driveway.) The solutions given here are specifically to cure driveway issues. Cures for the house itself when situated below the road can be found in the "Living high up or low down" section of Chapter 7.

Figure 9-1:
Steep drive
leading
down to
house
below road,
with light
cures.

Blind drive

In Feng Shui, a recurring principle is to be able to see what's coming towards you in life. A blind drive is one that prevents you from seeing who or what is approaching as you leave the site, and this constraint creates a psychological blind spot as well as physical security issues.

For a good cure, you can place a large convex mirror near the end of the drive so you can see the approaching street traffic as you come down the driveway. (The larger the mirror, the better.) You may need one mirror on each side of the drive to see the traffic coming from both directions.

Problematic neighbors' drives

A neighbor's driveway directly across from yours can affect you negatively if the driveway is wider than your drive or if it slopes down and away. If the neighbor's driveway is larger than yours, the opposing drive can eat part of your home's energy supply. If the neighbor's drive slopes down and away, you get the same effect: The opposing drive drains chi away from your property.

The solution is to mount a large convex mirror — a 24- to 36-inch mirror works well — above the garage door or at another position that's in line with the opposing drive. The mirror counteracts the effect of the larger driveway, pulling needed chi into your property. The same cure works for either opposing drive situation.

A shared driveway

A driveway shared with one or more other residents can affect your site by lessening its inflow of energy. A shared drive is one used by more than one residence, or a drive that leads to your house and also splits off to go to another home. If you share a driveway with a neighbor, you can mount a bright light (on a pole and the taller, the better) at the place where the neighbor's drive splits off from yours. The light marks a clear division between the two driveways. The light helps prevent the loss of chi (which translates to money, opportunities, health, and more) from your home and life. If you put lights on both sides of your drive at the splitting point, the cure is even stronger.

Clearing the Way for Natural Chi

Nature (trees, grass, air, sun, water, and so on) feeds us through its abundant chi. Lush, full, or verdant landscapes — oceans, forests, and jungles — are virtual reservoirs of chi.

Yet most people spend most of their hours indoors and so tend to be chronically chi-deficient. The rejuvenated, revitalized, and uplifted feelings you experience after spending a few hours (or days) out in nature were once the common human state. Humans felt so refreshed because chi, nature's energy, is the purest food that exists.

As I explain in Chapter 2, the house is a container for chi. The front door (main front entrance, or Mouth of Chi) is the main entry point for the chi. One Feng Shui master states that 80 percent of our access to natural chi is cut off once you go inside a house. The house insulates you from the outside chi, which your body continuously needs. So one purpose of Feng Shui cures is to overcome this unfortunate liability by introducing more of this vital natural energy into your home.

REMEMBER

Throughout this book, I use the terms *front door* and *Mouth of Chi* interchangeably. They both refer to the same place: the original, designed, front entry to the house.

Ask yourself these three questions about the energy that comes into your home via the front door:

- **Is enough energy (chi) coming in?** The amount and quality of energy is largely determined by the condition of your front door and entryway. If the front door and entry are clear, open, and easy to access, chi can enter in high quantity and positive quality. If the front door is hidden, dark, or cluttered (generally negative factors) chi flow can be drastically reduced, symbolically starving the house and its residents of greatly needed energy.

- **Is the energy positive?** This answer depends on the quality and condition of the chi as it enters and circulates through the home. If the chi is positive (healthy and beneficial), the energy is smooth, harmonious, balanced, strong, and lively. Negative chi is congested, stuck, blocked, conflicting, piercing, depressing, leaking, and so on.

- **Is energy circulating completely through the home?** The circulation depends on the smoothness and flow of the floor plan, shapes of rooms, and connecting elements throughout the home. If rooms lie in positive locations, the hallways and stairs conduct chi easily, and the layout is energetically balanced, among other factors, the chi flow assists the residents. If the opposite conditions prevail, you can lead a harried, frustrated life. Sound familiar? Chapters 8 and 10 are your resources for mastering this prinicple.

These three questions illustrate the prime importance Feng Shui places on the front door and how it allows energy to enter your home. The front door is a vital point in every home.

As I cover earlier in this chapter, your view of the front facade (first impression of the house) and your view looking out from the front door (first impression of the outer world) has a profound impact on you. But the path that leads to and from your front door is of equal importance. The path to your front door symbolizes your path in life, your comings and goings in the world. Also, the degree of ease or difficulty with which you can enter your house affects the way in which energy enters your life. To the degree that the path to your home is cluttered, or awkward, the energy coming into the house can be hindered, negatively influencing your finances, vitality, and career.

If you have the slightest feeling that an object near your door may be blocking your entry, it probably is. (Trust your feelings!) Test this situation by moving the object. How do you feel now? Less crowded or cramped? Do you breathe easier? If so, moving the object is probably good Feng Shui. And if you feel an immediate improvement, the energetic effect is clearly positive and can benefit you energetically over time. You can use this simple method to test the validity of almost any Feng Shui solution you implement.

Each residence has only one main door; all others are secondary — side, back, garage, patio doors, and so on. The main door is the chief energy entry point of a house, even if you enter more frequently by another door. Even if the front door is unused, this door is still considered the main door. The only way the front door ceases to be the main door is if you remove it completely and finish the wall. (Not usually recommended!) Then another door becomes the front door. I strongly recommend that you consult a Feng Shui practitioner before moving a front door.

Solving the hidden front door dilemma

Generally, the front door should be visible from the street for maximum energy flow. *Hidden front door* is a Feng Shui term describing a front door that can't be seen from the street, is recessed, is dark or in shadow, directly faces a hill, or is otherwise obscured.

If you have a hidden front door, you may find that moving ahead, receiving opportunities or income, and even selling the home can be very difficult. From the opposite point of view, if you can't see the street from your front door, your career can be energetically hindered, whether you work at home or out in the world. (This effect is minimized or nullified if you live on a very large estate, where the house is a long distance from the main street. In this case, ideally the main drive will be visible from the front door.)

Two cures for hidden front door problems are as follows:

 ✔ **If possible, mount a convex safety mirror (the kind used in parking ramps to see around corners) that allows you to see the door when approaching the house and to clearly see the street from the front door (shown in Figure 9-2a).** The larger the mirror, the stronger the cure. If the mirror is too small or incorrectly angled to see the approach clearly, the cure will not be highly effective. I recommend that you use a mirror at least 18 inches in diameter.

 ✔ **Line the path from the street to your door with lights or plants (shown in Figure 9-2b).** This cure guides the chi right up to the door.

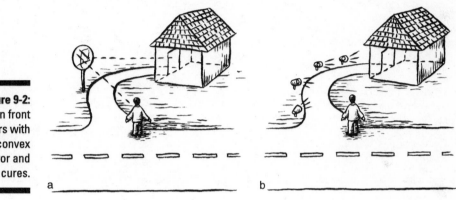

Figure 9-2:
Hidden front
doors with
convex
mirror and
light cures.

a   b

Curing common outdoor stairway dilemmas

Stairways leading to the front door, whether short or long, are an important aspect of your entryway. Reading the energy of your stairway is easy with your Feng Shui thinking (and feeling) cap on. If humans can flow easily and freely up and down the stairs, so can energy and income. The ideal entry stairway is wide and easy to ascend, not too long or steep, and free of sharp turns. The stairway is stable, with complete risers (the vertical parts of the stairs) and a solid hand rail.

Following are some common entry stairway problems and their Feng Shui solutions. (For more on stairways inside your home, see Chapter 14.)

Curing a tree or post in front of the front door

A tree growing in a direct line with the front door can promote bad luck because it obstructs the path to the door. An obstructed path can block income and inhibit career success. The following solution from Chinese folklore allows you to transform this bad tree luck to good, without chopping it down.

1. Buy a new unused ink pen, and a piece of red writing paper (most office supply stores sell red paper). From the red sheet of paper, cut a circular piece.

2. With the pen, write the following four words without a single pause on the red circle: "Raise head, see happiness."

3. Post the paper on the tree trunk or pillar at eye level or higher of the tallest person in the house.

4. Reinforce this cure with the Three Secrets Reinforcement (see Chapter 6).

As you write the words and perform the Three Secrets Reinforcement, visualize the God or deity of your chosen religion shining light on the words you've written. (If you're an atheist, visualize sunlight shining or the universal light/energy of modern physics.) Performing this cure helps neutralize the bad luck effects from the imposing tree. Another solution is to place a melodic metal wind chime over the front door, to deflect negative effects from the tree (as pictured here).

Long stairway

A stairway that's a long trip up to the front door has definite energetic liabilities. This type of stairway is common to second floor apartments or duplexes accessed by exterior stairs. Such a stairway makes it difficult for energy, income, and you to get to your front door. (Kind of like salmon swimming upstream.) The energetic effects can include difficulty resting or getting home. And you may end up traveling or being gone a lot. Steep stairways can also make opportunities more difficult to come by.

If the average person who visits you gets a bit winded climbing to your door, your stairs are probably too long. Curing them can counteract and improve the negative factors, even though your stairs may still give everyone a good aerobic workout. The suggested cure for a long staircase is to wrap an artificial green vine around the stair rail from the bottom all the way up to the top. (If the staircase has no rail, I recommend installing a good one. For further details, see the section "Missing or rickety banister" later in this chapter.) Ideally, the vine should reach the doorframe itself. The lively green energy of the vine adds health and vigor to the climbers, helping compensate for the long journey upward.

An alternate cure is to run pin lights (small holiday lights — white is good, multicolored is better) along the same path. The lights guide the energy up the long stairway, feeding the front door. (Light represents the energy of attraction as well as radiant energy itself.)

Missing risers

A riser is the vertical section that connects one stair (the horizontal part you step on) to the next stair up. Your toe points to each riser with every step unless the riser is missing or broken. A stairwell with missing risers potentially promotes the loss of income and life energy (chi) to the house and its residents. As energy ascends the stairs, it slips through the riser gaps, like water through a leaky bucket. (Less mojo for you!) As your feet are energetically connected to your career, missing risers can trip you up, both physically and in your life's work. On a practical note, missing risers are a safety issue. Twisted, sprained, or broken ankles and feet are bad personal Feng Shui. (Plus, they hurt.)

The cure for missing risers is straightforward and usually involves a carpenter or tradesman. You need to physically fill in or replace missing risers in your stairway. After completing this task, you can feel more solid and complete in life as well as every time you ascend or descend the stairs. Feeling solid and complete creates beneficial energetic effects that flow directly into your practical life. (And what is Feng Shui, if not practical?)

Stairway with a turn

A right-angle turn on a front door stairway creates an energy jam, robbing you and your home of vital chi. (If an actual robber stood at your door and stole your wallet every time you passed by, you'd do something about it pretty darned quick! Yet most people allow these Feng Shui robbers to steal their chi day after day, rarely doing a thing about it.) An excellent cure for a right-angle stairway is to place a healthy potted plant on the landing at the turn. The living chi of the plant nullifies the negative influence of the turn, attracts chi, and boosts the energy on its way to the door. Be careful that the plant doesn't block the way; otherwise, you've compounded one problem with another.

My clients Sam and Maureen had a narrow exterior stair leading to their front door that featured a 90-degree turn. Both residents were unhappy in their professions. They replaced the existing staircase with a much wider, more open, and completely straightforward one. Coincidentally — not! — Sam started a new and much happier career as a designer and consultant not long after. Maureen remarked on how much freer and more expansive the new stairway made them feel, and has now embarked on her dream career as well. Although this cure is virtually the only noticeable change they made, their friends rave about how more open, pleasant, and inviting the house now feels. They also feel connected energetically to their front yard for the first time.

Missing or rickety banister

A problem banister (one that gives at all when you grab it) creates unsafe feelings and lack of control in life. Also, subconscious uncertainties may creep into your mind for no apparent reason. The remedy is easy: Repair a rickety banister or install a good solid handrail that supports you completely when you hold it.

Dealing with pesky approach issues

The following barriers and impediments to a smooth entry are physical and energetic stumbling blocks in your life path. The more these obstructions lead into your home, the more your liabilities are compounded. Fixing them removes obstacles from your life's path, quells frustrations, and generally makes life an easier game to play.

- **Multiple gates, barriers, porches, and doors:** Having to go through these obstacles can produce frustration, mental blocks, lack of energy, and feelings of being stopped in life. Cures include removing some of the barriers, and placing wind chimes or faceted crystal spheres (check Chapter 4) between the doors and gates. When performing this cure, be sure to visualize abundant energy and finances flowing into your life as you apply the Three Secrets Reinforcement. Check Chapter 6 for details.

- **No walkway from your front door to the street:** This common situation is related to the dilemma in which the garage projects out from the house and blocks the front door. In many contemporary homes, the path to the front door connects to the driveway rather than to the street (or the sidewalk out by the street). The potential Feng Shui problem in this case is that you may receive less income and have fewer helpful friends in your life than you deserve, all because the front door feeds from the driveway rather than the street. The driveway is a secondary energy source for the front walk and front door, featuring less incoming chi than the street.

  The expensive cure for this problem is to build a new sidewalk from your front door to the street. If you're up for it, go for it. Several of my clients are now happily enjoying better incomes and careers after applying this new sidewalk cure. If not, you can use the walkway and chime cures in the next bullet point.

- **Projecting garage that blocks the front door:** This situation, also common, creates at least two problems. First, the structure of the house is unbalanced, usually in some form of an L-shape. Second, the garage hides the front door from view on at least one side of the house. I recommend these two cures:

- Build a second stone walkway to the street (shown in Figure 9-3) leading away from the garage. If your garage projects out, this cure has the important effect of balancing the house shape. Whether or not your garage projects, the new pathway has the additional benefit of bringing new (and more!) chi to your front door.

- For a more practical but slightly less powerful solution, place a wind chime along the side of the garage, or near the front door, to attract more chi into your home. (See Chapter 4 for important wind-chime tips).

✔ **Narrow, overgrown, or tunnel-like pathway to front door:** This scenario restricts your energy, making it harder literally and figuratively for you and the house to breathe. Ideally, your entry path should be at least as wide as the front door. Better still, have it wide enough for two people to walk side by side. Cures include widening the path and cutting back bushes and hedges to open the way. Also, make sure the path is well-lit, clear, clean, and bright.

✔ **Recessed front door from front line of house:** This situation results in less income and fewer career opportunities. The recommended solution is to brighten the exterior with powerful lights, or place a brass wind chime by the entryway. Doing so will activate the energy around the front door to attract more of the good things you deserve.

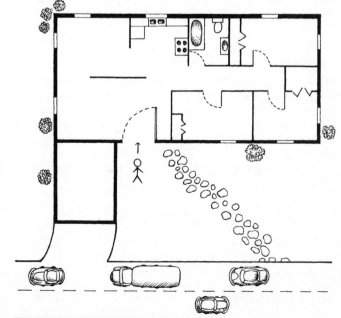

Figure 9-3:
Walkway cure for no path from front door to street or garage blocking front door.

✔ **Obstacles on the path to the entrance, near the front door, or on the porch close to the door:** Such obstacles can include bikes, boxes, trash, skateboards, buckets, and so on. Results include frustration, confusion, and finding it easy to figuratively stumble in your life as you could physically stumble over all the clutter. The simple cure: Remove and clean!

✔ **Decay or disrepair at entrance:** Decay and disrepair in and around the home symbolize death or stagnation. They can bring you down and make winning in life much harder. These signs, especially negative near the front door, include burnt-out or missing light bulbs, broken light fixtures, broken/missing doorbell, cobwebs around the entrance, birds nesting near the door, or a 4-foot-long pickaxe stuck in the front door. (Just take a look; you'll know it when you see it.) The cure: Fix, clean, replace, and repair.

Moving In: Interior Entryway Problems and Solutions

If energy flows from your front door through your house without obstructions or blocks, the chi of your entire house is fed and nourished, which promotes positive life results. If your energy is obstructed, problems may occur in the areas of career and physical and mental health. And some of these problems can occur right at the front entryway. I detail the solutions in the following sections.

Interior stairway facing front door

An interior stairway facing the front door signifies money rolling out of the house. The gravity force coming down the stairs pushes incoming chi back out the front door, symbolizing loss of wealth or income. As remodeling the stairs is usually impractical, an energetic solution is more pragmatic. The cure is to place a faceted crystal sphere or pleasant-sounding wind chime halfway between the front door and the base of the stairs. This cure diffuses the stairway's descending chi into the house rather than letting it escape out the door or repel incoming chi. (See Figure 9-4.)

The problem of an interior stairway facing the front door is less severe if the distance from the door to the stairs is greater than twice the height of the tallest person in the house.

Mandarin duck stairway

A main entry that opens directly onto a stairway landing, requiring you to go up one stairway or down another to proceed into the house, features a *mandarin duck* stairway. Under its influence, one partner in the marriage may go up in life while the other goes down; one may enjoy career success while the other struggles; or their life-paths may diverge, leading to separation or divorce. The unusual name stems from the Chinese custom of having a special dish — mandarin duck — at the wedding banquet. Apparently the staircase looks similar to the roasted duck at the feast. To cure this stair, place a plant at the juncture of the two staircases. Another effective alternative (or addition) is to wrap a realistic, silk, ivy, green vine (see Figure 9-5) around the banister of the stairway from bottom to top, imparting life and green energy to the stairway, and counteracting its negative effects.

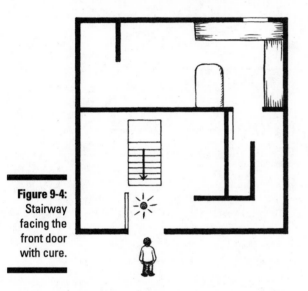

Figure 9-4:
Stairway
facing the
front door
with cure.

Split view on entering

A split view on entering (shown in Figure 9-6) is one where half of your field of vision is blocked by a close wall, while in the other half you can see much further into the house. One negative effect of this feature is a physical dissonance between your left eye and right eye, and between left brain and right brain. A psychological rift occurs when this sight continuously greets you upon entering your home. Repeated viewing can subconsciously stimulate anxiety, stress, schizophrenic tendencies, and other psychological problems, leading to bad decisions and even accidents. The cure for this is to place a mirror on the partially blocking wall to balance the view and restore harmony to the entrance. (See Figure 9-6 for an illustration of this solution.)

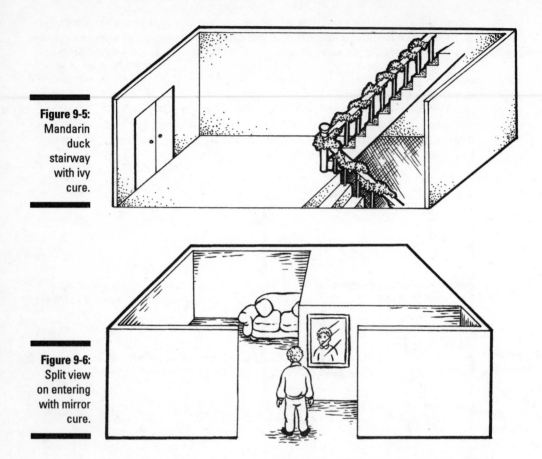

Figure 9-5:
Mandarin duck stairway with ivy cure.

Figure 9-6:
Split view on entering with mirror cure.

Making the Most of the Mouth of Chi

REMEMBER

The front door serves as the mouth of the house. Like your physical mouth, it takes in the sustenance that nourishes the house — chi or energy. If the mouth has trouble, you have trouble. "Health begins with the mouth," goes an old saying. The same is true in Feng Shui. The health of the house (and the fortunes of the inhabitants) begins with the front door and entry.

Principles of the ideal front door

An ideal front door adheres to three key principles. The front door requirements are as follows:

✔ **Well illuminated.** Your front door should be well lit and free of shadows and darkness. Good lighting at the entrance is a good energy principle for the door and the house.

✔ **Bright and clear.** The door, the approach, and the entryway should be cheerful, lively, and uplifting. Ideally, your front door invokes a pleasant, happy feeling and attitude. The front doorway should also be free of obstacles and obstructions to chi and to people entering.

✔ **Balanced to the house.** The front door should not be too large or too small compared to the front façade of the house. A door that is too small can't attract sufficient chi for the residents and can diminish their social stature. A door that appears too large for the house projects a boastful attitude and engenders subconscious dislike from your neighbors.

Solving front door problems

The following deviations from the ideal front door condition can be cured with properly applied energetic remedies. So carefully check your front door Feng Shui and make as many improvements as possible.

✔ **Squeaky door hinges.** The Chinese say, "Squeaky doors bring hungry ghosts," meaning that a door with squealing hinges attracts real or imagined spooks. At the very least, a squeaking door is subliminally scary. (That's why it's the most common sound effect in scary movies!) The cure? Apply WD-40 generously! I am amazed by how many of my clients fail to notice their squeaky doors until I point it out. (Only then they remember that "it's been that way for years.") This seemingly small cure of oiling a squeaky hinge can make a big difference. The same principle applies to all doors: front, side, bedroom, closet, cabinet, and others.

✔ **A window in the front door.** The front door protects your home. The ideal front door is solid and without windows. Front doors with windows in them are energetically, not to mention physically, weaker. They can be easily broken into and thus create vulnerabilities in your home's energy field. The best cure is to install a new solid door without windows. In some cases a highly skilled craftsman can create a solid piece of wood that fits the door. Another solution is to cover the window with cloth or a blind or curtain that matches the color of the door, making it look complete from the street (or you can use the Feng Shui power color: red). Even if you rely on this window for light, a solid door is still energetically better for your house and for you. Visualize protection and solidity when you perform this cure, and reinforce it with the Three Secrets Reinforcement.

✔ **Door swings closed or drifts open by itself (unaided).** A front door that swings closed automatically shuts out money and keeps people from coming to you. A door that drifts open on its own allows energy to leak out of the house and invites unwanted people in. The cure for both is the same: Get a carpenter to rehang or replumb the door so that it stands still wherever you put it.

✔ **Door doesn't fit right in doorframe and/or is loose on its hinges.** This awkward door situation creates confusion, mental blocks, and aggravation. The cure is to hire a finish carpenter or door hanging expert. The door may need to be reframed, replaced, or both.

Like all of these door suggestions (actually, all the suggestions in this book, pardner), this cure really works! One of my clients had a strong career and beautiful home but was perplexed by her lack of a meaningful relationship. Her home featured a door and frame combination that didn't fit correctly. (The door had been planed and shaved several times in partial attempts to make it fit.) After the consultation, she hired a craftsman to install a proper, new door and redo the doorframe. (She also, of course, reinforced this cure using the Three Secrets Reinforcement detailed in Chapter 6.) To her pleasant surprise, shortly after performing the cure, she happily moved to an even nicer house with a new partner.

✔ **Door doesn't close, latch, or stay closed on the first attempt, or latch sticks on strike plate, and anything similar.** These problems create subtle life blocks, making it difficult to complete things and keep them complete. Seemingly finalized deals can tend to pop out or come undone. To cure, replace or repair the strike plate and/or latch.

✔ **Dead/unused locks still on door, or door handle is loose.** These problems symbolize difficulty getting a grip in life, having weak energy, or hanging on to old and useless things in life. The cure involves repairing the door handle and removing or replacing outmoded lock fixtures.

✔ **Door scrapes on floor.** A scraping door obstructs or drags on your income and freedom. The ideal door swings freely at least 90 degrees without hindrances. This principle holds even if what scrapes on the floor is the insulator strip (to keep cold air out) on the bottom of the door. Because most thresholds sit an inch above floor level, the rubber insulation strip shouldn't scrape on your carpet or foyer floor. Plane or shave the bottom of the door so that it swings free to cure this problem.

✔ **Door is broken, worn, warped, or dilapidated, paint is peeling, and so on.** Replacing an old door can cure this situation! Here's the skinny: Dilapidated doors symbolize dilapidated lives. The front door represents the house, and the house represents your life. Ergo, a worn down front door can subconsciously influence you to feel (and maybe become) worn down as well. Sound attractive? No? I didn't think so. Fixing this right up can fix you right up, and a more worthy cure proves hard to find.

Changing your luck with front door colors

Door colors on most houses are white or a color that matches the house. These color choices are generally fine. However, you can boost your front door chi if you wish by painting it a particular color. The colors with the strongest energetic effects include:

✔ **Bright red:** This classic Feng Shui door color is said to confer power, protection, luck, and a sense of royalty to the house and its occupants. This cure is known in Feng Shui circles by the term "lucky red door." A great all-around cure for boosting your home's energy.

✔ **Green:** This color is another excellent choice, symbolizing life, health, and money.

✔ **Black:** Black is a fine color for a front door and is especially good if your front door is in the center, which represents career. Black symbolizes water, which equals money. Enough said.

Being Aware of Continual First Impressions

Feng Shui theory emphasizes the importance of first impressions, including the view of the house from the street, of the street from your front door, and others. In fact, these first impressions are also continual impressions. The first thing you see as you enter the house is a crucial first impression that sets the tone for your entire experience in the house, and surprisingly, for much of your life experience as well. A positive first entry impression creates uplifted spirits, hope, and positive expectations. A negative first entry impression, much like an unpleasant smell encountered when entering a restaurant, sets up lowered expectations. This continual first impression over time can make you a truly unhappy camper. Here's how to kick up your heels like a new filly.

Two levels of first impressions

This first impression principle has two important factors. One is the first room you enter (or if you enter into a foyer or entry hall, the first room you see or approach as you proceed into the house). Overall, the first room you enter impacts your psychology and physical health.

The second factor is the very first item or object your eye is attracted to as you enter the residence. Also, the first thing you see specifically affects your psyche, so carefully check out this aspect of your entrance. The implications of both of these aspects are detailed below.

The ideal entrance

The ideal entrance welcomes you in, greeting you with pleasant, uplifting sights, feelings, even sounds or smells, and makes you feel comfortable, peaceful, and at home. A wide, spacious, bright interior entryway gives you ample room to move forward and makes you want to move forward. You can easily see a place to sit or rest or at least see something pleasant and attractive ahead. An ideal entryway promotes career success and harmony at home — a positive attitude and a clear spirit. A less-than-ideal entryway is correspondingly less positive, or at worst, negative. If the first impression is one of a dark, cramped, cluttered or unpleasant space, the impact on you can gradually take its toll over time. In this section, I detail positive and negative rooms to enter, and positive and negative first things to see upon coming inside. Check out the following info to see how your entrance rates (and can be improved).

Positive rooms to enter by the front door

An ideal front door entrance leads into a foyer, entry hall, living room, den, family room, study, or office. Any of these rooms have either a neutral or positive energy, with corresponding life effects. Unless of course these rooms look like disaster areas! (Be aware that other factors in these rooms such as extreme clutter or negative furniture arrangements may counteract some of the positive effects of the room's location. See Chapters 13 and 16.) Specific qualities and effects of these positive rooms include:

- ✔ **Foyer or entry room:** This room is generally good and fine at the entrance.

- ✔ **Living room:** When you see a comfortable place to sit down as your first impression, you have a feeling of rest and relaxation.

- ✔ **Den or family room:** These rooms give you the same effect as the living room, inducing relaxation and comfort.

- ✔ **Study or library:** A study or library has positive effects; your family tends to be learned, intelligent, and studious and your children advance well in school.

- ✔ **Office:** When you see the office immediately upon entering, you can find it easier to achieve success in your business or career.

Negative rooms to enter by the front door

According to Feng Shui principles, unfavorable rooms to enter by the front door are the kitchen, bathroom, playroom, bedroom, or dining room. The following list details the negative effects of each room as an entry point and also

provides cures for each situation. (***Note:*** The negative effects still apply —
though slightly less harshly — if you see clearly these rooms ahead of you
when entering, rather than stepping directly into them.)

- ✔ **Kitchen:** The kitchen serves as a direct route to health issues, including
digestion problems and binge eating if entered from the front door. Your
finances can take a beating as well. To cure this situation, hang a wind
chime over the cook's position at the stove.

- ✔ **Bedroom:** If your bedroom is located just inside your front door, you may
find yourself feeling lazy, being tired constantly, and not wanting to work.
To cure, hang a wind chime halfway between the door and your bed.

- ✔ **Dining room:** Similar to entering the kitchen, but with less severity,
entering the dining room can negatively affect your eating habits and
personal energy. To cure the situation, hang a faceted crystal sphere
over the center of the dining table.

- ✔ **Bathroom:** Even though entering the front door directly into a bathroom
is virtually nonexistent in modern homes, entering the front door of a
house into an entryway and seeing a bathroom first thing is common.
This view can have psychological, physiological, and financially draining
effects, much more so if the toilet is visible upon coming in. The cure
involves keeping the bathroom door closed at all times, to retain precious energy. An additional cure which strengthens the first one involves
hanging a full-length mirror on the outside of the door, which helps psychologically eliminate the bathroom. This second cure only works when
the bathroom door is kept closed. (See Chapters 10 and 13 for more
information on bathrooms.)

- ✔ **Playroom, game room, or gambling room:** You can have rapid and
intense financial upswings or downfalls. To cure this situation, hang a
faceted crystal sphere 3 feet inside the front door.

Positive things to see on entering

What if books are the first things you see when you enter the house? A view
of books fosters excellent school performance and increased intelligence.
Also beneficial are positive images, scenes of nature or waterscapes, and
paintings or photos of peaceful and uplifting subjects. Additional positive
first impression objects are flowers, plants, and aquariums.

Negative first impression objects

Things you should avoid encountering as you enter the front door include:

- ✔ Any mess or uncleanliness
- ✔ Piles of undone work
- ✔ A toilet, the stove, or the bed
- ✔ Your mother-in-law or IRS agents

The cure for the first two items is easy and clear: Move them elsewhere. Toilet, bed, and stove cures are covered in Chapters 10 through 13. For the last problem, you're on your own!

Entering regularly other than through the front door

Using a garage door as a regular entry can negatively affect your life depending on conditions in the garage. A garage that is cold, unpleasant smelling, or messy creates corresponding effects in your life. If the garage door leads directly into the kitchen, a double problem exists. Fumes and noxious chi from the garage follow you into the kitchen and can negatively affect the kitchen's energy and, in turn, the food and your health. To perform a cure, you can always park outside and use the front door.

If this proves unlikely, you can hang a pleasant sounding wind chime (using a red ribbon) from the ceiling in the garage directly in front of the entryway to the house. The sound of the chime can act as an energy filter, helping to disperse the negative chi from the garage.

Entering the garage into a laundry room can also negatively affect your health. To cure this situation, I recommend keeping the laundry room clean or entering through another door.

Two separate doors on front of house

Two separate doors on the front of a house are a major source of confusion. A second door detracts energetically from the main entry and can cause career blocks, confusion, and other difficulties. To cure the situation, if possible use the originally intended front door to enter and exit. Mark the chosen front door with the house number and place plants on each side of it to attract energy. Hide the second door with a large potted plant and don't use the door.

Part III

Indoor Feng Shui: Boosting the Energy of Your Home and Office

The 5th Wave   By Rich Tennant

While practicing Feng Shui in a kitchen, Dwayne, the refrigerator repairman, causes a disharmonious event within the area of his attire.

In this part . . .

This part is bulgin' with incredibly easy-to-follow yet fiercely effective procedures for finding and curing problem areas in your home's individual rooms and overall layout. With each major problem feature, I fastball you one or more practical solutions that crank up the energy of your space and bring you tangibly higher levels of peace, satisfaction, and harmony.

I also discuss career Feng Shui in this part. Feng Shui at your office can balance your chi (or energy) and help you balance your workload.

Chapter 10

Making Sense of Your Home's Layout

In this chapter, I help you look at each section of your house in Feng Shui terms. Each part of your house has its own unique energy. But before you can adjust the Feng Shui of your residence, you need to find out what each area of your house represents and how the different areas relate to one another. I cover the basic structure of your home's interior and explain how each area of your home influences you.

I also show you how to analyze your floor plan and make the necessary Feng Shui changes. You can discover the difference between the front and back halves of your home and what fits best in each area. Next you can analyze the center of your home and find out why the center of your house is the most important area, the nucleus that energetically holds everything together. The center chi influences your health in particular and also connects to all other parts of your life. You can also see that some areas get along like compatible, friendly neighbors, and others rub each other the wrong way, like the Hatfields and the McCoys.

Looking At Your Home: Front and Back

An easy way to analyze your floor plan in terms of Feng Shui is to consider the front half and the back half of your house separately. For this exercise, you need a floor plan of your home, drawn to scale. On your plan, measure the length of the house from front to back. Then draw a line across the house from left to right, at the midpoint. For example, if your house measures 6 inches from front to back, draw a line dividing the house in half, at the 3-inch midpoint. (See Figure 10-1.)

The front door of your house is the orientation point. Therefore, the front side of the house is the half with the front door — even if this side of the house doesn't face the road. Whatever is in front of the midline is in the *front half* of the house; whatever is behind the line is within the *back half* of the house.

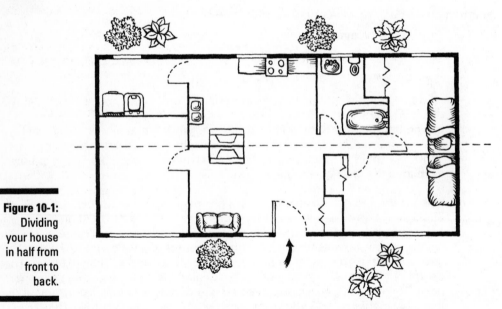

Figure 10-1:
Dividing
your house
in half from
front to
back.

In the following sections, I show you which rooms are best located in the front half of your house and which are best situated in the back half.

Good rooms for the front

The energy of your home enters at the front of the house through the front door. This part of the house involves movement, career, social life, and connecting with the outer world. The front is the *yang,* or active part of the house. The living room, family room, and den are good rooms to have located in the front of the house; their proximity to the front door enhances both your social life and family gatherings. However, these rooms are fine to have in the back of the house as well. Some other rooms that are especially well-suited in the front area include the following:

- ✔ **Office:** A home office that is close to the outside world and the street can assist your career and business and help keep the office energies separate from the rest of the house.

- ✔ **Guest bedroom:** If the guest bedroom is in the front of your house, your guests won't overstay their welcome. (But if the guest bedroom is in the back, they're probably still there!)

- ✔ **Child's bedroom:** Putting a child's bedroom in the front of the house can help them become independent. This placement is particularly beneficial for older children.

Good rooms for the back

The back half of the house is more naturally the *yin,* the quiet and receptive environment, ideally suited for privacy, rest, serenity, and connecting with the family. Nourishing activities such as relaxation, family activities, and preparing and eating food should occur in this half.

Pay close attention to the positions of the key rooms of your house: the master bedroom, and the kitchen. Ideally, the master bedroom, kitchen, and dining room should be located in the back half of the house. The closer either the master bedroom or the kitchen is to your front door, the more life problems you are likely to experience. A master bedroom positioned too close to the front door can result in separation or divorce. And a kitchen placed near the front door threatens your health and finances and can cause money to exit the house. The following sections provide you with a few simple cures to counteract negative effects if these rooms are located in the front of your house.

In Chapter 3, I show you how to draw the front line of the house on your home's floor plan. The *front line* of the house is the line or plane that contains the front door. If the master bed or stove sit in front of this front line, they are (in Feng Shui terms) located outside of the house. In this case, the problems mentioned in the following sections are magnified, and the cures given are even more vital.

Master bedroom

The ideal location of the master bedroom is as far back as possible from the front door. If the bed sits in the front of the house, the marriage can suffer and sleeping can be disturbed. You can cure the negative effects of a master bedroom located in the front of your house by placing a sizeable mirror (at least 3 by 4 feet, the larger the better) in the back of the house, directly in line with the bed. The mirror serves to symbolically pull the bed towards an energetically better position — the rear of the house. (See Figure 10-2 for an example.) The top of the mirror should be higher than the top of the head of the tallest resident.

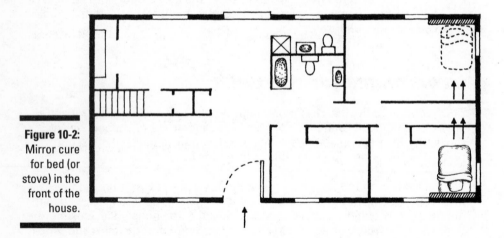

Figure 10-2:
Mirror cure for bed (or stove) in the front of the house.

Kitchen

A kitchen in the front half of the house can challenge the health and finances of the occupants because the energy of the stove can easily be disturbed by the active energies in the front. A kitchen easily seen or accessible from the front door creates the worst situation; the active, stimulating energies of the front portion of the house can symbolically attack the stove, leading to unfortunate life results. You can gain weight easily, experience stomach or gastrointestinal problems, and have a strong tendency to binge eat, especially soon after arriving home. Money problems are also associated with a kitchen placed too far forward in the house. To cure this situation, perform the mirror-pulling cure mentioned in the previous section (as shown in Figure 10-2), or you can hang a large faceted crystal sphere over the stove.

Dining room

A dining room in the front half of the house can also generate life problems, but not as severely as the kitchen. Visitors may habitually arrive, eat lots of food, and then quickly leave. Or worse, they may stay too long chatting. To cure a front dining room, hang a large faceted crystal sphere (at least 2 inches in diameter) over the dining room table.

Finding the Center of Your House

Although all areas of your house are important, the most important area (besides the front door) is the center. The center of the house is the most vital area on a home's floor plan. The energy in this area dramatically influences your health and impacts every part of your life. The center of your house is like the hub of a wheel: All action and energy pass through this area. This principle is true even if you rarely spend time in the center — even if it's a closet.

Recognizing the importance of the center

The following four characteristics make the center stand out from all the other house areas.

- ✔ **The center energetically connects to and interrelates with all other areas of the house.** The center affects and is affected by every area.

- ✔ **The center affects your health and well-being.** Good health and physical vitality allow you to achieve your fullest potential. If your health suffers, every part of your life suffers as well. To keep your life in balance, take a look at the center of your home or workplace.

- ✔ **The center affects every area of your life.** If you want to create overall life improvement, start at the center. Cures performed in the center spread energy outward to other areas. By the same token, if your home needs lots of Feng Shui work but multiple cures are beyond your budget, a single effective cure in the center can help you turn things around.

- ✔ **The center of the house can even make you centered!** At your wit's end? A cure in the center can help put things right by getting you centered.

Knowing the ideal energy condition of the center

Ideally, the center of the house should be open, airy, and free rather than stuffy, dark, and cramped. The center should feel bright, uplifting, healthy, and pleasant. The best room for the center is a living room, family room, den, or study.

Figuring out what's good in the center

Because the center of the house connects to all aspects of your life, performing cures in the center can solve your problems and create positive life benefits. The cures in the following sections can help enhance the center's effects on your life in multiple ways.

Attract vital energy with plants

Placing fresh, healthy green plants in the center of the house is a great all-around life cure. One plant can help, but more is even better. Odd, or yang, numbers are inherently more active than even, or yin, numbers. So an odd number of plants (3, 5, 7, and so on) can create more activity and change than an even number can create.

Display the color of health

Yellow is the color of health. For an excellent cure, place yellow objects in your center or paint the walls in the area shades of yellow or gold. (See Chapter 15 for more details on color.)

Apply a special life cure

If you're experiencing problems and really need relief, you can perform the special all-purpose "save me!" cure. Using a red ribbon cut to a 9-inch increment, hang a large faceted crystal sphere in the center of your house.

Curing troublesome central areas

Three rooms create problems in the center: the bathroom, the bedroom, and the kitchen. The bathroom drains the vital energy of the center, harming everything at once. On the other hand, a bedroom in the center poses a problem because the powerful energies of the center threaten the peace and safety of the bed. A kitchen in the center creates trouble; the strong, fiery chi of the stove adds too much intensity to the already highly active center area, so health can take a beating. Of course, building a fully compatible Feng-Shui dream house may not be an option for you. So the following section offers some easy-to-follow cures to calm the pesky negative energies.

Curing a bathroom in the center

According to Feng Shui, a bathroom in the center of the house can induce multiple adverse life effects. Bathrooms symbolize draining and loss — energy going down the drain. So a central bathroom can generate negative health, loss of money, and general life troubles. Big, Texas-sized problems.

For this situation, I suggest that you apply two cures, one for the exterior and one for the interior of the bathroom. First add a full-length mirror on the outside of the door (see Chapter 13) and keep it closed.

The second cure is to fully mirror all four interior walls of the bathroom. The four-mirrored-walls solution powerfully transforms the negative influence of a central bathroom. (An added bonus — you'll never feel lonely on the toilet again!) As with all cures, strongly visualize that your desired life results are materializing while you perform the cure. If you're hung up thinking that Martha Stewart may frown on such a design feature, just remember, she'll probably never use your bathroom.

If mirroring the walls isn't possible, an alternate cure is to hang four Feng Shui flutes in the bathroom. Hang the bamboo flutes vertically, one in each corner of the bathroom. (See the Feng Shui Resource page at the end of the book for a flute source.)

Make sure that the short sections of your flutes are toward the floor and the longer sections are nearer the ceiling. The top of each flute should hang at least at eye level or higher with the tallest person in the house. (See Chapter 4 for flute tips.)

The master bedroom

A master bedroom in the center of the house can generate havoc and confusion. The center's active, vital energies can disturb your sleep, peace of mind, marriage, and wealth. Unpleasant, you say? No problem. The mirror solution, shown in Figure 10-2, works dandy to help a centrally positioned master bedroom. Simply place the mirror in the back of the house directly in line with the bed. Visualize that the bed has been pulled back to a position of safety.

If you can't perform this cure, you can hang a wind chime in the center of the bedroom to calm and harmonize the room's energy. This cure performs a tad less powerfully than the mirror cure but substantially improves the situation.

The kitchen

A kitchen located in the center of the home can lead to accidents, major health problems, or even fires in the home. The mirror-pulling cure works wonders in this situation (see Figure 10-2). For an alternative cure, you can hang a large faceted crystal sphere (2 inches or larger) above the cook's standing position at the stove or in the center of the kitchen. The sphere harmonizes and balances the chi of the stove and the center, creating better luck and health. Also make sure the rest of the kitchen follows Feng Shui principles (see Chapter 12).

Spiral staircase

A spiral staircase acts like a corkscrew boring down into the earth. Downward spiraling energy in the center of your home can provoke a downward trend in your finances, health, and life fortunes. The antidote is to create upward, rising chi, so an appropriate cure is one that draws energy upward. I recommend two solutions. You can wrap a realistic green silk vine around the banister from the bottom to the top. You can also draw the energy upward by hanging a faceted crystal sphere from the ceiling above the center of the staircase. For a double-whammy cure, apply both solutions at once. (See Chapter 14 for additional staircase principles and cures.)

Noticing Neighboring Rooms

The two most vital rooms in a house are the master bedroom and the kitchen. Not to downplay the importance of your kid's rooms, but the master bedroom empowers the parents who literally and energetically feed the children. Therefore, the location of these two rooms affects the overall life and fortune of the occupants.

The bedroom and kitchen contain the all-important bed and stove, which create, nurture, and give life to the household. Ideally, the kitchen and master bedroom shouldn't be located near each other, because the energies of the bed and stove can conflict if they're too close. If the bed and stove are positioned back-to-back on a common wall or if the doors of these two rooms directly face each other, your marriage and/or health can suffer. In addition, neither the bed nor the stove should sit near a toilet.

Conflicts involving any combination of these three features — the bed, the stove, and the toilet — can lead to serious problems in the corresponding Life Areas (see Chapter 3 for details on the Life Areas). If these scenarios define your home environment, apply the cures in the following sections. Be sure to check out Chapters 11 through 13 to make sure the affected areas completely align with Feng Shui principles.

Toilet/stove and toilet/bed wall connections

A toilet should not be positioned back-to-back on a common wall with a stove or a bed, because the repetitive influence of the toilet flushing sucks life-force energy from either one. Potential toilet/stove consequences range from digestive problems to loss of wealth to serious illness or accidents. Toilet/bed consequences include not only these problems but also the possibility of divorce or even loss of life. If the sink sits on the wall behind the bed, the same problems may arise, though they aren't as severe.

To perform the toilet/stove cure, install a mirror on the kitchen wall behind the stove. Make sure that the mirror is the same width as the stove and extends from the floor to at least the top of the stove or up to the bottom of the cabinet above the stove. In addition, the reflective surface of the mirror should face the stove.

For the toilet/bed situation, place a mirror on the wall behind the bed, running from the floor to at least the top of the headboard. The mirror width should equal the width of the bed, and the shiny side should face the bed. If you don't have a headboard, the mirror can come up to the top of the mattress. When you perform this cure visualize peace, safety, and good health for the full results. (See Figure 10-3.)

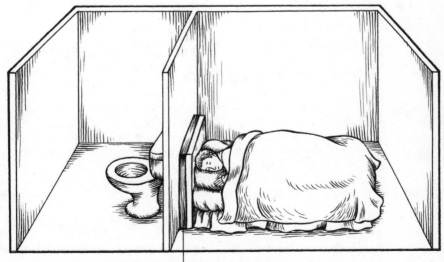

Figure 10-3:
Cure for bed and toilet on a common wall.

Mirror on wall behind headboard facing the bed.

A toilet located on the floor above and directly over a bed or stove can also mean potential disaster. To cure this situation, fix a small round mirror on the ceiling above the sleepers' heads or above the stove, directly under the toilet, shiny side down. An alternative or additional cure is to hang a faceted crystal sphere and/or a metal wind chime using a red ribbon (cut to a 9-inch increment) directly over the sleepers' heads or over the cooktop.

In an apartment building, a toilet located on the floor directly above your bed or stove, causes the same negative effects even if the toilet is located in another apartment. I recommend applying the previous toilet cures to this situation.

Stove/bed wall connection

If the stove and bed share a common wall, the potential problems are similar to the ones described in the preceding section, and the solution is virtually the same. Install a mirror behind the bed directly underneath the stove.

Curing Opposing Doors

Doorways of any two of these rooms — the kitchen, master bedroom, and bathroom — should not face each other. The following sections explain the potential pitfalls and cures for incompatible doors.

A bathroom opposite the master bedroom or kitchen

A bathroom door across from the bedroom door or kitchen entryway can stimulate stomach and intestinal problems or can result in depressed or negative states of mind. The situation worsens if the bathroom door is inside the kitchen or bedroom or if the bathroom door facing the kitchen is larger than the kitchen door. And if you can see the toilet from either the cook's standing position or the bed, watch out! For any of these situations, you can apply the following cure package.

- ✔ **Always keep the bathroom door closed.** Easy, basic, and foolproof.
- ✔ **Install a full-length mirror on the outside of the bathroom door.** This cure works only if you keep the bathroom door closed.
- ✔ **Hang a faceted crystal sphere midway between the two opposing doors.**

Bathrooms inside of bedrooms have their own Feng Shui issues; I cover bathroom/bedroom situations in Chapter 11.

Kitchen opposite a bedroom

Potential problems abound when the kitchen door directly opposes the bedroom door. Because you must always head toward the kitchen as you leave the bedroom, the sight of the kitchen influences you to overeat. Consequences include weight gain and digestive problems. Also, the fiery chi of the stove can overheat the marriage or relationship, creating arguments and discord. If you can see the stove from the bedroom, the problems get worse.

You can disperse these conflicting energies by hanging a wind chime halfway and directly between the bed and the stove. The healing sounds and energy of the wind chime diffuse and harmonize the energies, creating peace and abundance. As an alternative cure, you can place healthy new green plants on either side of the doorway.

Chapter 11

Jazzing Up Your Bedroom for Increased Health, Energy, and Romance

. . . .

In This Chapter

▶ Knowing the best locations for your bedroom

▶ Thinking about bedroom shapes and layout

▶ Examining the entry into your bedroom

▶ Seeing how the bed position can dramatically improve your life

▶ Recognizing the importance of the right bed

▶ Finding ways to boost the energy of your bed

. . . .

*T*his chapter covers the second Life Pillar — the all-important master bed — and its container, the master bedroom. The bed exists as a foundation for rest, health, and relationships or marriage. I present a wealth of principles and pointers that, if applied correctly, can lead to tangible and powerful improvements in many areas of your life. (For an overview of the Life Pillars, see Chapter 2.)

The master bedroom — the most critical room in the home — nourishes the chi of the adults. And the energy of the adults, in turn, feeds the children. If the chi of the adults suffers, so can the energy of the children. This situation makes the condition of the master bedroom important for the welfare of everyone in the home.

In addition to the master bedroom, you can apply the principles in this chapter to any bedroom in the house. (See Chapter 13 for more information on children's bedrooms.)

This chapter has a three-fold purpose: to set forth the ideal Feng Shui conditions for the bedroom, to explain how deviating from these ideals can create life problems, and to give you practical solutions to cure the deviations.

Placing Your Bedroom in a Powerful Position

The welfare of the entire household depends in large part on the placement, condition, and energy of the bedroom. Therefore, first consider the location of the bedroom in your floor plan. (Be sure to check out Chapter 10 for additional key issues regarding bedroom placement in the house.)

The ideal placement of the master bedroom is in the Commanding Position of the home. This principle says that the best place for the bedroom is the back of the house and as far from the front door as possible. (I explain this concept later in the chapter.) The front half of the house is less favorable for the bedroom because this area is closer to the front door — the active energy of the street. Choosing the back half of the house is more favorable; this area is generally quieter, more peaceful, and better protected. Moreover, the best areas for the bedroom are in the Commanding Position areas of the house; these areas lie cater-cornered to the front door of the house. For a front door on the left, the Commanding Position lies in the back right; for a front door on the right, the Commanding Position sits in the back left; and for a center door, choose either the back left or the back right of the house for your bedroom location. (Figure 11-1 shows the Commanding Position areas of the house for best bedroom placement.)

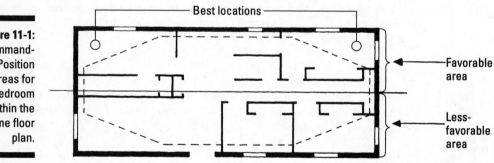

Figure 11-1: Commanding Position areas for the bedroom within the home floor plan.

Best locations

Favorable area

Less-favorable area

Rescuing a bedroom over the garage

An increasing number of people sleep in master bedrooms located over the garage — an unfortunate Feng Shui placement for several reasons. This location separates the bedroom from the vital grounding energy of the Earth and leaves you sleeping over an energetically cold, empty space. The garage feels colder, messier, and less friendly than the rest of the home, and it drains chi and warmth from the bedroom.

Another negative influence is the car itself. The chaotic, noisy energy of the car tends to disturb the tranquility of the bedroom; in addition, exhaust fumes inevitably find their way up into the bedroom and can negatively affect the respiratory system as well as the overall health of the occupants. The solution for this design feature involves using the symbolic energy of trees to help ground and stabilize the energy of the room. Under the bedroom and inside the garage (preferably but not necessarily under the bed), paint a large tree with brown roots that appear to go down onto the garage floor and a large powerful trunk that rises up the garage wall. The branches of the tree should bear a multitude of healthy green leaves and extend far onto the garage ceiling where they can flourish into an abundance of fruits and flowers.

You can perform a variation of this cure by decorating the bedroom with the same colors as the tree. (See Figure 11-2.) Paint the walls of the bedroom healthy shades of green and install carpet or flooring in brown or earth tone. Also, your ceiling should feature many flowers and fruits in multiple friendly colors.

Figure 11-2:
Cure for
bedroom
over garage:
Tree painted
on wall.

For an alternative or additional cure to the previous methods, you can place lively green plants in the bedroom to stimulate more-nourishing, living chi.

Protecting a bedroom threatened by a car

Cars that pull into an attached garage (or park directly outside of the house) and point towards the bed can subconsciously threaten the health and welfare of the sleepers. Over time, the continuous possibility that the car may come through the wall and harm the sleeper can negatively impact the sleeper's psyche. One of my client's teenage daughters inadvertently drove the family car through the garage wall into the house. (A quick thinker, she claimed to be starting some impromptu remodeling!) If the bedroom had been located on the other side of the wall, an expensive accident may have otherwise resulted in a tragedy.

To protect yourself in this situation, you can choose from two cure options. You can hang a large mirror facing into the room on the bedroom wall that is nearest the offending car. The mirror expands the bedroom and symbolically pushes the wall and car far away. Or you can hang a metal wind chime in the garage between the front of the car and the common wall. The chime diffuses the chi of the car and reduces the subconscious threat to the sleeper.

Considering Your Bedroom's Shape and Layout

The best shapes for bedrooms are squares or rectangles. If your bedroom is irregularly or oddly shaped, consult the "Shapes" section in Chapter 8 for the appropriate cures.

Positioning the Octagon on the bedroom

The Octagon is a basic Feng Shui mapping tool, which I explain in Chapter 3. The Octagon shows you which parts of your bedroom affect each of nine Life Areas. Apply the Octagon to the bedroom the same way you apply it to the yard or house. (See Figure 11-3 for a reference.)

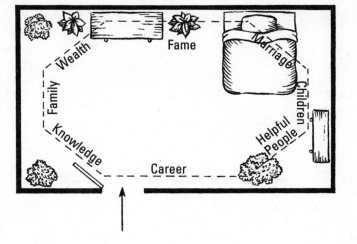

Figure 11-3:
Feng Shui
Octagon
placed on
the
bedroom:
The nine
Life Areas of
the room.

After you position the Octagon, you can analyze your bedroom to see how the Life Areas are affected. Then you can use the cures and principles within this book to correct any defects in your bedroom Octagon or improve any of the Life Areas you want. For example, if you have a missing part in the Marriage Area of your bedroom, your marriage can experience unnecessary stresses and problems. To improve your marriage, you can perform a cure by hanging a mirror to expand the Marriage Area.

Dealing with doors and windows in the bedroom

Ideally, the master bedroom should contain only one door (excluding closet doors) — the main entrance to the room. Multiple doors into the room lead to additional energy flows, which can distract you from rest and increase your vulnerability. These extra doors can also leak vital energy from the bedroom; consequently, they can drain your health and your money and also harm your relationship. I give you cures for extra doors in the bedroom in the following sections.

Windows provide needed natural light, but if located too close to the bed, they can be an energetic security issue as well as cause unhealthy drafts for the sleepers. If a window is positioned near your bed, you can hang a faceted crystal sphere in the window to diffuse the excess energy flows.

Curing a bathroom door in the bedroom

A bathroom door in the bedroom is a prime opportunity for you to experience energy loss in both your health and marriage. (But with opportunities like this one, who needs crises?) So I recommend keeping the bathroom door closed and hanging a full-length mirror on the outside of the bathroom door. In addition, I suggest that you check the other bathroom cures in Chapter 13 to remedy this vital Feng Shui situation.

Checking an outside door in the bedroom

An outside door in the bedroom symbolizes the frequent absence of one partner from the home as well as the possibility of divorce and loss of money. A door featuring windows only aggravates the situation; French doors are especially problematic. You can improve these doors in terms of Feng Shui by replacing them with solid ones and using the doors less often. If the door into the bedroom leads straight toward an outside door, money and marriage partners can quickly leave the site. To cure any outside door in the bedroom, hang a brass wind chime (with a sound you like) in front of the door. Also, use the door as infrequently as possible.

Curing multiple bedroom layout issues

This section demonstrates how you can apply cures to the entire bedroom at once. Figure 11-4 shows two examples of bedroom layouts that feature multiple Feng Shui problems. I've purposefully chosen rooms with several issues to demonstrate how multiple cures can work together in a room. Keep this tip in mind: You don't necessarily need to perform all the cures in this section to have good Feng Shui in your bedroom (although you may choose to do more cures!). Some rooms have great Feng Shui without adding any cures. The key is to be practical: Apply the cures that fit your needs.

Curing an oddly shaped bedroom

The following list describes the problems of oddly and irregularly shaped bedrooms as well as practical cures to remedy each situation. (See Figure 11-4a.)

 ✔ **An oddly shaped room:** This room shape can create confusion and stagnation, sleeping issues, and marriage problems. To cure the odd shape, you can hang a faceted crystal sphere or wind chime from the center of the room.

✔ **An angled wall in Marriage Area:** This problem can provoke arguments. You can cure this situation by putting a light on one end of the angled wall and a plant on the other. (See Chapter 14 for more specifics on angled walls.)

✔ **A pointed wall corner that juts towards the bed:** This condition can project threatening, arrow-like energy towards the legs and feet of the sleepers. To cure, you can hang a faceted crystal sphere directly in front of the projecting corner. (See Chapter 7 for information on poison arrows.)

✔ **A large window on the left wall and an exterior sliding glass door on the top wall:** This situation can cause excess chi to enter and leave the room. These factors can create a psychological lack of safety and protection for the sleepers. To harmonize these energy flows, hang a faceted crystal sphere at the midpoint between the window and exterior door.

✔ **A fireplace in the bedroom:** A fireplace can burn up the energy of the marriage, leading to exhaustion and strain. Cure it by placing a potted plant in front of the fireplace to cover its opening and refrain from lighting fires.

✔ **A closet door that hits the main door of the room:** Two doors hitting each other causes clashing doors, which can lead to arguments and personality clashes among the occupants. To cure this problem, hang two bright red drapery tassels, one on each doorknob, on the common sides of the doors. (See Chapter 14 for more details on clashing doors.)

✔ **A narrow entrance into a bedroom:** This tight spot can harm your career and prospects. Cure this problem by hanging a wind chime over the entrance inside the bedroom.

✔ **A door not visible from the sleeping position:** This situation makes succeeding in many areas of life difficult. Cure it by placing a wall or standing a mirror across from the bed that clearly shows the door. (I detail this problem in the section "The visibility of the bedroom door" later in this chapter.)

Curing a bedroom with a blocked entrance, skylight, or beam

The following bedroom positions make entry difficult and can create health challenges. For these examples, refer to Figure 11-4b.

✔ **Blocked entrance:** The closet wall provides only a small area to move forward as you enter. This constriction makes it difficult for energy and people to enter — and exit — the bedroom. Results can include blocked feelings in life, frequent absence from home (or sleeping alone for months on end), and difficulty finding a relationship. Cure this situation by placing a full-length mirror on the wall facing the doorway. This cure expands the entrance and draws additional energy into the room.

✔ **Beam over the bed:** A beam causes constriction and pressure on the sleepers; in this case, the heart. You can hang two Feng Shui flutes at 45-degree angles, one on either end of the beam. This cure relieves the pressure of the beam and creates better fortune in the Health and Marriage Areas of life. (See Chapter 14 for more information on beams and Chapter 4 for flute cures.) An alternative cure for this problem is to move the bed so the head of the bed is in the Children Area.

✔ **Skylight over the bed:** A positive aspect of a skylight is that it adds light to the room. On the other hand, a skylight situated over the bed can threaten the sleeper. To cure this problem, you can hang a faceted crystal sphere from the skylight. For best results, hang the sphere using a ribbon cut to a multiple of nine inches in length.

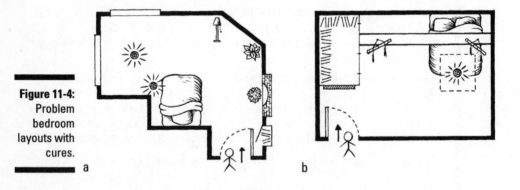

Figure 11-4:
Problem
bedroom
layouts with
cures.

a   b

Resolving the master suite dilemma

Large, beautiful, and convenient for owners, master suites reveal a major trend in today's home market. Amenities of a master suite often include the availability of a large closet and a bathroom integrated with the bedroom. However, a master suite can negatively affect the energy of its occupants in several ways.

A very large master suite can cause disorientation, confusion, and conflicts among the partners; a room that is too large lacks coziness and can make the occupants feel lonely. (Some partners end up communicating with each other by cell phone from different areas of the room.) Adding healthy plants to the space can make a large room feel more occupied and full of life.

Generally, an irregular space is an unwanted, persistent puzzle for your subconscious; in the same manner, an irregularly shaped room (see Figure 11-4a) causes confusion because the mind continuously attempts to make sense of its space. A room with multiple openings and odd shapes is like living inside a mystery — determining where the room actually begins and ends is difficult. "So what?" you say. So you're more tired, confused, and cranky, I reply. Thankfully, you can give your mind a needed rest with Feng Shui!

In addition, the opening to the bath area acts as a gaping hole in the room that inevitably draws precious energy away from the bed. The best cure for this situation is to place a curtain or door across the opening.

The most elaborate master suites (featuring multiple openings, doors to outside patios, and multileveled and/or slanted ceilings) are classic Feng Shui nightmares. These rooms can provoke multiple life problems and can make finding a good bed position quite a challenge. An overall good cure for a master suite is to hang a faceted crystal sphere from the center of the room to harmonize the disparate flows of energy. For a stronger cure, you can hang a high-quality leaded glass crystal chandelier (as long as you don't hang it over the bed).

Curing the master suite

Now you can find out how to apply cures for master suite problems. (You may want to take a look at the master suite example shown in Figure 11-5.) In the following sections, I analyze the Feng Shui problems and then explain the cures.

- ✔ **The room features an outside door in the bedroom.** This situation can lead to problems in a relationship (a partner joins the circus), drainage of money in the household, or loss of health. The outside door also introduces excess chi into the room, which induces additional problems.

- ✔ **The path of energy from the main door to the exterior door runs across the foot of the bed.** This condition can create challenges in the career area of life.

- ✔ **A huge opening in the room leads to the bath area.** This opening is directly across from the foot of the bed and can drain the sleepers' energies. The wet, draining energies of the bathroom, along with the gaping hole in the wall, can wreak havoc on the relationship and physical health.

A master suite with the previous three conditions doesn't afford a good place for the bed. In Feng Shui, bed position is the most important bedroom factor; it provides a foundation for health, strength, and life success. Three of the walls in this room contain an opening or doorway, which makes them impractical for the bed. The right hand wall is the only feasible alternative, but this position is a Feng Shui problem. You can apply the following cures to a master suite.

✔ **Place a curtain across the opening to the bath area.** This visual barrier reduces the effects of the opening and completes the room, which helps stabilize and solidify the marriage and health. Attaching a door to this opening makes a stronger cure, but for most people, the curtain is more feasible.

✔ **Hang a faceted crystal sphere in the center of the room.** This cure serves two purposes. First, a cure in the center is a good antidote to having concurrent multiple problems, and it can improve luck and fortune. Second, the energy flowing from the main door to the exterior door meets the energy that comes from the bath opening toward the bed (and vice versa). At this critical juncture, the sphere in the center helps balance and calm the energies, thereby protecting the sleepers and harmonizing the entire room.

✔ **Place a wind chime at the exterior door.** The wind chime regulates the flow of energy in and out of the exterior door. This cure helps retain energy and life in the room, and it protects the sleepers.

Note: Master suites usually include a closet, which isn't shown in Figure 11-5.

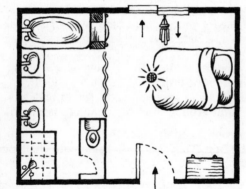

Figure 11-5:
Master suite
with cures.

Enlivening the Entryway into the Bedroom

The entry into the bedroom should allow a clear, straightforward path into the room. This principle applies to the pathways outside and inside the bedroom door. If the entryway — on either side of the door — is small, blocked, dark, or cluttered, problems can manifest in your health, relationship, and finances. The following cures can open up new prospects in your life and relationships.

Using a bright light to bring about good luck

A bright light is always helpful outside the entrance to the bedroom. In addition to brightening up a dark entryway, this cure can bring you good luck.

Widening the narrow path

If the entryway to the bedroom is narrow, you can hang two mirrors, one on each side of the entryway. This cure opens up energy flow into your life and stimulates creativity and lateral thinking. It can be effectively applied to the entryway either outside or inside the bedroom.

Making sure the door has a full swing

The door to the bedroom should open a minimum of 90 degrees. Anything located behind the door, hanging on the back of the door, or hanging on the wall behind the door can cause a block in your life — even if the door doesn't technically hit the items. (This principle holds true even if the door can swing open a full 180 degrees.) The cure is simple: Remove the things that come between the back of your door and the wall. If the door is blocked by a wall and can't open 90 degrees, you can hang a wind chime just inside the door to propel sufficient energy into the room.

Curing negatives seen when exiting the room

Facing a closet, bookshelf, or bathroom door when exiting your bedroom can frustrate your opportunities and career. If you walk out toward a closet or bookshelf, you can hang a convex mirror (the larger the better) directly ahead of you in plain sight, preferably at the eye level of the tallest person in the house. If you come out of the bedroom toward a bathroom door, the effect worsens; additional problems can include loss of money and poor health. I recommend these cures: Place a full-length mirror on the bathroom door, keep the door shut, and hang a wind chime halfway between the two doors. (See Chapter 13 for additional cures you can implement inside the bathroom.)

Remembering the Purpose of the Bedroom

The bed should be the main focus of any bedroom. Many people unfortunately (and unknowingly) turn their bedrooms into small apartments with lots of functions. Nowadays, bedrooms serve as places for office work, physical exercise, TV watching and entertainment, storage for extra stuff, a reading library, and even an eating area — all in addition to a place that provides (supposedly) rest and intimacy in the relationship. (You may as well fix your motorcycle in the bedroom, too.) In this hectic environment, the quality of your sleep (and health) can take a real beating. The busier and more connected your daily life becomes, the more you need a safe haven from the clamor of the outside world. Bringing media in all its wonderful forms (phone, TV, radio, Internet, alien civilizations) into your bedroom is indeed mentally stimulating and highly enjoyable, but exactly the opposite of the peace and calm needed for high quality rest.

Try to return the bedroom to its original intended functions. In case you've forgotten, these functions are sleep and relationship. (Try 'em out sometime. They're really great.) Let your other activities take place outside the bedroom (like in the living room and dining room) and watch your sleep and attitude improve remarkably and rapidly.

For Feng Shui bedroom décor, remember the *KISS* formula (pun intended): Keep It Simple, Sweetheart. Multiple functions and purposes in a room tend to breed confusion, and this concept is particularly true of the bedroom. If you want increased balance and better sleep plus more togetherness, romance, and passion in your relationship, I recommend the following quick and easy Feng Shui adjustments:

- ✔ **Get the phone and answering machine out of the bedroom.** This removal includes portable phones. At the least, unplug the phone at night.

- ✔ **Remove TVs, stereos, and entertainment centers.** The TV is relationship zapper numero uno in the bedroom. (Be honest: Late night talk show hosts aren't exactly erotic mood enhancers.) In addition, falling asleep while watching TV is a great way to turn you into a zombie. Just keeping these culprits in the room detracts from one's rest — even if they're not turned on very often. If you can't handle this cure, you can cover the TV — or keep it in a closed cabinet — whenever the TV is not turned on.

- ✔ **Haul out bookshelves and piles of books, magazines, bills, and paper.** They distract you from sleeping and keep your mind busy while you sleep. A few books on your nightstand, however, are fine.

✔ **Remove office equipment, computers, printers, and desks from the bedroom.** These critters offend for several reasons; they're noisy, clutter-prone, and emit electromagnetic fields that can sap your energy. (Because of these fields, I also recommend moving electric alarm clocks and radios at least 30 inches away from your body.) In addition, office items distract you from sleeping and from relating to your significant other. If you feel forced because of limited space to keep multiple functions in one room (such as an office in the bedroom), you can benefit from sectioning off the nonsleeping portion of the room with a screen or room divider.

✔ **Get the excess furniture out.** The KISS formula strikes again. Keep your bedroom simple, and you can feel more balance, peace, and calm. Also, excess furniture can stifle the energy of your bedroom and the people who sleep in it. You can still place other pieces of furniture besides the bed in the bedroom. But remember: Don't stuff the room with lots of furniture! Large amounts of tall, heavy furniture can dominate the bedroom and can even make you feel subconsciously dominated, oppressed, or frightened. Also watch out for *poison arrows,* angles and parts that jut out from furniture and point toward the bed. Poison arrows (see Chapter 7) can negatively affect your health. If your bedroom contains large or protruding pieces of furniture, do your best to rearrange or remove the offending items. If you can't, drape cloth in front of the angle or place a potted plant at a jutting corner to protect yourself.

I'm not saying that you can't have good Feng Shui if you don't follow all the previous tips. *Remember:* A bedroom really exists for health, wealth, and relationship or marriage; and then adjust your life accordingly — as best you can.

Taking the Best Position: Commanding Position Bed Placement

Feng Shui involves many principles for the *auspicious* (or favorable) positioning of your bed. To take advantage of as many of them as you can, use common sense along with the conditions of your individual room to make the best choices possible. In the following sections, I explain the five principles that comprise the Commanding Position concept, which shows you how to achieve the most powerful bed position in Grandmaster Lin Yun's Feng Shui school. If you see that your bedroom doesn't meet these criteria — don't panic! Keep reading: I show you cures you can implement to dramatically enhance your bedroom situation.

The position of the bed relative to the door

The first Commanding Position principle states that the position of the bed relative to the bedroom door rates more importantly than the compass direction the bed faces. Using the type of Feng Shui performed in this book, however, you don't analyze whether your bed faces east, west, north, or south. You can rest easy and position the bed according to the way it best relates to the other main feature of the room — the door.

The distance from the bed to the door

The second Commanding Position principle holds that the bed should sit as far from the bedroom door as possible. If the door is on the left, the best position is the far right corner of the room; if the door is on the right, the best bed location is the far left of the room; and if the door is the center, the best location is either the far right or far left corner of the room. (See Figure 11-6 for examples.) The farther your bed sits from the door, the more control you can feel over your space and your life. You aren't startled easily, and you have plenty of time to prepare for events as they unfold.

The sleeper's scope of vision

The third Commanding Position principle asserts that the bed position should allow the sleeper the widest possible scope of the room. A diminished range of sight within the room can restrict the sleeper's chi and his or her life vision. The larger the space in front of your bed, the more your life expands, breathes, and improves. For this reason, Feng Shui cautions against placing the foot of the bed against a wall, which can block your career and cause foot and ankle problems. Also, placing your bed directly against a side wall (with no space between the side of your bed and the wall) can make you feel cramped, stifled, and less flexible in life.

The visibility of the bedroom door

The fourth Commanding Position principle states that you should clearly see the bedroom door from the bed. This concept means that when lying on your back in bed — that is, in the center of the bed (if you sleep alone) or on your side of the bed (if sleeping with a partner) — you can open your eyes and immediately see the door of the room without repositioning your body. If you have to perform gymnastics or create new yoga positions to see who or what's coming in the door, your bed position does not meet this principle.

Not seeing who's approaching can keep you uncertain and on edge. Even if you think that you're accustomed to not seeing the door, you still likely experience ongoing subconscious stress, which can create imbalance and frustration. The possibility of always being startled can keep you on edge, and over time, the continual tension and unrest can cause an imbalance in the nervous system. Results can include nervous problems (think Uncle Fester), arrhythmia, and heart palpitations. In addition, repeatedly torquing the body to see whether someone's coming can cause neck and spinal problems in the long run.

If your bed position doesn't allow you to see the door and you can't move the bed, you can place a sizable mirror opposite the bed that allows you to easily see the door. (See Figure 11-7c.) If you need to angle the mirror to show the door, use a standing mirror angled to the appropriate position.

The direct line from the door

The fifth Commanding Position principle holds that the bed should not sit in the direct line of the path of the doorway. If your bed does sit in the direct line of the door, the chi of the door runs directly and too powerfully up the middle of the bed. This factor can create diseases along the midline of the body.

The farther you sleep from the door and the more of the room you see while in bed, the more you can feel in control of your environment and, therefore, your life. Seeing the door to your bedroom symbolizes that you know what life is bringing and feel prepared to deal with whatever comes. You're in command, and the results manifest positively in many areas of your life.

When following the Commanding Position principle, you can choose from three alternatives for good bed placement. (See Figure 11-6.) Choices 11-6b and 11-6c are both excellent; just be sure, if possible, to leave enough room on the side closest to the wall for your partner (or yourself) to get into bed. Position 11-6a (the bed angled in the corner) is the strongest choice of all; it gains support from two walls rather than one wall. If you choose this position, I recommend that your bed feature a solid headboard. Make sure the corners of the bed firmly touch the walls. You can strengthen this bed position by placing a plant and a light behind the headboard. (A real or an artificial plant works for this cure, and the light should be in good working order but doesn't need to be on at all times.)

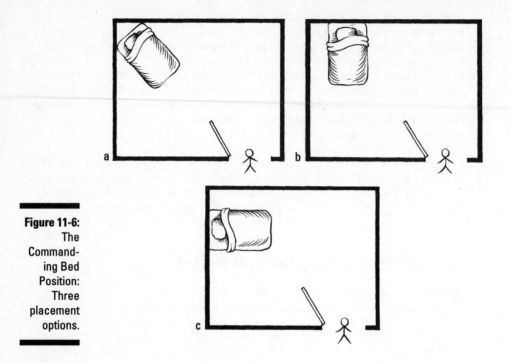

Figure 11-6:
The Command-ing Bed Position: Three placement options.

Exploring Additional Positioning Principles

Besides the Commanding Position principle, check out the following additional principles for good bed placement. Use your common sense to do the best you can in your situation. Oftentimes, following every Feng Shui pointer at once proves impossible; the trick is to adhere to as many of them as you can.

Of course, the ideal cure for almost every bed-positioning problem is to move your bed into a position that conforms to the Commanding Position guide-lines and the other bed position principles in this section. If you can't move to a better position, I provide you with cures that dramatically help your bed position and can also improve your relationship, health, and wealth.

Recruiting the power of the mountain

Positioning the head of your bed against a *solid wall* — your symbolic mountain — provides you with a strong sense of support, safety, and protec-tion. (Figure 11-6a obeys this principle; the two corners of the bed touch the walls.) If the head of your bed stands free in the room (not against a wall), your life and career tend to lack support. This position — for either the parents' or the children's bed — can also influence the children to do poorly in school and, in general, not receive strong parental support.

You can apply the easiest cure by pushing the head of the bed against a wall. If your bed already sits on a wall, check to see whether it physically touches the wall. You don't want any space between them; even a 1-inch gap between your bed and the wall can reduce your security, cause mental strain, and negatively affect your dreams and sleep.

Ideally, you shouldn't position the head of your bed against a window. The opening in the wall weakens the support of the mountain and can create health-challenging drafts during sleep. If a window must be positioned over the bed, cover the window with a drape or curtain. The best curtain gives you the visual illusion of a solid wall. For added strength, hang a faceted crystal sphere in the window. If a door stands behind your bed, the problem worsens significantly. For the best solution, move the bed away from the door if you can find a better position. If you can't, cover the door and hang a wind chime over the head of the bed to disperse and diffuse any harmful chi coming from the door.

Addressing a bed in the path of the door

If the straight-ahead path of any doorway in your bedroom — particularly the main door to the room — runs across the bed, you can encounter physical problems in the body parts in which the energy path crosses (see Figure 11-7b.) For example, if the energy runs directly across your heart and stomach, you can experience digestive problems or even heart conditions.

The worst version of this problem occurs if your feet (or head) point straight out the door (see Figure 11-7a). In this position, you lie in the "coffin ready to be carried out" bed position, a colorful Feng Shui metaphor alerting you to the dangers of this placement. You can apply a cure by hanging a metal wind chime halfway between the door and the bed. The sound of the chime deflects the onrushing chi of the door and creates safety and relief. Also, you can hang a large crystal (60mm) by itself or in combination with the wind chime.

Selecting cures for problem bed situations

The best option is simply to place your bed in the Commanding Position. But what if this cure isn't reasonable? Maybe the builder of your house or apartment forgot to cooperate with your Feng Shui goals, and you want to make the best of what's available. The following three situations, shown in Figure 11-7, give you a good idea of common bed position problems along with cures provided for each one.

Curing the coffin position

Figure 11-7a shows you how to perform cures to make a tough bed situation better. The bed lies in the dreaded coffin position; the incoming energy from the door can create health problems along the midline of the body and can split the relationship. Moving the bed significantly is difficult because of the closet door on the left as well as the large bay window on the right. I recommend hanging a faceted crystal sphere over the foot of the bed to disperse the oncoming energy from the door to protect the sleeper. Then hang a solid curtain over the smaller window behind the bed. The curtain makes the wall more solid and gives more support to the sleeper.

Fixing the exterior door

In Figure 11-7b, the outside door and huge window prevent positioning the bed in the Commanding Position (the upper left corner of the room.) Also, the location of the door in the Wealth Area (see Chapter 8) implies the possible loss of money. The situation worsens because a car parked right outside threatens the bed and sleeper. (The closet prevents the bed from being placed in the lower left of the room.) The outside door is cured with a wind chime; the sound of the chime disperses the attacking chi and helps to retain the wealth energy within the room.

This bed position involves another problem: The energy from the bedroom door runs right across the sleeper's body and can create health problems in the torso (heart, stomach, and so on). Hang a wind chime or faceted crystal sphere over the bed to cure this problem. This cure can also be placed halfway between the room door and the bed.

How to help your bedroom problems

Check out the following methods for improving your bedroom and your life:

- **Nightstands by the bed:** If you're single and looking for a partner, a helpful cure is to make sure a nightstand sits on each side of the bed.

- **Clashing doors:** If one door hits another door in the bedroom, arguments can ensue. You can hang bright red drapery tassels from each knob on the clashing sides of the doors.

- **Ceiling fan over the bed:** This situation symbolizes cutting energy over the bed that causes physical and emotional chaos. If the fan can't be removed, you can hang a faceted crystal sphere from the fan and, preferably, leave the fan turned off.

- **A slanted ceiling in the bedroom or a beam over the bed:** This situation causes mental and physical pressure as well as insomnia. You can cure this problem by hanging a faceted crystal sphere from the slanted ceiling or beam. Be sure to use a red ribbon, cut to a multiple of nine inches in length, to hang this cure. (See Chapter 14 for additional bedroom cures.)

For information on colors and lighting in the bedroom, see Chapters 14 and 15, respectively.

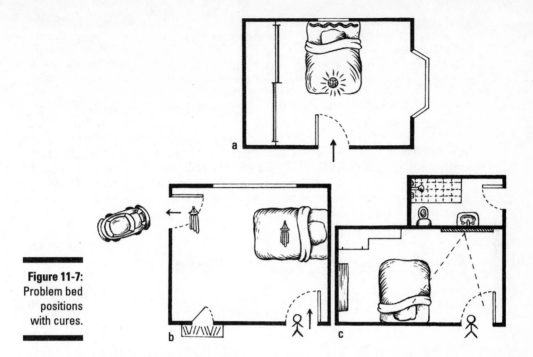

Figure 11-7:
Problem bed
positions
with cures.

Showing me the door!

Figure 11-7c details another tough bed situation. Built-in furniture on the left side of the room prevents placing the bed in the ideal position — along the left wall. The bed can't be placed on the top wall of the room, because this position shares a wall with the toilet and sink. The remaining available position is on the bottom wall of the room, which makes the door invisible to the sleeper. The cure for this situation is simple and effective: Place a mirror on the wall across from the sleeper so the door is visible from the bed.

Recognizing the Critical Importance of a Good Bed

In addition to the bed position and the ways in which the room's features relate to the bed, the nature and condition of the bed itself is also vital.

New versus used beds

For positive Feng Shui of the bed, the first criterion is the energetic condition and origin of the bed itself. A new bed contains fresh, unblemished energy that supports health and vitality. A used bed (one that comes from someone else and not new from a store) is a strong recipe for sexual problems, a lack of energy, and mysterious illnesses. This principle encompasses all parts of the bed: the mattress, the box spring, and the frame. And it applies even if you sleep on an antique bed that you really love and don't want to part with.

In a used bed, previous owners leave subtle energetic impressions; the bed can retain emotions, events, sexual energy, and sickness. So Feng Shui offers one word of advice about sleeping on a used bed: Don't. If you currently sleep on a used bed, I recommend getting a new one. The worst bed to inherit is one that belonged to someone who just passed over to the next plane (and I don't mean airplane). If getting a new bed is impossible right now, in the mean time, you can perform the Orange Peel Blessing on the bed (see Chapter 18 for details on this cure).

Good times to get a new bed

Feng Shui advises that you consider a new bed and bed clothing (such as sheets, pillows, pillowcases, and so on) when any of the following events occur:

- **The person you share the bed with dies:** A new bed can help you cope and keep you from living in the past.
- **A relationship ends:** Getting a new bed helps clear the old energy and bring in the new.
- **Anyone using the bed experiences a major sickness:** A new bed supports your health and protects you from illness.
- **You move into a new house:** This cure puts old energy behind you if you want to leave energy behind.
- **You get married:** In this situation, the new bed symbolizes a fresh, powerful, new start.
- **Someone steals your bed:** A real no-brainer.

If you can't afford to get a new bed, a substitute option is to change the mattress or even just the bedclothes.

The shapes and sizes of beds

You can fix a myriad of Feng Shui glitches in the following bed situations:

✔ **King-sized beds:** A king-sized bed can induce a split in the marriage or partnership. The box spring of a king-sized bed comes in two pieces that creates a division within the bed — a symbolic inducement for one partner to saddle up and flee the scene. The secret cure for this situation is to place a bright red cloth the full size of the bed between the mattress and the box springs.

✔ **Water beds:** A waterbed provides anything but a firm foundation for life, sleep, and success. The swaying and rocking motion may be comfortable, but you sacrifice security, groundedness, and career stability.

✔ **Storing things under the bed:** Stuff stored under the bed can induce subconscious blocks and stagnation plus stifle your creativity. Not exactly a barrel of laughs. Or monkeys. Large piles of stuff (actually anything) under the bed also can energetically hamper you if you're trying to conceive. The cure is simple: Get the stuff out!

✔ **Beds with drawers:** Beds with drawers underneath the sleepers confuse all parties involved. If you must use them, put only items concerning the bed and sleep inside, such as blankets, sheets, and pajamas. Books, guns, tax records, and other unrelated items (hot photos of ex-lovers, pints of whisky, and so on) are definitely not recommended.

✔ **Too-high or too-low beds:** A bed positioned too high or too low can throw off your energy patterns. I once had a client who positioned her bed so high that she used a small stepladder to get into the bed. Her complaint was that she couldn't find a relationship; I explained that it was because of the small population of pole-vaulters in her town. When she starting sleeping on a bed of a more reasonable height, she rested easier and found more prospects in her romantic life. If the bed sits too high to get into easily, it can block your chances of attracting a mate.

On the other hand, a bed sitting on the floor (or only a few inches off the floor) can symbolically keep you low in life, making receiving and keeping money more difficult. A bed that stands on actual posts energetically supports you better than one that sits on the floor.

✔ **Metal-frame beds:** A metal-frame bed can surround your body with a distorting magnetic field while you sleep. Wood frames, if possible, work better. Beds made from metal tubing (and mattresses and box springs containing metal coils) create an unwelcome magnetic field around the body and don't have the insulating quality of wood.

✔ **Built-in entertainment units or bookshelves:** Beds with built-in entertainment units, book shelves behind the sleeper, and other kinds of large multipiece bed units aren't recommended. Huge and heavy, these beds typically tower over the sleeper. Their shelves and cubby spaces are a prime inducement for clutter. (You may find yourself having a garage sale right inside the bedroom.) Many of these units leave an open space behind the sleeper's head — as with bookshelves behind the head of the bed — which can lead to insomnia, fitful sleep, or negative dreams. The best situation occurs when the sleeper's head lies next to the wall or the headboard of the bed.

✔ **Something rising above the foot of the bed:** Ideally, your bed should hold nothing above its surface at your feet — this principle includes chests, plants, and other items. Anything that rises above the foot of the bed blocks you and your progress. A bed with a footboard rising above the top of the mattress can block your travel and hamper your career and future. Sleigh beds aren't recommended. They violate several important Feng Shui bed principles; the footboard rises high above the mattress, and the headboard and the footboard curve toward the sleeper. This entire setup can create compression on the sleeper, causing one of the partners to want to flee the relationship.

If the footboard is in the form of bars (such as the footboard on a brass bed), the symbology worsens, foreshadowing legal troubles or even jail time. (Or at the least, a fondness for really large tattoos.) You can get a new bed or replace a too-high footboard with one that is even with or lower than the top of the mattress. However, you can attract bad luck by hammering, sawing, or using power tools on a footboard (or any other part of the bed) still attached to the bed. Follow the best route and gently remove the piece to be modified, have it corrected or ideally replaced, and then gently put back in place.

✔ **Moving and altering the bed:** Move or alter your bed with care. I recommend that you don't bang or harshly disturb your bed while moving it. This activity can create intense negative chi for the occupants of the bed that can lead to possible fights in the family. This commotion proves particularly harmful if the sleeper is a pregnant woman. For optimal health of both the mother and the unborn baby, the bed position should not be moved at all during pregnancy. Always handle the bed softly, gently, carefully, and respectfully when moving, changing, or otherwise altering the bed or its position.

✔ **Murphy, folding, or pull-down beds:** Murphy, folding, or pull-down beds (the kind that fold up into the wall when not in use) make the sleeper feel temporary, ungrounded, and not at home — even if left down all the time. On the other hand, a Murphy bed in your guest bedroom helps ensure that guests don't overstay their welcome — especially if you accidentally fold it into the wall while they sleep!

Improving the Power of Your Bed

All aspects of your bed affect your chi. The following tips give you additional areas that you can improve for greater health and comfort.

A strong headboard helps career and marriage

A headboard on the bed can help make you stronger in general and promotes growth in your career and solidity in your relationship. The headboard should attach firmly to the bed; when you grab the headboard and try to wiggle it with your hand, it shouldn't move. A headboard that feels loose or, worse, is separate from the bed (on the floor behind the bed) weakens the occupants. The best type of headboard is solid — made of one piece without major gaps or holes. The worst headboard is made of bars, which symbolically look like prison bars and can lead to legal trouble. If you can't replace the bars right away, a powerful cure is to wrap them with realistic green silk vines. The positive symbology of new life energy helps to negate the negative symbology of the bars.

Color your bed for vitality

Your bed sheets and blanket colors can help you create unique results based on your intentions. For instance, pink bed sheets attract love and romance, and red sheets spark passion and sizzle — but take them off if things get too hot to handle! Green sheets are good for health, healing, money, and new growth. Yellow represents another great healing color for bed sheets.

Avoid sweeping underneath when trying to conceive

Chinese energetic theory holds that as a woman attempts to conceive, the energy representing the new baby first coalesces underneath the bed. When the conditions are right, the fetal energy moves up into the woman's body, and she becomes pregnant. Therefore, sweeping or cleaning under the bed while trying to conceive can help prevent a successful conception. Also, avoid beds (for example, ones on wheels) that can easily move. If you have this type of bed, fix the wheels so they can't move.

Chapter 12

Nourishing Health and Wealth in the Kitchen

In This Chapter

▶ Identifying the subtle energy of food

▶ Paying attention to kitchen layout and stove location

▶ Looking at the stove — the energy generator of the home

This chapter details the kitchen and its star attraction — the stove, the third of the Life Pillars (see Chapter 2). The secret knowledge of Feng Shui holds that the energy flow in the kitchen greatly contributes to how food affects you. Food carries chi — life force energy — that enters your body when you eat. According to Chinese energy theory, the amount and quality of chi in your food rates more highly than its nutritional makeup. Energy theory doesn't ignore vitamins, minerals, and nutrients, but the food's energetic qualities are the number one consideration.

The stove — the most important factor in the kitchen — is where the cook physically and energetically creates the food. Food universally symbolizes health and nourishment, however, the Chinese make a further connection by saying that food also relates to money. Feng Shui refers to the stove as the home's *energy generator,* the place where the energy of the cook, the food, and the fire meet to create sustenance for physical health and the strength to earn money. Therefore, Feng Shui masters carefully scrutinize the energy conditions of the stove and kitchen.

In this chapter, I show you the principles of ideal kitchen layout and stove positioning and provide simple adjustments that you can perform if your stove needs Feng Shui help. I also cover vital aspects of stove Feng Shui including your stove's usage, quality, and condition.

Harnessing the Energy of Food

The energy of food affects not only your health but many other areas of life as well. Two factors help determine the energy in food: the origin of food and the preparation and cooking of food. The energy of food derives initially from the quality of the land and the way the food is grown, harvested, and handled. You don't need a Feng Shui master to tell you that purchasing the highest quality food available greatly benefits your health, vitality, and personal strength.

The second component of food's energy comes from preparation and cooking. In particular, the energy state and mood of the cook — on the conscious and subconscious level — while he or she cooks greatly impacts the chi of the food. Have you ever eaten a meal and remarked to yourself afterwards that something in the food tasted off? Well, an unhappy cook likely made your meal; the clashing or moody feelings a cook experiences can transfer to your body and emotions through the food. In fact, you can get sick by eating food made by someone who's upset or sick while they're cooking.

Positioning the Cook and the Stove

In the ideal kitchen layout, the cook can easily see the door of the kitchen while standing at the stove, so he or she is never startled while cooking. Whatever the cook feels can enter the food and profoundly affect the eater. If your back currently faces the kitchen door while you cook, you're probably being startled — whether or not you're aware of it. In the following section, I explain the two most important kitchen factors.

- ✔ **Kitchen Feng Shui Factor I: The relative energetic safety of the cook as he or she stands cooking at the stove.** The cook's standing position greatly determines the quality of chi he or she puts into the food. This position derives from the stove position itself.

- ✔ **Kitchen Feng Shui Factor II: The placement of the stove in the kitchen and the impact of the kitchen's energy on the stove.** At the stove, everything comes together to create nourishment and energy for the family. The energy that circulates in the kitchen affects the stove, so the position of the stove determines whether your raw ingredients are lovingly transformed into delicious meals for your enjoyment and health or unwittingly contribute to health issues and loss of money.

The stove not only impacts your physical health, vitality, and stamina, but also influences many other areas of your life. Chief among them is money! That's right, your stove affects your wealth situation. A family's financial welfare depends more on the energetic status of the stove than on almost any other Feng Shui factor. Surprising? Read on: The chi of the stove also correlates to the following areas:

- ✔ The quality of your marriage and the degree of family harmony versus upheaval and disagreement in the home.
- ✔ Your freedom from or involvement in lawsuits, legal trouble, or other major life entanglements.
- ✔ Your level of personal safety, security, and protection versus danger, accidents, mishaps, surgeries, and other problems.

As you can see from this list, the stove can greatly affect your well-being, and putting time and attention into the stove's chi can reap powerful rewards. Regardless of your status in life, you can improve your situation and prevent serious problems by adjusting the Feng Shui of your kitchen.

Maximizing Kitchen Location, Layout, and Stove Placement

In the Feng Shui floor plan, ideal kitchen placement is in the back half of the house. The back of the house is more protected, calm, and secure than the front, so kitchen placement in this area protects the sensitive energies of the stove and fosters health and wealth. The worst places for the kitchen are in the front of the house and the center of the house (the energetically more active areas). You can find cures for these situations in Chapter 10.

Understanding the ideal kitchen layout

A good kitchen layout prevents energy from attacking the stove or the cook. The best layout affords the cook a powerful standing position and protects both the stove and cook.

Ideally, the cook should see the doorway of the kitchen — and anyone approaching — while he or she cooks without needing to turn around. I recommend an island stove which the cook can stand behind and observe the kitchen doorway. (See Figure 12-1.) Of course, 90 percent or more of all American stoves sit against a wall, so in most homes, energy comes from the door toward the back or side (or both) of the cook. The best cure for this situation is the mirror-behind-the-stove cure. Read on for more details on this cure.

Figure 12-1:
Powerful
cooking
position
allowing
cook to see
the kitchen
door.

The energy from the main and secondary doors into the kitchen should not flow directly (straight toward) the face of the stove. In a pass-through kitchen, a path shouldn't run directly in front of the stove. In addition, the stove should be in balance with another kitchen feature, the refrigerator.

Even if you live and cook alone, you need to see the door when you're cooking because the position of the stove still affects your emotional, physical, and financial wellbeing. The symbolic relationship between you and the energy generator of the home — your stove — is more important than whether you share your home with other people.

Many cooks admit to me that they can't see the doors of their kitchens, so for years, they've subconsciously turned their bodies to avoid feeling vulnerable while cooking. Other cooks habitually put food on the stove and leave the kitchen and then return occasionally to check on the progress of the food. If this behavior sounds familiar, check out the following sections for useful advice.

Which direction should your stove face?

Unlike the Compass Feng Shui Method (a separate and valid way of practicing Feng Shui — see Chapter 1), Grandmaster Lin Yun's Feng Shui school does not utilize actual compass directions to determine which direction the stove should face, or in what part of the house it should reside. According to this book's approach, your stove should face the direction that allows you to see the door and who's approaching. If your stove doesn't meet this criteria, you can use the "mirror-behind-the-stove" cure in the following section.

Positioning your stove for wealth and health

This section is where the rubber meets the road — or the frying pan meets the fire. If any door into your kitchen is not visible when you're at the stove, you can solve the problem with one of the solutions in the following sections.

Seeing a kitchen door behind you

A single door behind you is the simplest version of the stove/door problem. (Note that if the door points straight at the stove, an accident involving visible blood can occur in the home.) Because remodeling the kitchen is impractical for many people, here's an easier cure: Hang a mirror on the wall behind the stove. This cure inexpensively allows you to see who's coming and effectively solves the issue of safety and protection of the cook. When installing the cure, visualize better physical health and increased income to achieve best results. (See Chapter 6 for more details on visualization.)

A mirror measuring a couple inches across and tacked to the wall behind your stove does not provide an effective cure for this problem. I recommend that you hang a mirror as wide as the stove that runs from the top of the stove to above your head or to where the extractor fan or hood begins. (See Figure 12-2.)

Figure 12-2:
Mirror
behind
stove
enabling
cook to see
the door.

What to do if you can't hang a mirror behind your stove

If your stove design (such as an all-in-one vertical unit featuring a built-in microwave) or other limitations prevent you from placing an effective mirror behind the stove, you can apply another option. Hang a pleasant-sounding metal wind chime from the ceiling halfway between the door and your standing position at the stove. The chime deflects the chi of the door away from the cook's back and ensures the protection and safety of the stove and the cook. (See Figure 12-3.) For best results, use red ribbon cut in multiples of 9 inches in length (see Chapter 4 for details). For another alternative, you can angle a standing mirror on the counter next to the stove so you can see the doorway.

If your mirror will sit within 2 to 3 inches of your burners, specify heat-tempered glass when ordering or buying your mirror to ensure that it doesn't crack.

Depending on the design of your kitchen, a mirror directly behind the stove may not show you the door. For this situation, you can hang a mirror on the wall to the side of the stove to solve the problem.

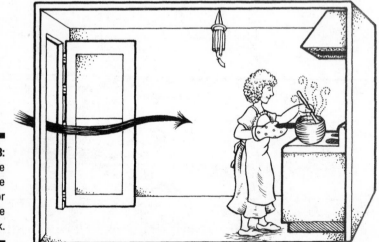

Figure 12-3:
Protective
wind chime
for a door
behind the
cook.

Curing a stove visible from the front door

Severe Feng Shui problems can result from seeing the stove as you enter the front door. If you can see the stove through one or more angled doorways, the trouble can intensify. (Worst case scenarios include violence and tragedy in the home.) To perform the cure, hang a door or curtain that visually separates the stove and the door. If a door or curtain doesn't work in your situation, you can strategically position one or two brass wind chimes or faceted crystal spheres along the path between the front door and the stove.

Curing multiple doorways and traffic patterns in the kitchen

When multiple doorways enter your kitchen, the picture becomes more complex. The following sections deal with the different situations, one at a time.

Pass-through kitchen or doorways leading in front of the stove

When a walkway passes directly in front of the stove, constant traffic can pull away the healthy chi of the stove. If the kitchen functions as a hallway, negative results can include fighting in the home and difficulty in holding on to your money. To cure this situation, hang wind chimes in the pathway — one between each door and the stove. (See Figure 12-4.)

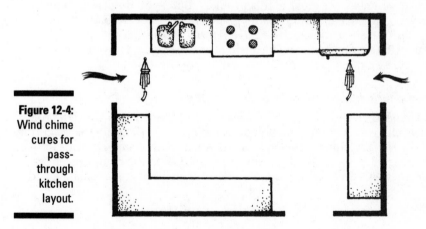

Figure 12-4: Wind chime cures for pass-through kitchen layout.

Outside door into the kitchen

If a door in the kitchen leads to outside the house, threats to health, safety, and money are heightened. I recommend two cures. First, use the outside door less often to reduce the effects of outdoor chi on the kitchen and stove. Second, hang a bamboo Feng Shui flute horizontally above the outside door frame (see Figure 12-5). The flute brings peace and safety, an effective antidote to the threatening energy of the door. Visualize these effects when you apply the cure.

Figure 12-5:
Bamboo flute over outside door in kitchen.

Garage door leading into the kitchen

A garage door that connects directly to the kitchen can carry noxious fumes and pollution directly into your food and body. Of course, if you don't park in the garage, you alleviate most of this problem. But if you do park in the garage, you can place multiple healthy plants in the kitchen to provide healthy chi. Certain plants such as Boston ferns and spider plants provide added benefits by purifying and cleansing the kitchen air. I also recommend the flute cure detailed in the previous section for this door.

Multiple doorways opening into the kitchen

If your kitchen has several doorways, excessive energy flowing into the room can cause chaos and confusion. I recommend applying the principle of curing the center: Hang a large faceted crystal sphere from the center of the kitchen. (See Chapter 10 for more on the center.) The crystal in the center balances the disparate energies that circulate in the kitchen, resulting in balance and calm.

Looking at the Stove: Your Home's Energy Generator

The stove is the energy generator of the home; it provides the food that gives nourishment and vitality to the residents. The quality and condition of the stove contribute to — or detract from — the chi of your home. Because of the symbolic connection between food and money, the stove is also one of the biggest overall influences on the wealth of the household.

Which type of stove cooks food best?

For the energetics of food, the best quality fire comes from cooking with wood or straw. In modern homes, most people generally cook at appliances, not hearths, so the choices are limited to gas, electric, and microwave (although new options are beginning to appear, including convection — or hot air — combined with electric, microwave, and other energies). Of the three available types of cooking, gas provides the best energy by far. (This information is an energetic analysis of stoves, not necessarily a scientific viewpoint.) Gas stoves cook with real fire, which cooks food better and puts stronger chi into the food itself. Electric stoves do not produce fire but cook the food with a hot electrical field, which creates at least two problems:

low-quality food energy and exposure of the cook to a high level of electrical fields. The human body is not energetically compatible with these fields, which can prove debilitating over time. The same goes for toaster ovens and electric ovens. Microwaves are further down the line of poor quality because they create deep energetic problems in the food, which can disturb both your emotions and physical body — no matter what scientific experts say on the subject. (And no, you shouldn't use your microwave to dry your poodle!) For a helpful cure, lose the microwave or hang a brass wind chime and a faceted crystal sphere above the microwave to protect you from radiation.

Choosing a new stove versus a used stove

Like the bed, the best stove is one you purchased new. A used stove inevitably retains the previous owner's energy and creates an energetic drag on your life and progress. Buying a brand-new stove when you move into a residence can give you a new start in health and wealth. If you can't afford a new stove, you can cure your existing one with a thorough physical cleaning, as explained in the following section. For even further benefits, you can energetically cleanse the stove by performing the Orange Peel Blessing (see Chapter 17).

Improving the cleanliness of your stove

Take a look at your stove's cleanliness. Feng Shui says that a dirty stove makes you tired and depressed and makes it harder to earn money. Old food particles (dirt to you and me) hold stale energy, which mixes with the chi of the new food you cook. The cure is simple: Clean your stove and keep it clean. The most important part is the top, which holds the burners. However, in order to experience the full benefits, clean everything: the oven, the broiler, the front of the stove, the controls, and the other areas.

You can also move the stove out from the wall and clean everywhere — all the sides, and the inside, including the back and bottom; the walls behind and to the sides of the stove; and the floor underneath. You may be amazed at what you find, and you may be pleasantly surprised at how much better you feel when everything's spick-and-span.

Inspecting the condition and use of your stove burners

The burners are to the stove like the engine is to a race car — the most important part that makes everything run. I cover two important burner issues in the following sections.

Repair broken burners

A broken or poorly working burner can cause a major Feng Shui problem. A broken burner is like losing one of your car's cylinders; the car may run, but you need repairs quickly if you want reliable transportation. The same holds true with your stove. If one or more burners don't work, it tops the list for immediate attention. The one and only cure: Fix defective burners. This cure includes fixing burners that technically work but show other problems including the following:

- The burners don't light reliably or mysteriously go out on a regular basis.
- You need to use a match to light them (because the pilot light is bad).
- The burner or grate is cracked or broken.

In San Diego, a therapist who invited me to do a Feng Shui consultation kept a broken stove for several years. After I gave her the stove repair cure, her landlord not only fixed the stove (which had several other problems) but approved a major remodeling and improvement of her home as well. Since applying this cure, she's enjoyed increased wealth, travel, and freedom.

Use all your burners for maximum earning power

The second important factor is how you use your burners. The Feng Shui trick is to utilize all the burners regularly. Many people use only their front two burners, and the back two sit idle most of the time. Rotate the usage regularly so all the burners stay active. The burners represent the wealth-generating potential of the home, but when they sit idle, wealth doesn't come as directly as it can. Strange but true, the way you use your burners affects your long-term financial picture.

Idle burners can directly affect your health as well as your finances. A Feng Shui colleague relates the story of a client who owned a large home containing three stoves in his kitchen, and he was consistently plagued by a mysterious stomach malady. Consulting with top-level doctors and nutritionists proved fruitless. During the Feng Shui consultation, however, he revealed that two of the stoves in his home worked just fine, but the third one hadn't worked since he purchased the house. After repairing stove number three, his indigestion quickly cleared up.

Examining the overall functioning of the stove

Although the burners are the most vital features of the stove, the working condition of the other parts of your stove is also important. Everything needs to work if you want to get the most benefits out of your stove. This principle covers all parts of the stove including:

- Missing, broken, or defective knobs and switches
- Light fixtures and light bulbs
- Fans and hood assemblies (attached to or above the stove)
- Broiler elements
- Clocks and timers on the stove
- Oven door hinges
- Anything you can find on the stove that doesn't work as perfectly as it worked when the stove was new

Visualize improved income and life circumstances when applying these solutions. (See Chapter 6 for more on visualization.)

My Feng Shui colleagues and I often shake our heads in amazement at how effectively the stove repair principle helps people get past sticky and drawn out money problems. The stories include legions (in fact, large stadiums full) of people who simply repair their stove and then receive new jobs, or people who get over nagging health issues or who suddenly hear from someone who owes them money and suddenly decides to pay up. Get the point?

Solving Miscellaneous Kitchen Problems

In the following sections, you can find some common Feng Shui kitchen problems along with simple solutions to ensure the best chi and good luck.

Remodeling the kitchen: A good time to be careful

Because of the sensitivity and importance of the kitchen in all areas of life, undertaking a remodeling job in the kitchen can bring misfortune to one's home unless the appropriate precautions are taken. I recommend two cures. First, choose a good date and time to begin the job (see Chapter 19 for timing details). Second, perform the house blessing in Chapter 17 (the Rice Blessing) on the day you begin the project and then on the day the project is complete. For a major house change, however, you may want to consult a Feng Shui professional to ensure that you receive the best outcome from the project.

Stove too close to the refrigerator

If your stove sits quite close to the refrigerator, you can have an energy conflict between the cold energy of the refrigerator and the hot energy of the stove. This placement can cause health and wealth problems. You can choose from several possible cures for this problem. You can mirror the side of the refrigerator nearest the stove; the mirror energetically expands the stove area, symbolically moving the refrigerator away. Alternatively, you can hang a wind chime or faceted crystal sphere between the stove and refrigerator to create energetic balance. If you have a small amount of counter space between the stove and refrigerator, you can place small potted plants on the counter as an energetic buffer.

A window over the stove

A window positioned over the stove creates a negative Feng Shui situation. However, the situation worsens dramatically when the cook sees one of the following through the window: bars, a grid, a grating, a trellis with a cross-hatched pattern, or a blocking wall. This arrangement can lead to family problems, exhaustion, legal problems, anemia, and blood diseases. The cure for this scenario calls for removing the offending symbolic feature. If you can't remove the culprit, you can plant ivy on the bars, or grates, or grid to add the color green — the energy of life. (You can even use artificial silk ivy.) Or hang a faceted crystal sphere in the window in order to expand your view and disperse the negative chi.

Small kitchen size

A large, spacious kitchen is favorable and portends wealth for the family. Try to avoid a cramped or stifled feeling. Mirrors work as the best tools for expanding small kitchens. You can also hang a faceted crystal sphere hung from the center of the kitchen.

A toilet or bed located on a common wall with stove

If your home's layout features a toilet or a bed on the opposite side of the wall from the stove, see the suggested cures in Chapter 10. For the toilet/stove combo, hang a mirror behind the stove, with the same width and height as the stove. (The shiny side of the mirror should face the stove.) For the stove/bed situation, hang a mirror on the bedroom side behind the bed. Use a mirror the width of the bed that runs from the floor to the top of the headboard (or mattress if you have no headboard). The shiny side of the mirror should also face the bed.

Light and color in the kitchen

The light level in your kitchen helps determine your mood and finances. Generally, bright light in the kitchen is better than dim light, but harsh light is negative. Incandescent lights are better than fluorescent. An easy light cure is to place small lamps on your kitchen counters to add cheer to dark corners. The best color for kitchens is white; dark colors are best avoided in the kitchen. (See Chapter 15 for expanded information on these factors.)

Knives visible in the kitchen

Visible knives in the kitchen symbolize accidents (especially cut fingers). This situation requires a simple cure: Keep your knives in drawers rather than displayed in plain sight.

Chapter 13

Applying Feng Shui to the Main Areas of Your Home

• •

In This Chapter

▶ Assessing living rooms and family rooms

▶ Choosing options for the dining room

▶ Improving the energy of children's bedrooms

▶ Performing Feng Shui in the bathroom

▶ Dealing with the garage

• •

*I*n this chapter, you discover how to apply Feng Shui to enhance the energy and beneficial effects of the main areas of your house. From the living room to the garage, each area of your house has an ongoing impact on your personal progress and emotional state. Read on to find out ways to keep the positive energy circulating in your home.

The Living Room, Family Room, and Den

The living room exists for relaxation, reception of guests, and social interaction. Family rooms and dens serve as informal, secondary living rooms for the family and intimate guests. If a living room is visible from the front door and/or the front hall or entryway, peace and comfort greet the weary residents as they arrive home. Therefore, a living room situated in the front of the house is positive. However, living rooms also fit well in other areas of the home. The principles of this section apply equally to your living room, family room, and den.

Positioning the group optimally

In the living room, the main activities involve sitting and conversing. The best seating positions for living rooms ideally afford both the guests and the residents clear views of the main door into the room. This arrangement makes everyone feel safe and comfortable.

Guests naturally feel honored if you give them the seats farthest from the main door of the living room; these spots are the safest and strongest positions. Residents of the home should also sit where they can easily see the door. In Figures 13-1, drawings a and b show examples of positive furniture placement.

Try to avoid placing a major piece of furniture with its back to the door (see Figure 13-1c). Sitting here can create a feeling of vulnerability, and the piece also blocks the door. If you can't arrange a main piece of sitting furniture to provide a view of the door, try placing a mirror on an opposite wall to reflect the door. Alternatively, you can add a table with lush, green plants behind the piece of furniture to create a sense of protection.

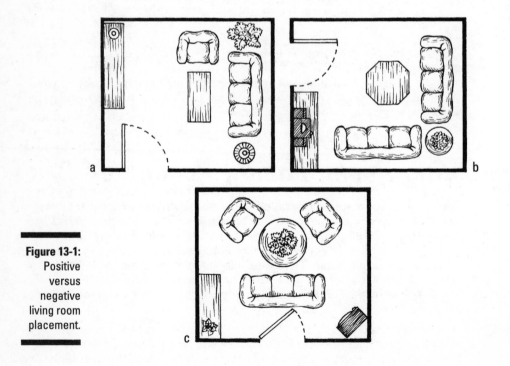

Figure 13-1:
Positive
versus
negative
living room
placement.

Placing furniture in conversational groups

The best living room arrangements make conversation comfortable and easy. If you need to talk across a walkway in the room, conversation is more difficult. Try to arrange your furniture so that groups of two to five (or more) people can converse in a single area. If your living room serves as a passage to other rooms, group the furniture so that coherent conversations can take place on either side of the pathway.

The Dining Room

The dining room correlates with both money and your career. Entertaining presents a great opportunity for you to build your network of associates and colleagues. (First you digest together, then you invest together.) The ideal Feng Shui location of the dining room is a practical one — next to the kitchen.

The larger the dining table, the better and stronger its energy — and the more your career can grow. The best energy comes from a dining table in one of these shapes: circle, square, rectangular, oval, or octagonal.

Large mirrors are very positive in the dining room, because visually doubling the plates and food on the table symbolizes doubling your wealth.

If the dining table sits under a beam, both your career and cash flow can suffer from extra pressure. To alleviate the problem, use the double-flute-on-beam cure: hang two special Feng Shui flutes, one on each end of the beam. Alternatively, you can move the table out from under the beam, or attach a green silk ivy vine along the bottom of the beam. (See Chapter 14 for more on beams.)

Feng Shui associates negative influences on health and money with seeing the stove while eating at the dining table. To cure this problem, place two special Feng Shui flutes over the door to the kitchen at 45-degree angles like symbolic swords. (See Chapter 4 for more on flutes).

Kids' Bedrooms

Favorable locations for children's rooms include the front of the house (especially for older children) and the Children Area of your home's Octagon (see Chapter 3). Less positive positions lie farther back than the master bedroom, or in the center of the house.

If a child's room sits further back in the house than the parents' room, the child may begin to run the household. The problem occurs because the child sits in a more Commanding Position than do the parents. (For more on the Commanding Position, see Chapters 10 and 12.) The cure for this problem is to hang a sizeable mirror in the front of the house, directly in line with and facing the child's bed. As a key part of this cure, visualize that the child's bed and energy are pulled toward the front of the house, and that the relationships in the home come into balance.

Another factor that can upset the balance in the home is if the child's room is larger than the master bedroom. Again, the child can exhibit out-of-control energy. One cure is to switch the two bedrooms. If switching rooms proves impractical, you can solve the problem by hanging a metal wind chime just outside the child's door, and a faceted crystal sphere in the center of the master bedroom ceiling. Use red ribbon, cut in 9-inch increments, to hang these cure objects.

Creating positive bed positions for children

The position of a child's bed is one of the biggest factors determining the child's progress, maturation, and safety. Two positive choices exist for bed placement: the Children Area (the center right area of the room) and the Commanding Position of the bedroom (see Chapter 10). Placing the bed in the Children Area gives the child strength, intelligence, and energy. (See Figure 13-2 for positive bed position choices.) Arrange the bed so the head rests against a solid wall.

Any of the factors that affect the master bedroom (such as a location over the garage, a slanted ceiling in the bedroom, and so on) can similarly affect a child's bedroom. Apply the cures in Chapters 11 and 14 to combat these problems.

Choosing the right bed for your child

The type of bed in which your child sleeps helps determine his or her strength and independence. Children are people too, and you can reap benefits by giving them the best possible quality of bed. In the following sections, I cover specific types of beds available for children, and the advantages and disadvantages of each type.

Getting rid of outgrown beds

Some parents keep their kids in beds they've long outgrown, thereby stunting their physical and emotional growth, as well as their advancement in school. Make sure your child has ample room to stretch out and sleep in his or her bed.

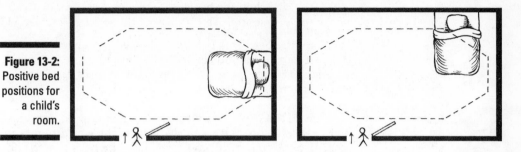

Figure 13-2:
Positive bed positions for a child's room.

Rethinking day, trundle, and temporary beds

A temporary bed gives a child feelings of instability and shakiness. If you can't afford a traditional bed right now, you can help stabilize your child's energy by using the special yu cure. Prepare a yu bowl, as detailed in the yu cure (see Chapter 18), and then place the bowl under the foot of the bed. Attach a red ribbon cut to a multiple of 9 inches long to the bottom of the bed and bring the ribbon down to the floor. Make sure the ribbon is long enough so the yu bowl can sit on top of the end of the ribbon. Reinforce this cure for the stability and tranquility of your child by using the Three Secrets Reinforcement (see Chapter 6). You can also perform this cure anytime you need help to stabilize a child's chi, even if he or she already has a good bed and bed position.

Letting go of bunk beds

Bunk beds save space wonderfully, but unfortunately do not benefit most children. Although the negative influence is generally greater for the child on a bottom bunk, both the top and the bottom bunk can oppressively affect the child's energy and health. Children sleeping on bunk beds can suffer from mental repression and show personality problems. A regular bed is definitely preferable, although bunk beds which reside in a guestroom, or that are rarely slept on are fine.

Buying a new bed is the easiest cure for this situation. For an alternative cure, hang a faceted crystal sphere directly over the heads of both children's sleeping positions. For the child who sleeps on the bottom bunk, hang the sphere down a few inches from the bottom of the top bunk. For the upper bunk, hang the sphere a few inches from the ceiling.

A client of mine expressed concern that her child was depressed, physically weak and performed poorly in school. To her surprise, I pinpointed the problem as the bunk bed her child slept on. Although she was initially hesitant when I prescribed the cure of getting a new bed for her son, soon after the new bed was installed, she reported that her son was remarkably happier and stronger.

Dismissing combination beds

A combination or an unusual bed design attempts to combine a desk, storage space, or a wardrobe into the bed. This type of bed does save space, but it doesn't provide the best benefit for your child in the long run. The combined energies are quite confusing, and the bed ends up doing none of its tasks well. A regular bed is a much better choice.

If you can't get rid of any of the bed types discussed in this section, you can apply this cure: Run a realistic-looking, green silk vine all the way around the edge of the mattress. Also, place healthy green plants in the bedroom to add living chi. The green life energy helps balance and harmonize your child's energy.

Looking at colors and special cures for kids rooms

Blue and green are good colors for a child's room. They promote growth, improvement, and a positive attitude. White is also a good color for a child's room, especially if you add accents of blue and green. For a very young child, multiple primary colors in the room help stimulate the brain functions and develop the sensory faculties. To settle down an overactive or unruly child, you can add darker colors like black, brown, or dark green to a white scheme.

Check out the following suggestions for improving a child's room and life, as well:

- **To help brighten a child's intellect:** Place a bright light in the Children Area of the room. This cure can assist a child any time.

- **To activate a child's awareness and mental capacity:** Hang a wind chime over the head of the bed and/or in the Knowledge Area of the room.

- **To balance a child's emotions and increase self-esteem:** Hang a faceted crystal sphere over the head of the bed.

The Bathroom

The bathroom, the home's place for cleansing and elimination, is a modern convenience that can instigate several Feng Shui problems. The bathroom impacts the family's wealth and the physical body's circulation of water. Grandmaster Lin Yun's Feng Shui school doesn't hold that the bathroom is a bad room with no proper place in the home — nor does it call for an idyllic return to primitive outhouses. However, I do recommend minimizing the Feng Shui problems of the bathroom using the cures given in this section. These solutions can make your home a healthier, wealthier, and happier place to live and love (and yes, go to the bathroom).

The bathroom presents two general Feng Shui issues. First, the bathroom exists for the purpose of waste removal, so it carries connotations of uncleanliness and dirt. Second, and more importantly, the bathroom features several drains, including the king of drains — the toilet. When addressing bathrooms, the chief goal is to keep the energy that circulates in the house from draining (or flushing) away, and therefore, to keep from depleting your life force. Another objective is to prevent the chi of the bathroom itself (sights, odors, and so on) from circulating throughout the house. Fortunately, you can successfully achieve these goals by performing Feng Shui cures.

Finding a place for the bathroom

I recommend paying particular attention to the position and layout of your bathroom if your intention is to improve any Life Areas of the Octagon associated with the locations discussed in the following list. The following bathroom locations can create particularly negative Feng Shui results.

- ✔ **A bathroom in the center of the house:** This rates as the worst bathroom location of all. The center is the single most important point in the home's interior; a bathroom in the center can drain your health and by extension, negatively affect every part of your life. If your bathroom lies in the center, see the four mirrored walls cure given in the "Curing Troublesome Central Areas" section in Chapter 10. I also recommend that you apply the standard bathroom cures given later in this chapter.

- ✔ **A bathroom at the front entrance or as the first room you see:** A bathroom at the main front entrance to the house can significantly drain the incoming chi from the front door, and therefore, debilitate the energy of the entire house. This arrangement can create significant problems for all areas of your life. (See Chapter 10 for additional bathroom location cures.)

- ✔ **A bathroom in the Wealth Area of the Octagon:** Humans possess a natural preoccupation with acquiring and keeping money, making the Wealth Area (the back left part of the house) a vital area of concern for virtually everyone. A bathroom in the Wealth Area can drain your current funds and lower your potential future wealth. Also keep an eye on a bathroom situated in the Fame or Marriage Areas of the Octagon. My experience has shown that either of these can also be a problem. Use the cures in the following sections for these bathrooms.

Considering positive bathroom layout

The layout of the bathroom hinges on one main factor — whether you can see the toilet when you stand in the bathroom doorway. If the toilet is immediately visible when you open the bathroom door (shown in Figure 13-3a), the effect is negative. The best location for the toilet is behind the bathroom door (as in Figure 13-3b), or behind a wall which makes it invisible from the doorway. Cure this by hanging a faceted crystal sphere from the ceiling halfway between the bathroom door and the toilet. (See Figure 13-3a.)

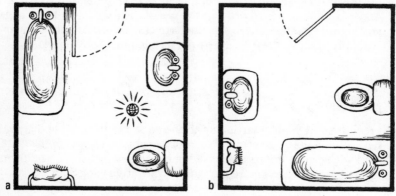

Figure 13-3:
Negative layout showing cure and positive bathroom layout.

Employing basic bathroom cures

The following simple Feng Shui solutions reduce the draining effects of any bathroom. These cures definitely apply to the three danger-level bathrooms explained in the previous section, but you can also apply them for good measure to any bathroom in the house. I recommend the following policy to my clients: When in doubt, apply the cure; you'll be covered — and amazed at the positive results.

Keep the bathroom door shut

Keeping the bathroom door closed is the most basic and fundamental of all bathroom cures. Simple, short, and to the point — yet it makes a real difference in the energy quotient of the home. If your children or hard-to-train guests constantly leave the door open, you can apply a special trick: Replace the standard hinges on the bathroom door with special spring door hinges from the hardware store. These hinges close the door even if others don't remember to.

Hang a full-length mirror on the outside of the door

This cure works in conjunction with the one in the above section: A full-length mirror yields very good effects if you keep the bathroom door shut, but it yields almost no positive effects if you don't keep the door closed. Hanging a full-length mirror on the outside of the bathroom door works for you in two ways. On the energy level, it reflects the chi of the house away from the bathroom so it doesn't get drained. And psychologically, the mirror makes the bathroom vanish from your attention, because the view in the mirror reflects another part of the house.

Keep the toilet lid down and drains closed

The main energetic problem posed by bathrooms involves their drains; stopping or blocking them up helps avoid the loss of chi. Men, this cure asks that you develop one teensy little new habit in your daily life, the same one your mother tried to teach you: "Keep the toilet lid down!" (You didn't know your mother was a Feng Shui master, did you?) In addition to keeping toilet lids down, I recommend that you keep a stopper in the tub and/or shower and sink drains when they are not in use. Both of these cures help to retain energy in the house, and in your life.

Using creativity in the bathroom

You can apply the following suggestions à la carte for your individual bathroom (and life) situations:

- ✔ **Install small round mirrors above the drains to provide additional lifting power.** The mirrors provide lifting power to counteract the downward-pulling effect of the drain, and retain vital chi in the household. The most important location for these mirrors is above the toilet, but they also help above the sink and tub and/or shower drains. Affix a 3-inch round mirror on the ceiling above each drain in the room (mirror side facing down), and visualize that the chi is being uplifted. (See Figure 13-4.)

- ✔ **Add plants for life.** Many bathrooms are somewhat grim and lifeless, but you can easily change their energy with healthy green plants. If your bathroom or green thumb doesn't support real plants, you can substitute realistic, artificial plants, which work as well.

- ✔ **Spruce up the place.** If your bathroom feels stark and bare, warm it up with some healthy and pleasant décor. The Chinese say that a clean and beautiful bathroom helps the household stay healthy and happy (and they're right!). Feng Shui color recommendations are black or white, with brigher colored accents. But you can apply your own taste and enjoy the results. Apply artwork, colorful candles, and/or positive scents to your bathroom and watch your health and attitudes take an upward turn.

Figure 13-4:
Mirror
above
toilet/drain
cure.

The Garage

An attached garage is actually part of the house, even though most people don't consider it as such. Based on its condition and chi, an attached garage can affect any Life Area of the Octagon. The continuous effects of vehicles going in and out of the house (including noise, fumes, and chaotic energy) can disturb the chi of any Life Area. Check out the Octagon of your floor plan to determine where your garage lies. For example, depending on its energy condition, a garage in the Marriage Area can put a strain on the relationship. (See Chapter 3 for more information on the Feng Shui Octagon.)

If you usually enter your house through the garage, according to the principle that the first thing you see affects you, the condition of the garage strongly conditions your personal energy. If you constantly view a messy, dark, and dirty garage you can feel frustrated and cranky, for no good reason. Apply old-fashioned elbow grease to the situation and spruce it up as much as possible. The whole house — and the family — will feel much better.

The ideal situation is to have an unattached garage, which (though more inconvenient) is better for the energy of the home in general. If the garage is unattached, the décor is not as important, but it still should not be a mess, or jammed to the gills with all those vital belongings (like those 12 year-old newspapers, and report cards from your third grade classes). Unattached garages affect the energy of your land more than your house. See more about these outbuildings in Chapter 7.

Utility Rooms and Basements

Utility rooms include mud rooms, back or side entryways, utility/mechanical rooms, and laundry rooms. The basic Feng Shui rule for all these rooms is the same: Keep them neat, clean, and free of junk and clutter.

Basements affect the entire house because they are the foundation environment that supports the upper floors. If your basement is damp, scary, wet, dark, cluttered, or stuffed, why not grab your shovel and clean it up? By doing so, you can resolve long-standing issues and problems and clear up life situations you didn't even know existed!

Chapter 14

Parts Is Parts: Other Important Areas of the House

• •

• •

In this chapter, I present a veritable potpourri of cures for the individual features that make up and adorn the living spaces in many homes. These parts include doors, windows, walls, hallways, stairways, skylights, beams, fireplaces, and appliances. All these parts affect the energy of a house.

In the following sections, I show you how to alter these elements to improve their energetic effects. Read on to gain the solutions.

Doors and Doorways

A door's primary purpose is to admit the good things we want; secondly it excludes bad, negative, and harmful things. A door relates to its respective house or room as the mouth does to the body, so the energy of your doors and doorways is a key important contributor to the overall Feng Shui of the space. Though the main door is the most important one (see Chapter 9), all doors in a home impact its energy — and your energy. The two key Feng Shui aspects of doors are: how the energy gets to and into the door, and how it flows into and affects the room.

The energy of a space is conditioned in large part by the way it enters the space, which is primarily through the door. The energetic function of a door is to channel energy into the space it addresses. The visible side of this function is the people who walk through the door, while the invisible side is the chi, or life force energy, that circulates into the space. Desirable energy characteristics in a house or room are smooth, balanced, and harmonious; undesirable energy characteristics include blocked, chaotic, stagnant, rushing, or piercing.

Door alignments: The good, the bad, and the inscrutable

In Feng Shui, doorways positioned across from each other in a hallway can either agree or disagree energetically depending on how they're aligned.

The following points offer a short course on door alignments and how they can affect you (see Figure 14-1).

- ✔ If the doors are the same size and completely aligned with each other (see Figure 14-1a), they agree, which is good — no problem.
- ✔ If the doors are the same size and completely unaligned, this is also fine. (See Figure 14-1b.)
- ✔ Doors that are the same size and slightly misaligned — called *biting jaw doors* — can result in disagreements and conflicts between the occupants of the rooms (not shown in figure). Cure these doors by hanging a crystal or wind chime in the hall between the two doors.
- ✔ If the doors are obviously misaligned, cure this by mounting mirrors at the two wall positions shown in Figure 14-1c.
- ✔ If one door is larger than another that is directly opposes it (as in Figure 14-1d), the larger door devours the smaller one. This negative situation impacts you much more if one of the two doors is a bedroom, a bathroom, or a kitchen door. The cure is to hang a faceted crystal sphere in the hall between the two doors.

Solving the empty door problem

A missing door (called an *empty door* in Feng Shui) is an interior door where the doorway exists, but with no physical door in place. This condition is okay in the living room, dining room, and kitchen, but is a big problem if it leads into the bedroom (or bathroom). A missing bedroom door can mean that a spouse is gone often, and the marriage can unravel. Fortunately, this situation can easily be cured by putting an actual door in the door frame. If this cure is impossible in your situation, you can also hang a curtain across the doorway. This variation has effect even if the curtains are kept drawn back from the doorway most of the time.

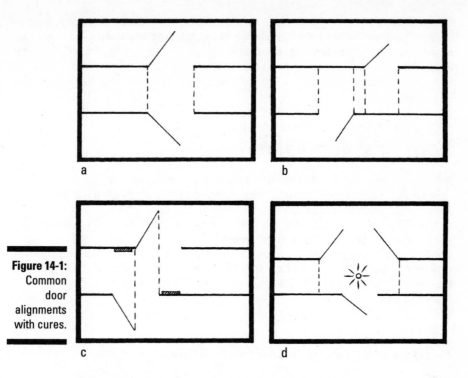

a

b

c

d

Figure 14-1:
Common
door
alignments
with cures.

Addressing more than three doorways in a row

As you proceed down a hallway, passing through three or more doorways can create a negative condition called *heart-piercing arrow,* a particularly harmful form of the poison arrow problem. Each doorway gradually compresses and focuses the chi until it functions like a shooting arrow that pierces the personal chi of the residents. If this hallway terminates at a bathroom or a bedroom, the situation becomes acute. The cure is simple: Hang two or more faceted crystal spheres between the doorways, along the pathway through the doorways.

Curing clashing doors

When one door physically hits another at any point of its swing, the condition is called *clashing doors.* Clashing doors can induce conflict, arguments, and misperception between members of the household. This principle applies to all inside, outside, closet, and cabinet doors in the house. For example, if the master bedroom door swings open and hits a closet door in the bedroom, the energy of these doors striking each other can create marital discord and confusion between the partners. Similar situations can ensue in any other area of the house. To cure this problem, hang a bright red drapery tassel from each doorknob of the clashing doors, on the sides where they touch. (See the "Hallways" section of this chapter to cure multiple doorways in a small space.)

Setting stuck doors free

If doors in your house can't open easily, don't work correctly, or get stuck on the floor or frames, the energy in the house can't flow smoothly. If one of these problems exists at the main front door, the entire household can experience problems (see Chapter 9 for more details). If the master bedroom door sticks, your career can be blocked or stifled. Restroom door problems can create havoc with your taxes and accounting. The door to the dining room relates to your financial welfare, and the door to the kitchen affects both wealth and health. The cure for this problem is realigning, repairing, or replacing the faulty door(s).

Relieving a "reversed" door

In Feng Shui, a door that opens near a wall, making the view very small at first, is called a *reverse door*. The cure is to change the door so it opens to the wider part of the room. If this proves impractical, you can apply a mirror to the wall near the door as shown in Figure 14-2. This mirror visually opens the space, providing a feeling of freedom and flow where constriction formerly prevailed.

Figure 14-2:
Door
opening to
tight space
with mirror
cure.

Treating angled doors

Whether you enter a space in a straight line or at an angle impacts both the quality of your experiences and your overall life course, profoundly conditioning your body, mind, and spirit. A straight entry symbolizes regular and balanced energies, while an angled one implies off-balance or off-kilter effects. Feng Shui refers to angled doors with the colorful phrase "wicked doors that bring evil chi." (To see an angled door, check out Figure 14-3.)

Problems created by angled doors include physical maladies (spinal, bone, and joint issues), emotional distortions, accidents, and big heapin' platters o' bad luck. From these examples, you can easily see the importance of curing angled doors. Although any angled door is unfortunate, the greatest problems result from an angled front, master bedroom, or office door. You can easily implement a cure for this problem by hanging two metal wind chimes or faceted crystal spheres, one outside and one inside the angled door. (See Figure 14-3.)

Figure 14-3: Angled door with cures.

Windows: The Eyes of Your House

How you see out your windows strongly influences your psychology, your energy, and your daily activities. Windows that open outward rate better in Feng Shui than those that open inward, sideways, or upward, because an outward opening window accepts more energy into the home. Also, windows that open widely allow more positive energy to enter than those that open only part way.

Your view out the window is a good metaphor for your relationship with the outside world. Windows represent how you see both your present world (literally) and (symbolically) how you view you your future. If the view is depressing, blocked, or chaotic, this influence finds its way into your psyche. Windows also symbolically connect to the eyes; damaged, stuck, or blocked windows can induce eyestrain and other vision problems.

Windows blocked from the inside or outside

If the view from your windows is blocked, both your career and future can suffer. In addition, blocked windows can promote depression, stagnation, and frustration. For the growth of your career — and to see bright possibilities in your future — I recommend that you remove obstructions that keep you from seeing the street (or any front view) from your front windows.

I also recommend that vegetation next to your house not extend above the bottom of the windows. If bushes, trees, or other obstacles cover your windows — even partially — from the outside, trim back the bushes to allow a clear view from the interior. If you have a large tree in front of your window, you can trim some of the branches, hang a faceted crystal sphere in the window (inside the house), or hang a wind chime with a pleasant sound between the tree trunk and the window (outside the house).

A designer client had tree branches blocking several of her front windows, blocking the view of her street and front yard. After trimming the branches to allow a much wider view, she felt more encouraged in life, moved ahead more quickly in her career, and experienced greater income.

Windows blocked from the inside of the house are just as bad as ones blocked from the outside. The simple solution: Move the offending bookcase, box, or other item away from the window, see the world more clearly, and have a smoother career and social life.

Stuck, malfunctioning, sealed, or broken windows

Windows in the home should work smoothly and easily for maximum visibility and good eyesight. Windows that malfunction, or are cracked or broken, are painted shut, can bring problems with your eyesight or for the children of the household. The cure is to repair the windows so they work perfectly. If a window proves impossible to fix, you can attach a 3-inch round mirror to the windowpane. This cure lets the window and house energetically breathe, relieving energetic pressure and stuffiness.

More windows than doors

In Feng Shui, windows symbolically represent the voices of children in the home, another good reason to fix any window problems soon. An overabundance of windows in comparison to the doors (which represent parents' voices) can cause the parents' voices to be unheard, and the children to start controlling the household. For this situation, it is necessary to determine the balance of windows to doors purely by intuition and feel, rather than by a mathematical ratio. (My standard recommendation is: If in doubt, do the cure — and see the benefits.) You can cure this by hanging a faceted crystal sphere in front of each window to balance their overabundant energies.

Windows that are too high, too low, or come down too far

If a window is positioned very high in a wall and prevents you from seeing out, you can feel uneasy, controlled, or stifled, especially if the high windows are located in the bedroom. This is not a major problem, so if these types of windows don't bother you, no cure is necessary.

But if you feel this situation is troublesome, hang a mural or painting that depicts an outdoor scene on the wall. Position it below a too-high window or above a window that is too low. You can also hang a mirror in either of these positions instead of a painting of the great outdoors. This is also a good cure to do if you have no or too few windows in a space.

A window that comes down "too far" (or has a bottom sill that is quite close to the floor) can make you feel overexposed and vulnerable. You can use potted plants to cover the window to at least knee height or higher. A client who always felt her neighbors were watching her performed this cure, and suddenly felt comfortable and free in her neighborhood.

Skylights

According to the Feng Shui principle that "the house represents the physical body," skylights represent having a hole (or other possible problems) in the back of the body or the head. This symbology can result in unfortunate accidents involving the back or head. The most dangerous skylight is one that is added to an existing house. Cutting a hole in the roof can foreshadow future surgery or accidents. Especially suspect are skylights near the entrance or center of the house, in the kitchen, and in the master bedroom. These situations can potentially affect both a person's financial and physical well-being.

Cutting a hole in the roof of the house without applying proper Feng Shui precautions can result in accidents involving the head. Recommended precautions include choosing a fortunate date and time to begin the project (see Chapter 19) and performing the Rice Blessing before starting the work (see Chapter 17).

You can cure a skylight by hanging a faceted crystal sphere from the center (see Figure 14-4). A clear suction cup is a good method for attaching the sphere.

Figure 14-4:
Skylight
showing
crystal cure.

Angled Walls

According to Feng Shui principles, angled walls (which run diagonally across a floor plan) are a negative feature in any home (see Figure 14-5). The angle tends to speed up the energy flow along the wall. The slant results in rushing chi, which can flow too fast and throw things off balance (out of harmony) in the home. It's important to remember that energy circulates throughout your house all the time — whether you see and feel it or not.

Make angled walls a high priority to cure if they're located in a room or Life Area where you currently experience life problems. For example, if an angled wall stands in the Marriage Area of your bedroom and your relationship has been plagued by arguments since you moved into the house, consider this angled wall a prime place to cure. Of course, you can physically move and straighten the slanted wall. However, this is not usually a practical solution, and excellent and easier choices are available. Two effective cures are given in the following sections.

Anchoring the energy of an angled wall

A good way to handle the chi of an angled wall is to place a cure at each end of the wall (see Figure 14-5). For example, place a healthy green plant at each end of the wall to anchor the energy of the angle. Or put a lamp at one end and a plant at the other. This method effectively controls and harnesses the powerful energy of the angled wall. The angled wall can become your friend and benefactor — rather than a troublemaker.

Figure 14-5:
Angled wall
with light
and plant
cures.

Slowing down or diffusing the flow of energy

The slanted wall creates an imbalance in the room, with increased pressure and restriction to the narrow end, expansion at the wider. To slow down or diffuse the flow of chi in your home, hang a wind chime or a faceted crystal sphere from the ceiling at the center of the angled wall. This cure makes the energy in your home flow more peacefully. Another effective method is to mirror the entire slanted wall to reflect the opposite wall, which gives the slanted wall the illusion and feeling of being square. If you use a partial mirror, mirror closest to the narrow side, especially if near an entry.

Hallways

Hallways are main energy arteries of the house that conduct chi, information, and people through the space. Consider these factors for a hallway: length, width, number of doors, lighting, and — most importantly — its feel. The best hallways feel open and clear, with a free flow of energy. In the following sections, I detail common hallway issues and simple, yet effective solutions. (For information on the best door alignments within a hallway, see the "Doors and Doorways" section earlier in this chapter.)

Hallways with too many doors

A hallway that contains too many doors in a small space can cause fighting within the family, and you can find yourself continuously using up all the money you earn. To cure this, mirror all the wall spaces in the hall (see Figure 14-6). You can place sizeable rectangular mirrors on each wall, or mirror the entire wall surface. Or, you can cure this problem by hanging one to three wind chimes or faceted crystal spheres in the hallway to calm and modulate the flows of energy. For a grander solution, install leaded crystal chandeliers.

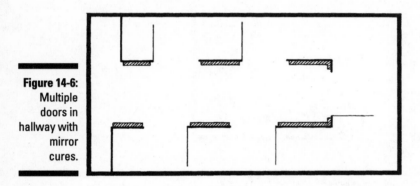

Figure 14-6: Multiple doors in hallway with mirror cures.

Long and narrow hallways

If a hallway is very long and narrow, people passing through can experience an oppressive or tight feeling. A long, narrow hall can conduct rushing chi that moves too quickly and can potentially harm the home's energy. To increase the feeling of space and freedom, hang sizeable mirrors (on one side of the hallway or both, square or rectangular, the larger the mirror, the better) along the walls of the hallway to add brightness and create an increased feeling of space and freedom.

A bedroom or bathroom at the very end of a long hall can bode ill for the occupants — even more so if the bed or toilet is visible from the hallway. To cure the rushing energy, you can apply the same cures as for a hallway that contains too many doors. Hang crystals or chimes from the ceiling, or, line the hall with mirrors.

Stairs

Stairways are pathways bearing chi and people. Stairways also connect levels of a residence or structure. Depending on the construction, the energy of a stairway either feeds the floors it connects, or prevents a free flow of energy between the floors. This section focuses on spiral staircases and how to cure their problematic affects. (For information on outside stairs leading to the front door, see Chapter 9.)

Transforming spiral staircases

Spiral stairways create many Feng Shui problems, more so if you install them after your house is built. Their energy drills down into the ground like a bore or augur, pulling chi and fortunes downward. This downward energy spiral affects the room and the Life Area where the stairway is located. Spiral staircases can also cause health issues. If the landing faces the front door, illness or brain disease can result. Or if the staircase is located in the center of the home, residents can experience heart problems. The following list details several options for curing a spiral staircase:

✔ **Wrap a green silk, ivy vine along the stair banister, from the bottom all the way to the top.** The symbolic living energy of the vine stimulates growth and life and counteracts the negative effect of the stairs. This cure is the best one to perform for this situation. (See Figure 14-7.)

✔ **Hang a faceted crystal sphere or windchime at the top of the stairway.** The cure draws the energy up the stairs and reverses the downward energy spiral.

✔ **Place a large, healthy green plant (live or artificial) at the base underneath the spiral stairs.** The rising energy of the plant provides a symbolic upward antidote to the downward spiraling energy of the stairs.

When performing these cures, visualize your life being dramatically uplifted and improved, particularly in the Octagon Life Area where your staircase resides.

Looking at assorted stairway problems and simple cures

The following stairway problems are easily cured; if left untouched, they can create unpleasant feelings and thoughts.

✔ **Dark, tight, or claustrophobic stairs:** These stairways are frightening, depressing, and oppressive to the residents who navigate their paths. Treat this problem by shining lots of bright and pleasing light on the stairs.

> ✔ **Rickety, unsafe stairs, or missing or broken banister:** These stairways can make your life unstable and can be a literal health hazard. The cure: Fix 'em!

See Chapter 9 for other stairway cures, including stairs with missing risers, the mandarin duck stairway (stairway at the front door where one stair goes up, the other goes down), stairs that lead to a blocking wall, and stairs with difficult turns (an energy jam). These cures apply equally to indoor as well as outdoor stairs.

Figure 14-7:
Spiral staircase with green vine cure.

Pillars, Columns, and Posts

Pillars, columns, and posts are all terms for the same physical structure. They can block flows of chi and send negative arrows throughout the rooms they inhabit. Cure pillars or columns that stand in the center of a space by mirroring all four sides of the pillar or column. If these structures stand near a wall, applying the cure is even more important.

Another cure is to place a potted plant, preferably with flowers, at the base of the post. A vine from the plant should be trained to grow circularly up the post. Or you can hang four potted plants, one on each side of the post. The plants should feature irregular lengths of vines hanging down to decorate the post. (A post that stands in the corner of a rarely used room is generally unharmful.)

Fireplaces

Fireplaces impact the household based on their location in the Life Areas of the Octagon. (See Chapter 3 for more information about the Octagon.) Fireplaces located in the Fame, Family, and Knowledge Areas are either good or neutral. On the other hand, fireplaces located in the Career, Children, Helpful People, and Health Areas are negative. The final two Life Areas, Wealth and Marriage, can be either positive or negative fireplace locations, so I recommend curing them as well.

To cure a fireplace located in any area of your home, simply place nine healthy green plants around the fireplace and on the mantel. The green energy adds life and balance to the area. For a smaller version of the cure, place just one plant in front of the mouth of the fireplace. Another cure option for a fireplace involves hanging a large mirror over the fireplace. The mirror, representing water, helps balance out the fire chi. (See Figure 14-8.)

Figure 14-8:
Fireplace with nine green plant and mirror cures.

Ceilings

The ideal ceiling is a flat ceiling, proportionate to the size of the room and the house — not too high, and not too low. For the best Feng Shui effects, I recommend curing multileveled, slanted, and other seemingly interesting ceilings.

Handling multileveled, slanted, and uneven ceilings

Multileveled, slanted, or uneven ceilings can cause confusion, mental instability, and differences of opinion among the residents. Specific results can include mood swings, and blood pressure and blood sugar level problems. A home with a one-level ceiling for the whole house (or per floor of the house) is preferred. One level of ceiling per room (rather than multi-leveled) is also important. If your ceiling issues seem difficult for you to handle even with the following information, consider contacting a professional Feng Shui consultant for recommendations (see the Feng Shui Resources page at the end of this book for consultant sources).

At a Feng Shui consultation, the ceilings of the condominium were extremely high (anywhere from 18 to 30 feet high) for a fairly small structure, and multileveled. The house felt like a tower, and the ceiling over the master bed was more than 15 feet high and slanted. I wasn't surprised when the client reported that the previous occupant became imbalanced and completely wrecked the house. These multiple design factors (small house, extremely high, slanted, and multi-leveled ceilings) likely conspired to create an unfortunate influence on the psyche of the resident. Using the cures given in the following sections helped the couple feel much more relaxed and mentally stable in their home.

Dealing with slanted ceilings over the bed

A slanted ceiling presses down on the heads of the sleepers, creating mental pressure, headaches, strife, troubled sleep, and the constant desire to get up and leave the room. Generally, a slanted ceiling over your bed can make for an unpleasant situation. The cure is to hang a wind chime or faceted crystal sphere directly over the head of the bed. (See Figure 14-9.) Or, you can place lights shining upward, or plants or Feng Shui flutes hung vertically under the slant to provide a lifting effect under the low portion.

Applying general ceiling cures

For a multilevel ceiling, you can install false ceilings to create the appearance of a more-level and more-even surface. A less expensive cure is to artistically drape fabric over head throughout the open space; this cure breaks up the lines and replaces the hard angles with softer flows of energy. For another option, hang large mobiles or crystal chandeliers from the ceilings. High-quality crystal chandeliers are an especially effective solution for a multilevel ceiling.

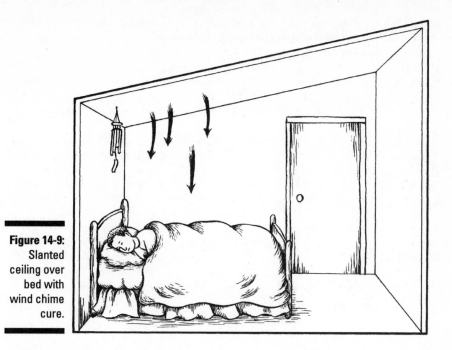

Figure 14-9:
Slanted
ceiling over
bed with
wind chime
cure.

Beams

Beams act as oppressive forces that can create division, repression, and a feeling of suffocation among the occupants of the house. Any place where people enter, sit, or lie down can receive negative effects from an overhead beam. A beam over the stove can depress your finances and physical health. Over the desk, a beam can block your career, and one over the dining table can hurt both your career and social life. The worst Feng Shui beams are ones that go over the bed; they depress both the marriage and health. (If a beam is very high, very small, or hard to notice, residents may receive little or no negative effects.) I provide Feng Shui cures for troublesome beams over your bed and in other areas of your home in the following sections.

Curing a beam over the bed

The ideal bedroom ceiling is flat across the whole room, is neither too high nor too low, and is beam free. A beam over the bed can create unseen pressures on the bed and on you — physically, mentally, and emotionally.

A beam that runs the length of the bed can exert unwanted pressure on the entire body. If you sleep with a partner, the beam can urge the partner under the beam to flee the relationship. If the beam runs between the partners, it can split them apart. And if a beam runs across the bed, it can create physical problems in whatever body parts it crosses. For example, a beam across the foot area of the bed can induce ankle and foot pain or even accidents, and a beam across the stomach can create indigestion and stomach pain.

Here's the best cure for most beam-over-the-bed situations. Hang two special bamboo Feng Shui flutes on the beam at 45 degree angles, placing one at each end of the beam. (Refer to Chapter 11, Figure 11-4 for visual guidance on hanging these flutes.) The symbolism of the flutes provides a powerful uplifting effect and creates relief from the pressure and oppression of the beam.

If the beam over the bed runs along a peaked ceiling, the cure contains two parts. First (if possible) move the bed so it's under the highest part of the ceiling. Second, hang two flutes at 45 degree angles on the wall over the bed, under the beam. See Figure 14-10. For best results, intensely visualize your desired outcome when applying the cures. (Visualization really works! And the details await you in Chapter 6.)

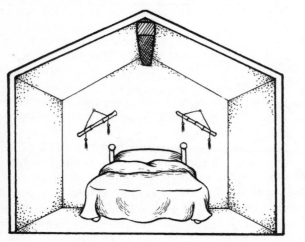

Figure 14-10:
Bed under peaked ceiling and beam with flute cure.

Resolving beams throughout the home

In my consulting experience, flutes have the most curing power for oppressive beams. If you don't want to hang flutes, you can hide the beams with fabric or a false ceiling, or even by painting the beams the same color as the ceiling. If the beams' color already matches the ceiling and still feels oppressive, hang a Feng Shui bamboo flute at both ends of the beam, as recommended in the previous section.

One of my consultations involved Larry, a real estate investor, whose wife had decided to leave the marriage. During the session, I discovered that a beam ran the length of his bed, directly over the area where his wife slept. A few days after Larry hung a bamboo flute at each end of the beam — the recommended cure — his wife returned to the house and the relationship.

Living with the Parts You Can't Live Without

Feng Shui is about finding the best way to live with society's current conditions and practices. Therefore, the practice is continuously updated to deal with factors that weren't present throughout the long history of Feng Shui's development. Modern conveniences and appliances are energy generators, and you can utilize them to better your home's energy.

- ✔ **Wall air conditioners and ventilation units:** A wall unit in any of these Life Areas could use a cure: in the Wealth Area (your money may blow away), in the Family Area (unity can suffer), or in the Marriage Area (cold water is symbolically thrown on the relationship). For this cure, start with a piece of fabric — large enough to cut into strips — of either solid red, ocean print, or a print of dancing human figures. Once you've chosen your fabric, cut it into strips; for the human figure print, cut out the individual little people (but don't cut them up). Hang the cloth strips in front of the air flowing from the unit so the pieces dance in the air. This cure will change the unit from a detriment to a positive influence. Visualize positive effects for the Life Area you cure with this solution.

- ✔ **TV and stereo systems:** Television sets, VCRs, and stereo equipment are energetically positive when found in the Knowledge or Helpful People Areas of your home's Feng Shui Octagon. These Areas are found in the right front and left front corners of your house. (See Chapter 3 to determine your home's Octagon.) If your audiovisual equipment sits in another area of your home, you can place healthy green plants anywhere within 3 feet of the units to balance their energy.

- ✔ **Computers:** A computer in the Knowledge Area can help make you smarter; in the Career Area, it can advance your career. With a computer in the Marriage Area, you may find computers involved in your marriage partnership — or you may find that special someone over the Internet. If your computer's in the Wealth Area, you're likely to obtain superior financial information by computer. The Family Area, however, is probably not the best location for a computer, because you want living energy of people rather than machine energy in this area. Computers are also beneficial in the Helpful People/Travel Area and in the Fame Area of the house. To strengthen any of these positive computer positions, use the Three Secrets Reinforcement, as explained in Chapter 6. (See Chapter 3 to determine where your home's Life Areas sit.)

✔ **Cords in the office:** If messy cords show behind your desk, information can become confused or snarled. Bunch unsightly cords neatly behind potted plants, or decorate the cords aesthetically with vines.

Chapter 15

Powerful Ways to Boost Your Home's Energy

• •

In This Chapter

▶ Recognizing the energy benefits of proper lighting

▶ Getting rid of your mess (and your problems)

▶ Feeling the magic of a clean living space

▶ Coloring yourself happy

▶ Keeping everything working

• •

From lighting up dark and dreary rooms to clearing the junk and useless clutter from your life, keeping your home clean and colorful can enhance your home's useful energies. In this chapter, I cover key areas that can perk up the energy of any home.

Lighting Up Your Life To See Positive Results

According to Feng Shui principles, adding light to an area increases its chi and can make positive changes in your home and life. In this section, I discuss the overall quality of the light in your environment. The type and quality of the lighting in your home and workplace can either improve or harm your health, moods, prosperity, and destiny. (See Chapter 4 for additional tips on applying light cures to specific parts of your home.)

A key area to infuse with good lighting is your entryway — both inside and outside your front door — because light levels in this area can set the mood for the energy of your entire house. In addition, bright light in the entryway can assist your career and fortune. Another good principle is to ensure that all key rooms of the house (the bedroom, kitchen, and dinning room) contain strong bright lights even if you don't keep them on all the time. These lights can have dimmer switches if you enjoy lower level lighting, as long as the lights can potentially be turned on brightly at any time.

Nurturing health and life with natural light

The light created by the sun is the best type of light for both your body and mind. Feng Shui Grandmaster Lin Yun regards the body as the primary environment for practicing Feng Shui; the body is even more important than your house or bedroom. One good way to take advantage of this principle is to receive more light from nature. You can enjoy natural lighting by going outside more often, such as during your lunch hour or, at a minimum, during your morning and afternoon breaks. This practice is especially good for people who work all day inside sealed office buildings with an absence of natural light. If you can see out a window while you work, the light helps immensely, but because of the way clear glass filters sunlight, this situation isn't as beneficial as being directly outside. Receiving direct sunlight is best (be careful not to burn), but even if the sky is cloudy, you can still gain many benefits from sunlight.

The latest findings by light researchers indicate that the body intrinsically needs to consume natural light on a regular basis. The sun's light activates, energizes, and balances your system. Sunrise, noontime, and sunset are particularly effective and mood-enhancing times to receive the sun's light. You can receive the sun's maximum energy at noontime (just be cautious about getting too much direct exposure). You can also get good quality light by walking through woods. The filtered and dappled light that comes through the trees creates a unique calming effect. This soothing activity is becoming more vital as people spend more of their time indoors and in front of computer terminals.

A little known but highly effective method for receiving light from nature is gazing at the moon — the longer the better. Moonlight produces calming, cooling, and refreshing effects, which increase feelings of hope, peace, and optimism. Seeing the moon during any part of its cycle is helpful, but the light of the full moon is most beneficial. In fact, the ancient masters prescribed the special practice of staring at the full moon all night — a method described as powerful enough to heal 108 diseases. Mental (or internal) uses of sunlight and moonlight give additional benefits to the body and spirit. See the sunlight visualization exercise in Chapter 18.

Taking advantage of natural-light substitutes indoors

Spending too much time exposed solely to artificial light can greatly affect your energy, moods, sleep patterns, and work abilities. If your environment receives little natural light or you spend lots of time indoors, you can supplement your light diet by using full-spectrum bulbs available for both incandescent and fluorescent lamps. Full-spectrum lights closely resemble the light of the sun, whereas fluorescent lights give off a cool blue light and emit less light from the warmer, yellow end of the spectrum.

For a better but more expensive solution, you can install special Ott lights, which specifically provide huge amounts of healthy light. Many people find that these lights work wonders for their depression or seasonal mood swings, a condition called *Seasonal Affective Disorder* (SAD), during the winter months. By providing exposure to full-spectrum light — the kind Mother Nature intended — natural lighting stimulates the pineal gland, suppressing melatonin, a sleep hormone overproduced by SAD victims. For further information on natural light and product sources, see the Feng Shui Resources page at the end of this book.

Recognizing the importance of improving interior lighting levels

The best type of interior lighting is bright and pleasant without feeling harsh. Dimly lit rooms are fine as long as you can turn on a bright light at any time.

Make sure that rooms are equally lit on both sides. A Western researcher found that people tend to feel comfortable and remain in rooms lit on both (opposite) sides, but they tend to leave quickly from rooms lit on only one side.

One key issue pertains to bedroom lighting: The bedroom should contain at least one light that brightly lights the entire room by itself. (This solution works even if you don't often use the bright light.) A bedroom containing only dim light can represent a bleak future, can make you depressed and moody, and can also create difficulties in finding a partner or enjoying a happy relationship.

Bright lighting is also essential in the kitchen. Aside from the practicality of needing enough light to cook well, be aware that dim light in the kitchen can depress your health.

Getting Rid of Things You Don't Need

Within the last few years, a big wave of books has surfaced urging everyone to get rid of their excess junk and clear the clutter. The experts' opinions vary on the merits of throwing out your stuff versus straightening and organizing your things. I advocate following both approaches, but emphasize throwing out things you don't need.

The problem with accumulated stuff is that the excess weighs you down, both literally and figuratively. A space filled with unnecessary belongings slows you down in life, making it more difficult for your life to flow, progress, and evolve. I suggest that you employ Feng Shui energy techniques to change the chi of cluttered spaces, so the areas don't automatically accumulate more loads of needless stuff.

Realizing that less is more

Working with clients, I notice that homes stuffed with many large items (like heavy furniture) also tend to gather lots of small items (books, papers, junk, and piles of all descriptions). This phenomenon obeys a basic principle — like attracts like. An already crowded environment tends to get even more jam-packed. Therefore, if you own too much stuff now, you are more likely to accumulate even more junk later. Talk about a vicious cycle!

Good Feng Shui requires that energy flows freely through your home. If you store too much stuff, energy doesn't move well. Take this hint: If moving from one side of your house to the other is difficult — or requires advanced acrobatics — you probably own a few things that you can do without.

You may have different clutter level needs than others. If you can't be creative in a super-neat office, don't try. Creativity is often stifled when your mind is busy observing the 101 things that you need to clean up. Clearing an area of clutter can free your mind — and your body will surely follow.

Families imprint patterns of keeping and saving during childhood, and these behaviors can be difficult to change. Unfortunately, the psychic clinging to the past holds you back from moving forward. In addition, having too many belongings reflects a level of subconscious clutter. What you don't want to look at in your space inevitably reflects what you don't want to see in yourself. By clearing your environment, you can substantially upgrade your mind, health, and financial flow. The choice is yours — hit the Freudian couch or start loadin' the dumpster!

If your space contains too much stuff, you can choose from three options: get rid of the excess, move to a larger house, or rent a storage space. I obviously recommend the first choice, but you can definitely benefit from the other two, depending on your needs. As you move through the junk, I suggest following a tried and true rule: If you haven't used the item for at least a year, you likely never will — and can profitably let it go.

Proclaiming independence: Clearing and removing your junk

My advice is to get motivated and ruthless with the clutter — right now. The more quickly you move, the more you can accomplish, and the more liberated you can become. Follow these simple tips to move the energy and drop the excess stuff — lickety-split!

- **Make a long-term commitment to keeping fewer material belongings.** You'll find that your mind and body (and many other areas of your life) will thank you, and the best thing is, you'll probably never miss 99 percent of the stuff you throw out.

- **Set aside a time every week to clear stuff out.** You probably won't get rid of everything in one session (no kidding!), but the important steps are setting aside the time to clear clutter and getting started as soon as possible.

- **Create destinations for the stuff you want to release.** To donate, give, and dump are the three big choices on the hit parade. Designate one box for each destination — and start tossin'. Give to friends the things that you think they can immediately use. Donate all other useful items to charitable organizations. Recycle as much as possible and trash the rest.

- **Invite over a friend (maybe one with less clutter than you!) and enjoy working as a team to quickly clear out the junk.** He or she may ask you to return the favor at their house — great!

- **Play some energizing music to move your chi.** Singing and dancing while you work helps you release the extraneous belongings.

- **Open all the windows and doors and let a fresh breeze blow into the house.** When new chi enters the house, you can let go of needless things more easily.

- **Focus on one area of the house at a time.** Don't try to tackle everything at once. A small victory in one session gives you the momentum to continue soon and get more done.

✔ **Move the big things out first.** Too many big things in a space magnetically attracts too many small things. Make your clearing job psychologically easier by getting the largest items out first.

✔ **Remove the stuff from the premises on the same day you clear it out.** A good way to solidify gains in this area is to pack the released items in your car and take them away. You end the cleaning experience on a high note, and you'll feel lighter and fresher when you return.

✔ **Remember that all the work is worth your while.** After successfully clearing out a lot of old stuff, people respond with a common reaction: "This freedom feels great! Why didn't I think of this a long time ago?" Why not? Good question. Try clearing the clutter for yourself — and find out!

Clearing the energy so clutter doesn't reappear

The same areas often get cluttered again after you clean. Follow these maintenance tips to help ensure this problem doesn't happen in your house.

✔ **Clean the area thoroughly right after removing the clutter.** Keep an eagle eye on the area for the next few weeks so it doesn't return to its old habits.

✔ **Hang a metal wind chime over the area that held the greatest concentration of clutter.** Visualize or imagine that the chime's ringing clears away stagnant chi and keeps fresh energy flowing in the area (see the visualization tips in Chapter 6).

✔ **Use the power of scent to keep areas fresh and clear.** The proper scent can work wonders for the feelings of a space. Good essential oils during and after cleaning include pine, lemon grass, citronella, tea tree oil, and rosemary. Use an *aromatherapy diffuser,* a device that propagates the desired scent throughout the space (see the Feng Shui Resources page at the end of this book). *Note:* High quality always pays off when purchasing essential oils. Alternatively, you can use high-quality incense or place fresh cut flowers in the area.

Paying attention to the most clutter-proned areas

No matter what you do, certain areas of the home — chiefly the closets, attics, and storage spaces — tend to draw clutter. In the following sections, I give you some useful tips for keeping these areas clutter-free.

Liberate your closets

The general Feng Shui guideline to keeping a closet clutter-free is simple: Clean it, keep it neat and orderly, and don't stuff it to the gills. If your closets adhere to this guideline, they're likely in order. But because closets are generally repositories of unused, unneeded, and unwanted stuff, attack these places first when removing clutter.

A stuffed closet can prevent energy from moving freely in any Life Area (see Chapter 3). For example, a closet in the Career Area of your home can make it rough to advance at work. Sound familiar? This closet is a prime place to apply remedies if you want that job promotion you really deserve. Therefore, clean out your closet. If your closet is already tidy or you want to make the cure stronger, you can install a bright light in the closet (if it doesn't already contain one). For a triple-decker cure, you can also hang a faceted crystal sphere or a wind chime to enhance the area's energy.

 A closet in the Marriage Area of your home can cause problems for you and your partner, so you may want to apply a cure. You can hang a special Feng Shui bamboo flute at the Marriage angle in the closet; hang the flute at a 45-degree angle, with the left end higher than the right end (see Chapter 4 for flute details).

Open up your attics and storage spaces

Some people — even some clutter experts — adhere to the philosophy that out of sight is out of mind. They pretend that stuffing junk into the attic, basement, closets, or storage space takes care of the clutter problem. Placing clutter out of sight definitely removes it from conscious attention, but the junk isn't gone and neither is its influence. Shuffling things around doesn't solve your excess junk problem, but merely hides it. Here's a wake-up call: What you can't see can actually hold you back. To enhance the energy flow in your home, keep your unseen spaces clean and organized.

Cleaning for Increased Freedom and Happiness

Cleanliness is a fundamental factor of the Feng Shui of your home. *Positive Feng Shui* (or good energy) is virtually impossible to enjoy if you live with dirt. Because hundreds of good books already cover the mundane aspects of cleaning, this section focuses on the energetic aspects of cleaning.

 To help yourself be neater and cleaner, you can hang a faceted crystal sphere in the Knowledge Area of your home (see Chapter 3). The brilliance and clarity of the crystal promote mental clarity, which helps you live cleaner and more organized. For a more direct application, hang the sphere directly over the head of your bed.

You can install a small tabletop fountain in any recently cleaned area. The moving water keeps the energy of the area flowing, making it more difficult for dirt to reaccumulate in the environment. You can also put a fountain in any pesky area that still needs cleaning; the moving water can help you get the job finished more quickly.

If you want to powerfully cleanse physical and psychic energy in an area, you can apply any of the ceremonial cures given in Chapter 17. These blessing ceremonies can significantly help keep the premises clean and free of extraneous belongings. A particularly good one for cleaning purposes is the Orange Peel Blessing (see Chapter 17). If getting started on a major cleaning is difficult, you can apply this cure to unstick the energy and bring fresh chi into the area to make your task easier. To ensure that the place stays clean, performing the ceremony after a cleaning project works wonders.

Adding Life with a Splash of Color

Everybody loves color! In this section, I explain the important benefits of color and the great fun involved in applying color. However, color does more than add wonderful aesthetics to an area. The energies of specific colors create different types of effects on humans. With Feng Shui, you can use colors to change your life circumstances in specific ways. Read on for all the details.

You can choose from many color options for your Feng Shui adjustments. These color methods — all covered in the following sections — include:

✔ Using colors associated with the Octagon Areas

✔ Choosing the best colors to adorn the individual rooms of the house

✔ Applying any of the three special Feng Shui color systems as taught by Grandmaster Lin Yun

Using the colors of the Octagon Areas

Cures using the colors of the Octagon's Life Areas are easy and effective to perform in Feng Shui. (See Chapter 3 for more details on the Feng Shui Octagon.) You can use color to positively adjust the energy of an Octagon Area. You can apply the following color cures as your personal needs and circumstances dictate. See Table 15-1 for a list of the nine Life Areas and their corresponding colors.

✓ **Place an item with a color of the Life Area in the respective area of the house.** For example, using Table 15-1, if you want to increase your wealth, you can place something purple in the Wealth Area of your home (or yard or bedroom.) This cure works! Five of the Life Areas have multiple colors; for example, the Wealth Area uses blue, green, red, and purple. Be sure to visualize positive, desired life results when applying your new colors (see Chapter 6 for tips on visualization).

✓ **Use the color or colors of the Life Area as the main color scheme for a room in the corresponding area of the Octagon.** Instead of placing a single object containing a Life Area color (as described in the previous cure) you can color an entire room. For example, to improve your marriage, decorate a room in the back right part of the house (the Marriage Area) with the color pink.

Table 15-1	Colors of the Octagon Areas
Octagon Area	*Colors To Use*
Helpful People	Gray, black, white
Career	Black, midnight blue
Knowledge	Blue, green, black
Family	Green, blue
Wealth/Money	Purple, green, blue, red
Fame/Reputation	Red
Marriage/Partnership	Pink, white, red
Health	Yellow, earth tones
Children	White

Recognizing good colors for the rooms of the house

Feng Shui advocates particular wall colors for main rooms of the house. From painting an entire room one color to accentuating a room with several colors, applying the following color principles to your most important rooms can enhance your health, moods, and good fortune. If your rooms don't match these colors, you don't necessarily need to change the colors. But if you want to improve an area of your life, you can benefit from enhancing the following rooms with their corresponding colors:

✔ **Master Bedroom:** The best colors for this room include pink, peach, light blue, and light green. Pink is the color of love in Feng Shui, and peach represents high attractiveness to the opposite sex. You can use either peach or pink to attract a mate, but if you use peach, switch to pink after the relationship solidifies to prevent a wandering eye.

✔ **Kitchen:** White is a good color for the kitchen because it shows off colorful food to the best advantage. Accent colors for kitchens include red and/or black. Lots of black — which in Chinese energy theory is the color of water — should be avoided, because it can put out the vital fire energy of the stove.

✔ **Children's bedrooms:** Kid's rooms are best in green and blue; these colors help them grow and flourish. White is also favorable for children. Use darker colors to settle down or calm a child.

✔ **Living room, den, and family room:** Multiple colors and shades work well in these rooms; they help you interact with many different types of people. Earth tones — especially yellow, gold, and shades of brown — are very agreeable, providing grounding and centering in these key rooms. Green and blue are also favorable, adding cheer, life, and growth.

✔ **Dining room:** Pink, green, and blue are the best colors for a dining room. These colors bring positive chi to social gatherings.

Using the three special Feng Shui color systems

Any Feng Shui color system in the following list can initiate powerful and dramatic life results in any Life Area of your home's Octagon. You can choose from the three methods to enhance your home's energy purely on intuition. After settling on a color system, you can select an item to decorate your home that contains all the colors of the method, or bring together multiple items by selecting a separate item for each color.

✔ **The Colors of the Five Elements:** This system uses all five of the following colors together — green, red, yellow, white, and black — to powerfully invoke harmony, balance, creation, and prosperity.

✔ **The Six True Colors:** This system uses white, red, yellow, green, blue, and black. The Six True Colors symbolize healing, blessing, and luck.

✔ **The Seven Rainbow Colors:** This system uses all these colors together: red, orange, yellow, green, blue, indigo, and purple. This rainbow of colors helps bring positive feelings, good luck, and harmony to everyone in the environment.

Keeping Things Shipshape and in Working Order

As I detail in the follow sections, the general maintenance and condition of the systems and appliances in your house directly affect your physical health, so care and attention should be paid to their maintenance and upkeep. Something that is seemingly insignificant to people without Feng Shui awareness, such as a burned-out light bulb in a bedroom light fixture, can create marriage problems or incidents of bad luck — forewarned is forearmed.

Interestingly, the build of the human body closely relates to the structure of a home: The head corresponds to the front entrance, the spinal cord to the beams, and the back to the ceiling and roof. (Outdoors, the bones and skeleton correlate with trees and fences on the property.) Although physical ailments often stem from multiple causes and factors, many individuals find significant relief from disease and environmental sensitivity by fixing problems that relate to faulty systems in their homes. This section provides simple cures that you can apply to the systems of your home to maintain a healthy flow of energy.

Keep systems moving

All the following systems relate to your physical systems as well as your Life Areas (see Chapter 3 for more information on the Life Areas). Plus, the advice is simply common sense and good maintenance.

Plumbing problems

The plumbing systems of the house correspond to the circulatory and digestive systems of the physical body. Problems in these areas can result in many physical ailments, sometimes of an unusual or puzzling nature.

Stopped and clogged drains

Problems with pipes and drains relate directly to the digestive and eliminative functions of the body, specifically the intestinal, excretory, and urinary systems. Clogged drains symbolize a difficulty releasing old things. The cure is easy: Clear the pipes!

Leaking pipes

On the physical level, leaks correspond to urinary and kidney issues. In addition, any leak in the house is immediately suspect for money problems or loss of wealth. Numerous people experience unexpected financial gains and clear up money problems by fixing their leaky faucets, problem toilets, or faulty pipes. Leaks don't need to occur only inside the house to cause problems — leaks anywhere on the property can affect you as well.

Foundation problems

The foundation is the basis for your house structure. Look out for problems including foundation defects and cracks, earthquake damage, excessive moisture, and water infiltration into areas such as basements. Problems in the basement can cause family and job instability and can bring unfortunate health problems.

Electrical problems

The electrical system of the home correlates to the body's nervous system. Fixing faulty wiring, lights, fuse boxes, transformers, phone lines, and computer systems is a good Feng Shui practice for restoring positive chi flow. These fixes can help eliminate physical problems including memory loss, nervousness, irritation, muscle spasms, and even more-serious nervous system issues.

Make sure air is flowing

The heating and air conditioning system in your house relates to your lungs and ease of breathing and blood circulation. The breathing link isn't simply a symbolic connection; proven relationships exist between dirty, debris-filled air ducts and residents who suffer from allergies, breathing difficulties, and respiratory ailments.

You can cure this problem by hiring a professional cleaning company to clear out the ducts at least once a year. Also be sure to clean or change your furnace and air conditioning filters regularly. Another remedy is to use a high-quality vacuum cleaner, preferably one that has a sealed canister system and uses *High Efficiency Particle Arresting* (HEPA) filtration.

Check the roof for potential problems

The roof of your home relates to both the head and the back. Leaks and holes in the roof can represent problems with the head or spine and are best fixed immediately. Take care when cutting holes in the roof; this activity can lead to unexpected accidents or problems involving the head or brain. If you plan to cut any hole (no matter how small) in the roof, you can ensure greater safety by performing the Rice Blessing (see Chapter 17) the day the project begins. A stronger method is to perform this cure both at the beginning and the end of the project. In addition, I advise making the first cut in the roof between 11:00 a.m. and 1:00 p.m., while visualizing that the workers and the home's family members experience freedom from harm. (Find visualization tips in Chapter 6 and cure-timing pointers in Chapter 19.)

Fix or replace malfunctioning or broken elements

Malfuncting items pose Feng Shui problems; anything defective in your environment creates the energy of decay, which symbolizes death on the property. Make sure that everything on the premises either works correctly or is thrown away, and fix anything that needs repair as quickly as possible. The following list of examples gives you an idea of how items in disrepair can affect you. The cure for each instance is quite clear: Fix it!

- ✔ **Burned-out light bulbs, missing bulbs, and broken fixtures reflect a dim future and indicate bad luck.** When bulbs go out, the best practice is to replace them rapidly with bulbs at least as bright as the old ones.

- ✔ **Broken and malfunctioning clocks symbolize that time is running out on you!** Clocks that keep time poorly encourage confusion and missed appointments.

- ✔ **A broken garbage disposal indicates digestive and excretion problems.** This situation affects all members of the household.

- ✔ **Stove problems harm the pocketbook and the body.** In fact, stove maintenance is so important that I devote an entire section to curing the stove in Chapter 10.

- ✔ **Broken bed elements are a top Feng Shui priority.** The bed affects just about every Life Area you can imagine, so repairs to the bed are essential for good Feng Shui.

And don't even get me started on rusting or derelict cars in the garage or yard!

Chapter 16

Using Feng Shui to Enhance Your Career

In This Chapter

▶ Relying on the Octagon and the Five Elements in the office

▶ Inspecting your office floor plan

▶ Assuming the Commanding Position at work

▶ Finding a good desk for a great career

▶ Using the Octagon to arrange your desk

▶ Sitting pretty in a good chair

This book is designed for practical individual and family empowerment, so in this chapter, I deal only with your personal workspaces. Here, you can find ways to improve your career by performing Feng Shui in your personal workspace and in your home office. After you've applied the solutions in this chapter, if you want to take further steps in using Feng Shui to enhance your career, you may want to consult a professional Feng Shui practitioner.

Using the Feng Shui Octagon and the Five Elements in Your Office

The Octagon and the Five Elements can help you maximize the power of your office space. Apply the simple methods in the following sections to implement these powerful systems.

The Octagon

On a scale drawing of your office or cubicle, draw in the existing furniture. Artistic skill is not required, and stick furniture drawings are fine. This drawing can help you place the Feng Shui Octagon on the floor plan. The Octagon is placed on your office, room, or cubicle exactly like any other room (see Chapter 3 for detailed instructions for placing the Octagon). After you map out the Octagon, you can apply cures to any Life Area to meet your intentions. Figure 16-1 shows you how to place the Feng Shui Octagon on your office.

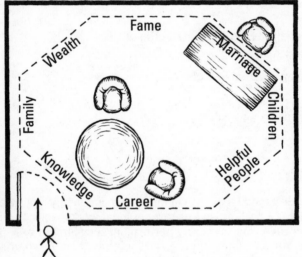

Figure 16-1:
Placing the
Octagon on
your office.

Refer to Chapter 8 for information that can help you determine whether your office contains projections or missing areas. For instance, if your office is L-shaped, one or more Life Areas are missing, which can negatively impact your business life. Missing areas in the shape of your office reflect missing energy in the Life Area affected. If the Wealth Area of your office is missing (for example, if a corner is "cut out" of the room in the back left area), you can find it much harder to bring in money. After you spot a missing area, you can correct its harmful influences by performing a cure, such as hanging a faceted crystal sphere to energetically complete the area. See Chapter 8 and Figure 8-3 for a clear idea of how to apply this cure.

The Five Elements

You can use the Five Elements in your home, your business, and your individual rooms, such as your personal office or even your cubicle. The Five Elements are natural phases of energy (Wood, Fire, Earth, Metal, and Water) that occur in every environment. Feng Shui gives you the opportunity to take advantage of their powers to further your career. Each Element's natural position corresponds to one of the Life Areas of the Octagon (as detailed in the following sections).

To discover more about the nature and uses of the Five Elements, see Chapter 5. And remember, Five Element cures are effective even if you don't fully understand the meaning of the Five Elements, just as you can taste spices in your food even if you didn't see the chef put them in. Apply the cures and find out for yourself!

Orienting the Five Elements in your office

Orienting from the main door of the office (or cube), the Five Elements should be placed on your floor plan in their natural locations on the Octagon.

- ✔ **Wood Element:** Center of the left side of the space, the Family Area
- ✔ **Fire Element:** Center of the back side of the space, the Fame Area
- ✔ **Earth Element:** Center of the space, the Health Area
- ✔ **Metal Element:** Center of the right side of the space, the Children Area
- ✔ **Water Element:** Center of the front side (the one nearest the door) of the space, the Career Area

Finding cures for your career

The purpose of the information in the following sections is to use the Elements that work for you. You don't necessarily need to empower all five of the Elements, although you can if you wish.

Wood

To increase the growth, expansion, and upward movement of your career, place Wood in its natural location. Wood helps you reach higher, grow into new areas in life, put down solid roots, and break through obstacles. To enhance your Wood energy, you can put any of the following items in Wood's natural location:

- ✔ A lively green plant
- ✔ Any object or piece of art containing the colors green and/or blue
- ✔ A rectangular or columnar object, especially one positioned upright, such as a stereo speaker or file cabinet

Fire

Fire provides you with lots of energy and movement, and can help you become more active, better known, and more powerful. To enhance the Fire energy of your career, place any of these objects in Fire's natural location:

- A candle or bright light (the brighter, the better)
- A red object or something triangular or pyramid-shaped, with the point directed upward

Earth

Earth creates balance, peace, connection, and stability. Earth cures are good if you are experiencing changes and transitions and need to feel solid and grounded. People and companies in rapidly moving industries such as Internet companies can benefit by applying Earth cures.

To invoke the increased presence of Earth in your environment, you can accentuate your office with one of the following objects:

- An earthen item, such as pottery, a ceramic statue, or a smooth stone
- Yellow or earth-colored pieces
- Any square or cube-shaped objects

If possible, put the Earth objects or colors in the center of the space, which is the natural location of the Earth Element. Otherwise, put them as close as is convenient to the center.

Metal

Metal is the agent of communication, creativity, codes, and keys. Metal unlocks doors and conducts energies from one place to another. If you need to make better connections with people or move more quickly and fluidly, the Metal Element is your friend.

You can put these cures in the natural location of Metal to enhance its power:

- Anything made of Metal — a chair, table, lamp, or an art object, for example
- An item or picture containing the color white
- An object or image with a circular or spherical shape

If a wall in the natural location of Metal (the center of the right side of your space) is already white, you may get a greater effect from one of the other two choices

Water

The Water Element is manifest in two types — moving and still. Moving Water brings money and people, making it a prime choice for any business. Still Water improves depth, wisdom, and clarity.

To increase either type of Water, you can

- Apply the colors black or midnight blue in Water's natural location
- Place something in the location with an undulating or wavy shape

To improve moving Water, two great cures include

- Installing a fountain in the natural location of Water
- Hanging a photo or painting of a waterfall, river, or ocean

To generate increased still Water, an image of a large calm lake is beneficial.

Working with Your Office Layout and Floor Plan

If you work in a corporation and aren't a top executive, you probably don't have much choice over where your office is located. However, knowing the good and bad positions in the building can arm you with knowledge. In this section, I include some cures that can work for almost any office or cubicle.

The positioning and quality of the office space

Generally, the farther your office is from the front door and toward the back of the building, the stronger your position is in terms of energy. First, power tends to accumulate near the rear of the building. And second, the people near the front take the brunt of the incoming traffic and noise. The energy of the space in the front influences people to serve, whereas the people near the rear of the building tend to rule. For individual offices located on floors above ground level, being located as far away from the main entry point to the floor — usually the elevator — is generally more powerful.

You can find exceptions in some offices, but over time, this rule plays out. Unless you run the company, someone else or the existing conditions dictate your office location. Of course, if you can choose your work location within a building, all other factors being equal, the one closest to the back is a stronger choice and can provide you with more power.

Be sure to use common sense when applying this principle. If you can choose between two offices — one in the front of the building that is large and spacious and also has great lighting and a good position for the desk, and one in the back of the building that is cramped, dark, cluttered, and depressing — the better choice is obviously the front office with the better conditions and feel.

What can you do if you want to increase the power of your office position and career, but you find it impossible to switch offices? Other than finding a new company to work for (or sneaking in at night and changing the location of your office building's front door), you can perform the symbolic mirror-moving-the-desk cure. You can apply the cure by hanging the largest possible mirror on your office wall that is closest to the back of the building. The mirror should face your desk. I recommend a mirror size of at least 3 feet across. You can hide the mirror behind a piece of art, if you want. This cure works great because it doesn't diminish the power of anyone else; it simply increases your power and energy. Visualize that this solution energetically places you farther back in the building to increase your power and stability.

Private offices versus cubicles

The continuous corporate emphasis on cost-cutting and profit maximization has led to a related yet unfortunate drive to squeeze the maximum possible usage out of every square inch of office space — not to mention out of the employees.

Corporate settings use two general seating arrangements: individual offices (one room per worker) and the dreaded cubicle (or office isolation tank). The move to more people sharing space, whether in cubicles or not, contributes to an admirable flattening of hierarchies within the corporation. But the downside is sterility, a lack of privacy and personal space; you may feel like a unit in a machine rather than a person with individual needs and desires.

Having a room of one's own

The ideal office is a room of your own with a regular shape (preferably square or rectangle), natural lighting (at least one window), a solid door you can close, and a good position for your desk. One of the great advantages of having your own office is that you can usually perform more decorative Feng

Shui adjustments than if you work in a cubicle. Of course, not every company can afford, or desires, to put every employee in his or her own individual space.

If your office deviates from these ideal conditions, try these cures:

✔ **Irregular room shape:** Use a faceted crystal sphere, mirror, or plant to correct the space. (Refer to Chapter 8 for shape cures and solutions.) If your office is extremely irregular, you can have inexplicable setbacks and continuous frustrations at work. If you can't switch offices, you can apply the special nine green plants cure. Add nine healthy new plants to your space all on the same day. The plants should be purchased new for the purpose of this cure. If convenient, you can place the plants near particular irregularities in the room, such as strange angles, posts, cramped areas, and so on. Otherwise, just stick them where they fit best. For full results from this cure, use the Three Secrets Reinforcement (see Chapter 6) and visualize your job and career going very well.

✔ **Projecting corner, post, pillar, column, soffit, or duct work:** Many offices contain features that break up the energy flow of the room or, worse, shoot poison arrows (see Chapter 7) at your sitting position at the desk. Place a sizeable plant in front of the troublesome feature, or hang a faceted crystal sphere between the feature and your sitting position at the desk. For more information, refer to the projecting corner and post cures in Chapter 15.

✔ **Solid versus glass walls:** If your office contains one or more glass walls that make you feel even a little vulnerable, try to hang mini-blinds to cover the glassed-in area. Blinds are effective even if you don't often use them; their presence gives you added protection. If you can't perform this solution, hang faceted crystal spheres from the ceiling with red ribbons cut in 9-inch multiples. Use one sphere for every 5 linear feet of window space.

✔ **Improper lighting:** Like the majority of office workers, if you suffer under fluorescent lighting, you can use a couple helpful hints. You may be able to replace the tubes yourself with healthier full-spectrum ones (also called "grow lights") from the hardware store. If you can't replace them, bring in some supplemental incandescent light in the form of floor or table lamps. Working solely with overhead light is uncomfortable for the eyes, and supplemental lighting is a source of relief for your eyes and mind.

Surviving and thriving in a cubicle

A cubicle is a much trickier Feng Shui situation than an office room. Cubicles are unfortunate paradigms of vulnerability for the individual worker. One of the chief problems is that you don't use a real desk but work from a countertop, unless you work in one of the large manager type cubicles. However, you can do plenty to improve your situation. By judiciously applying Feng Shui cures, you may find yourself in your own office sooner than you imagined. (See Figure 16-2 for cure placements.)

See that door!

The first and most important priority is to make sure you can see the entrance to your cube from your desk. Try to move your sitting position first, but don't seriously cramp your work style. If you can't move — you can't. If you are able to switch your sitting location, follow the tips in the following Commanding Position section.

If you definitely can't move your sitting position, you can place an 8-x-10-inch mirror in a picture frame or on a small stand to reflect the entrance of the cube to allow you to see if anyone is approaching. Many people subconsciously use the reflections in their computer monitor to see who's approaching them, because seeing the entrance is a basic human need. The problem is that the reflection in a monitor's screen is distorted, unclear, and unreliable.

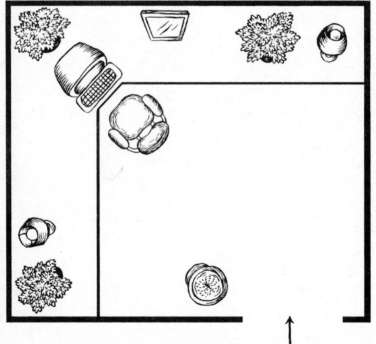

Figure 16-2:
Cubicle with plant, fountain, and mirror cures.

Living energy and water features

The second priority is bringing living and flowing energy into your workspace. These features are important ways of compensating for the small size of your space and the constant traffic flows that pass by your cube. If you can bring an odd number of healthy plants into your space, you can stimulate more-active, vibrant energy. Also, a nice fountain near the entrance of your cube can work wonders. Not only can it stimulate more salary coming your way, but also it can help uplift your mood and diffuse any negative flows of chi (human or environmental) in the vicinity of your work space. If space or social realities preclude a fountain, you can get some of the same benefits from a photo (the larger, the better) of flowing water, such as of a waterfall or river.

Uplift overhead storage

Many cubicles provide storage space starting about 30 inches above the desk space. This setup crowds your head and symbolically makes moving up the corporate ladder more difficult. I recommended hanging faceted crystal spheres from the storage bins, one for every 3 to 4 linear feet. They can help uplift the oppression of the space and brighten your outlook on work and life.

Putting Yourself in the Commanding Position at Work

In the interior of the home, bed position is the single most important factor; in your office, desk position takes the honors. An auspicious desk position can make the difference between an easy, smooth, and progressing career, and one filled with hardships, setbacks, and problems.

Using Commanding Position desk principles

The best Feng Shui position for the desk fulfills the principles of the Commanding Position.

- ✔ The position of the desk relative to the office door is more important than the compass direction the desk faces.
- ✔ The desk should be as far from the door as possible.
- ✔ The desk position allows you to see as much of the room as possible.
- ✔ The door of the office is clearly visible from where you sit.
- ✔ The desk should not be in the direct path of the door.

Seeing the door equals success

The most important aspect of the Commanding Position principle is that you can see the door from your desk position. Seeing who or what is approaching is a fundamental element of power and success at work. If your back is to the door, you're in the symbolic victim position, which makes it easier for others to take advantage of you. If your side is to the door, the effect is the same, but slightly less. *Note:* Seeing the door from your desk means that you can glance up from your work and clearly see the doorway without having to shift your position in your chair. Figures 16-3a and 16-3b are examples of powerful desk positions.

If you find it impossible to turn your desk to see the door, Feng Shui offers a solution. Arrange a small mirror on your desk or, even better, a larger mirror on your wall that allows you to see the entry. Simple and easy, this cure is a career (and life) saver. (See Figure 16-3c.)

Some people insist that facing the door is distracting. If you're one of these people, I understand your position. You don't like to be bothered by every passer-by because you need to get lots of work done. Some people think that they can find inspiration sitting with their back to the door, so they face out a window with a nice view. (On the contrary, a window view actually distracts from the tasks at hand.) However, as a minimum cure, I recommend that you use the mirror alternative so you can see the door whenever you want. Your control of the situation makes a real difference.

It is also important to be as far from the door as possible, which symbolically gives you more control over your space, and time to react to what comes in the door. This position makes you calmer, more resourceful, and more confident at work.

Understanding other key desk placement factors

Although the tips in the following sections don't carry the weight of the Commanding Position, they can help you gain success in the competitive world of work and career.

Keep yourself flexible: Access your desk from either side

For the most power and flexibility, I recommend that you don't push the side of your desk against a wall — if you can avoid it. You can experience more flexibility, creativity, and safety if you can approach your desk and leave it from either side (see Figure 16-3b). If the available space prevents you from having equal room on both sides of your desk, just make sure you have enough room to get out by the smaller side if necessary (at least 18 inches of space). However, if you fill up this space with books, files, or furniture, you cut off one avenue of escape, which makes for weaker positioning.

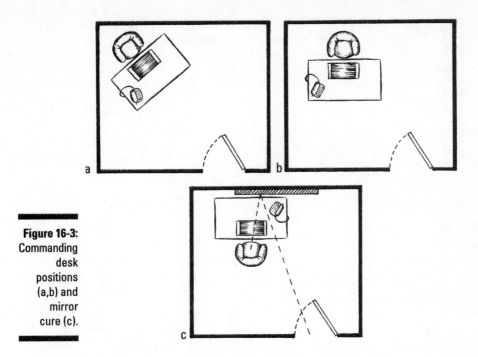

Figure 16-3:
Commanding desk positions (a,b) and mirror cure (c).

Don't back yourself too close to the wall

Unless you work in a very large office, you're usually better off with no furniture behind your desk. In addition, having at least 3 feet of space behind you while you're at your desk is good. If you hit the wall as you back your chair up, frustration and anger can result.

Don't sit with a door or threatening window behind you

Sitting with your back to a solid wall is ideal in an office setting. A window creates some vulnerability but is not a Feng Shui emergency. In fact, if the window affords good lighting, it can be helpful to your work. If the window makes you feel uneasy, you can hang a faceted crystal sphere or wind chime from the ceiling, about ⅓ of the way down the window. If the window is quite large, insecurity is probable; you can use drapes or blinds to make the window look smaller.

If the door is behind you, the situation is much worse; the crystal or chime cure for the previous window problem is a minimum recommendation. In this case, the best option is to hang the cure directly over your sitting position at the desk. (See Figure 16-4.) See if you can move your desk to a better all-around position. In addition, you can hang a curtain or tapestry or place a decorative screen to hide the door. (A door that leads to the outside behind you is particularly undesirable, and unless you have a really large office, you're better off without any outside door in the room.)

Figure 16-4:
Door behind
desk with
wind chime
cure.

Don't crowd your office with extremely heavy, large, or tall furniture

Furniture that dominates the space makes less room for you and your energy to flow; it can hold you down and can be depressing and even scary. (Ever feel like everything is falling on your head?) The cure is simple: Get rid of large bureaus or computer centers you don't often use, or trade them for more space saving and suitable items. Use your common sense, hold on to things you do need (like filing cabinets and bookshelves) and remember that you use only 20 percent of your items 80 percent of the time.

Making Sure You Have a High-Quality Desk

Second in importance to the position of the desk are the qualities and energy conditions of the desk itself.

The origin and energy of your desk

Your desk's history (who sat in it before you, how the person conducted his or her business, under what terms the person left or moved up in the business, and so on) can tell you plenty about its energy. According to Feng Shui practice, buying a brand new desk is generally the best way to ensure new, positive desk energy. Of course, in a corporation, asking the company to buy you a new desk is often not feasible. The following list shows you how to read the predecessor conditions of your desk to tell if a cure is in order.

Your desk houses positive energies if

- ✔ The person before you was promoted.
- ✔ The person before you moved to a larger office or retired after a long, successful, and prosperous career.
- ✔ The person before you left for a better job.
- ✔ The person before you was a successful, well-liked, and positive person.

If your predecessor has left the company, the best conditions result if the parting was amicable on both sides.

Your desk is home to negative energy and may be well served by applying a cure if

- ✔ The person who sat at the desk before you was fired or forced to resigned.
- ✔ The person before you was demoted.
- ✔ The person before you moved to a smaller office.
- ✔ The person before you left because of a disgrace.
- ✔ The person before you left because of sickness or death.

If you must use a desk with such negative predecessor chi, you can perform the Orange Peel Blessing on the desk (see Chapter 17 for details). This cure can remove lingering negative chi from your desk and provide you and the desk with positive new energy.

All these predecessor principles apply to another extremely important element of your work area — your chair.

Positive desk shapes

Most desks are strong, positive shapes — rectangular. Missing corners can definitely cause problems, so make sure your desk is a complete shape. Another good desk shape — although practically speaking harder to purchase — is one with a curved or rounded shape, such as a kidney-shaped desk or a desk with the back or Fame Area rounded.

As I explain in detail earlier in this chapter, the best position allows you to access your desk from either side. In addition, according to the Commanding Position concept, people are strongest and most productive when facing forward at their desk; this position enables them to see the door and who's approaching them. For these two reasons, I suggest avoiding an L-shaped desk or a desk with a return. Returns and L-shapes portions of the desk typically hold a computer. When you use the computer, your back may be to the door, which increases your vulnerability. These kinds of desks also limit your movement to one side of the desk and blocks your lateral movement and flexibility (coming and going), which translates into fewer options in times of stress and trouble.

The most powerful desk

The best desk is energetically solid and complete. A flimsy, weak desk can't support your career to the greatest degree possible. I find that my clients definitely benefit from buying the energetically and physically strongest desk (and chair) they can afford, a choice that pays them back in many career dividends over the years. If your workspace is large enough, go for an executive desk, which typically comes in two sizes, 30-x-60 inches and 30-x-72 inches.

Trying to use any of the following desk substitutes to pursue a serious career in business can block your progress:

- ✔ A writing table or dining room table
- ✔ A dormitory or miniature desk
- ✔ A door or piece of plywood mounted on filing cabinets

While a sturdy desk is key, using a desk that is extremely large and heavy can be impractical. Let common sense and your individual budget guide your desk selection.

The front and side panels

The desk protects your front and the chair protects your back. The front panel of the desk is a vital part for protection, strength, and security at work. The best front panel extends down to the floor. A partial panel leaves real vulnerabilities and weaknesses in your work life (see Figure 16-5).

The side panels are also important. Some desk models have only partial side panels, so check them when you're shopping for a desk. A vulnerable desk is one that has only legs to support a flat surface — no sides or front to the desk. With this type of desk, you can find yourself besieged from all sides and unable to gather and hold power in the corporate world.

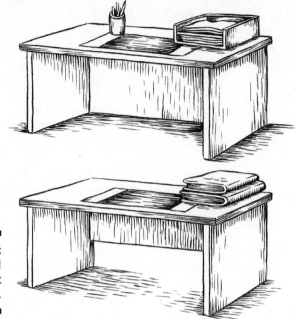

Figure 16-5:
Full and
partial front
desk panels.

Desk composition

A wooden desk is preferable to a metal one. Problems can occur if your desktop is glass. A glass-top desk lets deals and money fall from your grasp. Ideas, energy, and money metaphorically drop through the desk, finding no support. In addition, the glass reflects multiple light sources from within the room, causing confusion, stress, and even headaches. However, a glass topper, which sits on top of a solid wooden desk to protect the wood finish, is safe.

The kneehole of the desk (the area under the top where your feet and legs go) should be kept free and clear of all objects, including papers, books, trash cans, and so on. Objects in this area can block your legs and, therefore, trip up your career progress.

Computer position on desk

The ideal placement for the computer monitor is on the desk in front of you, in a position that still allows you to see the door of your office. Placing the computer on a credenza behind you generally detracts from your power to the degree that you work on the computer and cannot see the door of your office. If you must turn your back to the door to compute, you can restore good Feng Shui by arranging within eyeshot a mirror that gives you a clear view of the door.

Using the Feng Shui Octagon on Your Desk Surface

The Feng Shui Octagon is a versatile tool that you can use not only in your home, bedroom, yard, and office but also with good results on your desk. Place the Octagon according to Figure 16-6. The entrance of the desk is where the front of your body (belly) meets the desk. This area corresponds to the Career Life Area; the other Life Areas are placed around the desk accordingly.

Employing visible desk cures

You can profitably perform cures in any of the Life Areas of your desk.

- **Place your phone in the Wealth corner of the desk.** Your phone is more likely to ring with business in this corner, and each time it does, the bell sound of the phone stimulates more money coming to you.

- **Use a lamp to brighten your future or a plant for new growth and life.** You can place a desk lamp in any Octagon Area with the intention of activating and brightening the corresponding part of your life (except for the Career or Health Area, because the lamp would be directly in front of your face.) The Fame Area of the desk is a great place for a lamp and can really help your reputation inside — and outside — of the office. (When holding meetings in your office, make sure that the lamp doesn't block your visual contact with co-workers.) A healthy plant works well in the Family Area of the desk to promote harmony and cooperation.

- **Create more action and communication with a bell.** Place a brass bell in the Children Area to create increase quality communications — a perfect cure for salespeople, account executives, and telemarketers. Ring the bell nine times whenever you want or need to stimulate more business. This cure can also help any of the Life Areas of your desk.

Applying invisible desk cures

Colors and mirrors are two powerful weapons you can invisibly employ to amp up the power of the Feng Shui of your desk. These cures really work, sometimes with amazing results. Remember, however, that these solutions are less important than having a good Feng Shui desk placed in the Commanding Position. To implement these cures, simply place them in the desk drawer beneath the Life Area of the desk surface you want to empower, or tape them to the bottom of the desktop. (See Figure 16-6.)

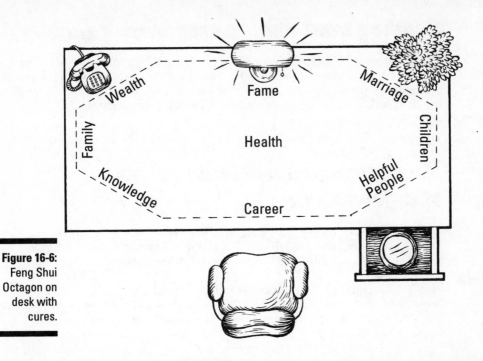

Figure 16-6:
Feng Shui
Octagon on
desk with
cures.

Fasten purple fabric or paper at the Wealth Area of your desk surface to
enhance your money (either on top of, or underneath the surface), red under
the Fame Area for a stronger reputation, and black under the Career Area for
general help in business.

Octagonal mirrors 3 to 6 inches across can be hidden under any Life Area for
activation and empowerment. The mirrors should be oriented with the shiny
side facing upward.

Sitting on a Firm Foundation: Your Office Chair

The part of your office Feng Shui that rivals your desk in importance is your
chair. The chair you sit on is literally your foundation at work. Your chair protects you, supports you, and holds you up. Positive chair qualities can help
you prosper rather than flounder.

Fortunately, getting a good business chair is a simple matter. Consider these
two main points when selecting your chair: where it came from and how
much protection it offers you.

Reading your chair's predecessor factors

The predecessor factors for your chair are the same as for your desk (see "The origin and energy of your desk" section earlier in this chapter). If you sit in a negative predecessor's chair, see if you can switch it for another one in the company. Some companies may even let you bring your own chair to work.

Recognizing characteristics of a good chair

The best chair has no gap between the seat and the back of the chair. Regardless of the quality or price of the chair, you are definitely more vulnerable than you should be in your career and work life if your chair has a gap.

Ideally, the height for the back of your chair should come to at least as high as the tops of your shoulders — up to the top of your head is even better. A chair back lower than the top of your shoulders weakens you. (See Figure 16-7.)

Figure 16-7:
Vulnerable
vs. powerful
office
chairs.

The newer office chairs made in the last few years are definitely superior in comfort, balance, and promotion of a healthy back and spine. The very best of these chairs can cost $500 to $1000, but you can get a reasonably good quality chair for $150. Make sure the chair is equipped with an adjustable height lever, and sit in the chair for a few minutes before deciding to buy it.

Part IV
Special Feng Shui: Performing Ceremonies and Personal Cures

The 5th Wave   By Rich Tennant

"Would you mind not sitting at that machine? It throws off the Feng Shui in this row."

In this part . . .

Some of the best Feng Shui methods have been kept secret for centuries. My job in life is to break the rules, spill the beans, and rip off the covers so you can get a whole lot more of what's comin' to you. In this part, I hand over the major artillery. If you want things to be incredibly better in your home, heart, and health, dive right in for some effective solutions. I start off this part with blessing ceremonies that can lift negativity, clear up the bad luck soap operas playing on *Your Life* TV, and generally help you feel happier, footloose, and fancy-free. They also bless your house so things can gradually improve.

If these benefits aren't enough, I give you another whole chapter cracking with higher-level cures that you can apply directly on your own energy; bypass the house and perform Feng Shui techniques right on yourself. Sounds freaky, but works wonderfully.

Chapter 17

Invisible Factors and Feng Shui Blessing Ceremonies

Grandmaster Lin Yun's Feng Shui school addresses both *visible elements* (physical features of the house and property) and *invisible elements* (energetic features such as wishes, desires, visualizations, intentions, existing energy flows, and so on) for practicing Feng Shui. This book mostly emphasizes the visible, practical features, because these areas are the most readily apparent as well as the most common the places to start. However, the invisible factors are the more significant of these two areas in terms of cause and effect.

Two key areas of so-called invisible Feng Shui are *predecessor factors* (energies of the people who came before you) and *invisible occupants* (energies, ghosts, and spirits) that may still reside on the property. (And the worst part is, they don't even pay rent!) A problem in either category can generate problems indeed. In addition, other types of invisible Feng Shui factors are invariably at work on most properties. These factors include intentions of current and previous owners, major positive and negative events that have occurred on the site, burial plots on the site, and other issues. Thankfully, this chapter can help you cure them without bogging you down in arcane details.

In this chapter, you find out about *blessing ceremonies,* which are highly effective cures for addressing and improving the invisible energies on your property. I also present several great blessing ceremonies that can counteract negative issues and enhance positive unseen energies. These cures include the Rice Blessing, the Orange Peel Blessing, the Vase and Flute Blessing, and the Constantly Turning Dharma Wheel.

Assessing and Addressing Predecessor Factors

Predecessor energies in your living and working environments vitally affect the Feng Shui of your home or office. The lingering energetic influences of the folks who occupied the space before you fall into the category of invisible factors because they can't be seen with normal vision. However, these energies can be felt and are directly experienced in daily life. Feng Shui methods allow us to notice or read these effects and then alter them to our advantage.

Feng Shui asserts that energetic influence is a two-way street: The energies of a house affect its occupants, and the energies of the occupants affect the house. Furthermore, occupant energies remain in a house even after the occupants leave. Any energetic influences the occupants generated — whether they had positive or negative energy, good luck or bad luck, suffered from poverty, or had the Midas touch — can subtly influence you when you move into the house. Starting with a clean slate is always better, so the cures in this chapter can greatly benefit you and all who live with you.

Predecessor energies deal with a large number of factors. To keep things manageable, I provide the most reliable methods that can help you check out and clean up a new property. Consulting a qualified Feng Shui professional is recommended in this especially important area, but the tips found in this chapter will stand you in good stead.

Most people looking to rent or buy are typically unconcerned with the predecessor factor. They tend to pay attention to how the house looks, but not to how it feels. The attitude is fairly nonchalant: "House looks fine, honey, let's move in! So what if Charlie Manson just moved out this morning! Gimme the keys!" Paying attention to Feng Shui factors is vital, so don't consider the appearance of a house as the most important factor. Take interest in the fortunes, characters, and life patterns of the person you are buying a house from, because these patterns start to impact you the minute you move in.

Dealing a one-two punch to predecessor energies

The first key factor in dealing with predecessor energies is knowing how to spot them or, rather, how to recognize good and bad energetic influences. I encourage you to find out about the history of the house and its previous occupants. Ask questions. If you don't know the predecessors and can't get any information about them, you need to rely on your all-important Feng Shui antennae, gut feelings, and intuition. (In other words, use the Force, Luke!) Unfortunately, apartments frequently abound in problematic predecessor energies due to frequent tenant turnover. With many people randomly moving in and out over the years, negative influences are almost inevitable — even if from only the constant disturbance of the continual moving.

The second key factor is what to do if the predecessor energies are negative. The first strategic maneuver is to try to avoid moving into a house where the predecessor energies oppose your life goals. But this plan isn't always possible or truly practical. If you do move into a house with negative predecessor chi, the tactical approach is to perform Feng Shui blessing ceremonies to remove or change the negative energy, thereby bringing blessings and prosperity to the site.

Taking advantage of Move-In Momentum

According to Grandmaster Lin Yun, your willpower and good intentions are at their strongest when you first move into a house. You tend to be enthusiastic, full of energy, and hopeful for the future. I call this excitement your Move-In Momentum. This momentum is real — a precious window of energetic opportunity — but it can't last forever. Why not? Because the second you move into the house, you become subject to its influences. These influences work on you night and day, without a break; they don't sleep even when you do. If these influences are positive, they're good for you. But if they aren't positive, guess what? They're already in your house! However, they tend to come on gradually, so time is of the essence.

The energetic effects in your environment are also cumulative; they build up and gain momentum like the proverbial snowball rolling downhill. Gradually, your subconscious mind adjusts to the new environment. And this adjustment — which typically happens outside of your awareness — affects any and all areas of your life to some degree.

Way back when

Technically, predecessor influences go back through the previous owners or residents of the house to the beginning. These influences also include the intentions with which the house was built and the energy of the builder. (Some Feng Shui professionals even analyze the way the land was used before any houses were built in the area.) For simplicity's sake, you can stick to the most important predecessor — the one who lived in the house right before you came along. The cures in this chapter can address any predecessor energies currently residing in your new home.

The Move-In Momentum generally lasts about two to three years. (Keep in mind that the two-to-three year principle is only a rough rule. As usual in Feng Shui, your mileage may vary depending on all the factors involved.) During this period, your ideas, thoughts, and ambitions prevail. At the two or three year point, your life results begin to adapt more fully to the Feng Shui of the house.

For example: You and your spouse, happily married for four years, move into a new home that was put on the market because the couple who owned it were getting divorced. (As you can see in Table 17-1, this example is not a positive predecessor factor.) For the first two to three years in this new house, your marriage is still pretty good. But in time, somewhere around the energetic turning point, the two of you may begin to argue, and one or both of you start to entertain thoughts of a trial separation — or even divorce!

This situation is not an unusual scenario; I've seen it happen time after time. And you know what? It isn't necessarily the two of you. The problems you're experiencing may be due to the lingering separation energy of the previous couple. The energy of their arguments, pain, and divorce seeped into the walls, carpets, and atmosphere of the house. You moved right into the thick of it, and you energetically managed on your own for a couple years. But now look at the mess you're in! Negative predecessor influences can gradually undermine the best of intentions. So why not nip this bud at the get-go with some simple Feng Shui cures? If your relationship is already suffering, better late than never. For help in this department, read on.

Reading the predecessor factors

Ask the following two questions first when considering a new residence to assess if the predecessor energies of the place are positive or negative. The third question can help you analyze the factors of the home you're currently living in.

Why did the previous occupants move out?

This question is the most important one to answer. The energy associated with moving is the final energy that the resident leaves in the house. The reason for moving is often a powerful factor that stirs up a great deal of energy and emotion, and the house resonates with these influences long after the family is gone. Table 17-1 shows the positive and negative reasons for moving out of a house. (All things being equal, avoid choosing a home with negative energies and lean towards choosing one with positive energies.) Keep in mind that if you currently live in a house with negative predecessor factors, you can perform Feng Shui blessing ceremonies to successfully remove and clear these energies. And if you move into a home where the previous resident died, pay particular attention to this section or skip directly to the Rice Blessing detailed later in this chapter.

Table 17-1	Negative and Positive Reasons Predecessor Moved
Positive Predecessor Factors	*Negative Predecessor Factors*
Growing family	Injury/death
Marriage	Divorce
Prosperity	Bankruptcy
Promotion/new job	Lost job
Good fortune	Lawsuit
Moved to larger house	Moved to smaller house

How did their life go while living in this house?

After finding out the occupants' reason for moving out, the next key factor to determine is the general behavior and emotional patterns of the occupants while they lived in the house. Pay special attention to the three key areas of wealth, marriage or relationship, and health. If possible, find out any significant incidents that happened during their stay in the residence, both positive and negative, including major accidents, sickness, bankruptcy, and death.

Of course, you can't always interview the previous occupant, and pressing them for intimate details about their life traumas is certainly awkward, not to mention in bad taste. But if you really want to find out such information, you often can. Realtors and rental agents often know things about their clients, and neighbors can be fountains of information. Getting even a little information is better than getting none at all. Ask point blank, and you may find out things that boggle your mind.

How has your life gone since moving in?

If you've been living in your current house for more than a few months, you're now your own predecessor. That's right, you've now infused your new house with the energies of all the events, inner and outer, that you've experienced since you moved in. These energies are added as casual factors to the energies of the previous occupants and now permeate your residential environment (visibly and invisibly). So if you've increased your wealth since you moved in, you are more likely to continue gaining riches due to your own residual influence. Conversely, any negative patterns you've experienced since moving in may also continue unless you do something to cure them. Life runs in trends and patterns that tend to self-perpetuate unless they are consciously and intentionally altered. (Improving the property's energy shows the real and invisible influence that Feng Shui has on people's lives.)

Significant negative incidents and patterns, if left uncleared, can gain a cumulative and powerful momentum. (Remember the snowball rolling downhill.)

My client Mary lived in a house for 25 years before our first Feng Shui consultation. Things went well for Mary over the first eight years in her home. Then her mother died in the house. Unaware of Feng Shui principles, Mary did nothing to clear from the homesite the negative energy of her mother's death, with all of its trauma, confusion, and grief. Without knowing it, Mary was living with a negative influence that weighed, day and night, on her health and emotions and affected the entire family. Two years later, her husband lost his high-paying job and couldn't find another one. Unable to continue paying for their daughter's college education, the daughter was forced to move back into the house, putting an additional financial and emotional burden on the family.

A negative cycle was in full swing, gaining momentum over time, and none of the family members knew it. A pattern was set in motion, starting with Mary's mother's death. The energy grew increasingly negative, with each negative incident accelerating the downward spiral. Eventually Mary's husband died, which made things very dark indeed. I learned these details as I interviewed Mary during our first Feng Shui consultation. Her situation was astounding — a clear pattern of tragedy spiraling down, event by event, to calamity. Every three to four years, with seeming regularity, some new trauma or life blow occurred. Mary seemed to be getting more than her share of hardships. (For brevity's sake, I've left out some of the unfortunate details.) The time clearly came to turn things around, and Mary was ready. The Feng Shui solution was simple: The Rice Blessing, which is presented step-by-step in the next section. As we performed the ceremony, the sense of energy lifting and feelings lightening in her home was palpable, and she continues to feel better and freer.

When you check the history of a house, also look for changes made to the original structure including remodeling, additions, rebuilding, demolitions, fires, and so on. If major remodeling is done to the house, the energy of the site can remain chaotic and nonintegrated for years — or at least until Feng Shui comes along.

Dealing with Unseen Occupants in Your Home

Many people are uneasy with the idea of unseen visitors living with them in the same house. People also tend to believe (perhaps wishfully) that ghosts are rare (and live with other people) and that most homes are free of invisible residents. Another common belief is that ghosts or spirits are inherently negative and everyone can be much better off if they are all cast out at once. If only it was that simple!

According to Feng Shui, most houses generally have one or more spirits living in them, and this condition is perfectly natural. From a Feng Shui perspective, you don't necessarily want to have a house completely empty of spirits. You just don't want negative spirits, or energies, disturbing your environment. Feng Shui posits two basic kinds of spirits or energetic influences: *benign* (positive spirits that promote harmony, good luck, and blessings) and *negative* (unhappy spirits that promote disharmony, bad luck, and unhappiness). The Feng Shui task at hand is to invoke positive spirits and energies and give the nasty ones their walking papers.

You guessed it, blessing ceremonies are the answer. Performing blessing ceremonies on a site allows you to communicate with the unseen realms through time-tested methods that help clear negative energies and strengthen positive ones, including your energy, your family's energy, and your home's energy — past and present.

Advantages of Blessing Ceremonies

Grandmaster Lin Yun's Feng Shui school includes many powerful blessing ceremonies, also called *Chi Adjustments,* for changing the chi (or *energy*) of your home, property, and life. Whereas regular Feng Shui cures — which I cover in this book — may powerfully impact one or two areas of your experience, blessing ceremonies can simultaneously improve all areas of your life and environment. Though the ceremonies in this chapter draw on multiple sources and influences, the specific methods are unique to Grandmaster Lin Yun's Feng Shui school.

I have found these techniques to be so effective that I refer to them as Feng Shui's Big Guns. Doing a blessing ceremony on your property can give you the same improvement that you can gain by performing numerous Feng Shui adjustments (proper placement, minor additions, and so on). Of course, both types are definitely recommended.

Suppose you find a negative Feng Shui situation in your residence, but for various reasons, you cannot perform the desired cure right now. In this circumstance, I recommend that you perform a blessing ceremony to change the energy and free things up substantially. Many of the cures given throughout this book work in specific areas of your house and life — although you may soon notice, their benefits often spill over unexpectedly into other areas of your life. These cures operate by changing the flow, nature, and quality of the chi in specific sites, such as your entrance, bedroom, kitchen, and other areas.

The blessing ceremonies, on the other hand, have the power to shift the energy patterns of an entire environment at once. They work holistically to provide powerful and comprehensive benefits in many areas of your life. Feel free to use them even if you have only one intention in mind, but don't be surprised if they give you more positive benefits than you bargained for. Blessing ceremonies are very powerful and often evoke unexpected positive life changes.

Always perform these ceremonies with an attitude of reverence, sincerity, and compassion and with the best intentions in mind for all the people involved. (See instructions for intention and the Three Secrets Reinforcement in Chapter 6.)

Reasons for employing Feng Shui ceremonies

Applying Feng Shui cures in as many ways as you find practical can produce positive results. But you may find in some instances that more is necessary. These blessing ceremonies are good for the following situations:

Changing the energy of multiple Feng Shui problems

Suppose you have a handful of Feng Shui problem areas. Maybe you're able to fix some of them but not others. If you're feeling overwhelmed by your Feng Shui situation, a blessing ceremony can help move the energy throughout your space and blow a powerful breeze of change and healing through the house.

Solving a pesky Feng Shui problem

Suppose you have a Feng Shui issue for which you either don't know the cure or can't afford to implement the optimal solution. A blessing ceremony may be just the ticket. In this case, a blessing ceremony is an effective solution that can remove some negative influences, compensate for other influences, and increase overall the positive energies of the site.

Alleviating a general feeling of negativity and depression in the house

Sometimes, a home has an overall feeling of gloom and doom, or it simply puts you down in the dumps. Maybe you perform these simple cures and notice some improvement, but the general feel of the place still doesn't change to one of overall cheer, health, and uplifted energy. In such cases, a blessing ceremony can help change the quality of the entire home's energy. You may notice a freer, lighter, and happier feel after properly implementing a blessing ceremony.

Setting the tone in a new residence or office

The crucial moving-in time is a prime window of opportunity for improving the energy of a site. Performing a ceremony to remove inauspicious energies before you move in to your new residence is the best way to set in motion positive energy in your new home, office, or business location.

Effects of Feng Shui blessing ceremonies

Performing blessing ceremonies in your home or office can remove the negative energies and improve the positive energies. Some of the many purposes Feng Shui blessing ceremonies can be profitably used for include:

- ✔ Inviting blessing, prosperity, and good fortune
- ✔ Blessing a homesite upon moving in
- ✔ Blessing the grand opening of a business
- ✔ Clearing negative predecessor energy
- ✔ Changing your luck from bad to good
- ✔ Improving your energy after an accident or any unexpected negative event
- ✔ Removing the chi associated with sickness or death
- ✔ Releasing negative ghosts, spirits, or other unwelcome visitors

Q and A on Feng Shui Blessing Ceremonies

Got a question on Feng Shui blessing ceremonies? This section should answer any puzzlers you may have on this important subject.

Do I need to change or go against any of my religious beliefs for these methods to be effective?

Definitely not! These practices work for anyone and everyone, regardless of their religion or faith (or lack thereof), just like gravity or other laws of physics. So don't worry, no conversion is required. In fact, I recommend that you incorporate your personal beliefs and practices into the ceremonies you do. And Grandmaster Lin Yun's Feng Shui school actually invites such eclecticism. So whether you're Christian, Hindu, Muslim, Buddhist, Jewish (or even atheist), incorporate your prayers in these Feng Shui ceremonies so they feel right to you. The practices that are most meaningful to you can have the greatest effects on your body, psyche, and environment. However, make sure you keep the basic structure and steps of the ceremony intact.

Do I need to perform a ceremony exactly right for it to be effective?

If you follow the essential steps of a blessing ceremony with a positive attitude, sincerity of heart, and clear intent (the ingredients of any powerful Feng Shui cure) you can experience corresponding positive effects. Do the best you can to follow the ceremony steps closely and hold positive expectations. Detail is important, but obsessing over results before they appear is definitely counterproductive. Apply the inner Feng Shui of self-control by adhering to the positive and relinquishing the negative influences within. As I tell my clients, Feng Shui is meant for stress relief, which requires stress release, not stress creation. So lighten up, have fun in the present, and look forward to the future.

Do I need special training to be able to implement these blessing ceremonies?

Yes, most definitely! What you absolutely must acquire to proceed are a human body (your own, by the way), the ability to read English, and a copy of the comprehensive Feng Shui manual called *Feng Shui For Dummies*. With these three elements in place you should have no problems! On a more serious note, these methods are part of the advanced levels of Feng Shui practice. Any art or skill always has details or nuances that can't be learned from a book but can only be learned from direct experience. Further levels of mastery can be gleaned only from direct training with a qualified teacher. While the steps in this chapter can enable you to perform these ceremonies and enjoy positive and life-changing results, direct training with a Feng Shui teacher brings the energy of the practices to a much stronger level. After your apprenticeship with this book, if you are interested in increasing your knowledge and skill in Feng Shui, you can always contact a teacher in your area to receive further training.

How do I know if the ceremony worked or was effective?

As with any method, art, or skill, results vary due to innumerable factors. Sometimes you may feel or notice immediate effects after performing Feng Shui cures. And sometimes results may come more gradually and improve your life over time.

Tips for Performing Feng Shui Blessing Ceremonies

If you've never performed a blessing ceremony, your first effort can feel a bit daunting. Following these tips can help you get the most out of any blessing ceremonies you perform.

- ✔ **Calm yourself down.** Get into a peaceful state of mind before beginning a blessing ceremony.

- ✔ **Begin fully prepared.** Gather all the materials you need for the ceremony before you start.

- ✔ **Have the steps of the ceremony in front of you.** Open this book to the appropriate page so you don't fumble and distract yourself as you perform the process.

- ✔ **Don't rush.** Dedicate the time you need to perform the ceremony properly. Your state of mind and ability to focus on the matter at hand makes a big difference in the success of the ceremony.

- ✔ **Make sure you won't be disturbed as you perform the ceremony.** I recommend that you turn off all phone ringers or beepers (and turn down the volume on the answering machine).

- ✔ **Call a trained professional if needed.** If you don't feel ready to perform a blessing or you want assistance, call a Feng Shui professional who can perform it for you.

Keep in mind that performing a blessing isn't absolutely necessary for your site to have good Feng Shui. Blessings are potent tools that are very helpful in time of need, but they aren't required practices.

Out with the Old, In with the New: The Rice Blessing

The Chinese name for the Rice Blessing ceremony is *Yu Wei*, which means Exterior Blessing or Exterior Chi Adjustment. The Rice Blessing adjusts the chi by shifting the energy to a higher level of dynamic coherence and harmony. In my consulting practice, this cure has demonstrated its effectiveness and power. My clients report a host of benefits including relief from financial and legal problems, improved family harmony, and better health.

What the Rice Blessing can do for you

The Rice Blessing is performed around the perimeter of your property, and it energetically uplifts everything on the site. Applied properly, this ceremony clears and changes the energy of these three realms:

- ✔ **Your land:** The Rice Blessing improves the energy of all parts of your property. The energies of the ground, water, air, vegetation, and wildlife are adjusted and improved.

- ✔ **Your house:** The Rice Blessing energetically upgrades the main living structure and any other buildings on your property.

- ✔ **You:** The Rice Blessing helps humans (and other living beings) on the property to live easier, happier lives by smoothing out the energy and circumstances.

How the Rice Blessing works

Rice is a symbol of blessing. (At Western weddings, handfuls of rice are tossed on the bride and groom to wish them good luck in their new life.) In the Rice Blessing ceremony, the rice is specially prepared and empowered and then is tossed around the perimeter of the property using three specific methods. The three-way tossing of the rice in the blessing performs three energetic tasks that are detailed in the following sections. See Figure 17-2 later in this chapter for a visual guide of the three tossing techniques.

Uplifting the chi

Uplifting the chi is accomplished by tossing the rice straight up in the air as high as possible (with the palm up) in a gesture called the Uplifting Mudra (a *mudra* is a spiritual or energetic gesture). This tossing method uplifts the chi and brings lightness, joy, and freedom to the site. Good things now come rushing your way!

Feeding the hungry ghosts

Hungry ghosts is a Chinese cultural term symbolizing all the problems, injustices, chaos, pain, negative emotion, and unhealthy energy that may reside on the site. When the rice is thrown with the Giving Mudra, a gesture that involves tossing the rice out horizontally to the ground with a Frisbee-like motion, the hungry ghosts can feed on the positive energy of the rice and become satisfied. Then the ghosts feel free to leave the site or even transform into beneficial guardians of the property. The result is diminished and cured problems and tribulation for the residents.

Planting new seeds of growth

With the Planting Mudra, you can plant new seeds for growth. This blessing involves tossing handfuls of rice straight down towards the ground. The Planting Mudra symbolically implants your wishes and intentions — along with positive fresh energy — into the soil so new things (the fulfillment of your needs) can spontaneously spring up and flower profusely.

Items to gather for the Rice Blessing

Before you begin the Rice Blessing, assemble and prepare the following items:

- ✔ **A large bowl:** A bowl such as a large-sized mixing bowl or salad bowl from your kitchen works well.

- ✔ **Five or more pounds of uncooked rice:** The amount of rice needed varies based on the size of the property. You can use 5 to 8 pounds for an average-sized yard and more rice for larger properties. Use regular white or brown rice, not minute or instant rice. (Sorry Uncle Ben!)

- ✔ **About a quarter teaspoon of cinnabar powder:** Cinnabar is a Chinese medical herbal mixture with special properties. This mixture has been ceremoniously scattered in ancient Chinese temples and imperial burial sites for thousands of years. To acquire cinnabar, ask a Chinese herbalist in your area.

    Unless you're a qualified Chinese medical professional, use cinnabar for external applications only.

- ✔ **A newly purchased, unopened bottle of high proof liquor:** One hundred proof or higher liquor (50-percent alcohol by content) is best to use for this ceremony. A particularly favorable choice for the cures in this book is Bacardi's 151-proof rum. However, if you can obtain only 80-proof liquor, it can also be effective. You can buy any size bottle you want.

Performing the Rice Blessing

The Rice Blessing is performed in two stages. Prepare the rice with the special methods outlined in the following section and then take the rice outdoors to do the ceremonial tossing. You can prepare the rice on the kitchen counter, a dining room table, or other convenient area. Please follow these steps when performing the Rice Blessing.

A *mudra* is a hand gesture that invokes a spiritual state in the person holding the position. A *mantra* is a word or phrase with spiritual significance and energy. (See Chapter 6 for more information on these two powerful Feng Shui elements.)

Preparing the rice

1. **Begin the ceremony by holding your hands in the Heart-Calming Mudra and recite the Heart-Calming Mantra nine times.** Place the left hand on top of the right with palms up and thumbs touching. (See Figure 6-1b in Chapter 6.) Then recite, "Gate gate, para gate, para sum gate, bodhi swaha," (pronounced gah-tay gah-tay, pair-uh gah-tay, pair-uh sum gah-tay, bo-dee swa-ha). A mantra or prayer from your own religion, such as Hail Mary (or personal prayer), also works fine; just be sure to repeat it nine times.

   Whenever a mantra is mentioned in this book, feel free to substitute a prayer or mantra from your own religion or heart. The point is to use one that has spiritual significance to you.

2. **Fill the large bowl three-quarters full with rice.**

3. **Add the cinnabar powder to the rice.** The cinnabar helps potentiate the mixture to remove negative forces and spirits from the property; it also adds powerful positive energies and auspicious blessings. (See Figure 17-1.)

4. **Add nine measures of liquor to the cinnabar and rice.** You can measure nine capfuls or pour nine splashes of liquor into the bowl — the nine measures don't need to be equal. The liquor helps to energetically strengthen the rice/cinnabar mixture. (See Figure 17-1.) Recite the Six True Words (pronounced Om Ma Ni Pad Me Hum) or another mantra of your choice while pouring the liquor into the mixture. (See Chapter 6 for more details on the Six True Words.)

5. **Mix the rice, cinnabar, and liquor together using the middle finger of the left hand for women, and the same finger on the right hand for men.** Yes, it's traditional. (See Figure 17-1.)

6. **Recite the Six True Words (or another mantra) 108 times while you mix the rice with your middle finger.** Visualize the God or deity of your choice entering the rice in spirit and infusing it with the power to bless and cleanse your property. As an optional aid to counting, you can use a *mala* (an Indian rosary), which contains 108 beads (a sacred number in many religious traditions). Count one bead for each repetition of the mantra and stop when you get to the end of the mala. Otherwise, you can just count any way you want.

Figure 17-1:
Rice
Blessing
ingredients
and mixing
procedure.

Tossing the rice

1. **Take your bowl of rice and go to the property's *Mouth of Chi*.** This area is the property entrance, typically where the driveway meets the street. If your house doesn't have a driveway, go to where the front walkway meets the public sidewalk or street (or the main front entry to the property).

2. **At the Mouth of Chi, start by vigorously tossing three handfuls of rice straight up and as high as possible into the air, using the Uplifting Mudra.** (See Figure 17-2.) Each time you toss a handful of rice, recite the Six True Words. Visualize the energy of your site — and your life — being raised, empowered, and uplifted.

3. **Toss three handfuls of rice outward, parallel to the ground, using the Giving Mudra.** (See Figure 17-2.) This gesture feeds the hungry ghosts. Visualize your problems disappearing and all negativity leaving the site. Again, recite the Six True Words with each toss.

4. **Toss three handfuls of rice straight down to the ground, using the Planting Mudra.** (See Figure 17-2.) This set of tosses plants new seeds of growth. Visualize the positive things you desire in life springing up all around you and growing strongly, starting now. Recite the Six True Words with each of the tosses.

Figure 17-2:
Rice
Blessing
tossing
methods.

5. **Proceed around the perimeter of the property in a clockwise or counterclockwise fashion, according to your choice.** (See Figure 17-3.) Wherever you intuitively feel you should, stop and toss the rice following Steps 2 through 4.

   For best results in this ceremony, each time you toss the rice recite the mantra and visualize according to the tossing method that you are performing, as described in Steps 2 through 4. Upward tosses clear and uplift the energy, outward tosses disperse and remove problems and negativity, and downward tosses plant new energies for growth.

6. **You can stop to throw three handfuls of rice against the front door of the house at any time during your trip around the property.** This step helps to bless the house as well as the land. When you've walked the perimeter of the property, you will arrive at your starting point at the mouth of the drive.

7. **Complete the tossing by throwing three final handfuls of rice towards the sky and ask for Heaven's blessings.**

Reinforcing the blessing

The final step of the blessing is to perform the Three Secrets Reinforcement: Flick nine times outward with your middle and ring fingers, repeat your mantra or prayer of choice nine times, visualize that your ceremony was effective, and see your desires coming true quickly and easily. (Check out Chapter 6 for more details on how to perform the Three Secrets Reinforcement.)

Figure 17-3:
Rice
Blessing
path around
perimeter of
property.

Q and A on the Rice Blessing

Check out the questions and answers in the following section to clear up any lingering mysteries on this powerful Feng Shui blessing ceremony.

What should I do with the rice that is scattered on the ground? And how long should I leave it there?

The best course of action is to leave the rice on the ground alone as long as possible; the rice is a blessing for the property. Ideally, the rice should remain outside for at least 24 hours. If you feel the need, you can sweep it off of your sidewalks and walkways during this period.

I live in an apartment building and can't perform this ceremony around my building unit. How can I bless my apartment?

You can perform the Rice Blessing around the apartment building's exterior or, if desired, around the whole city block. You can also perform a variation of the ceremony by tossing the rice around the interior perimeter of the apartment. In this variation, I recommend leaving the rice on the floor for a minimum of 24 hours before vacuuming it up. If you can't apply any of these options, you can perform the Interior Chi Adjustment (Orange Peel Blessing), as detailed later in this chapter.

What if pets or birds eat the rice?

I've never seen or heard of any animals being harmed by this ceremony, so this situation doesn't seem to be a problem. (If they do eat the rice, perhaps they can get the blessing!) An urban legend floats around that birds explode when they eat rice, so throwing rice at weddings is discouraged because of this apparent misinformation. Problems for wildlife only occur when you use pre-cooked rice, which specifically is not recommended for this cure. But if you're truly worried about the birds, you can also use other grains such as millet, wheat, or barley for this blessing.

What if I have extra rice left over?

You can ceremonially throw a few final large handfuls until you've used up the rice, or you can dispose of it anyway you want.

What should I do with the bowl after the cure?

Cinnabar should not be ingested internally unless you're under the supervision of a Chinese medical doctor. Therefore, take care to wash the bowl and your hands thoroughly after you perform this cure. Stone and jade artifacts removed from ancient Chinese burial sites were ceremoniously covered with cinnabar and commonly turned red from prolonged contact with this powerful herbal mixture. In other words, cinnabar's a strong substance — so wash the bowl out carefully.

Results from the Rice Blessing

Typically, the house and property feel lighter, freer, and more cheerful immediately after the ceremony, and the lighting in the house appears brighter. Some people mention that after the Rice Blessing, the house almost looks like it glows. Over the longer term, my clients report that they experience freedom from problems and blocks, their interpersonal relationships and health improve, and life just feels better. Increased flow of funds may also follow. Children, pets, and plants can also experience benefits from this blessing.

Using Citrus Magic: The Orange Peel Blessing

The Orange Peel Blessing ceremony is performed on the interior of a house or commercial building. Its purpose is to energetically cleanse and bless the building and its inhabitants. Moreover, this blessing removes a multitude of negative influences and helps to correct and compensate for known as well as unknown Feng Shui problems. The Orange Peel Blessing also helps to create new beginnings and fresh starts in life even in the most unfortunate circumstances. Performing this cure is also appropriate to bless a home or office upon moving in or to ensure an auspicious grand opening of a new business.

How the Orange Peel Blessing works

The Orange Peel Blessing is performed throughout the interior of a building. Whereas the Rice Blessing acts on the ground and the building, the Orange Peel blessing works only on the building itself and the lives of the people inside. Accordingly, it has great power to promote and enhance freedom and good fortune.

The Orange Peel Blessing uses the freshening power of citrus and water along with mantras (spiritual sounds) and visualizations to change and refresh the energies of the building.

Items to gather for the Orange Peel Blessing

For the Orange Peel Blessing, gather the following items in advance:

- ✔ **Nine oranges:** For a very large house, you can use eighteen or twenty-seven oranges.
- ✔ **A large bowl:** Any large mixing or salad bowl works well.
- ✔ **Fresh cut flowers:** Purchase fresh cut flowers specifically for this ceremony. Newly purchased ones are best, but flowers picked from your garden can also work. Put the flowers in water and place them in a visible spot in the house.

Performing the Orange Peel Blessing

The steps of this ceremony are similar to the Rice Blessing. First you prepare the orange peels and large bowl of water, as detailed in the following section. Then you perform the active phase of the cure throughout the house interior. Finally, you perform the Three Secrets Reinforcement to reinforce and further strengthen the blessing.

This ceremony is slightly different from others because you need to follow a couple of additional steps after you perform the Reinforcement.

Preparing the oranges and water

1. **Holding your hands in the Heart-Calming Mudra, recite the Heart-Calming Mantra (Gate gate, para gate, para sam gate, bodhi swaha) or your own mantra of choice nine times.** See Chapter 6, Figure 6-1b.

2. **Fill the bowl three-fourths full with water.**

3. **Tear the peels of the nine oranges into small pieces and place them into the water.** You can dispose of the pulp of the oranges any way you want; they are not used in the ceremony.

Sprinkling the orange peel water

1. **Take the bowl containing the water and orange peels to the front door on the inside of the house.** Hold the bowl of water in one hand. Dip the fingertips of your other hand into the water. With the Expelling Mudra (middle and ring fingers flicking out from the palm), sprinkle the water around the entryway, inside the house. (See Chapter 6, Figure 6-1a.)

2. **Sprinkle the water and recite the Six True Words (Om Ma Ni Pad Me Hum) or your own mantra.** Visualize and feel that all the bad luck and negative chi is being removed. Also see and feel new blessings and positive energy being infused into your environment. See your goals and desires coming true quickly and easily as you perform the cure.

3. **Proceed through the entire house, dipping your fingertips in the water and sprinkling the orange water throughout the house as you go.** (See Figure 17-4.) Continue to recite the Six True Words (or mantra of your choice). Visualize that all the negative energy is being removed. The visualization is the most important part of the process. The stronger your mental imagery, detailed imagining, and/or feeling of future results, the better.

   If you don't visualize easily, you can feel or internally hear the old, bad energy being removed and the good new energy and results flowing in.

4. **Sprinkle the water everywhere.** Sprinkle on all floors and rooms (including the basement and garage if they're attached to the house) and on walls, floors, furniture, ceilings, objects, and so on. As an extra step, you can include the closets, cupboards, storage spaces, and under the beds if you want.

   You can go through the house clockwise or counterclockwise as your intuition guides you.

5. **Return to the front door.** Don't attempt to use all the water. You can simply throw out any left over water.

Figure 17-4:
Orange Peel
Blessing
sprinkling
method.

Reinforcing the blessing

Next perform the Three Secrets Reinforcement (as detailed in Chapter 6) to complete the blessing. Visualize and feel that the blessing was completely successful and see your intentions coming to life.

Performing the final steps

These last steps are key parts of the cure. Please follow them closely.

1. **Place the flowers in a central location.**

2. **Open all the windows and doors in your house, including inside and outside doors, and leave them open for 24 hours.** (If windows are stuck or don't open, you can leave them alone.) At night, leave the windows and doors open an inch or so if you can't leave them completely open. Leaving them wide open for several hours during the day is beneficial. Also, the orange peels should remain on the floor for 24 hours.

3. **Change the flowers two more times after this blessing, once every 3 days, replacing them with fresh new ones.** If the flowers begin to wilt before their three-day period is up, go ahead and replace them. (Make sure they have sufficient water to help keep them from drooping.) Regarding the final set of flowers: They can stay in place after the nine days is complete but should be removed from the house as soon as they lose their freshness.

The Vase and Flute Blessing

The Vase and Flute Blessing is an excellent blessing ceremony to perform when moving into a house or office or when celebrating the grand opening of a business. This blessing can bring positive energies to the site and help maintain good fortune throughout the time of residence. The vase serves as a container of spiritual energy and a symbol of good fortune for the household; the flute conveys strength, peace, and blessing to the residents. You can use this blessing for your home or business anytime because it brings good luck, prosperity, and protection while expelling negative forces and ill chi.

Items to gather for the Vase and Flute Blessing

The following items are needed to perform this blessing:

- **A Chinese vase:** The vase should ideally stand about 3 feet tall.

- **A bamboo Chinese flute:** Preferably, the flute should feature two red tassels. Make sure the flute hasn't been blown, played with, or handled roughly. (See Chapter 4 for more information on ideal Chinese flutes and the Feng Shui Resources page at the back of this book for a flute source.)

- **Several pounds of uncooked rice:** Plain white rice is typically used for this cure, although any type is fine.

Performing the Vase and Flute Blessing

The steps of the Vase and Flute Blessing are similar to the Orange Peel Blessing. You prepare the vase and flute as detailed in the following section. Then you perform the active phase of the cure by carrying the vase and flute throughout the house interior. Finally, you perform the Three Secrets Reinforcement to complete the cure and reinforce the blessing.

Preparing the vase and flute

1. **Prepare a place near the front door where the vase/flute/rice container can be permanently left after the ceremony.** Ideally, this location is visible the moment you walk through the front door. You should prepare a place of honor where the vase can't be disturbed or treated casually. A shelf, ledge, counter, table, or other stable surface is a good location.

The vase should sit at least at shoulder height (or higher) of the tallest person in the house, but if this size isn't possible, the blessing can still be effective.

2. **Place the rice in the bottom of the vase.** You should put enough rice into the vase so at least half of the flute visibly extends above the top of the vase.

3. **Situate the flute in the vase so it extends out of the vase and sits on top of the rice.** See Figure 17-5.

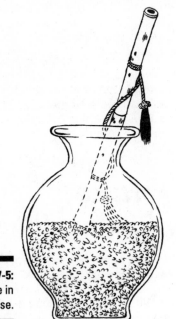

Figure 17-5:
Flute in
vase.

Performing the blessing

1. **Put yourself in a calm or meditative state of mind.**

2. **Begin with your hands in the Heart-Calming Mudra and recite the Heart-Calming Mantra (Gate gate, para gate, para sam gate, bodhi swaha) or other prayer nine times.** See Figure 6-1 in Chapter 6.

3. **Recite an assortment of 10 different mantras or prayers into the mouth of the vase or recite the Six True Words (Om Ma Ni Pad Me Hum) or other mantra into the vase 108 times.** As in all the steps, perform this action with respect and sincerity of heart.

4. **Carry the vase containing the rice and flute to the front door.** Visualize that the light, energy, and spirit of the God or deity of your religion or heart is accompanying you and shining out from you and the vase.

5. **Carry the vase throughout the house with sincere intention while reciting aloud the Six True Words (or mantra of choice) the entire time.** Visualize that the energy and light of the vase and flute are radiat-

ing out into the house, blessing the structure and the inhabitants and making your wishes and desires come true. Visualize that your deity is with you; see and feel that the deity's light is strongly blessing the site.

6. **Return to the front door after you have gone through every room of the house.**

7. **Place the vase in the honored position you prepared for it.** See Figure 17-5.

Reinforcing the blessing

Perform the Three Secrets Reinforcement (as detailed in Chapter 6) while visualizing and feeling that your entire house and life are blessed. Visualize that the vase is shining and blesses all the energy entering the front door and radiates its energy continually throughout the house. Also see your prosperity increasing, your health becoming more vibrant, your relationships becoming more harmonious and peaceful, and your other desires coming true.

Spin the Wheel of Good Fortune (The Constantly Turning Dharma Wheel)

The Constantly Turning Dharma Wheel Blessing spreads good energy throughout any site without using external implements. Like the Vase and Orange Peel Blessings, this blessing is also performed on the interior of the structure. The Constantly Turning Dharma Wheel performs a major house cleansing on the invisible level that continuously radiates thousands of positive impulses throughout the space.

Your own level of results may vary based mainly on your personal skill at performing detailed visualizations. If you practice diligently and gain some proficiency at the visualization portion of this cure before attempting it, you can perform the cure well. Most people don't receive a strong result from a casual approach (although you may!). And if you don't feel up to it just yet, you can look at visualization as something to aspire to in your Feng Shui practice.

Preparing for the ceremony

To perform the Constantly Turning Dharma Wheel Blessing properly, you first need to practice the visualization segment outlined in the following list of steps. If you are extremely good at practicing detailed visual imagery, you can read this section once and skip ahead to the performance section. Otherwise, I recommend practicing this exercise to hone your visualization skills:

1. **See in your mind's eye six colored balls of light arranged in a circular fashion.** The colored balls should always be in the following order: white, red, yellow, green, blue, and black.

2. **See the ring of balls rotating in orbit around an invisible central point.** They can orbit in any direction you wish.

3. **Visualize a smaller set of the six balls circling each of the balls in your first ring.** Each of the sets of six smaller balls is orbiting one of the larger balls. These sets of balls are also in the same color progression as given in step one. (See Figure 17-6.)

4. **Visualize a smaller third group of six balls orbiting each of the balls in the second smaller ring.** You can carry this progression as far as you are able. All the balls are spinning and moving constantly in their orbits. These colored spheres of light and their movement make up the Constantly Turning Dharma Wheel.

   The more clarity and detail with which you can visualize these balls and their movements, the more effective this cure can be.

5. **Visualize this complex orbital setup replicated in several additional versions around all sides of your body.** Perform this step if you can.

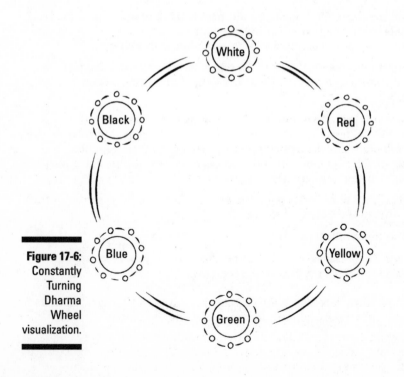

Figure 17-6:
Constantly
Turning
Dharma
Wheel
visualization.

Performing the Constantly Turning Dharma Wheel Blessing

Follow these steps to perform the blessing:

1. **Start the ceremony outside the house in front of your front door.**

2. **Place yourself in a calm state of mind.**

3. **Position your hands in the Heart-Calming Mudra and recite the Heart-Calming Mantra (Gate gate, para gate, para sam gate, bodhi swaha) or your mantra of choice nine times.** For more details on this mudra and mantra, see Chapter 6.

4. **Change your hand position to the Blessing Mudra.** Refer to Figure 6-1d in Chapter 6 for more details on the mudra.

   Optional step: Visualize an eight-petaled lotus blossom inside your body at your heart. See the deity of your religion sitting on the lotus flower and expanding to completely fill your body. You and the deity are now one and the same being. See your light shining out and blessing everything around you. Continue in this state for the rest of the ceremony.

5. **Visualize the three-dimensional color progression of orbiting balls.** See the clouds of moving balls all around you interpenetrating your body. (See the "Preparing for the ceremony" section earlier in this chapter.)

6. **Step into the house and see the blessing light and power from the colored balls shining everywhere at once throughout the house.** See Figure 17-7.

7. **Walk through the entire house while seeing the Constantly Turning Dharma Wheel moving with you.** See it clearing any negativity from the house and adding blessings and positive energy to the residence. Visualize problems fleeing the area and desired results springing into being right at the moment. (See Figure 17-7.)

8. **Recite the Six True Words (Om Ma Ni Pad Me Hum) or your mantra of choice during the entire ceremony.**

9. **Return to the front door.**

10. **Reinforce the blessing with the Three Secrets Reinforcement.** See Chapter 6 for details on the Reinforcement.

That's it, you're outta here! (Or your problems are at least.) Congratulations on performing a powerful and life-changing Feng Shui ceremony!

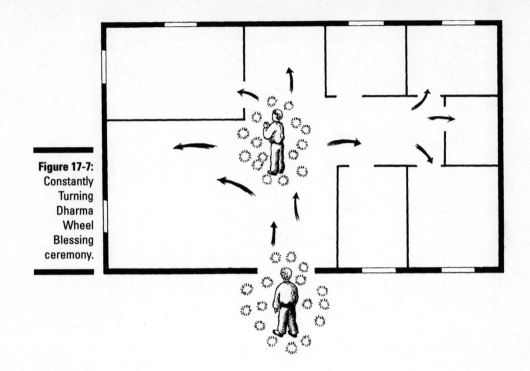

Chapter 18

Exploring Personal Feng Shui Adjustment Methods

This chapter reveals secret methods you can use to adjust your personal energy. Although the best results can come from applying both personal and environmental Feng Shui cures, these methods work whether or not you've performed any Feng Shui cures in your home. Grandmaster Lin Yun's personal cures use special, unusual, and, sometimes, seemingly nonlogical methods of changing and improving personal energy. These cures employ elements from multiple cultural and folklore domains, including Indian, Tibetan, Chinese, and Western influences. The eclectic nature of these cures adds to their potency and makes them priceless cultural treasures. The best part about these methods is that they are inexpensive though highly valuable and effective.

These methods are secret for two reasons: Many of them have never been publicly revealed and their potency is better retained if you don't reveal their procedural details or the fact that you're performing them. Secret cures strongly emphasize visualization and intention as catalysts for their unusual levels of effectiveness. Visualization involves using your mind's eye to see what you want before it happens; intention refers to the clarity and strength of your desire for the cure (knowing what you want and intending strongly for it to happen). See Chapter 6 for more details on visualization and intention.

The secret cures in this chapter are not meant to replace the Feng Shui cures your home may need to improve the corresponding areas of your life. They are part of inner Feng Shui, internal energy practices you can use to directly adjust and enhance your chi and change your life path in particular areas of need.

Preparing for the Cures in This Chapter

To perform the cures in this chapter, you may need to quickly refresh your memory of a few key concepts:

- ✔ **The Three Secrets Reinforcement:** This cure involves using aspects of your body (hand position), speech (sacred speech or mantra), and mind (visualization) to reinforce the effects of Feng Shui cures. See Chapter 6 for more details on visualization.

- ✔ **The Heart-Calming Mudra:** This *mudra* (hand position) brings a calming feeling of balance. To perform it, hold your hands in front of your body, palms up, with your left hand on top of your right and your thumbs touching. See Chapter 6, Figure 6-1b for details on this method.

- ✔ **The Heart-Calming Mantra:** This *mantra* (spoken prayer) is "Gate gate para gate para sum gate bodhi swaha," and it invokes peace and calm. Mantras invoke the energy of sacred speech while boosting the power of your Feng Shui cures. See Chapter 6 for more information.

- ✔ **The Six True Words:** This mantra is "Om Ma Ni Pad Me Hum," and is the mantra of compassion. It brings good luck and protection. See Chapter 6.

- ✔ **Using multiples of the number nine:** Feng Shui teaches that nine is the highest number, which symbolizes completion and power. Therefore, using its multiples in your Feng Shui can add potency to your cures.

Putting Bad Luck to Bed

In this section, I present two special Feng Shui cures for the bed — the Red Cloth Cure for vitality and stability and the Red Feet on Bed Cure for wealth and protection.

Giving yourself a boost

The Red Cloth Cure can enhance your life in a number of ways and can be used in relation to almost any intention or desire. First decide what you want to improve and then apply the cure with this intention. The purposes and effects of the Red Cloth Cure include:

✔ Improving your health and vitality

✔ Revitalizing or injecting passion into a marriage or relationship

✔ Boosting your spirits and energy

✔ Recovering from an unusual illness

✔ Gaining wealth and prosperity

To perform this cure, get a red piece of cloth as large as your bed. I recommend a bright red shade for this cure; this tone is more effective than off shades of red such as maroon. A red flat bedsheet purchased new from the store is a good choice because one whole piece of cloth is stronger than two pieces sewn together.

Place the cloth between the mattress and box spring of your bed. Reinforce the cure with the Three Secrets Reinforcement and visualize your results while you perform it. Parents can also perform this cure for a child using the child's bed. When performing the Three Secrets Reinforcement, visualize the needed results for the child.

Doing fancy footwork: Red Feet on Bed Cure

This cure is applied to the four feet (or bedposts) that hold up the bed. When performed, it helps strengthen one's ability to obtain money and provides strong protection for the occupants of the bed and the household.

How effective are these cures?

You may wonder whether the cures you perform in this book are as effective as getting them in a formal class. Suppose that you obtain the personal cookbook of a master chef whose recipes have delighted thousands of guests, and you want to produce the same meals in your own home. With the cookbook in your hand, all the basic information is available to you. The dishes you prepare may taste less desirable — or even tastier — than the ones prepared by the chef. If you're able to pick up the book and reproduce the meals, you can indeed cook without training.

On the other hand, you may want to get some training so you can make the dishes tastier. The same idea applies to practicing Feng Shui. Some variations and particular Feng Shui methods do need to be taught one-on-one to get the full flavor of the teachings, but with the methods given in this chapter, you can make a marvelous difference in specific and important Life Areas of your choice (see Chapter 3). Ready to get started?

Items needed for the Red Feet on Bed Cure

For this cure, you need:

- ✔ **Four 9-inch square pieces of new red cloth.** Bright red is the most effective.

- ✔ **Four old-style Chinese coins.** These coins are round with a square hole in the center; they usually measure about 1 inch in diameter. You can find them at Chinese gift stores or markets in many urban centers.

- ✔ **Four pieces of red ribbon.** Cut your ribbons to a multiple of 9 inches in length (typically 18 or 27 inches).

Performing the Red Feet on Bed Cure

To perform the Red Feet on Bed Cure, follow this simple procedure:

1. **Lay a red cloth square next to one of the bedposts.** Address one post of the bed at a time.

2. **Place a Chinese coin in the center of the red cloth. Lift up the bedpost and then slide the cloth underneath so the coin lies directly under the post.**

3. **Set the bedpost down so it rests on top of the coin.**

4. **Bring the red cloth up and wrap it around the post. Tie the cloth securely with one of the red ribbons.** The post will look like it has a red sock on it.

5. **Perform the same procedure for the other three bedposts.**

6. **Reinforce this cure with the Three Secrets Reinforcement.** (See Chapter 6.) See and feel yourself becoming wealthy and very protected.

Getting Personal with Feng Shui

The next group of cures includes special personal cures, which include the Traveling Cure to guard you on your travels, the Orange Peel Bathing Cure to restore your personal energy, and the Marriage Cure for enjoying a long and happy marriage or relationship.

Building strength with the yu

The yu cure involves preparing a special bowl called a *yu* (pronounced you). (For information on finding a yu bowl, see the Feng Shui Resource page at the end of this book.) A yu bowl is one with a shallow base, a wide body, and a shallow mouth (see Chapter 4, Figure 4-1). The body of the bowl, which is wider than the mouth, symbolizes accumulated energy. Before using the yu bowl as a cure, first put nine smooth, round or small stones inside the bowl. Fill it three-quarters with water and add in a fresh green leaf. Take the bowl outside and expose it to the sky for a few moments. Next place the bowl under your bed or on your nightstand. For nine consecutive mornings, change the water in the bowl, add in a fresh green leaf, and expose the bowl briefly to the sky. Then replace it under the bed or on the nightstand, and perform the Three Secrets Reinforcement (see Chapter 6). After performing this cure for nine days, return the stones to the earth. Now the bowl is ready for use in special cures, which can strengthen and stabilize your life, relationships, and career. To add strength to your life and positive weight to your endeavors, leave the bowl on your nightstand or under the bed indefinitely. Treat the bowl as a sacred object. If you want to empower your career, set the bowl on your desk. Be sure to reinforce either cure using the Three Secrets Reinforcement while visualizing your desired goals quickly being accomplished. To stabilize a child, perform the variation given in the "Rethinking day, trundle, and temporary beds" section in Chapter 13.

Traveling with good luck

Perform the Good Luck in Traveling Cure to bring you protection, prosperity, and good fortune on your travels. This cure symbolically evokes the protective power of walking on a magic red carpet when you leave for a journey. For this cure, you need a piece of red cloth 6 feet long and 3 feet wide, which you can buy at any fabric store. Bright red works best.

1. **Lay the 6-foot-long piece of red cloth across the threshold at the front doorway just before you leave home on your trip when you're packed and ready to go.** Three feet of the cloth stays inside the house, and 3 feet extends outside the door. (See Figure 18-1.)

2. **Take your suitcase and walk out the door on the red cloth.** Walk slowly and with great intention and awareness while reciting the Six True Words (Om Ma Ni Pad Me Hum) or another mantra of your choice nine times. Perform the Expelling Mudra nine times as you walk across the cloth (flicking the middle and ring fingers out from the palm, see Chapter 6, Figure 6-1a). Visualize a safe departure; see that your trip is beneficial, prosperous, and free of problems; and envision your safe return while you walk. Be sure to bring your red cloth with you on your trip.

3. **Before returning home, do the procedure again.** Place the red cloth over the threshold of the doorway of your hotel room (or wherever you're staying) 3 feet inside the door and 3 feet outside.

4. **Walk out on the red cloth and recite the Six True Words (Om Ma Ni Pad Me Hum) or another mantra nine times.** Perform the expelling mudra and visualize a safe return as you walk along the red cloth. This second performance of walking out on the red cloth helps insure your safety on the way home as well. Grab your cloth and head for home!

Because this special cure integrates into its performance all the elements of the Three Secrets Reinforcement (mantra, mudra, and visualization), you don't need to reinforce the cure separately at the end, as recommended with all the other cures in this book.

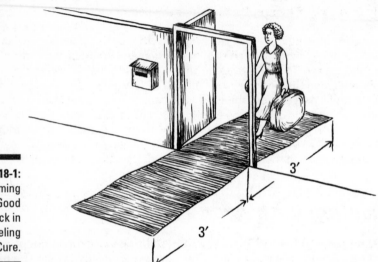

Figure 18-1:
Performing
the Good
Luck in
Traveling
Cure.

Restoring personal chi: The Orange Peel Bath Cure

This simple personal chi adjustment cure offers profound energetic help in times of real need. This cure calls upon the revivifying energetic properties of the orange; citrus is renowned for its power to freshen and purify and it can powerfully assist human chi. The Orange Peel Bath Cure is a highly effective way to restore personal energy, shed bad luck, protect yourself against spiritual or emotional attack, and recover from strange or difficult illnesses.

To perform the Orange Peel Bath Cure, follow these three easy steps to strengthen and revitalize your chi:

1. **Tear the peels of nine oranges into small pieces and put them into bath water.**

2. **Take a bath with the orange peels in the water.**

3. **After your bath, perform the Three Secrets Reinforcement (see Chapter 6) and visualize yourself free from harm, disease, and ill will.**

Promoting a long and happy marriage

With over 50 percent of marriages ending in divorce and with many relationships never reaching the marriage zone, many people have clearly mastered the art of short intense relationships. But maybe you're ready to try something new and different, for instance, a long and happy marriage. (Particular emphasis on loooong and haaappy!)

If you're someone who desires a long fulfilling marriage (or if you simply find the concept intriguing and want to give it a shot), the Marriage Cure may be the one for you. Although this cure can't get you a new partner, it can promote relationship longevity and happiness with your current partner. And this cure is very potent when performed properly with great intention.

Items needed to enhance your marriage

For this cure, gather the following items:

- ✔ **One photo of you and one of your partner:** Ideally, the photos should be approximately the same size. Each picture should show only one person (Figure 18-2a).

- ✔ **A really long red string or ribbon, all in one piece (not tied together):** To determine the length of ribbon needed, multiply the width of the picture times 100. For example, if the photos are 3 inches across, the string needs to be at least 300 inches.

- ✔ **A red envelope:** Make sure your envelope is big enough for your photos to fit inside. Most stationery stores offer red envelopes in various sizes. (As a last resort, you can take a white envelope and color it red with crayon or marker.)

Performing the cure

To perform this cure, follow these steps:

1. **Place the photos face-to-face.**

2. **Write your full name and the word "matrimony" on the back side of your partner's photo.** On the back side of your photo, write the word "matrimony" and your partner's full name.

3. **Under the light of the moon, bind the photos together (face-to-face) by wrapping a red-colored string around them 99 times.** See Figure 18-2b.

4. **Visualize that you and your beloved are perfect mates brought together from many miles apart.**

5. **Place the photos wrapped with red string in a red envelope.** See Figure 18-2c.

6. **Put the envelope beneath your pillow.** Sleep with the envelope in this spot for nine consecutive nights. See Figure 18-2d.

7. **On the tenth day, take the red envelope to a place with moving water.** Find a river or go to the ocean. Throw the envelope into the water. The water should carry it away; a barely moving brook or stream that can't carry away the envelope doesn't have a strong enough current for a good cure. If you go to the ocean, make sure you throw in the envelope when the tide is going out. See Figure 18-2e.

If you can't get to a body of flowing water, you can alternately bury the photos in the back yard — the Marriage Area is a good spot — and, at the same time, plant a new thriving tree on top of the envelope. The Marriage Area of the yard is the far, back-right portion of the lot (see Chapter 3 for more details on this area).

8. **Visualize that your marriage or relationship is made in heaven and will last forever.**

9. **Reinforce the cure with the Three Secrets Reinforcement.** See Chapter 6.

If you perform this cure, your relationship can move to a new depth of love and commitment that may surprise and delight you and your partner in many ways.

Figure 18-2: Marriage cure steps.

Letting the Sun Shine In

The next cure is the Great Sunshine Buddha exercise, a physical energy practice that helps your body circulate its energy in a more healthy and vibrant manner. It purifies, clarifies, and strengthens your energy system and promotes physical and mental health. This cure is easy, requires no training, produces tangible results — and it feels great! You can perform the Great Sunshine Buddha Cure as many times per day as you want.

The Great Sunshine Buddha exercise has three parts (which are shown in order from left to right in Figure 18-3). In Grandmaster Lin Yun's Feng Shui school, visualization is the most important part of Feng Shui. If visualization is not easy for you, you can physically feel or internally hear the corresponding sensations according to the following visualizations:

Great Sunshine Buddha: Part 1

1. **Stand with your feet shoulder width apart and with your hands at your sides.**

2. **Visualize a bright shining sun 2 to 3 feet above your head and directly in front of you.**

3. **Raise your arms over your head and slightly in front of you with the palms facing this sun.** Visualize that the sun contains positive, spiritual, and healing energy as well as sunlight. For extra power, visualize a spiritual figure in the sun that is shining his or her light through the sun's rays.

4. **Inhale.** As you draw in air, visualize the healing golden light and warmth from the sun pouring into your body through three points — the centers of your palms and the point between your eyebrows. See the healing golden sunlight flooding and filling your body. See the light fill you and also feel it energetically.

5. **Start to exhale when your body is full of light.** As you exhale, visualize all the golden light going straight down through your feet and into the ground.

6. **Return your hands to your sides.**

Part I   Part II   Part III

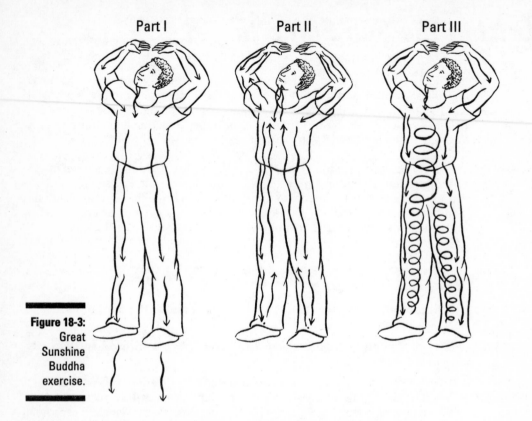

Figure 18-3:
Great
Sunshine
Buddha
exercise.

Great Sunshine Buddha: Part 2

1. **Raise your hands over your head again, palms toward the sun.**

2. **Inhale energy from the sun into your body through three points — both palms and the mid-eyebrow point.** Visualize and feel the warm sunlight flooding into your body.

3. **See and feel the light immediately bounce back up and shoot upwards through your body and out through the three points toward the sun.**

4. **Return your hands to your sides.**

Great Sunshine Buddha: Part 3

1. **Raise your hands over your head again, palms toward the sun.**

2. **Inhale energy from the sun into the body through the three points — both palms and the mid-eyebrow point.** Visualize the warm sunlight flooding into your body.

3. **Start to exhale when the sunlight has filled your body.**

4. **Exhale and visualize that the light begins to swirl in a spiral manner upwards through your body.** As the light swirls upward, it collects these negative energies:

    • Sickness and harmful chi

    • Negative emotions and thoughts

    • Bad luck and negative energy or negative potential of any kind

5. **Continue to exhale and visualize the light exiting the three bodily points and returning to the sun.** When the light hits the sun, the negative energy is instantly, completely, and permanently burned up.

6. **Return your hands to your sides.**

Performing the three-part cure one time through is one repetition of the Great Sunshine Buddha Cure. After you complete one (or more) repetitions of the exercise, perform the Three Secrets Reinforcement while visualizing and feeling yourself refreshed, clear, and revitalized.

Cleansing and Curing with Meditations

In this section, I present two special meditation methods: Supreme Yoga Stage 1 and the Five Elements, Five Colors Meditation. Both of these practices can help improve your health and physical energy circulation. Supreme Yoga Stage 1 positively adjusts your energy by increasing intelligence and stability. The Five Elements, Five Colors Meditation helps heal the organs by restoring them to proper functioning and returns the body to health.

Supreme Yoga Stage 1

Supreme Yoga is the highest form of meditation in Grandmaster Lin Yun's school of Feng Shui. Nine stages of Supreme Yoga exist, each of which cultivates different areas of the body and psyche. The method in this section is the first stage of the set.

Benefits of Supreme Yoga Stage 1

Supreme Yoga Stage 1 is good for healing insomnia and clearing neuroses. It improves the health and cultivates one's spiritual development and psychic abilities. This meditation can benefit anyone of any religion. It can restore energy when you are tired and can also help you to recover from so-called incurable diseases. Potent and highly effective, this method operates purely on the inner level (it entails no furniture placement) and rearranges the most important Feng Shui environment of all — your energy and bodymind system.

Performing the meditation

The steps of Supreme Yoga Stage 1 are as follows:

1. **Sit, stand, or lie down in the most comfortable position of your choice with your hands in the Heart-Calming Mudra.** (See Chapter 6, Figure 6-1.)

2. **Repeat the Heart-Calming Mantra (Gate gate para gate para sum gate bodhi swaha) or your mantra of choice nine times.**

3. **Imagine everything around you becoming very still and quiet.**

4. **From a far distance, hear the sound "Hum" gradually approach you, getting louder and louder as it grows near.** (See Figure 18-4a.)

5. **Hear and feel the sound enter your body at the point between your eyebrows and see the sound become a small white ball of light.**

6. **See the white ball drop down inside your body to a point 2 inches below your navel, in the center of your body.** In Chinese medicine, this point is called the *dan tien,* or energy field.

7. **Visualize and feel the small white ball making nine small circles in a clockwise direction.**

8. **Visualize the white ball dropping to the bottom of the torso and then moving up the front of your body, over your crown, down your back, and to the bottom of the torso again.** Visualize the white ball traveling around your body in this manner two more times for a total of three circulations. (See Figure 18-4b.)

9. **Visualize the white ball returning to the dan tien.**

10. **See and feel the white ball becoming very hot and bright like the sun, radiating heat and light.**

11. **See the white ball circulating all throughout the interior of your body, still radiating heat and light.** (See Figure 18-4c.) The white ball can circulate rapidly or slowly; it can move in a random or precise manner. The details are up to you.

As the ball circulates, visualize its movement, heat, and light opening up the body's circulation on these multiple levels:

- **Physical circulation:** The flow of blood and lymph, nervous activity, air, water, digestion, and chi throughout the body is enhanced. The body is energized, clarified, and healed.

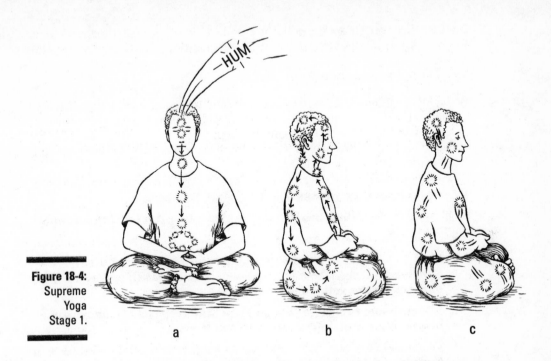

Figure 18-4:
Supreme
Yoga
Stage 1.

a   b   c

- **Mental and emotional circulation:** Old and stagnant emotions such as fear, anger, and hatred are cleared; mental stagnation including rigid ideas, ignorance, and confusion is replaced with clarity, wisdom, and free-flowing awareness.

If any areas of your body need extra healing, allow the small white ball to circulate in these areas a little longer.

12. **Allow the small white ball to return to its position at the dan tien when you feel the circulation is complete.**

13. **Complete the meditation by holding your hands in the Heart-Calming Mudra and recite the Six True Words (Om Ma Ni Pad Me Hum) or another mantra of your choice nine times.**

Five Elements, Five Colors Meditation

This meditation applies the power of the Five Elements and their corresponding colors to five internal organs of the body. Chinese medicine believes that these five organs are the most important ones of the human body. Each organ correlates to a particular energy of the Five Elements as follows:

✔ The lungs relate to Metal.

✔ The kidneys relate to Water.

> ✔ The liver relates to Wood.
>
> ✔ The heart relates to Fire.
>
> ✔ The spleen relates to Earth.

When all Five Elements are balanced and functioning normally in your body, your life achieves profound balance and harmony. This harmony greatly enhances and energizes your being on the physical, emotional, mental, and spiritual levels. In other words, this meditation brings you profound benefits on every level of your being.

Performing the Five Elements, Five Colors Meditation

To perform the Five Element, Five Colors Meditation, perform the following internal steps:

1. **Hold your hands in the Heart-Calming Mudra and chant the Heart-Calming Mantra (Gate gate para gate para sum gate bodhi swaha) or other mantra of your choice nine times.**

2. **Visualize that everything around you is in deep silence. Imagine that everything has dissolved into a complete void.**

3. **Visualize every part of your skeleton from your skull downward turning into red-hot molten iron.** Inch by inch, heat moving downward from your skull to your jaw, to your neck, then to your spine and ribs, pelvis, thighbones, calf bones, arms, fingers, and finally to your toes — all the bones of your body are turning steadily into molten iron — hot, strong and red, like steel in a smelting furnace. Your skeleton is radiating heat and light intensely.

4. **Envision, through the molten heat of your skeleton that the following is occurring:**

   • All negative causes and effects that have accumulated from your previous, current, and next lifetime are cleansed and purified.

   • Negative energies stored in your bodymind through wrong actions of body, speech, emotion, and thought are also being cleansed away.

   • All negative chi, bad luck, and illness of body are being removed and burned away.

5. **Imagine a pink, eight-petal lotus flower arising from the bottom of your feet.** The lotus flower begins to wrap its petals around your red hot skeleton, moving up from your feet to your legs, pelvis, chest, back, arms, and so on.

6. **Visualize that all your vital organs (lungs, heart, stomach, liver, and so on) are emerging as 100 percent newborn pink lotus flesh.** Also see your skeleton being reborn from this new pink lotus material. Composed entirely of pink lotus flesh, your body is completely new and pure.

Purifying three lifetimes

Buddhist practitioners of inner Feng Shui believe that negative causes and effects have accumulated through multiple lifetimes. However, you don't have to believe in past lives to receive tremendous "this lifetime" benefits when performing the Five Elements, Five Colors Meditation. Just visualize that all negativity from the past, present, and future portions of this life are being cleansed away. This concept is called *three lifetime purification.*

7. **Envision a smaller eight-petalled pink lotus blossoming in your heart.** On the blossom appears a small Buddha (or the deity of your own religion). See the image of the deity growing gradually and filling your body completely until you and the deity are one. You now have the deity's same image, color, and shape. You are one with the deity, and the deity is one with you. You possess the deity's perfect wisdom, great compassion, and infinite power.

8. **Starting with your lungs, visualize the color of each key organ gradually changing according to the Creative Cycle of the Five Elements, as described in the following sections.**

Lungs: Natural color white (Metal)

Visualize your lungs changing color from white to black (Water) to green (Wood) to red (Fire) to yellow (Earth) and back to white (Metal) again.

Visualize that all lung disorders are gone and both lungs are emitting light and radiating heat and you are breathing normally.

Kidney: Natural color black (Water)

Visualize your kidneys changing color from black to green (Wood) to red (Fire) to yellow (Earth) to white (Metal) and back to black (Water) again.

Visualize that any kidney disorders are gone and your kidneys are emitting light, radiating heat, and functioning normally.

Liver: Natural color green (Wood)

Visualize your liver changing color from green to red (Fire) to yellow (Earth) to white (Metal) to black (Water) and back to green (Wood) again.

Visualize that any liver disorders are gone and your liver is emitting light, radiating heat, and functioning normally.

Heart: Natural color red (Fire)

Visualize your heart changing color from red (Fire) to yellow (Earth) to white (Metal) to black (Water) to green (Wood) and back to red (Fire) again.

Visualize that any heart disorders are gone and your heart looks like a sun emitting light, radiating heat, and functioning normally and strongly.

Spleen: Natural color yellow (Earth)

Visualize your spleen changing color from yellow (Earth) to white (Metal) to black (Water) to green (Wood) to red (Fire) and back to yellow (Earth) to again.

Visualize that any spleen disorders are gone and your spleen looks like a sun emitting light, radiating heat, and functioning normally.

The entire body

Next visualize that your entire body is now filled with the light of the deity in your heart. All your internal organs are metabolizing healthily and are radiating spiritual light towards the following:

- **Millions of deities (or any angelic beings of your own religion) in the universe:** Their spiritual light radiates back toward you.

- **The six realms where sentient beings exist:** In Buddhism, these realms are named the heavenly realm, jealous gods realm, human realm, animal realm, hungry ghost realm, and hell realm. If your religion differs, you can broadcast the light to the realms that fit with the cosmology of your religion (such as heaven, hell, earth, and other variations). Visualize that all the beings in these realms go from suffering to happiness, and from happiness to ultimate peace. Now their spiritual light radiates back to you.

- **Your spiritual teacher (if you have one) or a spiritual mentor or friend:** His or her spiritual light radiates back to you.

- **Your family, friends, and relatives from afar:** Bless them. Their spiritual light radiates back to you.

- **Your house and office:** Eliminated of evil spirits, bad luck, illness chi, and negative chi, your house is cleansed and purified and radiates positive luck.

Now make a wish for whatever you like. As you visualize your wish coming true, with your hands in the Heart-Calming Mudra, recite the Six True Words (Om Ma Ni Pad Me Hum) or your personal prayer or mantra nine times.

When you finish this meditation, your circulation is enhanced, your organs function more smoothly, and your energy is positively adjusted. Your internal energies are balanced and harmonized, creating a centered body, mind, and feelings. You feel calm and peaceful — probably like you're ready to do some more Feng Shui cures!

Part V
The Part of Tens

In this part . . .

*I*f you hate wasting time and want to hastily waltz into better times, this part is for you. Tens and tens of Feng Shui methods to end the madness and mend the sadness. From ten essential pointers to ensure that your Feng Shui packs a punch to ten special art pieces created by the Feng Shui master, this part helps bless your life, bliss your loft, and blow away your loss. All in all, a treasure trove tried-and-true, a bounty basket through and through.

Chapter 19

Ten Principles for Success with Your Feng Shui

In This Chapter

▶ Paying attention to your surroundings

▶ Following your Feng Shui instincts

▶ Keeping the energy flowing

▶ Getting help with your Feng Shui cures

▶ Using special timing to enhance your cures

*I*f you've read most of this book, you have a good idea how to begin apply-ing Feng Shui. Hopefully, you're already breaking ground and reaping the benefits. But reading a book on Feng Shui and performing some cures doesn't yield the full results. Feng Shui is not a one-trick pony — some gimmick you use once or twice and then put away in the closet with your ab machine. Instead, Feng Shui is a multifaceted tool that enables you to see beneath the surface of your environment, understand how your environment affects you, and rearrange your life on a whole new level. Beginning Feng Shui is like embarking on a journey — it leads you to new discoveries, knowledge, and more of what you really want and need in life!

Use the best materials you can find and afford for your cures. Consider your Feng Shui remedies an investment in your future. (Hey, it's only your life I'm talkin' about here!) Just like everything else in life, you get out of Feng Shui what you put into it. So use high-quality materials to implement your cures.

By the same token, if options exist, choose the strongest cure you can for the situation at hand. In many cases, I've sprinkled tips throughout the text to indicate which cure is the most potent. In other cases, stretch a little and use your intuition to select the best one. Why settle for a partial solution? By applying your full commitment to each cure, the results you see can be pro-found and highly gratifying.

Every journey in life needs guideposts. Let the following ten guiding principles help you refine your new skills so you can take your Feng Shui all the way home.

Follow Your Intuition and Act with Urgency

Allow your intuition — the inner knowing — to guide you when deciding which cures to perform, and when, where, and how to apply them. (If you don't believe in intuition, by all means, use the Force.) After all, you're the one living in your home, and your feelings are connected to its energy. The key is to pay attention to your feelings — and act on them!

I recommend that you perform cures within three days of recognizing the need for them — the sooner the better. The three-day period is a special opportunity window that significantly increases the effectiveness of cures. A Feng Shui problem area is like a wound to your environment's energy, and this condition directly affects you whether you realize it or not. The longer you wait, the more damage the situation does. For example, if you cut your finger with a rusty knife, would you think, "Hmm. . . I really ought to wash and bandage this cut, but a football game is on TV right now, and tonight is the dinner party at the Wilsons' house, and I'm kind of busy at the office this week. Maybe I'll do it next Saturday." Not! Well, the same idea applies when dealing with Feng Shui wounds. (Feng Shui solutions are called cures, hint hint.) So don't procrastinate — fix the problem as soon as you discover that something is broke. (If you can't complete your cure within the three-day period, at least try to get it started within this time.)

Pay Attention to Life's Feedback

Life itself is the ultimate, unerring feedback mechanism for the Feng Shui process. The events of your life are inseparable from and interactive with your environment. Take notice of your life events and actions after you perform the cures and look out for signs of the changes you seek. If you're not getting the desired results or if the effects aren't coming fast enough, you may need to perform additional cures in the corresponding areas of your life.

Fine Tune Your Feng Shui

Use the feedback that life gives you to help reach your goals. What happens in your life after you apply a cure tells you how to fine-tune your Feng Shui. If you perform a wealth cure and your funds increase just one-third the amount you desire, be encouraged — this result is progress! In addition, you learn the art of using energy to create new wealth. So maybe you're not Picasso, yet. But if you keep practicing, you can profit the rest of the way as your skill improves.

Retain Your Energy

Feng Shui recommends that you keep the specific details and purposes of your cures to yourself. Keeping the particulars of your cures private is a way of containing their energy. (Loose lips don't just sink ships, they also leak energy.) You can safely discuss the subject of Feng Shui and let others know that you use it, but telling people outside your household the fine points and purposes of your cures, or teaching them cures without receiving red envelopes, unnecessarily leaks energy from your life. (And do they really need to know?) See the Red Envelope information at the end of Chapter 6 for more details on protecting your energy.

Keep on Keeping On

Continue performing cures, cures, and more cures! Feng Shui is a perpetual process, not a one-way trip to your destination. The need for Feng Shui arises every time you leave your shoes in the hallway, buy new furniture, turn your garage into a junk pile, or simply notice the need for change in any area of your life. The more cures you perform, the more the energy of your home aligns with your needs and supports your goals. You gain skills with cures over time. And remember, a positive frame of mind works wonders both in life and in Feng Shui, so expect results before they appear and then celebrate when they come. As you continue to make positive changes (and your Feng Shui eyes sharpen), you may notice new parts of your home that pop out at you because they need balancing. Go after 'em with a vengeance!

If you feel stuck or unclear about a Feng Shui issue, you can seek spiritual guidance from whatever source you feel connected to — your heart, God, Jesus, Mary, Buddha, Allah, the Tao, Scooby Doo (even Obi Wan Kenobi!). Ask for help in selecting and performing the right cures. Visualize that this source is coming to your aid and guiding your actions and thoughts. You may be surprised at what you receive, and your cures can produce great results.

Work on the Mundane as Well

This principle is more or less a common-sense disclaimer: Put diligent attention and effort into fulfilling the mundane requirements of your life as well as into your Feng Shui practice. If you desire wealth, diligently study and practice the principles and techniques of creating wealth. Feng Shui is not a substitute for gainful employment; it can't magically fill your bank account while you drink beer and watch soap operas in your perfectly Feng Shui-ed home. Feng Shui enhances your life's work in progress and creates a supportive environment in which you can further your dreams. So perform cures in your home and do your work in the world. The combination of intelligent effort, dedication to self-improvement, and powerful Feng Shui cures is the best recipe for your success.

Continue to Learn

If you practice Feng Shui attentively, your ability to notice Feng Shui trouble spots and adjust them to your advantage continuously increases. Eventually, you become like the captain of a well-organized, smoothly operating, and aesthetically pleasing ship. And this ship is your living and working environment — your life as a whole. Attending classes on the subject and reading additional books can help you keep progressing in the world of auspicious placement.

Keep the Faith

Keep an open mind with your Feng Shui work. There is no such thing as a cure that doesn't work. What matters is that you do enough and you do it in the right direction. (For every action, there is an equal and opposite reaction.) Some people perform cures and feel disheartened if they don't get immediate results, but they experience powerful and desired life shifts weeks or months later. Predicting the precise results from any specific cure is impossible. However, God is in the details of the cure, and details are what Feng Shui is all about. So continue to perform cures with sincerity and great intention and use the Three Secrets Reinforcement (see Chapter 6). Then you can patiently and confidently expect the well-deserved results to appear in time.

Enlarge the Team

If you need help performing a Feng Shui cure, enlist your partner or other members of your household. Numbers mean synergy — a combined force — so the more positive intentions involved in your cures, the more the Feng Shui problem can be transformed. Seek qualified help if you feel the need. If a Feng Shui situation seems out of your league or you simply want to advance to the next level with professional help, you can probably find a qualified Feng Shui practitioner in your area.

Employ Special Timing for Stronger Cures

Feng Shui teaches that special timing can make your cures stronger. Two special time periods each day provide windows of opportunity: 11:00 a.m. to 1:00 p.m., and 11:00 p.m. to 1:00 a.m. These periods — when day turns to night and night turns to day — add significance to any solution you perform, giving extra momentum to a Feng Shui cure. You can also consult the Chinese almanac for auspicious dates and times. Good dates to perform cures include the day of the new moon or full moon, your birthday, New Year's Day, Chinese New Year's Day (which differs every year so check an almanac or the Internet for the exact date), or any other day with special significance to you. Performing cures on special dates and times is especially helpful for enhancing the effects of the special cures (blessing ceremonies and personal cures) given in Chapters 17 and 18. But remember: If these dates or times aren't convenient for you, perform the cures whenever you can. Better to move ahead now and see progress than to wait for a special date or time.

Chapter 20

Ten (+1) Ways to Increase Wealth and Stimulate Cash Flow: Show Me the Money!

• •

In This Chapter

▶ Clearing a path for wealth energies to enter your home

▶ Positioning your desk to increase your wealth

▶ Shaping your lot and home to invite weath

▶ Stopping money from leaking out of your home and wallet

▶ Keeping visible so money can find its way to you

• •

Chances are, you're standing in a bookstore right now, reading this section to see if *Feng Shui For Dummies* is really worth buying. (Next, you'll probably flip to the chapter "Better Sex with Feng Shui" — oops, my editor cut that one!) Or maybe you've actually read the whole book, and you want extra tips on how to get mo' money! Well, you're in luck: I've saved the caviar for last. In this chapter, I lay down ten powerful, hard-hitting money cures that can help if you need more money, and they can't hurt if you've got plenty already. The three key wealth areas are the front entrance, the Wealth Area of the Octagon, and the kitchen (especially the stove); I give several cures for the first two areas in this chapter. (For more on the front entrance, check Chapter 9. For Octagon information, see Chapter 3. And for additional stove tips, see Chapters 12 and 22.)

Keep Your Front Pathway Unblocked

The pathway to your front door and the space around the door primarily affect how the chi (energy) is — or isn't — attracted into your home. The condition and quality of the energy that circulates inside your house (and affects you directly) is determined by how much energy can come through the front door. So keeping this path clear allows more energy to enter and circulate in your home, and more importantly to circulate in the Wealth Areas of your home. So clear a path for the wealth to enter! Remove items such as shoes, bikes, toys, newspapers, dead shrubs and trees, and other obstacles. Trim back living plants so the path to the door is free and open. Perform the Three Secrets Reinforcement (see Chapter 6) to strengthen the power for your intention, and watch as more and better energy flows into your home and life.

Put Life in Your Wealth Area

Growing energy is a lovely way to generate growth in your financial situation. A properly placed plant in the Wealth Area is a great money cure (see Chapter 3 to find out where the Wealth Area is located in your home). Try it! Buy a healthy, strong, beautiful new plant for the Wealth Area of your house and apply the Three Secrets Reinforcement (as detailed in Chapter 6). Money may not grow on trees, but trees (and plants) can enhance your money-growing chi. If your Wealth Area doesn't have enough light to support a plant, be creative. Put in a light, or buy a shade-loving plant, or get a realistic artificial plant. (Yes, artificial plants work, too. And so does this cure!)

Place Your Desk in the Commanding Position

You can more easily achieve success when your desk is placed in a Commanding Position in your home or office (see Chapter 16 for more details and illustrations on the Commanding Positions). Repositioning your desk helps make the energy in your Wealth Area work for you, not against you. (Ever notice that you can run faster and further with the wind at your back than you can with the wind at your face?) Placing your desk in the Commanding Position (farthest from and facing the door) is like running with the wind, and it gives you several possible advantages. You may find that your decision making flows easier; you feel more relaxed, focused, and in control; your confidence naturally increases; and things just seem to improve around you. In addition, your moneymaking power may increase (along with your chi) due to this auspicious — need I say lucky — shift to the Commanding Position in your Wealth Area. Not bad for a cure that requires no monetary output and only minor muscular investment.

Brighten Up Your Front Entrance

A dark entrance implies a dark future, a difficult career, and difficulty in attracting money. (Not to mention a difficulty getting your key in the door!) The ideal entrance creates positive and bright feelings. Many entrances have only one 60-watt bulb. Adding light is an easy and effective way to up the chi of your entrance, lighting the way for wealth to find your door. The cure is simple: Put bright lights (the brighter the better) near your entrance. This cure also increases the energy level of the whole house.

Increase the Flow of Wealth into Your Home

In Feng Shui, water signifies your wealth, and flowing water creates your cash flow. The ideal water condition is one in which water flows towards your front door. Therefore, an exterior fountain arranged with water flowing towards the front door is highly beneficial. Water flowing away from the front door symbolizes money flowing away from the house. (Not good!)

The greater the flow, the better the benefits. Even if you can't run your fountain in the winter due to freezing temperatures, the fountain is still a wealth enhancer if properly placed. (To compensate, you may choose to place an additional fountain indoors — again, with water flowing into the body of the house.) However, a broken fountain or one in disrepair is a negative Feng Shui feature.

Fountains that circulate water from a gathering pool symbolize money gathering and entering into your life. This kind is more beneficial than a fountain that allows water to disappear as it circulates (trickle down between rocks, for example). If water pools visibly, it's easier for you to accumulate the money the fountain brings.

Even Out the Lot

The shape of your lot is a prime factor determining your destiny and your luck (good or bad). An uneven lot shape means uneven opportunities — life is hard work, and cash harder to come by. Looking at a drawing of your lot, if your lot shape is a square or rectangle, good for you. If not, correct missing areas by installing lights, planing trees, or raising flagpoles. (See Chapter 8 for more on identifying and filling in missing lot areas.) Correct angled sides of the lot (those that look angled or leaning on the lot drawing) by installing lights at each end of the slant. Correct lots with more than four sides or that are oddly shaped by placing a tall green flag at each corner of the lot. (See Chapter 8 for more on these points.)

Seal Up Those Money Leaks

As I mention earlier in this chapter, water flowing toward the house (barring leaks, floods, or fire hoses) signifies money entering the home. In contrast, water flowing away symbolizes money leaving the home. Drains inside your house, therefore, automatically signify money leaving the premises. Clearly you're not about to give up your precious indoor plumbing. So what's a reasonably minded person to do? It's really quite simple: Apply ye olde Feng Shui cures, of course! Wherever you find a drain, seal in the energy by keeping the drain plugged or covered, and visualize your wealth increasing (see Chapter 13 for more on drains). Drains are especially problematic in the Wealth Area, at the entrance, and in the center of the house (see Chapters 3 and 10, respectively, for information on how to find the Wealth Area and the center of your house). But for good measure, I recommend sealing any drains on the premises.

Keep bathroom doors closed and place a full-length mirror on the outside of the bathroom door. This will prevent vital chi from unnecessarily "leaking" from the premises, draining both health and wealth. Sink, tub, and shower drains should be stoppered or covered when not in use. (And hey, guys, remember to put that toilet lid down.) I also suggest placing a seal on any other drains in the house (in the garage, laundry room, and so on). Many people can feel the energetic shift in their bodies immediately after applying these leaky drain cures. And before long, your wallet should also experience a profitable shift.

Multiply Your Abundance

Food and dishes on the dining table represent wealth. So energetically increase this factor by keeping a large, decorative bowl of fresh fruit or other appealing edibles on the table. A more powerful cure involves placing a large mirror in the room so that it reflects the dining table. The mirror symbolically doubles the dishes, multiplying wealth and fortune. Another method — which can be applied with or without the mirror — involves purchasing a larger dining table with more room for these cure items.

Balance the Shape of Your House

If your house shape is missing some areas (for example, if your house is L-shaped rather than a square or rectangle), pay close attention — particularly if the missing areas are in the Wealth, Career, or Helpful People Life Areas (see Chapter 3 for more information on applying the Octagon to your home to identify your Life Areas). Interior cures for missing areas include mirroring a wall in the missing area to energetically expand the house, or placing living plants, or hanging a faceted crystal sphere in the missing area. Adding any one of these items to a missing area in your home will create balance and strength, making it easier to attract and retain money.

Hit the Hot Spot in the Bedroom

The Wealth Area of the bedroom is a major money zone! (See Chapter 3 for details on applying the Feng Shui Octagon to your bedroom to identify its Wealth Area.) The Wealth Area of your bedroom — the room where you spend roughly a third of your life — powerfully influences your monetary fate. Hanging a wind chime in the Wealth Area of your bedroom is a very effective cure for activating this area. Hang the chime from a red ribbon cut in multiples of 9 inches in length.

Make Your House Numbers and Mailbox Visible

If it's hard for people to find you, then it's probably tough for money and energy to find you as well. Hiding out is not generally the best way to enrich yourself. The simple cure is to put your house number in plain view. Placing it in multiple locations — on the house, mailbox, and curb — can't hurt.

House numerals arranged flowing upward (at a 45 degree angle is good) invoke a more positive influence than those arranged slanting downwards. Also make sure your mailbox is visible and in good repair. *Muy importante!* An invisible or decrepit mailbox is just another energy barrier to receiving income and wealth. Remember, the check really is in the mail! More than simple maintenance cures, these solutions make it easier for you to receive money, information, and connections.

Chapter 21

Ten Ways to Create Harmony in Your Marriage (Or Find That Perfect Partner)

*H*o-hum — another wonderful Friday night watching reality TV while all your friends are out having an incredible time in their real lives with their fabulous partners. It's enough to drive you . . . to Feng Shui! A small percentage of people in this country are in a happy, long-term relationship. Everybody else is waiting to hit the jackpot — meaning they either find their perfect partner or move their presently unsatisfying relationship to a whole new level of love, respect, and intimate communication.

So what does it take? I suggest Feng Shui (not surprisingly) as the quickest and easiest place to start, which if properly applied, can work wonders. Right now, Feng Shui is one of the most powerful factors influencing your relationship. The energy of your home and bedroom may be keeping your ideal companion at bay, or it may be blocking the flow of energy between you and your current partner. Something as simple as correctly positioning your bed in relation to the bedroom door can be half of the battle. (Of course how you dress, talk, and smell has a wee influence as well . . . but that's a subject for *Dating For Dummies*.)

This chapter walks you through ten homegrown, handpicked cures for spicing up your love chi. Apply with a sprig of intention, a dash of Reinforcement, and a dollop of visualization, and watch your love life blossom!

Position Your Bed for Good Fortune

Bed placement is a prime factor determining the quality of your marriage and love life. It also plays a key role in the quality of your sleep, which significantly affects your personal strength, including how strong you are throughout the day — and throughout a date.

The ideal position for the bed is farthest from the door. If your bedroom door is in the front right part of the room (viewed from standing just outside the bedroom door), the best position for your bed is in the back left corner. If the door is in the left front corner of the room, the bed should be in the back right corner. And if the door is in the front middle of the room, the bed can be positioned in either corner farthest from the door. Also, place the bed with the head firmly against the wall, with the door in plain view. (If your bed doesn't fit in any of these position options, see Chapter 11 for remedies.)

The principles I detail in the previous paragraph are indeed important. They all count, so make the best choice (using logic and intuition) after taking all factors into consideration.

Place your bed in the strongest position possible, and watch your romantic life gradually — or even suddenly — take a turn (hopefully on the dance floor!) for the better.

Remove Distractions from Your Bedroom

The watchwords for bedroom Feng Shui are simplicity, peace, and beauty. In the bedroom, an important rule of thumb is that anything not directly connected to resting and relating to your partner detracts from the relationship. A few items to remove from your bedroom include work-related materials such as your briefcase and miscellaneous papers, your telephone and answering machine (do you really want to sleep with a beeper under your pillow?), and your TV and radio (you can survive without them). Bookcases and large piles of books stacked around the room are also distractions. Although the books contain many interesting ideas, few of them really involve sleeping and relationships — the intended functions of the bedroom. Removing most of the books and all of the shelves from your bedroom helps reduce mental turbulence, improve sleep, and make relaxing and relating much easier.

Extract Clutter and Extra Furniture from Your Bedroom

For energy to flow between you and your mate (that's "love" if you live outside of California!), the bedroom must have enough space for the flow to, well, flow. If you need to perform a special version of the limbo to get through your bedroom, guess what? You've got too much stuff! Clutter can stifle the vital energy of a relationship and may even cause your partner to look for a new place to sleep, or worse — leave the relationship! Less is usually more in the bedroom, so any tall, large, heavy furniture items — particularly ones positioned near the bed — should be removed. If the room seems too empty after removing the blocking items, fill the spaces with healthy plants, nice lamps, or much smaller furniture items.

Hang a Flute for Strength

Special bamboo Feng Shui flutes symbolize peace, safety, and strength — desirable qualities for any relationship. To encourage these characteristics to flourish in your relationship, try hanging a flute in the Marriage Area of your bedroom and see how it feels. (See Chapter 3 for details on how to find the Marriage Area of your bedroom, and Chapter 4 for flute tips. Check out the Feng Shui Resources page at the back of this book for places to purchase bamboo flutes.)

Upgrade Your Marriage Areas

Try a holistic approach. Try what? Well, a good idea is to assess all the Marriage Areas in your space (see Chapter 3 to determine these areas). Important places to check out include the Marriage Area of your yard, house, and bedroom. Look for these negative contributors: broken or useless items, leaks, dirt, spare boards from that still-incomplete home improvement project you're still "working" on, upside-down lawn jockeys, and so on. Repair and/or remove these items. Cleanse and beautify the area and then reinforce these cures using the Three Secrets Reinforcement detailed in Chapter 6 to enhance clarity and love in your relationship.

Fit Your Bed with Pink Sheets

The color pink empowers qualities such as love and tenderness, so putting this color close to you (or better yet, sleeping in between pink sheets) can create harmony in your relationship. Applying the pink sheet cure requires you to fit your bed with — what else? — pink sheets! Hey guys, your wife may love that you're getting in touch with your "feminine side," and if your friends find out, just slouch with your thumbs hooked in your belt and mumble, "Oh yeah, it was my wife's idea." Single men, unfortunately, can't use this disclaimer to explain the new pink sheets to friends, but rest assured that your new partner will really dig them. (Tell her you bought the sheets for her.)

Release the Old, Bring in the New!

If you have sad momentos from a previous marriage or relationship, don't keep these momentos in the bedroom, or anywhere else on the property for that matter. According to Feng Shui, they represent psychic obstacles and could keep you from welcoming a new and healthy relationship into your life. Build a fire (safely), and place old pictures, articles, scrapbooks, locks of hair, and other things that stir up painful emotions in the fire. (If the fire marshal lives next door, or your mother doesn't like you to play with matches, just toss out the keepsakes.) Cry if necessary and then put out the old flame! Perform the Three Secrets Reinforcement (detailed in Chapter 6) and be on the lookout for your new partner, or new happiness with your current partner.

One client kept his ex-wife's bridal gown under his bed. It wouldn't have been so bad, except the relationship ended after she cheated on him, stole his money, and fled the scene of the crime (in this case, the marriage). Needless to say, the energy improved (along with the unfortunate gentleman's spirits) soon after he removed this noxious momento from his home.

You Light Up My Life

Because this cure helps virtually every area of your life, I feel odd putting it in a marriage section — oh, well! The cure is to install a single light fixture in the bedroom, bright enough to vividly light the whole room. As I like to say, "Bright light means bright life. Dim light means dim future." (I also moonlight writing catchy phrases for fortune cookies.) Insufficient light exerts a subtle depressing effect in your marriage and life. You don't need to keep the light on for this cure to work, but it does need to be functional.

Multiple lamps that can brightly light the room when turned on at the same time are not as effective as one lamp that can brightly light the entire room by itself, unless the multiple lamps are wired to a single switch. If you already use the one-switch-turns-on-all type of bedroom light, you can further empower its energy simply by using the Three Secrets Reinforcement (detailed in Chapter 6).

Plant a Healthy New Tree in the Marriage Area

A new tree means new life, so try planting a healthy tree in your yard to attract a new partner or add new life to your current one. (And who doesn't want oomph in the relationship department?) First, get a tree. Then heigh thee ho to yonder right back corner of your property. Dig. Plant. Water. Love. Now watch as the growing energy of the plant adds growth and new energy to the Marriage Area of your property, which in turn empowers your relationship with that special someone.

If the tree has colorful flowers, so much the better. Any color is good, but pink is especially effective.

Use the Double Happiness Symbol

Double Happiness is an ancient Chinese symbol that represents unity and mutual happiness for two parties. This symbol (usually painted in gold on a red background) is quite lovely to look at, and it is prominent at Chinese weddings even today. You can find them in most Chinese groceries and markets; just ask. Feel free to place one or more anywhere in the bedroom. But the Marriage Area of the room is, of course, a prime location for this cure.

Chapter 22

Ten Ways to Enjoy Better Health with Feng Shui

Tired of feeling down, drained, and depressed? Or perhaps you're ready to lose those extra 15 pounds? Well, if you're interested in quick and easy Feng Shui cures that can immediately improve your spirits and your health, you've certainly come to the right place. Your physical and emotional health is strongly influenced by the condition of your house and the placement of the objects within it. Simple changes can often bring about big benefits for your health — not to mention your state of mind. So try any of the following cures that jump out at you and see how they make you feel.

Feng Shui health cures are not a substitute for proper medical care. They are supportive energetic remedies only. Check with your physician *tout de suite* (that's French for "right now") regarding all health issues. And freely use Feng Shui cures as a supplement to necessary medical care.

Placing a Mirror Behind Your Stove

Your kitchen stove is a primary factor in determining the health of your home's occupants. According Feng Shui, you should be able to see the doorway of the kitchen to avoid being startled while cooking, because your feelings while cooking can affect your food and in turn your body. By extension, these feelings can also affect your entire life and the lives of those living in your home.

For this simple yet profound reason, ideal stove placement — so that you can see all entryways to the kitchen when cooking — keeps you protected, a helpful factor indeed for positive life results.

An island stove — a stove located in the center of your kitchen — can be ideally placed in the Commanding Position of the kitchen. A stove in this position faces the door coming in to the kitchen. Because this position is quite rare, the cure for the more common stove position (against a wall) is to put a mirror behind the stove. The mirror should be at least as wide as the stove — the taller, the better. Installing a large mirror behind your stove will show you the doorways into the kitchen, and also symbolically double your stove's burners — two potent effects from one cure. Reinforce this cure by visualizing greater health and happiness. This cure and the following two cures can benefit your wealth as well as your health.

Hanging a Crystal Sphere over the Cook

Whether the cook can see the door, and regardless of your stove position, this cure can improve the health of your home's occupants. The positive chi and prismatic light created by the crystal brings good energy, luck, and opportunity to the household. Hang a wind chime or faceted crystal sphere with a red ribbon cut to a 9-inch multiple directly over the cook's position at the stove. The flow of the kitchen's chi, particularly the chi around the cook, is harmonized by the chime or sphere, resulting in better-quality chi in the food.

The crystal also harmonizes and calms any chaotic chi that may be circulating in the kitchen, thereby helping to reduce kitchen accidents and mishaps — a clear health issue, as any chef knows.

Keeping Your Stove in Good Working Order

Clean and perfectly working stove — good! Dirty or broken stove (grimy stove top, malfunctioning burners, and so on) — not so good! Enough said.

Just kidding! Seriously, because of the stove's symbolic relationships to your mouth and body, maintaining a clean, perfectly functioning stove helps maintain good health. If the stove malfunctions or looks filthy, something inside — that's inside you pardner! — probably doesn't look so good either. The cure is quite simple: Keep your stove clean and in good working order.

Boosting Your Health by Using a Bright Red Cloth

Need a vitality boost? Place a bright red cloth or a flat new red sheet between your mattress and box springs. (Whatever type of cloth you use should cover the entire surface of the box springs.) This cure is effective whether or not the sheet is visible after its placement. If you apply this cure, expect powerful results, 'cause it invokes 'em. (This cure helps the ol' sex life, too – the energy of red helps invoke passion and start the sparks a-flyin'. Feng Shui even works in the dark. Cowabunga!)

Perform the Three Secrets Reinforcement to enhance the cure's effects on your energy and health. (See Chapter 6 for more information.)

Increasing Energy Circulation with a Mobile

The center of the home relates to the residents' health and is a prime place to apply Feng Shui health cures (see Chapter 10 for more on the home's center). Because mobiles invoke energy circulation and flow, hanging a mobile in the center of your home can be an effective health cure. Reinforce the mobile by visualizing greater health and perfect circulation in your body and your home.

Keeping House Systems in Good Working Condition

A home's circulatory systems directly affect your body's systems. Repairing these systems not only enhances your home's energy flow but also avoids breathing and respiratory problems.

The main systems to pay particular attention to are the plumbing, electrical, heating and air conditioning, and duct systems. Immediately repair all system problems.

For best results repair the systems correctly and completely. Makeshift, haphazard, or partial repairs produce correspondingly weakened cures.

Deflecting Poison Arrows

Poison arrows are a real health threat. ("But I don't have any poison arrows," you say. Read on.) A poison arrow is any sharp angle, point, or protruding corner aimed at a front door, bed, crib, stove, desk, couch, armchair, or other common habitat. These arrow-like points can be anything from a neighbor's protruding roof ridge, a tree branch or post aimed at the front door, sharp edges of sculptures or furniture, or even wall corners that stick out into the room.

Effective cures for poison arrows are usually quite simple. For outside arrows, place a Ba-Gua mirror over the front door (see Chapter 7 for more details about the benefits of Ba-Gua mirrors). For interior poison arrows, remove (or redirect the point of) the offending object, or cover the object with cloth, a curtain, or a silk vine. Another possible cure involves hanging a faceted crystal sphere in front of the point to diffuse its sharpness. (In some cases, you may simply want to move the affected object away from where the poison arrow is pointing.) Be sure to visualize greater health when applying any of these cures. (See Chapter 6 for more information on visualization.)

Curing Exposed Beams

Exposed beams can create oppressive downward energetic flows that can induce health, psychological, and other life problems. The beams needing the most attention include beams over the bed, stove, desk, dining table, or front door. The best way to cure such beams is to hang two Feng Shui flutes at 45-degree angles on the beam, one at each end. (See Chapter 14 for more on beams.)

Other beam cures include painting the beams to match the ceiling, hiding the beams with a false ceiling, or camouflaging the beams with decorative cloth.

Freshening Air and Filtering Water

Because Feng Shui means wind and water, the quality of the air and water in your home is clearly important. Yet the average home is host to hundreds of toxic chemicals and substances, which wage continuous airborne assaults on your immune system and health. The average kitchen, garage, basement, and bathroom are storehouses of chemical pollutants. Most people bring home many of these substances themselves, because they are unaware of how much airborne poison they inhale on a daily basis. Surprised? A full treatment of this subject can fill an entire book.

Here's a partial list of common household chemicals that release toxins and pollutants into the air you breathe: oven cleaners, air fresheners, disinfectants, furniture and floor polishes, fabric cleaners and stain repellents, and drain cleaners. These modern wonders have the advantage of being highly effective and easy to use; they have the disadvantage of exposing your lungs to toxic chemicals that human bodies simply were not designed to deal with. Remember that what you breathe is a vital component of daily health.

What can you clean with, you say? Consider some natural and environmentally safe cleansers and detergents, which — though requiring slightly more "elbow grease" — are much healthier to be around. They're not only better for you, but they are much kinder to the environment and the planet's precious water supply. Baking soda, vinegar, Borax, and citrus-based cleansers can tackle just about anything. Instead of toxic commercial air fresheners, you can use white vinegar in a pump sprayer with a drop or two of peppermint or other essential oil to freshen the air. The next step is to take a look at the toxic chemicals and poisons stashed in the garage and the rest of the house.

Most homes can use a high-quality air filter as well as a negative-ion generator to recreate needed electrical charges in the air. These charges can help better your health and mood.

Remember that water plays a big part in Feng Shui because it affects your body's energy and health. Therefore the quality of the water you drink and bathe in (because your body absorbs many ounces of water during each shower you take) rates highly on the list of health concerns. For water quality, a high-quality, full-house filtering system is the best choice. One with additional filtering for drinking water is excellent.

Watching Out for Harmful EMFs

Electromagnetic fields (EMFs) known to surround such common appliances as alarm clocks, radios, clock radios, computer central processing units and monitors, and stereos undeniably impact humans. A debate currently rages whether the impact is negative or neutral, yet prudence suggests reducing exposure until the final verdict is in. The hot-spot EMF areas are present in places where you spend significant time, so pay attention to the EMFs around your desk or workstation and your bed. The general rule of thumb is to move electrical objects and appliances to at least 30 inches or more (farther is better) from any part of your body. (For greater precision, you can buy an inexpensive EMF meter on-line at www.lessemf.com.)

Heated waterbeds and electric blankets are particularly problematic and ideally should be avoided altogether. Also watch for power mains and circuit panels behind your bed or desk.

For computer monitors, I have two key recommendations: First, insist on a monitor that is certified as TCO-99 compliant, which means it has much less radiation than other models (see `www.tco-info.com` for details). The difference is noticeable, and you may find it easier to work for longer periods without fatigue. Second, get a good combination glare screen/radiation shield for your monitor. Glare produces headaches and eyestrain, an increasing problem in most corporate environments (see `www.lessemf.com` for more information).

Chapter 23

Ten Tips for Selling, Finding, and Buying a House

- -

In This Chapter

▶ Removing obstacles from your front entrance to invite potential buyers

▶ Getting organized for a stress-free move

▶ Finding a new home with a well-positioned bedroom

▶ Scoping out the previous tennants

▶ Avoiding landforms and locations that may drain you and your home's energy

- -

For many people, moving out of a residence into a new home is a stress-fest that falls somewhere between living with your in-laws and outright torture. But Feng Shui can lessen the pain of the dreaded moving game, and leave you feeling just about none the worse for wear. This chapter helps you deal with selling your existing house, deciding what belongings should make the move, and finding a new home that has good Feng Shui features to begin with.

Selling a house first requires getting qualified buyers to show interest and view your home. The Feng Shui cures in this chapter help activate energy to attract the right people to buy your home. These cures mainly address the entrance because this is where people first come to view the house.

Once you find a buyer and are preparing to leave the property, it's time to address your powerful energetic attachment to your home. This step is necessary even if you consciously want to move. One way to face this psychological obstacle is to dispose of the mountains of unused belongings tucked in your closets and garage. Such accumulated baggage can be emotional and physical deadweight that anchors you in your current residence, and it should be tossed overboard before heading to your new home.

Finally, this chapter gives you pointers to help you find a new home complete with good Feng Shui.

More factors than I can cover in this short chapter need to be considered when selecting a home. I recommend contacting a Feng Shui professional when choosing your next residence.

Take Care of Business

When selling a house, the following three main factors are as important as any Feng Shui cures you can apply. In order of importance, I suggest that you make these preparations:

✔ Set the right (<u>realistic</u>) price

✔ Employ a good realtor

✔ Keep a good marketing plan

To clarify, the lack of these factors definitely makes selling your house a tough job. Price is the most important factor of all. Feng Shui cures can't induce buyers to act against their own best interest (for example, overpay you for a house or take the place of a qualified realtor). So even more importantly than using Feng Shui to help sell your house, securing the three kings in place is vital. The following cures can be applied in addition to handling these practical matters.

Send Out Your Message

An effective Feng Shui house-selling cure is to activate your entrance with sound energy. Sound, especially clear, bell-like tones promote the energy of awakening, alerting, calling, and sending messages. So when you put your home up for sale, hang a wind chime near your front door. The sound of chimes awakens and draws the chi to your entrance, and the sound attracts people to your front door as well. It also greets the visitors and makes them feel welcome. When hanging your chime, visualize the house selling rapidly and easily — and for the right price.

Enhance the Visibility of Your Entrance

If your entrance isn't visible from the street, you have a natural block to selling your house. For a good cure, you can install bright lights to illuminate the front area. If the main entrance to your home is dark or shadowed or set into the front of the house (a funnel-like entrance), mount a bright light just outside the door to light the front entrance. Adding light to the front of your house energetically "activates" the entrance, the most important part of the house. If energy is lively at the entrance, buyers are much more likely to view and purchase the home.

Remove Obstacles from Your Entryway

If the entryway (or Mouth of Chi) is blocked, possible buyers tend to stay away. If your trees or shrubs block the entrance, I recommend trimming them back so the chi can flow freely towards the front door. When the chi can flow freely towards the entrance, buyers are much freer to visit the home, greatly increasing your chances of making a sale (sometime within this millennium!).

Activate Your Helpful People and Money Energy

The Helpful People Area of the house is extremely important at sale time (see Chapter 3 for details on how to locate the Helpful Please Area in your home). To sell a house and close escrow requires many helpful people, including realtors, bankers, brokers, family members, escrow agents, and, of course, the buyer. So the best cures for this area are ones that create activity. You can install a fountain in the Helpful People Area of your house and/or lot for tangible benefits. The energy of the fountain creates flow, which is very helping for bringing the first key ingredient of home sales your way — a qualified buyer. Visualize the house selling rapidly when you install the fountain(s) and be sure to use the Three Secrets Reinforcement to fully activate the cure.

The other important ingredient in the sale of a home is money. Thus, the Wealth Area is also a prime area for house-sale cures. A chime in this area can effectively attract money. (See Chapter 21 for more details.)

Applying cures in either the Helpful People or Wealth Areas of your home can also help you find a good realtor, and gather the necessary funds when you're buying a new house.

Start Moving Now

Selling a house, in the outer realm, is based on the price and the market, but in the inner realm, the sale largely depends on the seller's personal energy and willingness to move. Many sellers consciously think that they want to leave, but they subconsciously hold on to their homes through fear, resistance to change, and emotional attachment. To keep this mindset from holding you back from selling your home, get some energy moving as soon as possible.

Start by lightening your load. Detach yourself from all material things you don't need, and free yourself of stuff you won't be taking with you when you move. The more deadweight you toss off your property and out of your life, the more energy you free up to move yourself out. So do whatever it takes — have a garage or yard sale, donate goods to a local charity or halfway house, give things to friends and neighbors, or simply throw it in the back of a truck and take it to the dump. Also evaluate the personal value of the stuff you keep in rented storage space. Every object you let go of decreases your unconscious attachment to your home. The sooner you clean house, the sooner you'll find yourself emotionally — and energetically — ready to move into a new home.

Finally, you can get a good start by boxing up in advance the things that you will move into your new home. The more ready you are to move, the easier (and more urgent) it becomes to find a new residence.

Find a Master Bedroom in the Commanding Position

Because the bedroom is the key room in any house, its position in your new home is highly important. Finding a home with a bedroom in the back of the house is always preferable. A bedroom located in the front of the house can generate chaos (and even unfortunate separations). Assessing the bedroom's other Feng Shui characteristics such as shape and availability of a good bed position when buying a new home is also high priority. (See Chapter 11 for more details.)

If you find your dream house but the bedroom isn't auspiciously located or shaped, you can remedy any defects with specific Feng Shui cures found in this book. (See Chapter 10 for bedroom location solutions, Chapter 8 for bedroom shape cures, and Chapter 11 for other bedroom cures.)

Investigate Predecessor Chi Wisely

Predecessor chi, the energy of the people who lived in the house before you, constitutes a significant Feng Shui factor that affects your experience in the new residence. Negative effects may come from predecessors who moved due to bankruptcy, divorce, illness, death, job-loss, and so on. (If the previous resident got divorced, fell ill, lost his job, then went bankrupt, and died, maybe you should choose a different house!) Additional negative predecessor chi is also generated through chronic poverty, sickness, or conflict, including physical or emotional violence. Although blessing ceremonies are effective in clearing these energies from a home, the recommended course is to avoid such negative predecessor chi if possible. To remove negative predecessor chi, perform one of the blessings in Chapter 17, or contact a professional Feng Shui consultant for professional attention (see the Feng Shui Resources page at the end of the book for a referral).

Choose a Favorable Terrain

A lot that slopes down and away from the rear of a house can cause financial troubles or other calamities for a home's occupants. The home's energy drains (or flows) away from this land formation and can rob you of money, health, and valuable connections with important people. A better lot choice is land that lies flat behind the house or, better yet, that slopes up gently to the back, thereby retaining chi — and money.

A house located on ground that is below street level can inhibit your career or social life, make money hard to come by, and negatively affect your health. The lower the main floor of the house is in relation to the street's surface, the more pronounced these effects can be. I recommend choosing a house situated evenly with or slightly above the street. This location puts you in more of a Commanding Position and bodes better all around for your destiny. This position sets you "above the situation," following the age-old wisdom that higher ground is usually stronger in life than lower ground.

Look for a Street with Positive Energy

The energy of society (people, money, mail, and so on) connects to your house mainly through the energy of the street. Therefore, a strong flow of energy to the house is very positive. On the other hand, a too-busy street can have the reverse effect, disturbing your home's chi and actually pulling energy away from the house. In this situation, you can lose career energy, opportunities, and money. (Not to mention that the street is extremely noisy!) The ideal street allows activity and movement and feeds the driveway and property, but the street is not too heavily trafficked.

Steer clear of lots on T-intersections and Y-intersections (they can threaten your safety), one-way streets (they often pull away your opportunities), dead ends (things in your life can come to a halt), and steeply sloping streets (these make it easy to feel off-kilter in life).

Chapter 24

Ten Tips for Apartment, Condo, and Townhouse Living

· ·

In This Chapter

▶ Boosting your owner energy

▶ Living over a garage

▶ Dealing with neighbors in your complex

▶ Clarifying uses of rooms to clarify your life

▶ Bringing nature inside for health and comfort

▶ Solving apartment kitchen dilemmas

· ·

*L*iving in a multiple-unit residence has its own challenges, dilemmas, and benefits. Whether you rent or own your apartment, condo, or townhouse, Feng Shui can help you make the most of the situation. In this chapter, the word *apartment* refers to condos, townhouses, and other forms of multiunit living (duplex, triplex, and so on). These units can pose many Feng Shui challenges. Luckily, you can find solutions for most of them throughout this book. But the top-notch cures for apartment living are sitting right before you.

So, what are some of the problems? For starters, units tend to be smaller than houses. Neighbors are closer. Walls are thinner. (And dang, if some oaf isn't blowing his nose two feet away on the other side!) The unit has fewer green spaces — not to mention less psychic space. But never fear — Feng Shui is here. Say "Kibosh!" to such petty problems! Or in Feng Shui-speak, perform the cures given in this chapter to smooth the little snags in your life's ongoing apartment saga and make long-term residency much easier and happier. And if getting out as soon as possible is your current mission, light the fuse on the relevant cures and you can soon head for greener pastures (and thicker walls!).

Act Like an Owner, Dagnubit!

The first suggestion for renters is to adopt an inner Commanding Position. In other words, act like you own the whole darn place! (Your unit, that is.) Too many renters throw in the psychic towel and act like renters, thereby giving up the Commanding Position and their personal power with it. ("Oh, I just rent here, so why invest in the place and make it look all nice and everything? It's like giving money to the landlord! I'll just lie here watching TV and snorting canned cheese until I get my own place.") This abdication weakens a renter's chi in his or her own home and generates chronic renter's malaise. And if you perform Feng Shui with this attitude (no gusto), expect to reap what you sow — mediocre results.

Feng Shui cures are not just an investment in a location, they are an investment in your life. So don't hold back on your cures and think you're outsmarting the landlord. (He doesn't live there, remember? You do!) Going halfway on cures and succumbing to renter's malaise can keep you energetically stuck in locations and life situations that you might otherwise outgrow. When you invest in quality solutions, you gain power and invest in yourself. They can help you flourish in your surroundings, and you can either move on to a better location or turn your present location into such a homey paradise that your landlord couldn't drag you out. And if you do move, you can always take many of your cure items with you, and bring good Feng Shui to your next location.

Resolve Entrance Issues

Entrances are perhaps the most important Feng Shui area in every home or apartment, and multiple units can have more-complicated entrance situations. Entrances that are convoluted, dark or poorly lit, narrow, confusing, and pressed nose-to-nose with the entrance across the hall can cause many Feng Shui problems, and in some cases, can even be dangerous. To reach the front door of many units, you almost need to crawl through serpentine labyrinths of passageways, halls, and turns. These conditions can cause you to experience greater energetic obstacles if you're trying to get ahead in your life, career, and relationship. So, what to do?

If moving or even getting the landlord to perform an overall building cure isn't possible, you can choose from many options. Given the previous entrance scenarios, making the most of your unit entrance isn't merely an option but a necessity. I suggest the kitchen sink method, which means throwing everything at the situation. As much as possible, make your entryway clear, open, and free — both inside and outside the front door. You can give it better lighting; use mirrors to open the space if needed; install fountains to create flow; and hang chimes to encourage the flow of energy to your front door. Choose cures from the above menu that fit your needs, and enjoy the energetic shifts that come when your entryway cures start working!

Sittin' on Pins: Pillars in the Garage

Many complexes feature a gigantic garage that takes up the whole first floor. This amenity is supposed to enhance security and convenience for the residents. The problem, however, comes to the tenants who reside on the floor directly above the garage. Sitting on top of a large vacuous space in which vehicle movement constantly disturbs the area's chi can create energetic havoc in your life. In addition, the entire building may be energetically precarious, because it sits on pins (support pillars in the garage). The solution is to perform grounding cures in your unit to solidify and stabilize your life. Placing plants or large smooth stones in all four corners of the apartment or just in the four corners of the bedroom are good locations for this cure.

Way Up High in the Sky

For millions of years, humans have evolved — on the earth. Modern building techniques now make it possible for millions of people to live and work high above the ground in multilevel apartments and high-rise offices. (Say, if your building burns down, do you still own that little square space in the sky where your unit used to be?) So now that many people live umpteen stories above the earth, the key is to figure out how to make the best of it.

From the Feng Shui point of view, living in a high unit affords at least one advantage: You typically get a commanding view of your surroundings. Having made it to the top, you feel on top of the world. But you also get a down side: You can feel too high, ungrounded, and precariously perched. Human energy cycles are actually tuned in to the earth's magnetic rhythms. So anything higher than the third floor can make many (but not all) people subtly feel wobbly and ungrounded. Living in a tall building can also cause mental confusion, a spaced-out feeling, and uneasiness, because the body has a basic need to be closer to *terra firma* (that's solid ground to you and me).

What can you do? Besides moving to a lower unit, three good solutions involve installing plants, plants, and more plants. (With lots of dirt or earth in them, of course.) Other cure items that also contain earth element energy are items such as earthenware (pottery), objects of earth tone colors, and cubic shapes. And the cures can work fully after you apply the Three Secrets Reinforcement on these items (see Chapter 6 for more details on this cure enhancing procedure).

Itsy Bitsy Teeny Weeny Yellow Polka Dot — Living Unit

Size (or lack there of) is the common bugaboo of apartment life. To counter the boxed in feeling that a small unit causes, I suggest performing these three cures:

1. **Get rid of some of your stuff.** If it isn't absolutely necessary, heave it overboard.

2. **Employ large mirrors wherever possible to expand the space.** This cure creates the pleasant illusion of more room.

3. **Apply faceted crystal spheres to energetically create the feeling of expansion, cheer, and lightness.** These spheres have the powerful quality of expanding the feeling of a space, psychically providing more room for the occupants. The centers of rooms are good spots for these crystal cures. Reinforce them with the Three Secrets Reinforcement (see Chapter 6).

Give Yourself Some Breathing Room

Neighbor problems got you down? Paper-thin walls shivering when the fan blows? Seems like your next door neighbor is living on your lap? ("Say, would you mind snoring a little louder over there!") What, you can smell them too? Sheesh! Neighbors, neighbors, neighbors — you gotta love 'em if you got a lot of 'em. Anyway, mirrors are a multipurpose cure for closed-in unit living. You can choose from two ways to bring the power of mirrors to bear: First, if neighbor energy is particularly obnoxious — or even scary — you can mount a Ba-Gua mirror on the adjoining wall surface, facing the other party. Hang it with a feeling of compassion, and intent of harmony for all concerned. The mirror won't hurt them or you, but it can help deflect any unwanted energy missiles that are launched your way.

If the neighbors are friendly but a bit too close for comfort, perform the cure in the previous section. Large (non–Ba Gua) mirrors placed on adjoining unit walls serve to push your walls out further. This expansion symbolically places the other party much farther away. They also brighten, lighten, and cheer up the space. These mirrors should face into the room. The larger the mirror, the better. (Use high-quality, nondistorted, or rippled mirrors, please.)

Multi-Use Rooms — They Can Bamboozle

Because apartments often contain fewer rooms than houses, using your rooms for multiple purposes is natural. Unfortunately, this routine can lead to boundary issues within your home. One solution is to separate the spaces with large attractive screens (a favorite because they're moveable), curtains, or faceted crystal spheres. Screens and curtains provide important visual blocks that supply needed separation. If putting up a curtain or screen isn't possible, you can apply the faceted crystal sphere cure to energetically divide spaces, balance your brain cells, and harmonize energy flows.

Bring the Outside In

A key issue with many units is that they provide little or no yard or garden space. The lack of natural energy can be depressing as well as confining, so bring some natural energy inside. I recommend photo-quality wall murals, which have powerful and awe-inspiring natural scenery. Search the Internet for the term "wall murals" for hundreds of options, many in the neighborhood of $100. Thanks to wonders of modern technology, you can enjoy Niagara Falls, the Grand Canyon, Mount Fuji, or the Serengeti in the comfort of your own condo. All you need is a little patience and *lots* of glue. (Actually, most murals come with self-adhesive already installed.)

Is looking at a picture of Mt. Fuji the same as climbing it? Not really. (But at least you can't fall off.) And you can enjoy indoor plumbing and Chinese takeout and cable and 24-hour grocery stores and . . . well, you get the picture. So make the most of what you don't have and appreciate what you've got. Liberally toss in a few fountains, murals, plants, spring for an aquarium, and stick a few bird feeders on the deck. Before long, you'll need to go outside to get away from all the natural energy in your cozy little unit!

Fix Stubborn Windows

Landlords often have a funny way with windows. Some like to paint them shut. Others prefer nailing them closed. Some think prison-chic looks nice, so they barricade them with tacky iron bars. Whatever your situation, if your windows don't slide open easily, they can cause needless frustration, hassle, and even claustrophobia. A simple solution: Open the window! If the window is broken, get it fixed. If the edgings are painted shut, try to loosen the paint around the window. And if the windows are covered with opaque material or unneeded bars, see if you can remove these materials as well. Don't suffocate in your living space. Cure the problem and then reinforce it with Three Secrets Reinforcement (detailed in Chapter 6) for better vision, flow, and freedom. You'll feel better and breathe easier to boot. (Of course, if you live on the ground floor in a dangerous neighborhood, think twice before removing any security bars. As usual, let your common sense be your guide.)

Help Out in the Kitchen

Apartment kitchens present a couple major issues. First, they're small. To expand the kitchen space psychologically and energetically, strategically install mirrors between cabinets and counters, or any available walls — the more, the better. The mirrors give you a greater feeling of freedom and expansion in your life. (Helps out in the ole bank account, too.) Second, apartment kitchens tend to be in the front of the unit and can create havoc on your career and your health. And your pocket change can suffer as well! For this situation, I recommend hanging a wind chime with a soothing, pleasant ring halfway between the front door and the stove.

Chapter 25

Ten Unique Calligraphies to Bless Your Life

In This Chapter
▶ Discovering the significance of the calligraphies
▶ Using the calligraphies to enhance your life

*T*his chapter contains a special bonus: ten works of art created especially for the reader of this book (that's you!) by Grandmaster Lin Yun, master of Feng Shui and traditional Chinese calligraphy. Chinese culture reveres calligraphy and painting as the only two true art forms, and highly skilled masters of the brush are few and far between.

Each of the ten calligraphies contains a special meaning and energy. Grandmaster Lin Yun imparted great energy while he created this art; each calligraphy has the power to adjust your energy simply by you viewing it. The calligraphies can also help energize your environment. You can enjoy the calligraphies in this chapter as works of art, or you can apply them as cures for your home.

You can use any of these calligraphies as cures to improve any Life Areas or specific rooms of your house for any intention. To apply a calligraphy as a cure, you can photocopy it or cut it out and hang it on the wall (with or without a frame). I recommend that you apply the "Auspicious As You Wish" calligraphy to any area where you have a specific wish or desire that you want to come true; "Treasure Box" for acquiring wealth (for instance, in the Wealth Area of the house); and "Taoist Talisman For Wealth And Safety" for wealth as well as safety and protection. (Check out Chapter 3 to discover the Life Areas of your home.)

Each calligraphy is titled and followed by the English translation of the Chinese characters. (Calligraphy translations provided by Crystal Chu.) Traditionally, Chinese calligraphy includes the place and/or date where the art was composed. In the following pages, this information succeeds each calligraphy translation.

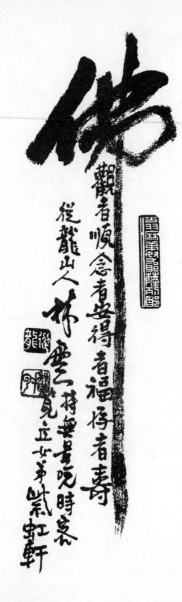

Buddha

May the observer [of this calligraphy] be blessed with a smooth life. May the chanter be blessed with peace. May the receiver be blessed with prosperity. May the keeper be blessed with longevity.

Composed by Grandmaster Lin Yun while chanting infinite numbers of mantras at the study of disciple Crystal Chu.

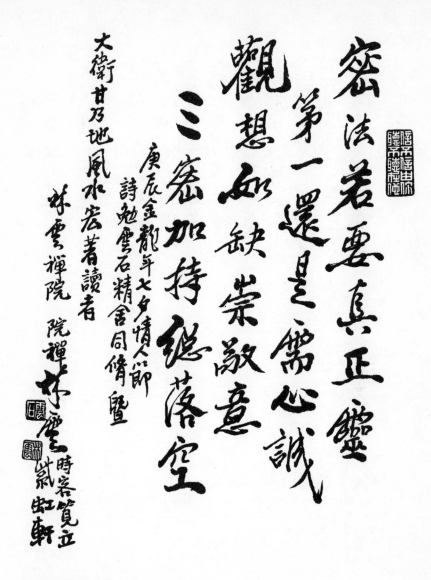

Secret Cures Poem

If you want your secret cures to be really effective,
First you have to have a faithful heart;
If your visualizations lack respect and sincerity,
Even with the Three Secrets Reinforcement, you will still come up empty.

Written by Grandmaster Lin Yun on the Seventh Day of the Seventh Lunar Month, also known as Chinese Valentines Day, to encourage all disciples of Grandmaster Lin Yun, as well as the readers of David Kennedy's book on Feng Shui.

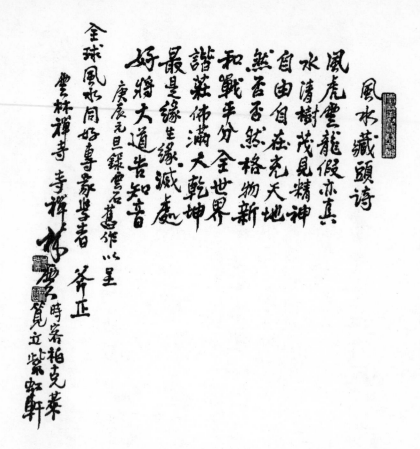

Hidden Title Poem on Feng Shui

Tigers appear in wind, and dragons emerge from clouds,
These images seem real yet untrue.
Water is clear and trees are lush,
From these we sense vital energy.
Freedom and ease fill the heaven and earth
Whether this is true or not,
We will get new knowledge after we've analyzed it.
Peace and warfare are spread equally throughout the world;
Humor and seriousness also fill the entire universe.
The ultimate is when karma begins and karma ceases
So it's best to share this teaching with those of common interest.

Grandmaster Lin Yun composed this poetry while visiting the study of disciple Crystal Chu. Written on New Year's Day, 2000, from a previous poetic composition. This poem is presented to all the Feng Shui founders, experts, and scholars in the world.

Good Karma Should Be Widely Connected

To bestow blessing upon the reader, author, and user of this book. May they receive prosperity, lucky chi, wealth chi, good health, and peace.

This calligraphy was composed by Grandmaster Lin Yun while visiting the study of disciple Crystal Chu.

One Shall Receive Great Benefits from Opening This Book
To bestow blessings upon the readers of David Kennedy's Feng Shui book.

This calligraphy was composed by Grandmaster Lin Yun while chanting mantras on New Year's Day at the study of disciple Crystal Chu.

Auspicious As You Wish

To bestow blessing upon David Kennedy's Feng Shui book. May its author, readers, publisher, and their family members all receive prosperity, wealth, wisdom, and safety.

Composed by Lin Shi while chanting infinite numbers of mantras, at the study of disciple Crystal Chu. (Lin Shi is the other given name of Grandmaster Lin Yun.)

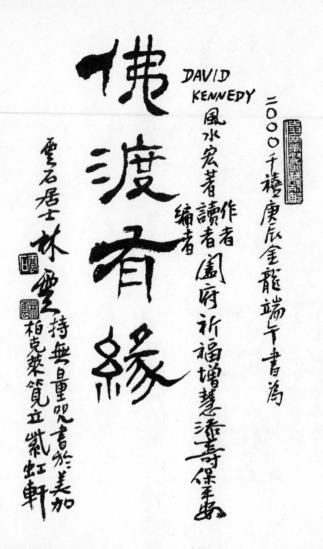

The Buddha Liberates Those with Good Karma from All Suffering
Written in the Millennium Year of the Golden Dragon for David Kennedy's Feng Shui book.

May its author, readers, publisher, and their family members all receive wisdom, longevity, and safety.

Composed by Grandmaster Lin Yun while chanting infinite numbers of mantras at the study of disciple Crystal Chu.

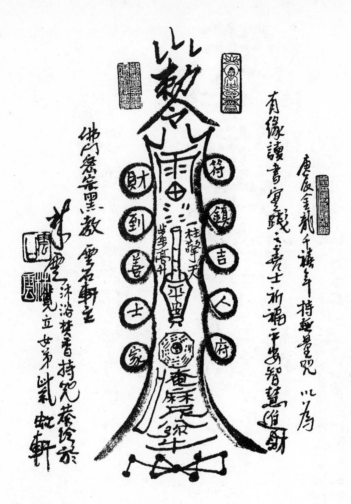

Taoist Talisman for Wealth and Safety

Taoist Talisman [showing the following blessings]: "Highest Supreme Order,"
"Five Thunder Protectors," "Bamboo Flute in Vase" to bring safety, while cata-
pulting and elevating your success and well-being, "Eight Trigrams," "Six
Syllable Mantra: Om Ma Ni Pad Me Hum," and "Tracing of the Nine Star Path."

This Talisman will bring safety to the residence of the blessed one. Wealth
will arrive to the residence of those who do good deeds.

Respectfully composed by Grandmaster Lin Yun at the study of disciple Crystal
Chu. Written in the Millennium Year of the Golden Dragon while chanting infi-
nite numbers of mantras to bestow blessing upon readers and users with good
karma. May they receive prosperity, safety, wisdom, and wealth.

Treasure Box

To bestow the acquisition of wealth upon the author, readers, and publisher of David Kennedy's Feng Shui book.

Regarding Wealth

Don't assume that seeking wealth is the same as being greedy.
Money just may bring relief
In hard times when you're needy.
Yet if it is acquired and used
Without a proper method,
It'll be easier to capsize a boat
Than to carry it afloat.

Composed by Grandmaster Lin Yun while chanting infinite numbers of mantras at the study of disciple Crystal Chu.

為本書讀者作者及修持者

闔府祈福納吉增慧

道通天地

林雲題並持呪時客覓立戠虹軒壬襄端午二〇〇〇年元旦

The Tao Reaches Heaven and Earth

For the readers and author of this book, as well as spiritual cultivators. May their whole families be blessed with prosperity, auspiciousness, and wisdom.

Composed by Grandmaster Lin Yun while chanting mantras at the study of disciple Crystal Chu on New Year's Day, Millennium Year 2000.

Feng Shui Resources

The following sources offer Feng Shui products, training, and further information:

Yun Lin Temple Feng Shui Objects

Many authentic Feng Shui objects are available through the Yun Lin Temple, most of them exclusively designed or chosen based on Grandmaster Lin Yun's Feng Shui school. Following the principle of Minor Additions, Grandmaster Lin Yun's Feng Shui school uses special objects for Feng Shui cures. These items include bamboo flutes, 10 emperors' coins, Ba-Gua mirrors, Buddha statues, wind chimes, ceremonial firecrackers, yu bowls, faceted crystal spheres, crystal bracelets and necklaces, and many others. All Feng Shui objects have been blessed by Grandmaster Lin Yun at the Yun Lin Temple to enhance their effectiveness as remedies. To order these Feng Shui objects or for more information, please contact:

Yun Lin Temple
510-841-2347
510-548-2621 (fax)
E-mail: info@yunlintemple.org

David Daniel Kennedy

David Daniel Kennedy offers Feng Shui classes, home and business consultations, and practitioner trainings nationwide. Feng Shui training is available by classroom, Internet, telephone, and correspondence. Classes include basic, intermediate, and advanced Feng Shui courses, as well as training for Feng Shui practitioners with an emphasis on techniques for success in one's career, family life, and personal growth. Visit Mr. Kennedy's Web site for Feng Shui information, manuals, classes, and schedules. To inquire about classes, finding cure items, or locating a consultant in your area, please contact:

David Daniel Kennedy
PMB 127
1563 Solano Avenue
Berkeley, CA 94707
888-470-2727 (toll free)
510-237-7374 (fax)
Web site: www.daviddanielkennedy.com
E-mail: info@daviddanielkennedy.com

Index

• D •

Notes

FOR DUMMIES
BOOK REGISTRATION

We want to hear from you!

Visit **dummies.com** to register this book and tell us how you liked it!

- Get entered in our monthly prize giveaway.

- Give us feedback about this book — tell us what you like best, what you like least, or maybe what you'd like to ask the author and us to change!

- Let us know any other *For Dummies* topics that interest you.

Your feedback helps us determine what books to publish, tells us what coverage to add as we revise our books, and lets us know whether we're meeting your needs as a *For Dummies* reader. You're our most valuable resource, and what you have to say is important to us!

Not on the Web yet? It's easy to get started with *Dummies 101®: The Internet For Windows® 98* or *The Internet For Dummies®* at local retailers everywhere.

Or let us know what you think by sending us a letter at the following address:

For Dummies Book Registration
Dummies Press
10475 Crosspoint Blvd.
Indianapolis, IN 46256

FOR DUMMIES

BESTSELLING BOOK SERIES

Feng Shui For Dummies®

Enlivening Your Environment with Color

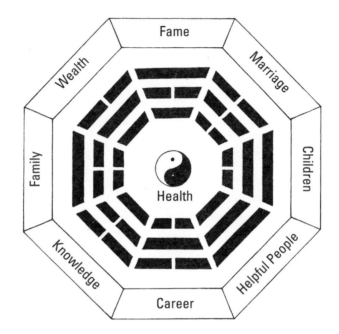

Feng Shui uses the Octagon pictured here to map the life energies of a house or lot. Place the Octagon over a drawing of your home. Then refer to the following table for areas to apply color to magnify the energy of each Life Area. From painting the walls yellow in the Health Area of your home (for better health and physical well-being) to positioning a healthy, green plant in the Family Area of your home or lot (to encourage unity and a stronger family bond), Feng Shui encourages the use of color to enhance your life energy.

Color	Home or Lot Area to Place Color	Life Area Helped	Specifically Improves
Green	Center left	Family	Unity, Bonding
Purple	Back left	Wealth	Money, Prosperity
Red	Back center	Fame	Reputation
Pink	Back right	Marriage	Relationships, Partnerships
White	Center right	Children	Kids, Creativity
Gray	Right front	Helpful People	Assistance, Travel
Black	Center front	Career	Promotion, Job Change
Blue	Left front	Knowledge	Learning, Spiritual Growth
Yellow	Center	Health	Physical and Mental Health

Feng Shui Improvements on the Spot

The following list includes practical Feng Shui improvements that you can make right here and now.

✔ **Spice up your love life.** Place 3 or 9 new plants in the bedroom to enliven the energy of your bedroom, adding hope and cheer. And if the plants have pink flowers, they're even stronger!

✔ **Let the good times flow.** Enjoy more cash flow and connections with key people. How? Simply place an energetic fountain near your front door. The flowing energy of the water symbolizes cash, which helps more of the green stuff come your way.

✔ **Bring more energy and better luck into your life.** Let the chi (or energy) flow right into your home and life by ridding your home's entryway of obstacles. Such things as looming plants or vines, old newspapers, bikes, and toys clutter your front path and limit the amount of energy entering your home. Clear out anything behind your door for even more benefits.

✔ **Make sure your home makes a good first impression.** Put books where you can see them when you come in the front door to stimulate learning in both you and your children.

✔ **Position your bed to feel safe, loved, and great.** Place your bed in the Commanding Position of your bedroom. Position your bed in the farthest possible area from the door where you are still able to see the doorway and anyone approaching while you are lying in the bed. You can be stronger, calmer, and in charge.

✔ **Keep more dollars from draining out of your pockets.** To keep your funds from being drained, keep your bathroom doors closed, hang full-length mirrors on the outside of your bathroom doors, and keep your drains closed (cover the sink drain, stop the tub, and keep the toilet lid closed).

✔ **You against the world? Not for long!** Hang a pleasant-sounding metal wind chime in the right front area of your home, office, or bedroom. The sound activates more people to help you, and gets you more help from the people already at your side.

✔ **Get rid of unwanted frustrations.** Make sure your front door is in good working order. For example, make sure the door doesn't scrape the floor or squeak and the doorknob, hinges, and locks are secure. This improvement releases frustrations and anxieties, and smooths your life path.

✔ **You're the boss — or you can be soon.** Set yourself up for success with the best desk position at work. This adjustment helps you encounter more opportunities, go farther in your field, and lose less often. Position your desk catercorner to and facing the office or cube door. If you can't turn your desk to face the door, arrange a mirror on your desk or wall so you can see who's coming. Be sure that you sit in a high-quality chair — one without a gap between the back and bottom and one with a back as high as the top of your shoulders.

For Dummies: Bestselling Book Series for Beginners